Respect for the Ancestors
American Indian Cultural Affiliation in the American West

Peter N. Jones

Bäuu Institute Press
Boulder, Colorado

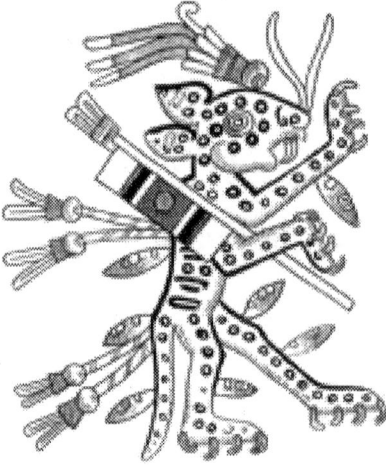

Library of Congress Cataloging-in-Publication Data

Respect for the Ancestors: American Indian Cultural Affiliation in the American West
    / by Peter N. Jones
        p. cm.

    Includes bibliographic references and index.
    ISBN 0-9721349-2-1. (hdbk.)
    1. American Indians-North America. 2. American Indians-Cultural Affiliation. 3. Plateau- United States. 4. Great Basin- United States. 5. Anthropology- Cultural Adaptation. I. Jones, Peter N.

Printed in the United States

10 9 8 7 6 5 4 3 2 1

Respect for the Ancestors:
American Indian Cultural Affiliation in the American West

by

Peter N. Jones

Dedication

To my wife Tara

Table of Contents

Preface...5
Chapter 1: Introduction...7
Chapter 2: An epistemological praxis of epoché 15
Chapter 3: NAGPRA and the Guidelines for Inquiry.......................21
Chapter 4: A Brief History of the Kennewick Man and the Spirit Cave Mummy....27
    Kennewick Man
    Spirit Cave Mummy
Chapter 5: The Plateau and Great Basin Culture Regions.......................33
Chapter 6: The American West During the Pleistocene and Holocene..................37
    Paleoenvironmental Reconstruction
        Northeastern Asia
        Alaska
        Northwest Coast
        Canada
        Plateau
        California
        Great Basin
        Southwest
        Plains
        Summary of Paleoenvironmental Record
Chapter 7: Ethnographic Evidence...75
    Plateau
    Great Basin
    Summary of Ethnographic Evidence
Chapter 8: Biological Evidence..85
    Dental Evidence
    Craniometric Evidence
    Genetic Evidence
    Trichological Analysis
    Summary of Biological Evidence
Chapter 9: Archaeological Evidence..115
    Northeast Asia
    Pleistocene Megafauna and the First Americans
    Early First American Subsistence Lifeways
    Plateau and Great Basin Archaeological Synthesis
    Summary of Archaeological Evidence
Chapter 10: Linguistic Evidence 151
    Linguistic Evidence Summary

Chapter 11: Oral Tradition Evidence 165
    Summary of Oral Tradition Evidence
Chapter 12: Migrations, Diffusions, and Subsistence in American Prehistory.......179
Chapter 13: Synthesis of the Evidence...191
Chapter 14: Anthropology and American Indians...197

List of Figures

Figure 1: Map of American Indian Reservations within the Contiguous United States...24
Figure 2: Map of the Plateau Culture Area 29
Figure 3: Map of the Great Basin Culture Area 31
Figure 4: Map of Glacial Coverage of Alaska during the Pleistocene.......................44
Figure 5: Map of the Northwest Coast Culture Area 48
Figure 6: Map of the California Culture Area...57
Figure 7: Map of the Southwest Culture Area..65
Figure 8: Map of the Plains Culture Area...69

List of Tables

Table 1: Table of Major Geologic Periods..39
Table 2: Table of Tree Species 72
Table 3: Table of Flora Species...74
Table 4: Table of CTUIR Tribal Affiliation...108
Table 5: Table of Common Themes from U.S. American Indian Oral Traditions..174
Table 6: Table of Summary of Evidence...195

PREFACE

Ever since anthropology dedicated itself to becoming a "hard" science instead of a "human" science, American Indians, their culture (materially, physically, spiritually), and their ancestors have been treated as objects. This has resulted in the fundamental lack of acknowledgement by a majority of anthropologists that American Indians are just as human as the anthropologists studying them. Furthermore, all that they create, believe in, and interact with are deeply tied to what it is to be human. When anthropologists simply reduce these very human processes to "objects" that are only understood and recognized on a qualitative level, not only are the processes denied their essential humanness, but American Indians are denied the same equal humanness as the anthropologist. This is a form of racism that has been prevalent within anthropological circles ever since it was formed, though I am sure most will be unwilling to acknowledge this very simple fact. Most are too comfortable in their reality; they have solidified their reality to the point that such issues as the Kennewick Man and the Spirit Cave Mummy repatriation cases are not about anthropology, but are about who's reality is more correct. This, if any of the anthropologists would take a moment to realize, is axiomatic with the very premise of science itself. (They are no longer searching for a truth, through a scientific method, but instead are simply asserting one.)

This book has attempted to take a very unique, purely scientific approach to the question of cultural affiliation in the American West. By this, I mean that I did not step into this process with any set goals, any *a priori* theory or methodology that I wanted to test, nor did I step into the process wanting to disprove anthropology. I am an anthropologist, but I am also a human. Thus, my fundamental goal in writing this book was to begin from an epistemological praxis of epoché. This means that my method of action came from a theory of knowing of emptiness. I chose to focus specifically on the Kennewick Man and the Spirit Cave Mummy repatriation cases because both of these cases exemplify the current situation between anthropologists and American Indians. The Kennewick Man legal battle has nothing to do with anthropology, despite what is claimed, but is purely about political power, and as is discussed in this book, those who control power control knowledge and thus reality.

Therefore, the Kennewick Man (a.k.a., the Ancient One) and the Spirit Cave Mummy repatriation cases are used as representative examples to explore question of cultural affiliation that have been long-standing in American Indian studies for the Plateau and Great Basin culture regions of the American West. The guidelines of inquiry established by the Native American Graves Protection and Repatriation Act (NAGPRA) of 1990 are followed in addressing this question, because these are the binding guidelines of inquiry in discussing cultural affiliation. This book, as a result, is an in depth anthropological inquiry focusing on the subfield areas of ethnography, biological anthropology, archaeology, linguistics, and oral traditions. This unifying approach allows for a comprehensive understanding of the two case examples specifically and questions of cultural continuity and cultural affiliation in the Plateau and Great Basin in general.

The book begins with an introduction and a chapter on the premis of the methodology. A brief overview chapter of NAGPRA follows, as well as a brief chapter on the Kennewick Man and the Spirit Cave Mummy. These last two chapters are not ment to be comprehensive in nature; there are several books that chronicle the unfolding of these two cases. They are, however, ment to be a refresher for those who have followed these cases, as well as to introduce those unfamiliar with these two landmark cases to their history. Chapter six is an in-depth paleoenvironmental reconstruction of the American West, focusing primarily on the Pleistocene to Holocene boundary. Many readers may wish to skip this chapter since it seems irrelevant and they will not disrupt their overall understanding it they do. However, this chapter is provided for the purpose of giving the reader a greater understanding of how peoples subsistend and interacted with the environment during this time, a time when both the Kennewick Man and Spirit Cave Mummy were alive. Following this chapter, chapters seven, eight, nine, ten, and eleven delve into the data of the ethnographic, biological, archaeological, linguistic, and oral traditions. A chapter discussing the requirements necessary for establishing whether a migration event has taken place in prehistory follows this large overview of the data. Finally, following this, chapter thirteen is a synthesis of the data provided in the proceeding chapters, and the final chapter offers a discussion on the future of anthropological research among American Indians.

CHAPTER 1
INTRODUCTION

S ince the passage of the Native American Graves Protection and Repatriation Act (NAGPRA; Public Law 101-106) in 1990 and the subsequent Rules (43 CFR 10) in 1995, the issue of cultural affiliation between today's American Indian tribes[1] and the peoples of the archaeological, paleobiological, and historic record has gained considerable attention and importance. The question of cultural affiliation concerning American Indian tribes, however, is not a new topic within anthropology, but one that has been around since the development of the field. Likewise, the issue of today's tribe's relationship with the past has always been a topic of discussion, both in academic circles as well as among the general public, and can be traced back to the initial arrival of Europeans in the Americas.

When Europeans first encountered American Indians in the late 1400s and early 1500s, the question of cultural affiliation was raised concerning who American Indians were in context of the then present European epistemology, ontology, and cosmology. Initially, early European explorers thought that American Indians were possibly culturally affiliated to one of the "Ten Lost Tribes of Israel," that is recorded in the biblical literature (2 Kings 17) as championed by Diego Duran in the early 1500s (Huddletson, 1967). Another popular theory during this time was that perhaps American Indians were culturally affiliated with the European idea of the mythical lost world of Atlantis, as suggested in 1530 by the poet Fracastoro and in 1535 by Gonzalo Fernandez de Oviedo y Valdes (Wauchope, 1962). However, these notions were short lived in the minds of Europeans, for this was the beginning of the period in European history known as the Renaissance (which was, ironically, partly the subsequent result of the discovery of the "New World"). The term "Renaissance" means rebirth, and is commonly used to refer to an intellectual, literary, and artistic movement that began in Italy in the 14th century following the

Middle Ages, spreading throughout Europe, and eventually culminating in the 16th century in France and Belgium. During this time, scholars, writers, and artists redis-covered and reinterpreted the great classical heritage of the Roman Empire — its architecture, sculpture, philosophy, art, and literature.

As the Renaissance began to unfold and Europeans began to rediscover the clas-sic Roman and Greek writings and philosophy, a more empirical tendency to the understanding of the world was instilled in the European epistemology. "The New World provided, as it were, a gigantic laboratory in which the speculations of Renaissance man could be tested, modified, and developed" (Crone, 1969, p. 176). As the Renaissance continued to unfold, and as a result of the broadening of the European epistemology through exploration of the Americas, new ideas about epis-temology developed. This resulted in the dawning of the scientific revolution cham-pioned by Francis Bacon (1561-1626), and culminated in the empirical and social philosophies of such thinkers as Thomas Gresham (1519-1579), Rene Descartes (1569-1650), John Locke (1632-1704), and Voltaire (1694-1778). A direct result of this scientific revolution and the advocation of empiricism was the idea that knowl-edge, and thus "Truth[2]," could no longer be innate or self-evident, but that knowl-edge must be acquired, and "Truth" must be discovered, tested, and proven. These ideas came to bear on the issue of American Indian cultural affiliation at this time through the impetus of Thomas Jefferson (1743-1826).

During the period between the late 1500s and the late 1700s many new and fleet-ing theories arose concerning the cultural affiliation of American Indians, particu-larly associated with the numerous archaeogical sites that were being discovered all across the Americas. However, it was Thomas Jefferson who in 1784 took the step of embracing the new Renaissance epistemology sweeping Europe by carrying out a relatively well-controlled (i.e., scientific) excavation of one of these sites. Jefferson's excavation was "the first scientific excavation in the history of archaeology" (Wheeler, 1954, p. 6). This excavation revealed to Jefferson and the world that the site under study was built by the ancestors of the American Indians of the region, and not by mythical Atlantians or one of the lost tribes of Isreal. Thus, it was empir-ically demonstrated with Jefferson's excavation that American Indians were the direct descendents (culturally affiliated) of the prehistoric peoples who built the mounds and the numerous other archaeological sites found throughout the Americas, and were not the work of some other peoples.

As further excavations under this new methodology were carried out it became more evident that American Indians had been in the Americas for a very long peri-od of time. Thus, new questions arose such as for how long and from where did the American Indians originally come from. These two questions played a guiding role in the development of the field of anthropology at the time, and continue to be of relevance as demonstrated by recent court cases such as that concerning the Kennewick Man skeleton (also known as the Ancient One) (Jones, 2004a; Jones & Stapp, 2003). Thus, in the late 1800s and early 1900s with the development of anthropology as a formal field of scientific investigation, the question of cultural affiliation took on two new, yet very separate directions: 1) which American Indian tribes were more related to each other and what were their similarities and differences (dominated at the time by the Diffusionists and Cultural Particularists); and 2) how did American Indians come to the Americas and when (dominated by the Clovis-first followers)?

It was also during this time, and partly as a result of these two similar yet very different questions concerning American Indian cultural affiliation, that the field of anthropology was formally codified, developed, and subsequently fractionated. This last aspect, the subsequent splitting of the field into various sub-disciplines was never part of the vision of the founders of the field, and has been both a hindurance and a benefit to the field of anthropology and the questions of American Indian cultural affiliation and cultural continuity ever since (this will be discussed in more detail below).

Alfred Kroeber, one of the founders of American anthropology, and the field of anthropology in general, noted in his classic treatise that, "Anthropology is the science of man. This broad and literal definition takes on more meaning when it is expanded to 'the science of man and his works'" (Kroeber, 1923, p. 1). By this, Kroeber (1923) meant, "the interpretation of those phenomena into which both organic and social causes enter" (p. 3). Why did Kroeber break down anthropology into this dichotomy? Because, as he noted earlier in this classic work,

> If anthropology were to remain content with an interest in the Mongolian eye, the dwarfishness of the Negrito, the former home of the Polynesian race, taboos against speaking to one's mother-in-law, rituals to make rain, and other such exotic and superseded superstitions, it would earn no more dignity than an antiquarian's attic. As a co-laborer on the edifice of fuller understanding, anthropology must find more of a task than filling with rubble the temporarily vacant spaces in the masonry that the sciences are rearing. (1923, p. 2)

Thus, for Kroeber, the key to anthropology and the promise of the field in general, lay in its encompassing embrace and interpretation of both the organic and social causes of human nature. Under the organic causes Kroeber placed physical/biological anthropology, and under the social causes Krober placed language (linguistics), cultural anthropology, and archaeology (the essential historical component necessary to study cultures).

As is well documented in the history of anthropology, Kroeber, as well as other such founding luminaries as Robert Lowie, Edward Sapir, and Clyde Kluckhohn, among others, were all students of Franz Boas (see Barnard, 2000; Harris, 1968 for a discussion of this history). Boas, as one of the major propounders of anthropology in the Americas, and especially of ethnography, was particularly interested in questions of race, ethnicity, and thus, in a sense, cultural affiliation. Boas, in exploring these questions, initially turned the field of anthropology and the question of American Indian cultural affiliation further away from general areas of inquiry and more towards particulars. Boas' rejection of evolutionism, his downplaying of diffusion, and above all his insistence on the meticulous gathering of ethnographic data, all contributed towards changing the agenda of anthropology as a whole, from historical questions to other ones. (Barnard, 2000, p. 55)

These "other ones" were such theories as historical particularism (which, although Boas initially advocated, he eventually came to move away from this theory), culture personality, and cultural relativism. However, throughout the development of these theoretical orientations that have now fallen by the wayside, it is important to note that Boas maintained that anthropology must consist of "'complete descriptions' [which] were to be carried out by 'all available techniques,' and explanations were to be provided by embracing a wide variety of theoretical assumptions" (Harris, 1968, p. 284)

Thus, from the first formation of the field, Boas, Kroeber, and their students viewed the driving questions of anthropology to be centered on *cultures* (which in this case are the different American Indian tribes). In 1871 E.B. Tylor borrowed the word culture from the German *Kultur*, where it had become well recognized since its first appearance in the 1793 German dictionary of Adelung (1793). The original use in the German language meant the process of cultivation or the degree to which it has been carried (stemming from the Latin *cultura*, which means "growing, cultivation," from *colere*, meaning "cultivate"). Tylor (1871/1924; 1881/1924), however, radically changed this definition to one that meant a state or condition, sometimes described as extraorganic or superorganic, in which all human societies share. Later, as anthropology solidified into its own academic discipline in the late 19th century, the American school, under the guidance of Franz Boas took on a strong four-field approach to the study of "culture." Boas, who took Tylor's definition for granted, was in search of natural laws that governed the state or condition of cultural phenomena, and although he originally defended a geographical particularist viewpoint, he would later broaden that particularist viewpoint in his search for nomothetical laws. To this end, language came to be considered an important component in the study of the concept of "culture," along with archaeology and human remains, largely as a result of the Bureau of Ethnology and the direction of John Wesley Powell (1834-1902). As Duranti (2003) has shown, it was Powell who supported the young Boas's study of Chinook and other American Indian languages and commissioned what then became the *Handbook of American Indian Languages* (1911a). Thus, the concept of "culture" within the American school of anthropology came to mean a state or condition that could be operationalized through the four-field approach of ethnology (which would later become ethnography and cultural anthropology); archaeology; human remains (later to be called physical anthropology); and language (later to be conjoined with linguistics).

Although Boas would later become skeptical of the possibility of a direct correlation between language and culture (and he certainly rejected any correlation between language and race), he would maintain that the historical particularist method, in conjunction with the comparative method, was the proper approach at arriving at such laws.

> When we have cleared up the history of a single culture and under-
> stand the effects of environment and the psychological conditions

that are reflected in it we have made a step forward, as we can then
investigate in how far the same causes or other causes were at work
in the development of other cultures. (Boas, 1896/1948, p. 279)

Boas would later revise this historical particularism, arguing that there may not be
nomothetical laws governing cultures that can be comparatively analyzed, instead
arguing for the occurrence of similar institutions throughout the world that reflected something inherent in the human mind (Boas, 1911b).

Though this is not the place to discuss the particulars of Boas' view or how it is currently being interpreted by neo-Boasians (e.g., Bashkow, 2004; Bunzl, 2004; Duranti,
2003; Handler, 2004; Orta, 2004; Rosenblatt, 2004), it is important to realize that
Boas' views were fundamental in the shaping of American anthropology and its
grounding in a four-field approach to the study of the concept of "culture" and cultural phenomena. In all, Boas offered a very loose nominal definition of the concept of "culture" that was to heavily influence the students he trained:

> Culture embraces all the manifestations of social habits of a com-
> munity, the reactions of the individual as affected by the habits of
> the group in which he lives, and the products of human activities
> as determined by these habits (Boas, 1930, p. 79).

Furthermore, this loose nominal definition of the concept of "culture" and the goal
of operationalizing it was carried forward as anthropology solidified and spread
throughout various United States institutions. The diffusion of this understanding
of the concept of "culture" can be seen in the fact that the next generation of
anthropologists in America were all trained by Boas: Alfred Kroeber, Robert Lowie,
Fay-Cooper Cole, Edwin Sapir, Melville Herskovits, Alexander Goldenweiser,
Alexander Lesser, Paul Radin, Clark Wissler, Leslie Spier, J. Alden Mason, E.
Adamson Hoebel, Ruth Benedict, Margaret Mead, Ruth Bunzel, Jules Henry, M.F.
Ashley Montagu, T.D. Stewart, and Frank Speck. These students took on the proj-
ect of operationalizing the concept of "culture," primarily as a result of the strong
logical positive influence spreading through American academia at the time
(Leahey, 1987) through the newly established four-field approach.

However, as the field of anthropology has grown over the subsequent decades, the
sub-disciplines have grown further and further apart, becoming more specialized in
the development of their own respective methodologies and ultimately epistemologies. This specialization of the sub-disciplines has been both a benefit and a hindurance to the field of anthropology in general and to questions of cultural affiliation and cultural continuity in particular. It has been a benefit in that it has allowed
each sub-discipline to develop, refine, and gain command of particular techniques
and methodologies that have greatly contributed to our understanding of "the science of man and his works" (Kroeber, 1923, p. 1). Notwithstanding, this splitting
and specializing of the sub-disciplines has also greatly hindered the field of anthropology by allowing the sub-disciplines to become overly specialized to the point that
they have developed their own epistemologies, so much so that these epistemologies
are virtually mutually exclusive and there is a lack of an overarching epistemology

or praxis for the field of anthropology in general. Furthermore, because each sub-discipline has specialized to the point of being grounded within their respective epistemologies, there is no longer any (or very little) dialogue between the sub-disciplines resulting in a general lack of understanding between each discipline's data.

However, with the passage of NAGPRA and the guiding Rules, the field of American anthropology is "forced" to become a unified field of scientific inquiry once again as it was historically conceived and developed by its founders. As NAGPRA mandates in Section 7c:

> such Native American human remains and funerary objects shall be expeditiously returned where the requesting Indian tribe or Native Hawaiian organization can show cultural affiliation by a pre-ponderance of the evidence based upon geographical, kinship, bio-logical, archaeological, anthropological, linguistic, folkloric, oral tradition, historical, or other relevant information or expert opinion.

Thus, as discussed above, the founders of the field clearly imagined what NAGPRA has subsequently mandated to be the driving epistemology for the field of anthropology. Each sub-discipline is consulted according to the NAGPRA mandated guidelines of inquiry, and a unified perspective is presented based on the "preponderance of the evidence" into questions of "the science of man and his works" (Kroeber, 1923, p. 1).

It is the purpose of this book to attempt to fulfill both the historical objectives of the fields founders, as well as the current legal mandate of NAGPRA by examining the question of cultural affiliation between the present-day American Indian tribes and the peoples of the ancient past from a four-field approach. Furthermore, in an attempt to examine the question of cultural affiliation as empirically as possible, I follow an epistemological praxis of epoché throughout this book. Finally, to operationalize the area of inquiry, I specifically examine the question as it applied to the Plateau and Great Basin culture regions of the American West, focusing in particular on the issue of cultural affiliation of the Kennewick Man skeleton and the Spirit Cave Mummy.

Accordingly, chapter two goes into a more in depth discussion of what it means to examine cultural affiliation from an epistemological praxis of epoché. This epistemological stance of inquiry advocates for a much deeper suspension of *a priori* assumptions than the standard anthropological practice of "suspending judgement." Instead, not only does an epistemological praxis of epoché necessitate a suspension of judgement, but also a suspension of knowledge. As I will discuss in chapter two, this means that I have attempted to look at the data without any *a priori* assumption as to which type of data is more valid than another. That is, I have considered oral tradition evidence as equally valid as archaeological data, and so on.

Chapter three follows from the discussion in chapter two by discussing both NAGPRA and its mandated guidelines of inquiry, but also how an epistemological praxis of epoché is in line with these guidelines. Furthermore, chapter three also discusses how this framework of inquiry is in line with a four-field approach as originally advocated for by the founders of the field of anthropology.

Before I discuss the data, which I cover to some length in chapters seven through eleven, I spend a chapter discussing the history of two ancient skeletons, Kennewick Man and Spirit Cave Mummy, respectively. These two skeletons and their respective histories are used to operationalize and contextualize the focus of this book. The legal case surrounding the Kennewick Man has proven to strain the already fragile relationships between American Indians and anthropologists, and the historical and sociological neuances of the case will not be discussed. For an excellent review of the historical and sociological history of this court case, see Fine-Dare (2002) and Richman and Forsyth (2004). Instead, I use the examples of the Kennewick Man skeleton and Spirit Cave Mummy to discuss the issue of cultural affiliation and cultural continuity within the Plateau and Great Basin regions of the American West. Furthermore, both cases have already been through the NAGPRA process, and in both cases a finding of no cultural affiliation has been arrived at. There are numerous misunderstandings and fallacious conclusions within each case (see Jones, 2004a; Jones & Stapp, 2003 for a discussion of some of these misunderstandings), and this book argues that if a truly four-field approach as mandated by the NAGPRA guidelines had been followed, both cases would have resulted in different outcomes.

The following chapter discusses the anthropological operationalization of the Plateau and Great Basin regions. It is important to establish both the history of these culture regions, as well as the anthropological boundaries based on these cultural regions, for this will not only limit the scope of this book, but will also help us develo a solid background to analyze the questions of cultural affiliation and cultural continuity with.

Chapter six further establishes this background baseline by discussing the paleoenvironment of the American West. This chapter is fairly data rich, but will prove to be necessary information if we are to properly understand the issues of cultural affiliation and cultural continuity, especially when we need to distinguish between culture change or diffusion and culture migration or abandonment. Likewise, this paleoenvironmental reconstruction helps inform how far back it is theoretically possible to establish cultural affiliation, for prior to the late Pleistocene much of the Plateau and Great Basin were covered by ice or large amounts of water.

At this point, the book turns to the first of the four fields of inquiry, discussing the cultural anthropological data. Under the NAGPRA guidelines this covers the geographical and kinship evidence, as well as the historical and ethnographic data for these regions. Chapter eight turns to the physical/biological anthropological data, covering the dental, craniometric, genetic, and trichological evidence. The third field of inquiry covered is that of archaeology, where I spend some time discussing such issues as Pleistocene/Holocene subsistence lifeways and the possibility of when American Indians first arrived in the Plateau and Great Basin, as well as whether other peoples also at one time possibly lived in these regions. Chapter ten concludes the four-field approach by discussing the linguistic evidence, spending a fair amount of space focusing on the linguistic Numic Expansion Hypothesis. The final chapter that covers data important to the question of cultural affiliation is chapter eleven, in which I discuss the oral tradition evidence. This line of inquiry is not necessarily thought of as its own field, usually being placed under the general field of ethnography. However, under NAGPRA, and in line with an epistemological praxis of epoché, it is a necessary and legitimate form of data that must be given equal weight as the traditional four fields.

Before I attempt to synthesize the data discussed in chapters seven through eleven (which I cover in chapter thirteen), I spend a chapter discussing the differences between migration/abandonment evidence and theories and diffusion/evolution theories. This chapter is necessary because several confusions concerning the differences between these two radically opposing interpretations of the data has lead to fallacious readings in both the legal and academic arenas. Once I have delineated these differences, I then synthesize the data. Because I have attempted to come from an epistemological praxis of epoché throughout this book, I place the burden of proof in my a priori assumptions on discontinuity and a finding of no evidence of cultural affiliation. That is, I presuppose that until the evidence can demonstrate otherwise, it would seem both illogical and question begging to assume that the present-day American Indians of the Plateau and Great Basin have not resided in these regions since illotempore.

I conclude the book with a discussion of the future of anthropology's relationship with American Indians. As a result of the implications stemming from this work, I discuss how anthropology must learn to embrace other epistemologies in its quest to investigate and understand "the science of man and his works" (Kroeber, 1923, p. 1).

CHAPTER 2
AN EPISTEMOLOGICAL PRAXIS OF EPOCHÉ

As discussed in chapter one, I have attempted to come from an epistemolog-ical praxis of epoché throughout this book. In this chapter I discuss in some depth why it is necessary to follow such a praxis, especially in light of developments in both the theory of anthropology as well as the philosophy of epis-temology. Furthermore, this praxis will prove to be fundamental for investigating the question of cultural affiliation as the framework outline by NAGPRA specifies.

As has been mandated with the passage of NAGPRA, the now disparate fields of soci-ocultural anthropology, physical/biological anthropology, archaeology, and linguis-tics are once again "forced" to re-engage in a dialogue that was originally envisioned by the founders of the field as one of its guiding principles. There are many instances throughout history where the various sub-fields of anthropology have worked together, for example where archaeologists and cultural anthropologists, or physical anthropologists and archaeologists have come together to fulfill specific research agendas or projects. Likewise, there are also many instances throughout history where cultural anthropologists have used archaeological data, or where archaeologists have used physical anthropological data, and similar such situations. However, these examples are few and far between when one considers the entire body of literature within the field of anthropology, or how anthropology is current-ly taught within the academy.

Furthermore, because the sub-fields of anthropology have become so focused through the development of their own highly specialized and "limiting" methods and theories (for a recent discussion, see McGimsey, 2003), the majority of NAGPRA mandated cases have relied on an "out-sourcing business model" by commissioning out each area of study to specific experts within the various sub-fields (for a discus-sion of the costs associated with such a practice see Schneider, 2004). This has left the job of synthesizing these various commissioned sub-field reports/studies to lawyers, judges, or governmental officials — individuals who lack the necessary experience, training, and expertise within the field of anthropology to properly address the complex question of cultural affiliation.

In an attempt to honor and follow both the founders of the anthropological field and the guidelines of inquiry established under NAGPRA, this book is an attempt to present a unified anthropological understanding of the data concerning cultural affiliation within the Plateau and Great Basin. The epistemology taken in this book — the method and theory of knowing — is one of epoché (the suspension of all belief). This means that I have attempted to not have any *a priori* presuppositions, assumptions, or projective stances when examining the data and the questions of cultural affiliation and cultural continuity. If such an *a priori* position is taken, as is the general requirement in most anthropological research (and for that matter, all scientific research), biases are introduced at the most fundamental of levels. For example, when one begins a series of inquiries into some question with a particular epistemological stance, then they are already limiting the possible types of knowledge and the data that stems from that knowledge, as well as their interpretation and the subsequent analysis of that data. This would be no better than attempting this project with the idea in mind of either finding cultural affiliation and cultural continuity or not, despite what the data evidences. In essence, this praxis is an attempt to avoid any essentialist argument, be it for or against the finding of cultural affiliation. Instead, by coming from an epistemological praxis of epoché, I am attempting to come from a stance of emptiness in which the data (all forms of data) can stand for themselves, and no *a priori* interpretations, projections, or perceptions influence what the data actually evidence.

The idea of an epistemological praxis of epoché is foreign to most in the fields of anthropology. Though anthropology preaches the "suspension of judgement" in its data gathering and data analyzing endeavors, rarely does this "suspension" deal with epistemic issues. Instead, it usually centers on ontological, ethical, and moralistic subject matters, staying within the bounds of Occidental epistemological possibilities. Logical positivist notions, notions that have been seriously challenged by postmodern, deconstructionist, and critical theory scholars have heavily circumscribed these epistemological possibilities, until the last twenty years or so. Historically Francis Bacon outlined the essential components of Occidental "operative science" as the observation of phenomena, the formation of hypotheses concerning the phenomena, testing the hypotheses to see whether they are valid or not, and the conclusion of what the phenomena are and a validation or reformulation of the hypotheses. This "scientific method" was to inform the range of epistemic possibilities, and to help bring human understanding out from underneath syllogistic paradigms. As a result, scientists (including anthropologists) have attempted to construct theories and methods to investigate the phenomenon of humankind; "the science of man and his works" (Kroeber, 1923, p. 1). There is not, however, the space nor the need to cover the history of these theories and methods for the purposes of this book. Furthermore, as a built in component of the process of the scientific method, a continuous critique of various methods and theories has taken place.

Therefore, anthropologists, along with their methods and theories, have always been the subject of criticism, either through the continuing development of new theories that either build on the established paradigm until it fails (e.g., Kuhn, 1970), or that come from the outside and criticize the previous held theories outright. Several recent examples of the latter for anthropology include relativism, poststructuralism, Orientalism, Occidentalism, and postcolonialism. The latter three are of particular importance to this book, because these theories and their critiques have proven particularly relevant to issues of American Indian cultural affiliation. Furthermore, by briefly reviewing the central critiques of these theories, my argument will be made as to why it is critical to come from an epistemological praxis of epoché if one is to begin to truly come from an unbiased presumptive stance, as opposed to asserting that either the anthropological or American Indian perspective is "more" accurate.

The poststructuralists, along with the feminists, Orientalists, Occidentalists, and others have the common desire to move away from the more formalist ideas of functionalism and structuralism towards a looser, yet more complex (and some argue deeper), understanding of relations between culture and social action. Poststructuralism is in essence a critique of structuralist thought played out mainly in structuralist terms, with a reluctance to accept the distinction between subject and object that is implicit in structuralist thought, especially that of structuralisms founder Saussure (1916/1974). The idea of "poststructuralism" is most closely associated with the literary criticism of Jacques Derrida (1976; 1978), who is also well known for his discussions on deconstructionism. One of poststructuralisms primary critiques is that of the idea of structures, in the sense that structures are not preexisting (as structuralism assumed), and discourse should be paramount over cultural grammar. Furthermore, order is created by the anthropologist who writes about an event, not by the actor in a given time and space. Much of this understanding comes from the work of Michel Foucault (1974; 1977; 1980), who came to focus on the ways in which power and knowledge are linked. Power, according to Foucault is not something to possess, but rather it is the capability to manipulate a system. In other words, neither social nor symbolic structures are to be taken for granted, nor should they be seen as culturally agreed schemata that each member of society understands in the same way. Instead, by acknowledging that cultures are constructs of the viewer, and not the viewee, anthropologists were made aware of the interpretive nature of their work. This resulted in the development of interpretivism (Geertz, 1973).

Interpretivism represents the opposite of structuralism by claiming a rejection of meaning as embedded in structure in favor of the intuitive and interactive creation of meaning. By claiming that the creation of meaning is intuitive and interactive, interpretivism turned the standard linguistic analogy of structuralism and poststructuralism sideways. Clifford Geertz (1973) is one of the most important propounders of this theory. For Geertz, cultures can no longer be considered metaphorical "grammars" to be figured out and written down; instead they must be thought of as "languages" to be translated into terms intelligible to members of other cultures, or more often than not, to the anthropologist's culture.

As a result of interpretivism as well as its fellow theory of postmodernism, the theoretical paradigms of Orientalism, Occidentalism, and globalization emerged. These paradigms are primarily concerned with power, derived, as was noted, primarily from Foucault, the poststructuralists, and others. This resulted in the identification of power as a manifestation of colonial and postcolonial discourses through the paradigm of "Orientalism." Orientalism was largely introduced by Edward Said (1978; 2000), who attacked the West for creating a notion of the East, the Orient, in order to dominate it by trade, colonialism, imperialism, and other forms of exploitation. The West, Said pointed out, needs the Orient in order to define itself, for without the East there can be no West.

Many of these ideas were previously championed by several anthropologists (e.g. Asad, 1973; *sensu* Goody, 1996) who pointed out that during colonial times, anthropological studies were embedded in unequal relationships between the West and the "Third World." It is interesting to note that this argument has been turned on its head in recent years, resulting in Occidentalism. Occidentalism has pointed out the fact that "Oriental" peoples are just as likely to have biased and generalized visions of the West as "Occidental" peoples are of the East (e.g., Carrier, 1992; 1995). Furthermore, there are many instances where the East willingly embraced the imperialistic drive of the West. Such examples as the open industrialization of China and Japan and their own subsequent economic exchange with the West, as well as the examples of Argentina, Chile, Saudi Arabia, India, and many other countries' acceptance of Western ideologies surrounding economics, privatization, and society, readily come to mind.

Postmodernism, which in a large part embraces much of Oriental, Occidental, and globalization paradigms, constitutes the critique of all "modern" understandings. Postmodernists define what is "modernist" as what is all-encompassing in the sense that they reject both grand theory in the social sciences and the notion of completeness in any type of description. On the latter aspect, postmodernists reject the presumption of authority on the part of the teller. Thus, reflexivity, and ultimately embodiment, have come to the fore. In a wider sense, then, postmodernism in anthropology takes its cue from critical studies of "Orientalist" writing and levels its critique at the creation of the "other" (and consequently at the "self") as the driving force of all previous positions in the field. Postmodernism is also a logical development of both relativism and interpretivism, so much so that it is difficult to isolate these perspectives except superficially — i.e., by chronology, vocabulary, or style of writing.

Postmodernists often stress the arbitrary in culture, descriptions of culture, theorizing about culture, and ultimately of culture itself. As Crapanzano (1992) has noted, "Not only is the arbitrariness of the sign in any act of signification paradigmatically proclaimed but so is the arbitrariness of its syntagmatic, its syntactic, placement" (p. 88). In other words, whereas some poststructuralists (such as Bourdieu) oppose Saussurian (e.g., 1974) distinctions altogether, postmodernists expand the Saussurian notion of arbitrariness to cover not only signs themselves, but even signs in relation to other signs. Therefore the distinction which Saussure, and virtually every anthropologist has recognized, that between observer and observed, has been called into question.

Ernest Gellner attacked relativism and postmodernism as subjectivist and self-indulgent (1985; 1992). Postmodernism is the most prevalent form of relativism today, and Gellner saw it as especially problematic in its misplaced attacks on, for example, the stated objectivism of European colonial anthropological research. For postmodernists, anthropological research in the colonial era represented a tool in the hands of oppressive colonial governments and multi-national corporations. For the anti-postmodernists, postmodernism's attempt to liberate anthropology is misguided, its attacks on earlier anthropological traditions misplaced, and its subjectivity downright nonsensical. The postmodernist, says Gellner, sees anthropology as a movement from positivism (i.e., a belief in objective facts) to hermeneutics (i.e., interpretation). Yet the postmodernist movement is really a replay of the romanticist one two centuries before, in their overthrow of the classical order of Enlightened Europe.

To the "soft" postmodernists (including Geertzian interpretivists), society and culture are like a text, to be "read" by the anthropologist as surely as his or her own text will be read by his or her readers. Other postmodernists seem to see culture as "shreds and patches," each shred and each patch a play on another one. To some, culture is a series of word plays or "tropes." This leads us to the semi-nihilistic perspective that all anthropological research is relative, i.e., there is no Truth, only truths (or to put it another way, there is no History, only histories)[3]. According to this paradigmatic approach, anthropology should dissolve into literary criticism, or at best into a brand of literary criticism that has taken over a big piece of anthropology's subject matter — called cultural studies (e.g., Bratlinger, 1990). However, I do not believe that anthropology is semi-nihilistic in its perspectives, and in fact, can be used to arrive at both Truth and History, instead of claiming either one truth and history are correct while those of others are not, or that all truth and history are correct.

To lead us out of this apparent conundrum, we must go back to the origins of the scientific method. As noted, the scientific method, and thus all anthropology, rests on the four basic premises of the observation of a phenomena, the construction of a hypothesis concerning the phenomena, testing of the hypothesis, and either validation of the hypothesis or a reformulation of the hypothesis. It is the first premise, however, that is of importance for understanding an epistemological praxis of epoché and for finding a way out of the postmodernist maze. According to the current scientific method all anthropology rests on the observation of phenomena. Only upon observation of a phenomenon can the anthropologist begin to construct theories concerning the phenomena. However, if the act of observing, the observation itself, is misguided, then the theory constructed on that observation will also be faulty. This is the point of departure I take in advocating for an epistemological praxis of epoché, and that goes much deeper than the standard "suspension" of judgement. I believe, and as I attempt to follow throughout this book only by coming from an active method and theory of knowing that suspends all presuppositions can an accurate observation of the phenomena as possible be met.

Thus, in essence there is no theoretically hypothesized outcome for this book other than what the data for the Plateau and Great Basin regions actually can evidence. Or, to put it another way, the theoretical outcome of the book is that the data will be left alone so that they can stand for themselves on their own ground, and not those of a particular theory or methodology, which has actually biased the data to support the particular epistemological stance taken.

CHAPTER 3
NAGPRA AND THE GUIDELINES FOR INQUIRY

As I discussed in the introduction, I have attempted to approach the data from an epistemological praxis of epoché, as well as by following the guidelines of inquiry established under NAGPRA[4]. In the last chapter I discussed both the necessity for an epistemological praxis of epoché approach, as well as what this approach means according to anthropological theory. In this chapter I discuss NAGPRA and the guidelines of inquiry established under this law. There is not the need nor the space to cover the anthropological or legislative history of this law, other scholars have already covered this topic in detail (see, e.g., Fine-Dare, 2002; Richman & Forsyth, 2004). Instead, in this chapter I merely plan to outline the framework of inquiry established by NAGPRA and show how this framework is in accord with both an epistemological praxis of epoché, as well as a four-field approach as outlined by the founders of American anthropology.

Under the guidelines of inquiry established by NAGPRA, the following terms have been defined as follows:

> "cultural affiliation" means that there is a relationship of shared group identity which can be reasonably traced historically or prehistorically between a present day Indian tribe or Native Hawaiian organization and an identifiable earlier group. (NAGPRA, Sec. 2(2))

> "Federal lands" means any land other than tribal lands which are controlled or owned by the United States, including lands selected by but not yet conveyed to Alaska Native Corporations and groups organized pursuant to the Alaska Native Claims Settlement Act of 1971. (NAGPRA, Sec. 2(5))

"Indian tribe" means any tribe, band, nation, or other organized group or community of Indians, including any Alaska Native village (as defined in, or established pursuant to, the Alaska Native Claims Settlement Act), which is recognized as eligible for the special programs and services provided by the United States to Indians because of their status as Indians. (NAGPRA, Sec. 2(7))

"Native American" means of, or relating to, a tribe, people, or culture that is indigenous to the United States. (NAGPRA, Sec. 2(9))

"Native Hawaiian" means any individual who is a descendant of the aboriginal people who, prior to 1778, occupied and exercised sovereignty in the area that now constitutes the State of Hawaii. (NAGPRA, Sec. 2(10))

NAGPRA also clearly lays out the guidelines for determining cultural affiliation, which are as follows:

c) Criteria for determining cultural affiliation. Cultural affiliation means a relationship of shared group identity that may be reasonably traced historically or prehistorically between a present-day Indian tribe or Native Hawaiian organization and an identifiable earlier group. All of the following requirements must be met to determine cultural affiliation between a present-day Indian tribe... and the human remains, funerary objects, sacred objects, or objects of cultural patrimony of an earlier group:
    1) Existence of an identifiable present-day Indian tribe... with standing under these regulations and the Act; and
    2) Evidence of the existence of an identifiable earlier group. Support for this requirement may include, but is not necessarily limited to evidence sufficient to:
    i) Establish the identity and cultural characteristics of the earlier group,
    ii) Document distinct patterns of material culture manufacture and distribution methods for the earlier group, or
    iii) Establish the existence of the earlier group as a biologically distinct people; and
    3) Evidence of the existence of a shared group identity that can be reasonably traced between the present-day Indian tribe... and the earlier group. Evidence to support this requirement must establish that a present-day Indian tribe... has been identified from prehistoric or historic times to the present as descending from the earlier group. (43 CFR § 10.14)

As with other legislation that attempts to appropriate scientific concepts for legal purposes, there is a large degree of misunderstanding and misemployment in this process. Two of the most important concept that have been confused in the process of implementing NAGPRA are "shared group identity," and "identifiable earlier group." These two concepts are central to the effective power of the NAGPRA legislation and to the ideas of cultural affiliation and cultural continuity.

The word "group" has been difficult to fathom for those not familiar with anthropological theory when dealing with issues that are contingent upon a diachronic, deep-time perspective (for example, see the confusing interpretations Magistrate Jelderks takes, "Robson Bonnichsen et al. Vs. United States of America et al.," 2002). Many have taken the stance that when dealing with American Indians "tribe" equals "group" and they have applied this understanding nomothetically. However, this is a very limited understanding of these terms within general anthropological theory. For example, while we refer today to the Yakama Nation, Nez Perce, Shoshone-Paiute, and Confederated Tribes of the Umatilla Indian Reservation (CTUIR) as "tribes," in reality they are assemblies of smaller groups that the U.S. Government organized from the 1850s until the 1890s through the treaty or executive order process (see Figure 1).

However, at no point in prehistory were these "tribes" autonomous, isolated, self-limiting groups. In the past, and still today, these "tribes" were in contact with each other, traded goods and technologies with each other, and intermarried on a regular basis (Anastasio, 1972; Carlson, 1994; Dobyns, 1992; Erickson, 1990; Galm, 1994; Hayden & Schulting, 1997; Stern, 1998; Vehik, 1994).

Furthermore, as has been well documented in Plateau and Great Basin ethnography the present-day reservation "tribes" are a construction fabricated by the federal government, and that prior to the construction of these reservations, the "tribes" of the Columbia Plateau and Great Basin were split up into many groups who all shared a similar cultural identity, ontology, and epistemology (see Claims Commission, 1974; Commission, 1973-1975; D'Azevedo, 1986; United States Indian Claims, 1974; Walker, 1998; Wilkinson, Buffalohead, Hart, & Johnson, 1986 and articles therein). For example, the Palus and Joseph Bands of the Nez Perce reside on the Colville Reservation, and some Palus reside on the Yakama Reservation, further emphasizing this larger "group identity." In a very real sense, all of the Plateau tribes are related, and therefore all have a "shared group identity" with prehistoric American Indians of the same region.

A similar situation is also true for the Great Basin. For example, the people who are today called the Walker River and Yerington Paiute are part of the larger Northern Paiute peoples, a designation that at the time of Euroamerican contact, consisted of several linguistically homogeneous but culturally and politically distinct populations. Included among them were numerous geographically and ecologically defined subgroups for whom a consciousness of common language and a general appreciation of the geographic extent of that language constituted the principal tie. The recognition of a Northern Paiute people was historically based principally on linguistic evidence. They were not for any practical purpose politically integrated, nor did they constitute a single "tribe," prior to Euramerican contact (Alley, 1986; Claims Commission, 1974). Furthermore, the Northern Paiute peoples that make up the present-day Yerington tribe consist of three groups: *Tu-pus'-ti-kut'-teh*, which means "Cyperus bulb easters" who historically resided in the Mason valley area; the *Poat'-sit-uh-ti-kut'-teh*, which means "clover eaters" who historically lived in Antelope Valley; and the *Pam'-mi-toy*, which means "salt eaters" (Fowler, 1986a; Fowler & Fowler, 1970, 1971; Stewart, 1939, 1941, 1966).

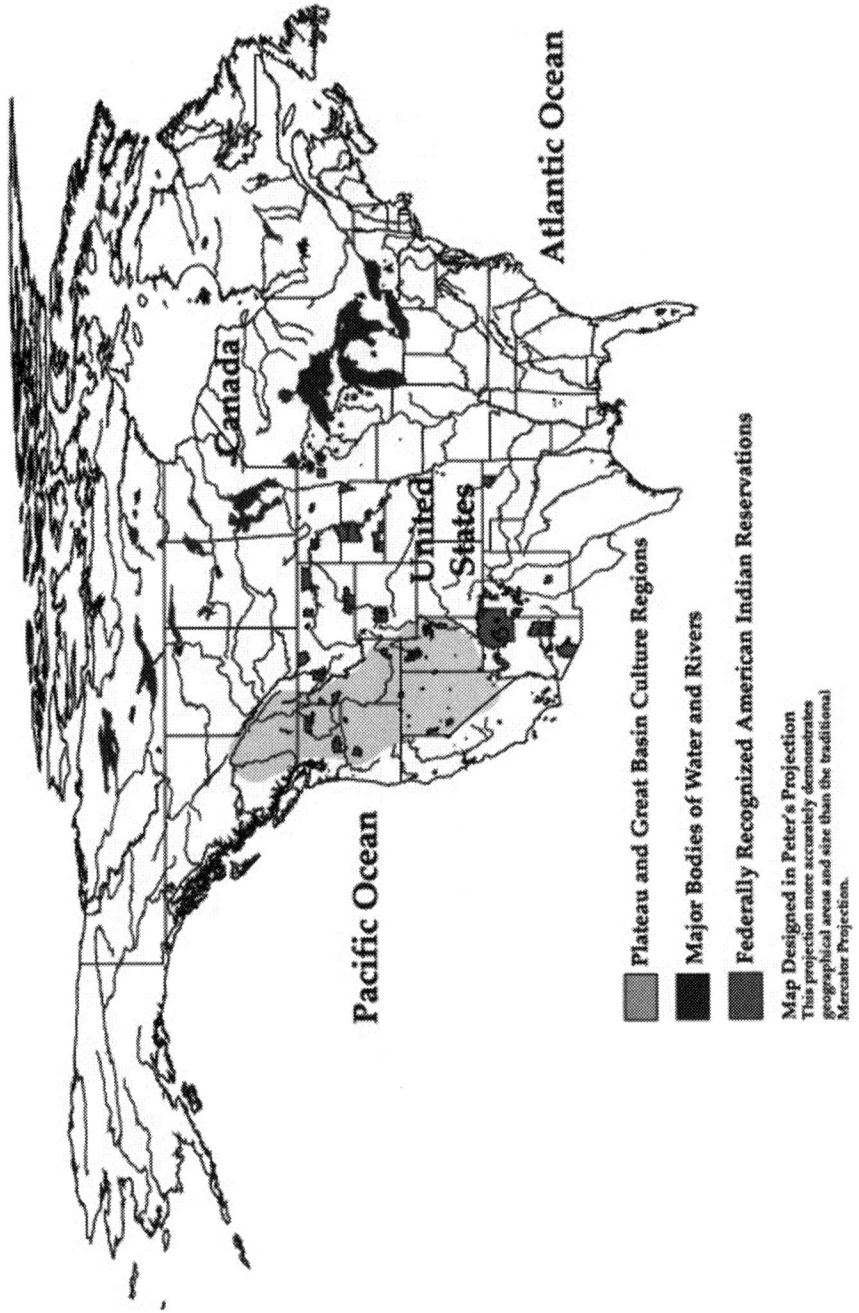

Figure 1. Map of the Lower 48 United States showing contemporary federally recognized American Indian reservations, as well as the Plateau and Great Basin culture regions.

Furthermore, it is these tribes' shared group way, with ties to places where long-standing cultural epistemologies, ontologies, and ideologies have persisted through time that ties the present-day American Indian "tribes" to prehistoric "groups." Therefore, an interpretation of the language above can be grounded in anthropological theory as requiring the existence of an earlier "tribe" (which would be composed of smaller groups) that shared a particular cultural identity, and which can be reasonably traced to the present-day Indian tribe(s) who also share this particular cultural identity, or what may be reasonably attributed to them given cultural change and cultural evolution. NAGPRA states that this must be done by looking at geographical, kinship, biological, archaeological, anthropological, linguistic, folklore, oral tradition, historical, and other relevant information and forms of evidence, along with expert opinion in determining cultural affiliation and identity.

This proves to be the most parsimonious understanding because it accords anthropological theory with the NAGPRA guidelines. In the specific cases used throughout this book to contextualize the discussion, NAGPRA makes it necessary to identify the "earlier group" of which the skeleton or item was a member, specifically the "group" of which Kennewick Man or Spirit Cave Mummy was a member. Unfortunately, as we have seen, by using "group" the language of NAGPRA does not fully express the anthropological nuances necessary for this identification to take place. If we are to accord anthropological theory with the NAGPRA guidelines, this identification should take place by examining all of the guidelines of inquiry to see if the "preponderance of the evidence" can demonstrate a link between an "identifiable earlier group" that shares a similar cultural identity, ontology, and epistemology, with a present-day American Indian "tribe."

Under Section 3 of NAGPRA and its implementing regulations the standard of proof is the "preponderance of the evidence." As Secretary of the Interior Bruce Babbitt described in his letter,

> this is a threshold that many scholars hesitate to use for interpretations based upon archaeological, anthropological, and historical evidence. The determination to be made here is informed by, but not controlled by, the evidence as a scholar would weigh it. Instead, the determination is for the Secretary of the Interior to make is the one that, on the evidence, would best carry out the purpose of NAGPRA as enacted by Congress. (Babbitt, 2000, p. 4)

This threshold thus must also attempt to strike a balance between the interest in scientific examination and investigation and the recognition that American Indians, like people from every culture around the world, have a cultural, religious, and spiritual reverence for the remains of their ancestors and their cultural patrimony. Thus, science must not divorce itself completely from the objects that it studies, nor can it forget its human foundations. These issues will be discussed in greater depth in the final chapter. Finally, by striking a balance between all lines of inquiry, the NAGPRA guidelines are also in accord with a four-field approach to the scientific study "of man and his works" (Kroeber, 1923, p. 1).

CHAPTER 4
A BRIEF HISTORY OF THE KENNEWICK MAN AND THE SPIRIT CAVE MUMMY

A s one story goes, many, many years ago, when humans first came to this land, the world was inhabited by powerful animals, monsters, and other creatures. The land that the first humans came to understand, live in, and respect was a vast and wild place. It was a time in which dangerous monsters were slain, the features of the landscape were formed and implanted with "gifts" to sustain body and spirit, and the ceremonies, social practices, and "teachings" necessary to bring order and happiness to humankind were brought forth.

As the people moved across the land, learning to hunt, fish, and gather in a proper and respectfull way, they came to call parts of the land home. Oral traditions were developed and told to be handed down from generation to generation concerning the proper way of conducting one's self towards the animals, other people, and the land. Through the years, the people continued to revisit the same places on their annual rounds, developing a strong physical, cultural, and spiritual bond with the land. Outside of their known area, the world was still a dangerous place, and people rarely left their kin, the larger community group, and the area of land that they had come to call home. As part of this continued lifeway, as time passed and people passed away, individuals who had walked before were treated with respect for their actions and wisdom in this world, and allowed to rest in peace so that they could carry on their legacy into the next. Individuals were buried, some simply, others with gifts and offerings for the future, in places of importance such as along rivers, near cliffs or bluffs, or perhaps on the side of a sacred mountain. Here these individuals were left, with the assurance that their fellow humans would not forget them. Perhaps the Kennewick Man (a.k.a., the Ancient One) or the Spirit Cave Mummy were such individuals.

Kennewick Man

In 1996, a 9,300-year-old skeleton was found on the banks of the Columbia River by a group of teenagers going to a boat race that would prove to be the impetus for the first major legal assault on NAGPRA (see Figure 2)[5]. This skeleton was found just outside Kennewick, Washington, from which the name was derived. After the Army Corps of Engineers (Corps) took possession of the remains, because the skeleton was found on federal land, they gave them to James Chatters for analysis. Chatters initially announced that the skeleton resembled that of an early European settler based on physical features. However, after an x-ray examination and CT scans, a lithic point was found embedded in the upper hipbone of the skeleton. Because of Chatters initial designation of the skeleton resembling a Caucasion, the public and media became very interested, and several destructive types of analyses were planned. At this point, several American Indian tribes opposed the study of the skeleton and requested that it be repatriated to them under NAGPRA. The Army Corps announced their intentions to repatriate the Kennewick Man, as the skeleton came to be known, to four federally recognized tribes and a non-federally recognized band. These five tribes had historically and prehistorically inhabited the region where the remains were found. At this point eight prominent scientists (the Plaintiffs) filed suit in the federal district court of Oregon to prevent the repatriation of the skeleton and demanded that they be allowed to study the remains under NAGPRA, the Archaeological Resources Protection Act (ARPA; 16 USC § 470aa-470mm), and their alleged Constitutional right to do so. The Plaintiffs primary argument was that NAGPRA did not apply to this skeleton because it could not be shown to necessarily be Native Americn as NAGPRA necessitates for its application. The lawsuit resulted in several hearings, which reversed the Corps decision to repatriate the remains and imposed de facto court oversight on the NAGPRA process. The Corps delegated its responsibility to determine whether the remains were Native American to the Department of the Interior (DOI), and if so, whether they were culturally affiliated to any of the five modern-day tribes.

The DOI then commissioned a series of lengthy and expensive studies as it attempted to determine the cultural ancestry and cultural affiliation of the skeleton (Service, 2003). These studies were then used by the Secretary of Interior to make his September 2000 determination (Babbitt, 2000) in which he found the remains to be Native American under NAGPRAs definition, as well as culturally affiliated with the tribal coalition. Subsequently, the Plaintiffs filed an Amended Complaint challenging the DOI's decisions, and asserted additional claims.

At this point the case was brought before Magistrate Jelderks of the United States district court for the Ninth District of Oregon. Legal hearings were carried out, and Magistrate Jelderks deliberated on the evidence for over nine months. Finally, on August 30, 2002, Magistrate Jelderks issued his "Opinion and Order" in which he overturned the DOI's earlier decision and claimed that "NAGPRA does not apply to

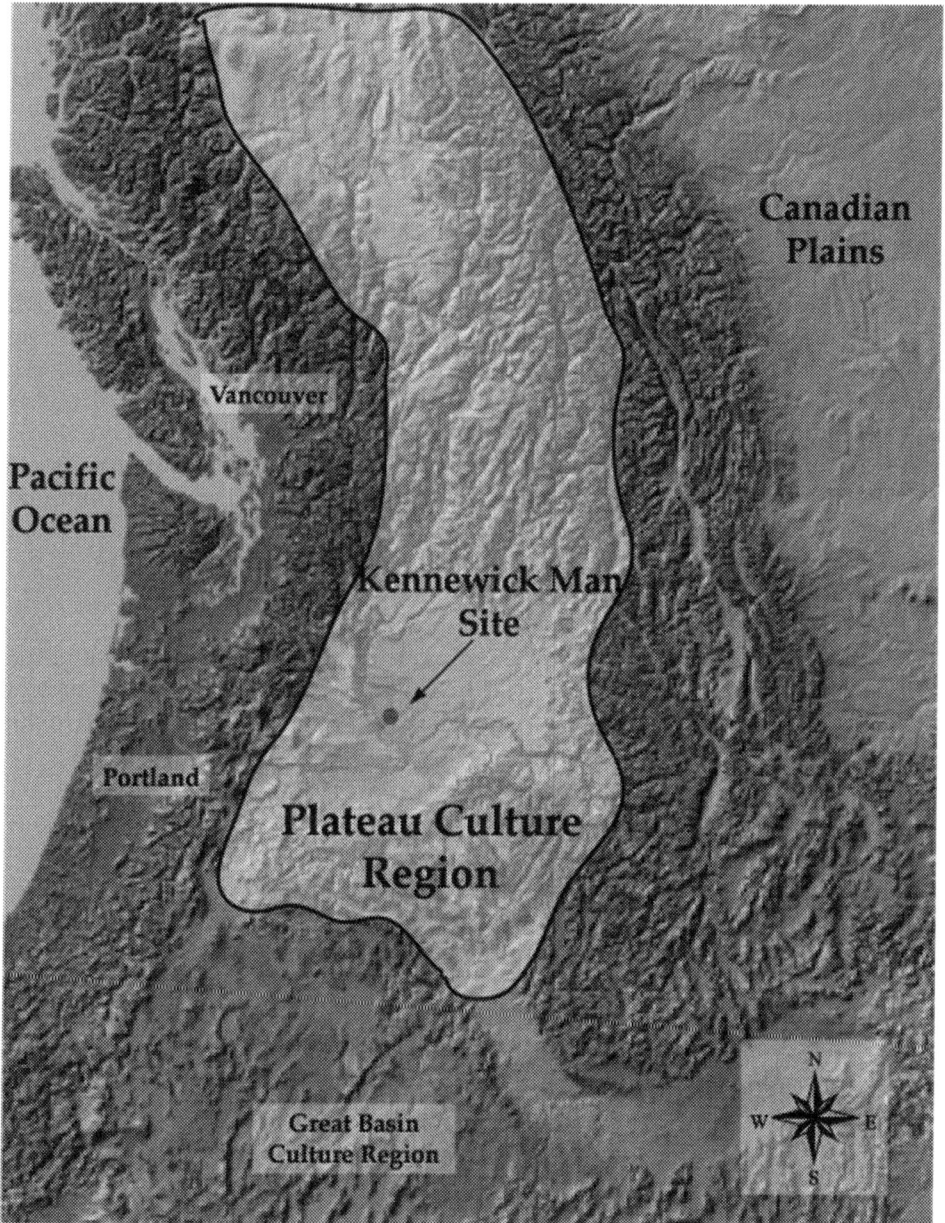

Figure 2. Map showing the Plateau culture region and the approximate location of the Kennewick Man archaeological site, located outside of Kennewick, Washington.

the remains of the Kennewick Man" ("Robson bonnichsen et al. Vs. United states of america et al.," 2002, p. 70). Furthermore, Magistrate Jelderks ordered "that Plaintiff's request for access to study be granted," ("Robson bonnichsen et al. Vs. United states of america et al.," 2002, pp. 72-73). However, briefly after Magistrate Jelderks' decision, the defendants appealed the decision to the United States Court of Appeals for the Ninth Circuit. On February 4, 2004, Judge Gould issued his opinion concerning his case. He declared that the Magistrate Jelderks had properly ruled concerning the legal proceedings and that the skeleton should be open to study by qualified scientists.

Briefly after Magistrate Jelderks reversal decision, the defendants appealed the decision to the Ninth Circuit Court of Appeals. The Ninth Circuit Court of Appeals, after another long deliberation, ruled in favor of the plaintiffs and Magistrate Jelderks opinion. The Ninth Circuit Court of Appeals found that NAGPRA did not apply to the Kennewick Man skeleton because the skeletal remains do not bear some relationship to "a *presently existing* tribe, people, or culture to be considered Native American" (Court, 2003, p. 1596). Furthermore, the Ninth Circuit Court of Appeals also found that "Human remains that are 8340 to 9200 years aold and that bear only incidental genetic resemblance to modern-day American Indians, along with incidental genetic resemblance to other peoples, cannot be said to be the Indians' "ancestors" within Congress's meaning" (Court, 2003, p. 1603).

Fifty-six years before the Kennewick Man skeleton was found eroding out of the Columbia River, archaeologists in the Great Basin discovered a similarly ancient skeleton in Nevada. This skeleton was removed from its burial site and stored in the Nevada State Museum where it came to be known as the Spirit Cave Mummy.

Spirit Cave Mummy

In March of 1996, the Nevada State Museum was approached by physical anthropologists from the University of California, Davis with a request to investigate early human remains from western Nevada. As part of this proposed investigation, 41 sets of human remains from Bureau of Land Management (BLM) managed public lands were to undergo various forms of consumptive testing, including DNA analysis and radiocarbon dating. Some of these remains had been housed in the museum for over 50 years, including the Spirit Cave Mummy that was originally excavated in 1940 by S.M. Wheeler and Georgia N. Wheeler (1940; 1969). Spirit Cave, located in the Grimes Point/Stillwater area, is located about 75 miles east of Reno, Nevada adjacent to the present-day Fallon Paiute reservation (see Figure 3).

As part of the mandated NAGPRA consultation process, the BLM contacted the Northern Paiute tribal governments and began consulting with them concerning this request. From the first consultation meeting, "the tribes strongly opposed consumptive testing and asserted their cultural affiliation with the human remains from Spirit Cave" (Barker, Ellis, & Damadio, 2000, p. 3). In March of the following year, the Fallon Paiute-Shoshone tribe formally asserted a NAGPRA claim of cultural

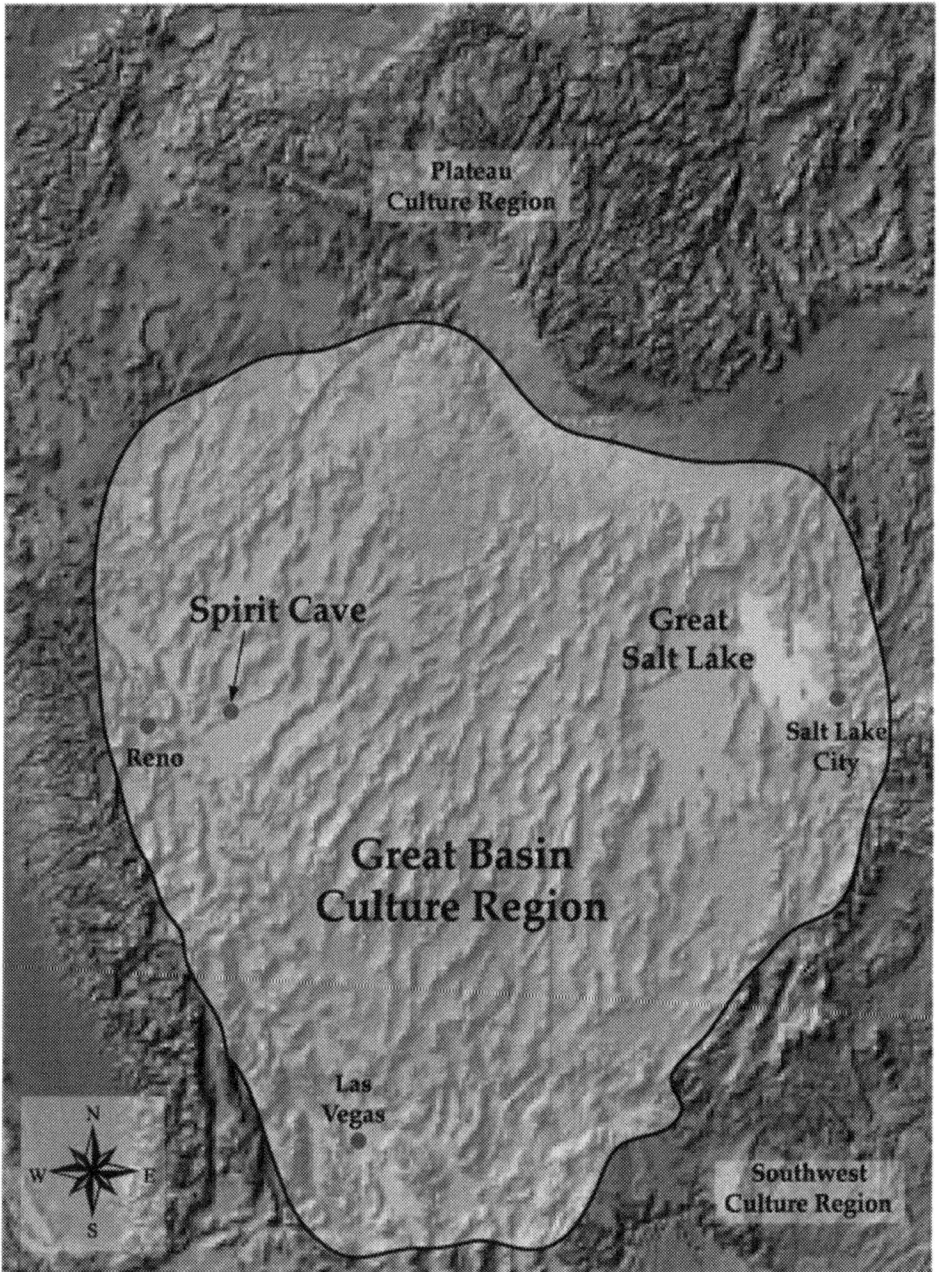

Figure 3. Map showing the Great Basin culture region and the approximate location of the Spirit Cave archaeological site, located near Fallon, Nevada.

affiliation for the Spirit Cave Mummy, representing all Northern Paiute tribal governments. In the fall of 1998 the BLM reached the preliminary conclusion that the remains from Spirit Cave were Native American, but that they could not be culturally affiliated with any living individual or contemporary human group, primarily based on its great age. In January of 1999, during a meeting to inform the tribes of this preliminary decision, the Fallon Paiute-Shoshone asked for more time to develop and present evidence of affiliation, which they were granted until December 17, 1999. On December 16, 1999 the Fallon Paiute-Shoshone tribe, through counsel, provided their response to the preliminary conclusion of non-affiliation. Finally, on July 26, 2000, the Nevada State Office of the BLM issued their final *Determination of Cultural Affiliation of Ancient Human Remains from Spirit Cave, Nevada*, which stated that:

> Based on a review of the evidence from the tribe, as well as the evidence gathered from other sources, the BLM has concluded that the preponderance of the available evidence demonstrates that the human remains from Spirit Cave are appropriately considered to be unaffiliated with the Northern Paiute, i.e., the remains predate contemporary Northern Paiute tribes and cannot be culturally affiliated with any of them. Thus, the BLM has determined that the remains from Spirit Cave are unaffiliated with any modern individual, tribe, or other group and are therefore culturally unidentified. (Barker, Ellis, & Damadio, 2000, p. 63)[6]

Both the Kennewick Man and the Spirit Cave Mummy cases are no longer involved in legal proceedings. The cases have been decided, and in both cases the skeletons were not repatriated. In the Kennewick Man case, the courts determined that the skeleton was not Native American, while in the Spirit Cave Mummy case the skeleton was found to be Native American, but not affiliated with any tribe.

As I will argued in chapter thirteen, based on a four-field approach, as well as an epistemological praxis of epoché, both the Kennewick Man and the Spirit Cave Mummy can be found to be Native American. Furthermore, as I will argue in this chapter, the preponderance of the evidence indicates that both the Kennewick Man and the Spirit Cave Mummy are culturally affiliated with the present-day American Indian tribes of the Plateau and Great Basin. First, however, it is necessary to spend some time discussing the history of the recognition of the Plateau and Great Basin culture regions, as well as the paleoenvironment of the American West.

CHAPTER 5
THE PLATEAU AND GREAT BASIN CULTURE REGIONS

In this chapter I outline the two culture regions that are the focus of this book. I first cover the Plateau culture region, followed by the Great Basin culture region, which is locted directly south of the Plateau. My aim is to briefly cover the history of the development of these culture regions within anthropology, as well as to list the present-day American Indian tribes located within each culture region. Finally, I mention the characteristics that led to the recognition of each culture region. By no means is this an in depth discussion of these topics, in fact the chapter is relatively brief. Instead, this chapter is intended to provide background information that will help contextualize the data covered in chapters six through eleven.

The Plateau culture area is a well recognized delimited area that can be defined as the region drained by the Columbia and Fraser rivers excepting certain portions of the northern Great Basin drained by the Snake River, itself a tributary of the Columbia River (Walker, 1998). The Plateau culture region encompasses the northern two-thirds of Idaho and eastern Oregon, all of Washington east of the Cascades, and the southern half of British Columbia east of the Coastal Range and west of the northern Rocky Mountains. The Plateau culture area includes the Interior Salishan peoples, the Sahaptian peoples, several cultural isolates, and Athapaskan outliers, as well as the Kootenai and Cayuse whose exact linguistic affiliations remain unclear. Current American Indian tribes located within the Plateau culture area include the Lillooet, Thompson, Shuswap, Nicola, Kootenai, Northern Okanagan, Lakes, Colville, Middle Columbia River Salishans, Spokane, Kalispel, Flathead, Pend d'Oreille, Coeur d'Alene, Yakama, Palouse, Wasco, Wishram, Cascades, Western Columbia River Sahaptins, Cayuse, Umatilla, Walla Walla, Nez Perce, Molala,

Klamath, and Modoc. It is within the Plateau culture region that the Kennewick Man skeleton was found.

The Plateau has been recognized as a distinct culture area ever since Otis T. Mason (1896) first suggested that there were 12 "ethnic environments" or "culture areas" in North America. Later, Holmes (1914) provided a map that delineated the Columbia-Fraser Rivers area, essentially following Mason's earlier designation. At the same time Wissler (1914) provided a map of the "Plateau Area" but excluded the Oregon Coast and included the Flathead-Pend d'Oreille. He also included the Chilcotin (now placed within the Subarctic culture area), but placed the Molala in the Northwest Coast, the Klamath and Modoc in California, and the Shoshone over-lapping the Plateau and the Plains. Subsequently, Wissler published his general textbook, *The American Indian* (1917), in which he did not map the Plateau area but revised his earlier map by indicating that the Kootenai, Flathead, and Nez Perce overlapped into the Plains. In 1923 Kroeber presented a map of culture areas "mod-ified from Wissler," where the Plateau extended further north, apparently including the Carrier and Sekani (now placed within the Subarctic culture area). By 1939 Kroeber was more specific, although by then his "Colubmia-Fraser" was a subarea of the larger "Intermediate and Intermountain areas," which included the Great Basin and much of California. This subarea included all those tribes in the Plateau as fol-lowed in this book, with the exception of the Klamath and Modoc (located in Kroeber's Great Basin subarea), and the Wasco, Wishram, and Cascades (placed in Kroeber's Northwest Coast). It also included the Chilcotin and, more doubtfully, the Carrier (both now located in the Subarctic culture region). Verne Ray's (1936) "Plateau Culture Area" included those treated in this book, except that the follow-ing were omitted: Klamath, Modoc, Molala, Wasco-Wishram-Cascades, Flathead, and Pend d'Oreille, and in the north the Thompson, Lillooet, Shuswap, and Kootenai. Later Ray (1939) added the last six and the Molala, and probably also the Sekani, Carrier, and Chilcotin.

For Murdock (1941) the Plateau included the same groups as those included here, with the exception of the Klamath and Modoc, which he placed in the California culture area. The definition of the Plateau culture area used here, therefore, fol-lows Driver and Massey (1957), Kroeber (1939), and Murdock (1941).

Among the distinguishing characteristics that anthropologists have used to delin-eate the Plateau culture region are:

1) Riverine (linear) settlement patterns.
2) Reliance on a diverse subsistence base of anadramous fish, as well as extensive use of game and root resources.
3) A complex fishing technology similar to that found on the Northwest Coast.
4) Mutual cross-utilization of subsistence resources among the various groups comprising the populations of the area.
5) Extension of kinship ties through extensive inter-marriage practices throughout the area.
6) Extension of trade links throughout the area through institutionalized

trading partnerships and regional trade fairs.

7) Limited political integration, primarily at the village and band levels, until adoption of the horse, at which time political integration significantly increased.

8) Relatively uniform mythology, art styles, and religious beliefs and practices focused on the vision quest, individualistic spirituality, life-cycle observances, and seasonal celebrations of the annual subsistence cycle.

Located just south of the Plateau culture region is the Great Basin culture region, where the Spirit Cave Mummy was buried and subsequently recovered. The Great Basin region comprises 400,000 square miles of western North America between the Sierra Nevada and the Rocky Mountains. It includes all of Nevada and Utah, most of western Colorado, and portions of southern Oregon, Idaho, and Wyoming, as well as of eastern California, northern Arizona, and New Mexico. Though encompassing almost one-tenth of the conterminous United States, it was the last major frontier of North America to be explored and settled by Euroamericans.

Present day American Indian groups that are located in the Great Basin culture region include the Western Shoshone, Northern Shoshone and Bannock, Eastern Shoshone, Ute, Southern Paiute, Kawaiisu, Owens Valley Paiute, Northern Paiute, and Washoe. The designation of the Great Basin culture area is based upon a synthesis of prehistoric and historic cultural and linguistic features characteristic of the human populations native to the region. Excepting for the Hokan-speaking Washoe, the cultural boundaries of the region are coterminous with those peoples who speak languages of one or the three widespread branches of Numic, a division of the Uto-Aztecan language family.

The Great Basin culture region is an area of distinctive cultural and environmental distributions, yet it has been delineated in various ways over the years. Mason (1896, pp. 646, 650-651), though providing no maps, was among the first to distinguish a Great Basin area in his classification of twelve North American culture areas or "ethnic environments." He noted what he perceived to be a close correspondence between the linguistic map that had been prepared by John Wesley Powell and the geographic distributions posed by C. Hart Merriam.

Next, Wissler (1914, pp. 449-454, 466-467) attempted to construct culture area divisions, but this initial effort suffered from a misconstrual of the historical situation, and consequently disolved the Great Basin as a distinct area. Later, Wissler (1917, pp. 16-17) presented a diagrammatic map based upon the distribution of the use of acorns and other seeds in which central and southern California and most of the central Great Basin are included in an "Area of Wild Seeds." These depictions were significantly altered by Kroeber, who first suggested a "California-Great Basin" area of general culture (1920, pp. 167-169), but later posited an "Intermediate" area among six basic "areas of native culture" in North America (Kroeber, 1923). Subsequently Kroeber (1939, p. 49) commented that "California has generally been reckoned a distinct area ever since American culture began to be classified geographically; but the Great Basin has been bandied about." Steward (1940) commented in a similar vein about the problem of classifying the region. The close relation between natural vegetation and cultural distribution was noted by Kroeber (1939, p. 13-14), a correspondence that has largely determined the boundaries of the region.

The first maps to show a detailed and accurate placement of groups and distribution of languages were those of Steward (1937; 1938), based primarily on his own fieldwork and informed to some extent by the work of Lowie (1924) with the Northern Shoshone and Kelly (1932; 1976) with the Surprise Valley Northern Paiute and the Southern Paiute. Subsequently, Kroeber (1939, map 6) became the first to delineate a Great Basin culture region in a revised version of his earlier "Intermediate and Intermountain Areas." Four subareas are identified in this map that define the extent of the culture region as generally accepted by later scholars (Driver & Massey, 1957; Fowler & Fowler, 1970; Stewart, 1966). Kroeber's inclusion of the most northeasterly Klamath-Modoc and Achumawi-Atsugewi groups was later not accepted by some scholars, who placed the Atsugewi-Achumawi in California and the Klamath and Modoc in the Plateau. The definition of the Great Basin culture region used here, therefore, follows Driver and Massey (1957), Kroeber (1939), and Murdock (1941).

Among the distinguishing characteristics that anthropologists have used to delineate the Great Basin culture region are:

> 1) Cyclical settlement patterns rotating between riparian and upland environments.
> 2) Reliance on a diverse subsistence base including seeds, fish, rabbits, and roots.
> 4) Mutual cross-utilization of subsistence resources among the various groups comprising the populations of the area.
> 5) Extension of kinship ties through extensive inter-marriage practices throughout the area.
> 6) Extension of trade links throughout the area, especially with the California, Plateau, and Southwest regions.
> 7) Limited political integration, primarily at the village and band levels.
> 8) Relatively uniform mythology, art styles, and religious beliefs and practices focused on the vision quest, individualistic spirituality, life-cycle observances, and seasonal celebrations of the annual subsistence cycle.

CHAPTER 6
THE AMERICAN WEST DURING THE PLEISTOCENE AND HOLOCENE

A s chapter four discussed, both the Kennewick Man and the Spirit Cave Mummy lived during the Late Pleistocene and Early Holocene transition in the American West. More specifically, they lived in what is now called the Plateau and Great Basin culture regions, respectively. As this chapter will discuss, this time was a period of great climatic change as glaciers melted, rivers formed, lakes dried up, and the vegetation shifted from one of a cooler/temperate biotic makeup to one more closely resembling that of today's arid, xeric biotic makup.

In order to understand how these dramatic environmental changes effected the peoples of the American West, and whether the "preponderance of the evidence," as mandated by NAGPRA, supports or does not support cultural cultural affiliation in the Plateau and Great Basin between the present-day American Indians and those peoples of the ancient record, I conducted a comprehensive review of the available data from the traditional four-fields of anthropology. Furthermore, for reasons discussed above (see chapter two) concerning an epistemological praxis of epoché and a unified four-field anthropological perspective, no particular theoretical or methodological *a priori* assumptions have been taken when conducting this research. Each of the lines of evidence contains an in-depth, epochétic review of the data along with a concluding summary of its individual findings. These summary findings are then synthesized in chapter thirteen. First, however, as discussed in chapter one, it is necessary to cover in some depth the paleoenvironmental record from the Late Pleistocene until the historical period for the American West. This chapter provides an important background context for properly interpreting the anthropological lines of evidence. I begin the paleoenvironmental reconstruction with a short discussion of major geologic periods and the paleoenvironment in Northeast Asia. This is followed by discussions of the paleoenvironment of Alaska, the Northwest Coast, Western Canada, the Plateau, California, the Great Basin, the Southwest, and the Plains. This overview allows for a comprehensive understanding of the possibility of when American Indians first possibly came to the Americas and populated certain regions, as well as helping constrain the possibilities of how far back cultural affiliation may be possible to establish. Furthermore, as will be discussed below, recent research in the Siberian arctic has revealed that humans were, in fact, subsisting above the Arctic Circle by 27,000 ybp (Pitulko et al., 2004). Thus, by including an overview of the paleoenvironmental record, this book allows for a more comprehensive understanding of the data within each line of evidence.

Paleoenvironmental Reconstruction

For the purposes of this book it is only necessary to cover the paleoenvironmental record of the latter part of the Quaternary. The Quaternary is a geologic time period that began some 2.5 million years ago with the cooling of the earth's climate and large glacial expansions across much of the northern and southern latitudes. Mid-latitudinal glaciers also formed at this time and have been present ever since then, fluctuating greatly over time. During the most recent 900,000 years these fluctuations have been amplified due to the forming of the largest mid-latitudinal ice sheets in the last 2.5 million years. It is these fluctuations, some relatively rapid, which make the later Quaternary so complex paleoenvironmentally.

The cause for these fluctuations is not well understood. There are many hypotheses, one of the more widely recognized being the Milankovitch cycles. It is thought that the Milankovitch cycles serve as triggers that start the stages of glacial and interglacial periods. Milankovitch cycles are cycles in the Earth's orbit that influence the amount of solar radiation striking different parts of the Earth at different times of the year. To explain this phenomenon three types of variations in Earth's orbital patterns have been utilized. These are the eccentricity of the orbit, obliquity (axial tilt), and precession. Based on oxygen-isotope analyses, there is evidence for as many as 21 glacial cycles that have occurred during the Quaternary period, all of which have been given various names by geologists (Bryant & Holloway, 1985b; Pielou, 1991; West, 1996; Wright & Frey, 1965). However, there are only a few that are of relevance for the purposes of this book, and they include:

> Wisconsin glaciation (80,000 years ago to 12,000 years ago)
> Sangamon interglaciation (225,000 years ago to 80,000 years ago)
> Illinoian glaciation (325,000 years ago to 225,000 years ago)
> Yarmouth interglaciation (600,000 years ago to 325,000 years ago)
> Kansan Glaciation (700,000 years ago to 600,000 years ago)
> Aftonian interglaciation (900,000 years ago to 700,000 years ago)
> Nebraskan glaciation (1,000,000 years ago to 900,000 years ago)

All of these periods were initially constructed by using terrestrial data, which has been difficult to interpret. Recently, geologists have turned towards using oxygen isotope analyses which has proven to be able to provide much more specific data. This method of reconstructing the paleoenvironmental record has produced a more complex stratigraphic sequence than any terrestrial evidence previously inferred. As a result, there has been somewhat of an abandonment of at least the

ERA	PERIOD OR SYSTEM	EPOCH OR SERIES
Cenozoic (65 million years ago - Present) "Age of Recent Life" An era of geologic time from the beginning of the Tertiary period to the present. Its name is from Greek and means "new life."	**Quaternary** (1.8 million years ago - Present)	**Holocene** (10,000 years ago — present) An epoch of the Quaternary period. It is named after the Greek words "holos" (entire) and "ceno" (new).
	The second period of the Cenozoic era. It contains two epochs: the Pleistocene and the Holocene. It is named after the Latin word "quatern" (four at a time). The several geologic eras were originally named Primary, Secondary, Tertiary, and Quaternary. The first two names are no longer used. Tertiary and Quaternary have been retained but used as period designations.	**Pleistocene** (1.8 million — 10,000 years ago) "The Great Ice Age" An epoch of the Quaternary period named after the Greek words "pleistos" (most) and "ceno" (new).
	Tertiary (65 — 1.8 million years ago) The first period of the Cenozoic era (after the Mesozoic era and before the Quaternary period).	**Pliocene** (5.3 — 1.8 million years ago) Final epoch of the Tertiary period. It is named after the Greek words "pleion" (more) and "ceno" (new).

Table 1. This table briefly summarizes the major geologic periods relevant to the discussion of this book.

early time period terminology describing glacial periods above, notably the Nebraskan, Aftonian, and Kansan interglaciation. Instead glacial and interglacial stages are now commonly referred to by their isotopic stage. However, because the names are more commonly used within the anthropological literature, continued use of the traditional naming scheme will be maintained in this book.

The current glaciation began at least 1.5 million ybp (years before present) in the Northern Hemisphere, and continues to the present. This period is known as the Pleistocene, during which time glaciers dominated the Northern Hemisphere's climatic system. Lengthy interglacial periods (times of little or no ice cover, other than around the Arctic Circle), however, occurred during the Pleistocene. The present interglaciation (often termed the Holocene) has lasted for about 10,000 years. Prior to that, climates were glacial for about 70,000 years, with two major glacial stades (a short period of time, less than 10,000 years, characterized by climatic conditions associated with maximum glacial extent) about 25,000 and 70,000 years ago that were separated by an interstade (a short period of time, less than 10,000 years, characterized by climatic conditions associated with minimum glacial extent). At the Pleistocene maximum, ice covered approximately one third of Earth's total land area with the most extensive ice sheet, the Laurentide of North America, covering the vast majority of Canada and extending southward into the United States to Long Island and the Ohio and Missouri rivers. About 130,000 to 75,000 years ago there was an interglaciation, initially slightly more intense than the modern one (i.e., the Holocene), but towards the end was marked by minor glacial stades, before which a glaciation slightly more extensive than the previous one had covered the landscape.

Thus, as can be seen, the Quaternary period has been quite complex and glacially dynamic, with various glacial stades and interstades throughout (see Table 1). For the purposes of the paleoenvironmental reconstruction that follows, only the latter part of the Wisconsin glaciation (30,000-10,000 ybp) will be covered, for it is widely held that some time during the last 40,000 years the ancestors of today's American Indians arrived in the Americas.

Northeastern Asia

Though the paleoenvironmental record of Northeastern Asia is not directly applicable to the questions of this book, it is necessary to include a brief review of this region because it is widely acknowledged that at some point in prehistory, the ancestors of today's American Indians originally came from this area (Anderson & Gillam, 2000; Bonnichsen & Steele, 1994; Bonnichsen & Turnmire, 1999; Dixon, 1999; Fix, 2002; Gibbons, 1996; Gruhn, 1994). Furthermore, it is necessary to discuss this region in order to help contextualize processes of cultural evolution and development, processes that are particularly important for addressing questions discussed in this book. Likewise, I also focus the discussion on the areas of the Bering land bridge and the coastal regions, for it is believed that the ancestors of today's American Indians migrated to the Americas either across the Bering land bridge or along a coastal route (Bonnichsen & Steele, 1994; Bonnichsen & Turnmire, 1999; Dixon, 1999; Gruhn, 1994; Rogers, Rogers, & Martin, 1992; Steele & Powell, 1999; Wright, 1999).

As has been well demonstrated, much of Northeast Asia was either wholly or partially covered by ice during much of the Pleistocene (Brantingham, Krivoshapkin, Jinzeng, & Tserendagva, 2001; Goebel, Waters, & Dikova, 2003; Ikawa-Smith, 1982;

Zhu et al., 2001). The ice-spreading center of the North Asian ice sheet appears to have been on the Arctic shelf, in the vicinity of the New Siberian Islands, with a historic maximum height of 1,700 meters (Grosswald, 1999; Grosswald & Hughes, 1999). Furthermore, this ice sheet appears to have been coalescent with the Kara ice sheet in the west and with another great ice sheet, the Beringian, in the east. This reconstruction of glacial paleoenvironments is in conflict with the usual concept of Mega-Beringia as a terrain remaining ice-free throughout the entire glacial hemicycle. Instead, it implies that parts of Mega-Beringia were predominately covered in ice, while other areas, especially during the various glacial intervals, remained ice free (Grosswald, 1999; Grosswald & Hughes, 1999).

For example, evidence indicates that glaciers were restricted to mountainous areas like the Verkhoiansk, Cherskii, and Kolyma ranges in the southwest, and Anui range in interior Chukotka, as well as the Koriak and Sredinnyi ranges in Kamchatka, while much of the lowlands of Western Beringia remained ice-free and were suitable for human habitation during the Late Pleistocene (Astakhov, 1998; Isayeva, 1984). Likewise, palynological and paleontological evidence from the Kolyma basin suggests that full glacial vegetation in many places was dominated by wormwood (*Artemisia*) (see Table 2 for a full list of flora discussed in this section), various grasses, and tundra plants, indicating areas that were not covered by glacial ice (Goebel & Slobodin, 1999).

As Grosswald and Hughes (1999) have tentatively reconstructed the Beringian paleo-ice sheet, it appears to be grounded on the Chukchi and Bering continental shelves. This Beringian ice sheet is believed to have reached an altitude of 2,000 meters, and its northern margin, buttressed by the Central-Arctic ice shelf, was thick enough to ground on the submarine Chukchi Borderland (i.e., on the Arlis Plateau, Northwind Ridge, and Chukchi Cap) at depths of 300 to 800 meters (Edwards et al., 2000; Grosswald, 1999; Grosswald & Hughes, 1999; Porinchu & Cwynar, 2002).

The Bering ice shelf floating in the deep basin of the Bering Sea fringed the southern margin of this ice sheet. The exceptionally great depths of the sea's "canyons" are hypothesized to imply the abnormally thick nature of the ice shelf, which in turn suggests that the Commander-Aleutian Ridge buttressed the latter. It was across this ridge, through deep straits and shallow saddles, that the Beringian ice was released into the North Pacific Ocean, completely covering the Aleutian Island chain during the late Pleistocene and early Holocene (Edwards, Anderson, Brubaker, Ager, Andreev, Bigelow, Cwynar, Eisner, Harrison, Hu, Jolly, Lozhkin, MacDonald, Mock, Ritchie, Sher, Spear, Williams, & Yu, 2000; Grosswald, 1999; Grosswald & Hughes, 1999).

Furthermore, stratigraphic records from coastal cliff sections on the Yamal peninsula, Russia, date the Kara glaciation to greater than 40,000 ybp (Forman, Ingolfsson, Gataullin, Manley, & Lokrantz, 2002). However, data also indicates that by the Late Pleistocene the Yamal peninsula was free of ice from this glaciation (Forman, Ingolfsson, Gataullin, Manley, & Lokrantz, 2002). Likewise, sediment evidence from Smorodinovoye Lake, Northeastern Siberia (the area to the east of the Verkhoyansk Range) indicates that vegetational and climatic changes in the upper

Indigirka basin resemble those in Eastern Siberia (Lena basin and westward), bordering Beringia (Anderson, Lozhkin, & Brubaker, 2002). It is interesting to note that maximum postglacial summer temperatures at Smorodinovoye Lake probably occurred 6,000-4,000 ybp, an age more in accordance with Eastern than Northeastern Siberian records. *Larix* appears to have arrived in these environments by 9,600 ybp, approximately when forests expanded in the east but approximately 1,500 years later than forests were established in the neighboring upper Kolyma basin. Paleobotanical data further suggest that *Larix* possibly migrated southward from populations in the arctic lowlands of eastern Siberia and did not originate from interior refugia of the upper Kolyma basin. Although a Younger Dryas cooling has been noted in Eastern Siberia, Smorodinovoye Lake provides further evidence from the Northeast for a similar climatic reversal. Climatic variations seemingly have persisted between the Indigirka and Kolyma basins over at least the last 11,000 years, despite the proximity of the two drainages and the occurrence of major changes in boundary conditions (e.g., seasonal isolation, sea levels) that have influenced other regional climatic patterns (Anderson, Lozhkin, & Brubaker, 2002).

This paleoclimatic distinction between two neighboring valleys demonstrates the difficulty in attempting to reconstruct the paleoenvironmental record for such a large area as Northeastern Asia. Briefly, it is possible to note that the Kara diamicton reflects regional glaciation of the Kara and Barents seas with the ice sheet overriding the Yamal Peninsula approximately 40,000 ybp, possibly during the early Wisconsin 80,000-60,000 ybp or earlier. The ice-sheet configuration and limit associated with the deposition of the Kara diamicton remains unresolved, but may approximate maximum reconstructions. The Varjakha peat and silt subsequently accumulated on top of the Kara diamicton approximately 45,000-35,000 ybp and reflects regional warming. Further, there is no geomorphic or stratigraphic evidence to indicate coverage or proximity of the Yamal Peninsula to a Late Pleistocene ice sheet (20,000-10,000 ybp). The Late Pleistocene ice sheet margins lie between Novaya Zemlya and the Yamal Peninsula, with eastern expansion possibly limited by the 400-m-deep East Novaya Zemlya Trough. Finally, the discovery of birch trees (*Betula spp.)* 10,000-9,000 ybp, rooted in the upper Baidarata sand, indicates at least a 200-km shift northward of treeline from present limits, which reflects a 2-4°C summer warming across this region (McDonald, Carmack, McLaughlin, Falkner, & Swift, 1999). This warming resulted in permafrost degradation and deepening of the active layer that permitted the rooting of the birch trees (Forman, Ingolfsson, Gataullin, Manley, & Lokrantz, 2002).

To summarize, the paleoenvironment of Northeastern Asia was much like that of Alaska during the same time, though as we will see, perhaps slightly more glaciated. At no time during the Pleistocene does it appear that the entire Northeast region was covered in glacial ice. The two main ice sheets, the Beringian in the east and the Kara in the west, were coalescent, covering large amounts of Northeastern Asia during much of the Pleistocene. However, many of the valleys and sections between these ice sheets remained ice free, each with a highly variable and distinct climatic regime, such as was discussed for the Kolyma and Indigirka basins. This allows for the possibility that peoples could have inhabited particular areas of Northeast Asia during the Middle and Late Pleistocene, and that by the time birch and *larix* (larch) forests were established, much of the land would have been readily habitable, as the archaeological evidence suggests (see chapter nine).

Alaska

Similar to Northeastern Asia, the Alaskan region experienced drastic environmental changes during the Pleistocene and Holocene. A brief overview of the Alaskan region during this time reveals that the paleoenvironment for the region was actually quite diverse, and not as glaciated during the Pleistocene as Northeast Asia. Similarly, as a whole, there were several intervals during this time when eustatic lowering of the sea level exposed large tracts of the shallow Bering and Chukchi Sea floors. This vast plain formed a broad land connection (known as the Bering Land Bridge) between Northeast Asia and North America, permitting extensive biotic interchange between the two continents. During these times of eustatic sea level lowering half the area of Alaska remained unglaciated, and provided important refugia for plants, animals, and people (see Figure 4). Because it has generally been understood that the Bering Land Bridge provided a key route for the migration of biota during the Pleistocene, much of the palynological and paleoenvironmental research in Alaska has been directed towards reconstructing the history of the Beringian environment, and the postglacial development of modern vegetation. Briefly, pollen data suggest that boreal forest and tundra vegetation had developed in much of Alaska by late-Pliocene times. A few sites from which pollen data of middle-Pleistocene age are available suggest that tundra vegetation existed in areas now covered by boreal forest. Late-Pleistocene records further suggest that tundra and boreal forest environments coexisted in Alaska during the Sangamon Interglacial (225,000-80,000 years ago), but the severe climate of the Early Wisconsin (80-75,000 years ago) glacial interval reduced many of those forests and replaced them with herbaceous tundra. This was followed by the long Middle Wisconsin interstadial that was characterized by oscillating climates and widespread tundra vegetation, along with boreal forest or forest-tundra that appears to have been restricted to either the interior or various coastal refugias of Alaska during the warmer intervals of the interstadial. The subsequent Late Wisconsin glacial interval appears to have been cold and arid, with trees and shrubs becoming less frequent while herbaceous tundra covered most of unglaciated Alaska. By 14,000 years before present (ybp) data indicate that shrub tundra began to replace herbaceous tundra as climatic warming began. At the Pleistocene/Holocene boundary *Populus* (cottonwood) spread widely in Alaska, followed by *Alnus* (alder) in early-Holocene time. Finally, boreal *Picea* (spruce) appeared in interior Alaska 9,500 ybp and spread to Cook Inlet by 8,000 ybp and to western Alaska by 5,500 ybp (Ager & Brubaker, 1985; Anderson, 1984; Anderson, Bartlein, & Brubaker, 1994; Briner & Kaufman, 2000; Heusser, 1965; Kaufman, 2001).

Taking a closer look at specific data for the Alaskan region, it becomes evident that many of the inlets of the coast were quite habitable during the Quaternary and that they acted as biotic refugia during the glacial periods. For example, investigations indicate that a boreal forest of *Picea*, *Alnus*, and *Betula* (birch) with *Polypodiaceae*

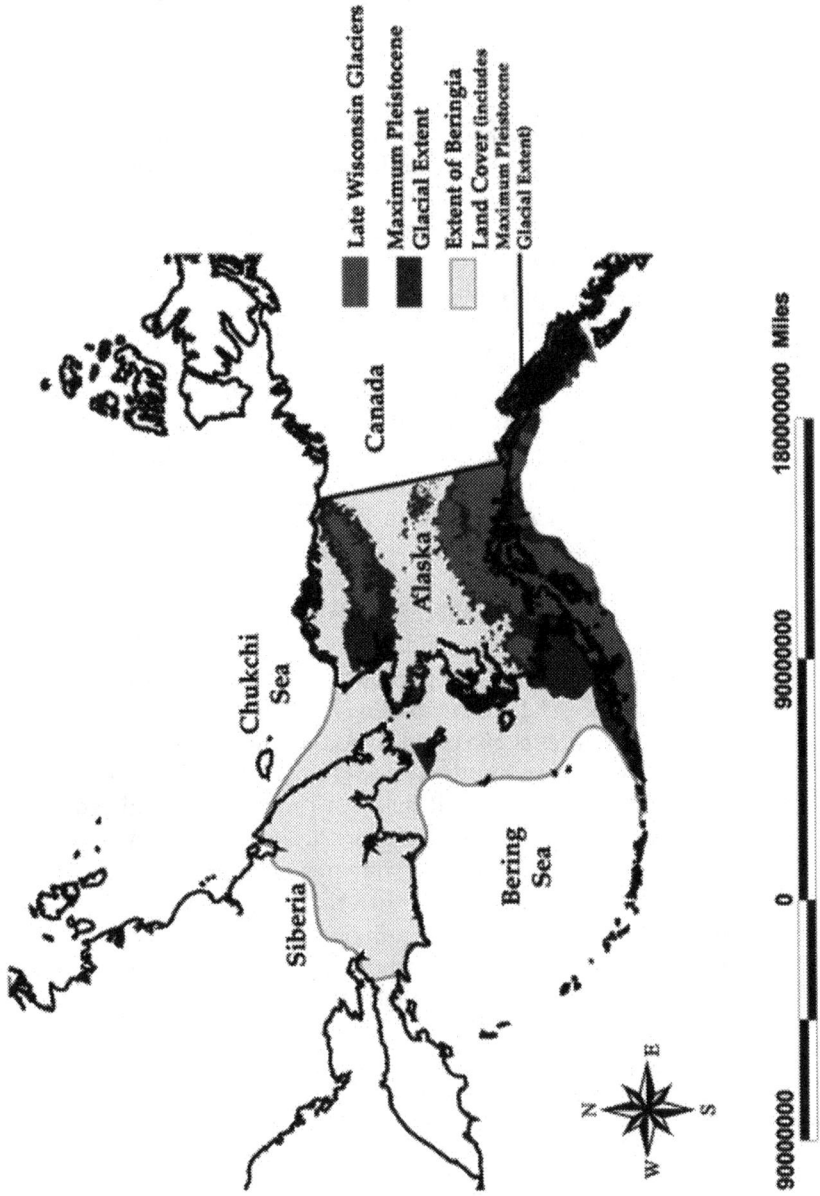

Figure 4. Map showing the glacial coverage of Alaska and Northeast Asia during the glacial maximum of the Pleistocene.

(fern) existed in Upper Cook Inlet in southwest Alaska prior to the Naptowne Glaciation (25,000-9,000 ybp), when it appears that the climate was probably quite similar to that of the present day. Furthermore, glacial deposits in the southwestern Ahklun Mountains, southwestern Alaska, record two major glacier advances during the late Pleistocene. Known as the Arolik Lake and Klak Creek glaciations, these events took place during the Early and Late Wisconsin, respectively. During the Arolik Lake glaciation, data indicate that outlet glaciers emanated from an ice cap centered over the central portion of the Ahklun Mountains and expanded beyond the present coast. During the Klak Creek glaciation, ice-cap outlet glaciers terminated roughly 60 km up valley from Arolik Lake moraines (Briner & Kaufman, 2000). Thus, at times inlets were glaciated while at other times large portions were ice free (Kaufman, 2001; Mann & Peteet, 1994).

Turning inland, the paleoenvironmental data indicate that the climate during the Quaternary was quite different than that of the southwest coastal area just described. The available data suggest that the Sangamon interglacial was a complex climatic event during which various boreal forests of interior Alaska expanded into and retreated from tundra zones paralleling the western and northern coasts (Anderson, Bartlein, & Brubaker, 1994). For example, the Goose Bay peat north of Anchorage is thought to be of Sangamon age, and suggests that boreal forest vegetation occupied upper Cook Inlet during the interglacial. However, a little further inland, the Late Pliocene vegetation at Lost Chicken in eastern interior Alaska indicates the area was covered by boreal forest of *Picea*, *Betula*, and *Alnus*, but with the addition of *Pinus* (pine) and *Larix,* which do not grow in the area today (Hofle, 2000; Kaufman, 2001).

In northwestern Alaska much of the same vegetation seems to have been present, though in a slightly different pattern. Pollen analysis of a core from Joe Lake indicates that four tundra and two forest-tundra types characterized the Quaternary vegetation of northwestern Alaska. Over a span of the last 40,000 years it appears that a *graminoid-Salix* tundra dominated during the later and early portions of the glacial record, while the middle glacial interval and the transition from glacial to interglacial conditions were characterized by a *graminoid-Betula-Salix* tundra. A *Populus* forest-*Betula* shrub tundra existed during the middle portion of this transition, being replaced in the early Holocene by a *Betula-Alnus* shrub tundra. The modern *Picea* forest-shrub tundra found in the region today was established by the middle Holocene. This data suggest that the composition of modern tundra communities in northwestern Alaska developed relatively recently and that throughout much of the late Quaternary, tundra communities were unlike the predominant types found today in northern North America (Anderson, Bartlein, & Brubaker, 1994).

It is important to note that much of our knowledge of this time period is still incomplete. Early Wisconsin records are rare, but the data suggest that the climatic episode was very cold and arid, and sparse herbaceous tundra vegetation occupied most of unglaciated Alaska. The Middle Wisconsin, a long interval of oscillating climates that ended about 26,000 ybp, seems to indicate that tundra vegetation was widespread, but that *Picea* forests and forest-tundra existed in the valleys of interior Alaska at least during the warmest intervals of the interstadial.

The Late Wisconsin glacial interval was again a cold, arid period where large tracts of *Picea* forests and forest-tundras retreated and were replaced by predominately herbaceous tundra. By 14,000 years ago data indicates that the climate changed towards warmer, moister conditions, and shrub tundra vegetation with dwarf *Betula* spread rapidly into many parts of the region where only herb tundra or glacial ice had existed previously. By around 11,000 ybp *Populus* stands developed in many parts of the region, even in areas beyond the present tree limit in western and northern Alaska. This nearly simultaneous spread of *Populus* suggests that a climatic threshold had been crossed that permitted small populations of *Populus* (probably *Populus balsamifera*) that had survived in biotic refugias during the Late Wisconsin to quickly expand into previously unsuitable habitats. By about 9,500 ybp *Alnus* began to invade southern Alaska from the coastal refugias. *Picea* first appeared in Holocene age pollen records in eastern interior Alaska by about 9,500 ybp, then spread southward, reaching Cook Inlet around 8,000 ybp, and westward, nearing the present tree limit by 5,500 ybp. In general, vegetation types quite similar in composition to those of today reached their approximate modern distributions in many areas of interior Alaska by the mid-Holocene time (Ager & Brubaker, 1985; Anderson, Bartlein, & Brubaker, 1994; Wiles, Post, Muller, & Molina, 1999; Zazula et al., 2003).

Further north, on the arctic coastal plain of northern Alaska, data indicate that during the Late Pliocene (2.5-1.8 million ybp) *Picea*, *Betula*, and *Ericaceae* forest-tundra existed along with small amounts of *Pinus* and *Larix*. This suggests that boreal forest vegetation grew in northern Alaska at that time, whereas today the vegetation is wet tundra (Ager & Brubaker, 1985). During the Middle Pleistocene the pollen data suggest that the vegetation shifted between shrub tundra and herbaceous tundra. Furthermore, a few samples from interior Alaska thought to be of Middle Pleistocene age suggest that treeline was significantly lower than it is today in the region, and that tundra and shrub communities covered much of the landscape.

Closer to the Bering Sea coast in northwestern Alaksa data indicate that Cordilleran ice from the south did not retreat from the Aleutian terminus of Beringia until some 11,000 years ago (Aigner & Del Bene, 1982). Access to the terminus was limited to a northern route since the Cordilleran ice remained longer to the south and southeast. However, at the same time, the south Beringian coast from the Gulf of Anadyr to Bristol Bay lacked glacial ice (Aigner & Del Bene, 1982; Anderson, Bartlein, & Brubaker, 1994).

Data for this region along with the Alaskan peninsula and Kodiak Island indicate that a glacier complex composed of confluent alpine glaciers, island ice caps, and piedmont lobes covered much of the area during the last glacial maximum (LGM). Because this glacial complex formed the southeastern border of Beringia, its dynamics may have been important in the timing and feasibility of the Northwest Coast route for human migration into lower-latitude North America (Mann & Peteet, 1994). Like much of the rest of Alaska during this time, it appears that the area had a combination of glacial complexes intermixed with forest-shrub-tundra environments and biotic refugias. Furthermore, it appears that at no point in time was the entire area completely covered by glacial ice. However, this does not appear to be true for the eastern Aleutians. Prior to 12,000-11,000 years ago the eastern Aleutians (including Anangula) were under an extensive ice cap. Any flow of land-based biota between the mainland and the central Aleutians would have been difficult. Deglaciation is now determined to have begun about 11,000 years ago, thus dating the opening of the Aleutians for the first time to human occupation to the Early Holocene.

On the other side of Alaska in the Homer area, which connects southwest Alaska and many of the inland and coastal biotic refugias to the Northwest Coast and interior British Columbia, data indicate an early post-glacial tundra-like vegetation with low shrubs, ferns, and *Umbelliferae*, followed by the development of *Alnus-Betula* shrub/scrub vegetation. Later, during the Early Holocene, a *Pinus-Alnus-Betula* forest dominated the region. It is unknown whether the invading *Picea* was boreal *Picea mariana* or the coastal spruce *P. sitchensis*, both of which grow in the Homer area today (Ager & Brubaker, 1985).

To summarize, therefore, it appears that during Illinoian, Wisconsin, and recent times glaciers were much more extensive in southern Alaska than in northern Alaska and were nourished chiefly by air masses moving north-northeastward from the northern Pacific Ocean. The Wisconsin glaciation in Alaska was clearly a complex event, consisting of at least two major advances and including several minor oscillations during the last major advance. However, as has been discussed, large sections of Alaska remained ice-free throughout the Pleistocene, including both large inland sections and coastal refugias. Therefore, though parts of Alaska may have been too inhospitable for people and certain types of fauna, much of inland Alaska, and various coastal refugias along the valley floors of fjords remained ice-free and quite hospitable during the Pleistocene, possibly allowing humans and fauna to slowly migrate into the Americas either through the "ice-free corridor" route or along coastal refugias.

Northwest Coast

The Northwest Coast paleoenvironmental record is less well known than that of Alaska, especially along the upper British Columbia coast and among the Queen Charlotte Islands. However, at the same time it is not nearly as complex as the Alaskan record because the region lies along the Pacific Ocean and the entire region is affected by the same ocean currents and weather patterns.

Briefly, pollen records dating back to the Early Wisconsin in Washington indicate a contrasting paleoenvironment of tundra, parkland, and closed coastal forest. Tree line in the Pleistocene apparently fluctuated across southwestern Washington and, as has been discussed, during the Early Holocene advanced to higher latitudes in Alaska and to higher altitudes in the cordillera of British Columbia. Advance of forest environments northwestward along the coast was from unglaciated biotic refugia located in Washington, southeast and southwest Alaska, and possibly in the Queen

Charlotte Islands of British Columbia and other places along the Pacific slope. Lodgepole pine (*Pinus contorta*) and alder (*Alnus*) invaded deglaciated ground in British Columbia and southeast Alaska during the late-glacial Pleistocene, followed in the Holocene by Sitka spruce (*Picea sitchensis*), western hemlock (*Tsuga hetero*

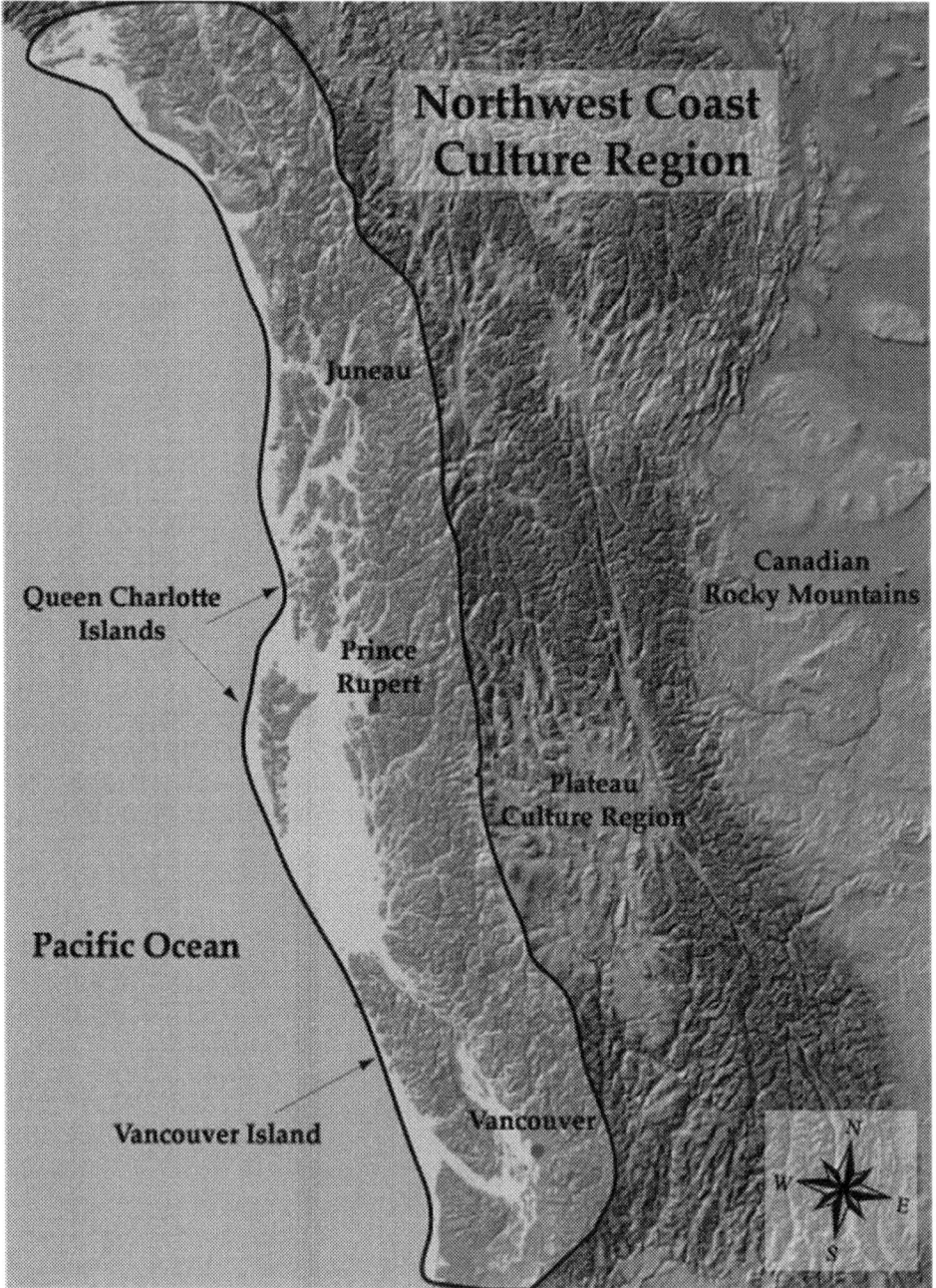

Figure 5. Map showing the Northwest Coast culture region.

phylla), and mountain hemlock (*Tsuga mertensiana*), which within approximately the past 2,000-3,000 years reached south-central Alaska.

During this expansion of forest environments in the Late Pleistocene and Early Holocene, records indicate relatively warm, wet intervals at 47,000 ybp and around 30,000 ybp, with the coldest and driest conditions between 28,000 and 13,000 ybp. Holocene warmth and dryness became pronounced about 8,000 years ago, after which the climate became cooler and more humid. During earlier interglaciations, temperatures comparable to the Holocene are evident in records of the Alderton and Whidbey Formations, whereas the record of temperature for the Puyallup Formation is about 2 degrees Celsius lower than for the Holocene (Heusser, 1965, 1985).

More specifically, looking at the paleoenvironment beginning in the north, knowledge of the Queen Charlotte Islands, as well as the upper British Columbia coast during this time is sparse, though recent studies indicate changes in tree line and climate during the Early Holocene. These studies suggest a warmer-than-present climate accompanied by higher-than-present tree lines in the early Holocene (between 9,600-6,600 ybp). For example, basal ages at SC1 Pond and Shangri-La Bog located in the Queen Charlotte Islands indicate that basins did not hold permanent water before 7,200 ybp, consistent with a warmer and drier Early Holocene. Furthermore, pollen and plant macrofossils indicate the initial establishment of subalpine conditions by 6,090 ybp in parts of the Queen Charlotte Islands, which is similar to the 5,790 ybp age for cooling inferred from Louise Pond. Furthermore, conditions similar to present were established at SC1 Pond by 3,460 ybp, confirming the previous estimate of 3,400 ybp for similar conditions at Louise Pond (Pellatt & Mathewes, 1997).

Likewise, the paleoenvironmental data indicate that the regional pattern of ocean circulation off the west coast of North America was further south 15,000 ybp than it is today, and reached its present location around 13,000 ybp. That is, the North Pacific Drift and Transition Zone were further south as a result of a more southerly North Pacific high-pressure cell prior to 13,000 ybp. These data indicate that changes in the past latitudinal position of the North Pacific Drift played a significant role in controlling continental climate immediately to its east (i.e., in the Northwest Coast region), as it does in the present environment (Sabin & Pisias, 1996).

Further south, the paleoenvironmental record from Washington and Oregon is better known, and several glacial complexes have been identified that appear to have covered large extents of land during the Quaternary period. For example, the Puget Lobe reached its maximum southern extent around 14,500-14,000 ybp and appears to be asynchronous with the Purcell Trench Lobe of the Cordilleran Ice Sheet. This suggests that advances of glacier lobes off the southern margin of the Cordilleran Ice Sheet were nonsynchronous, as the Purcell Trench lobe east of the Cascade Range advanced to its maximum southern extent before the Puget Lobe west of the Cascades reached its maximum southern extent (Beget, Keskinen, & Severin, 1997).

Geologists have divided the Cordilleran Ice Sheet in the Fraser lowlands and the Strait of Juan de Fuca for the last glacial period into four distinct phases.

> Phase SI: 12,500-11,400 ybp; glaciers receded dramatically, and the climate warmed.
> Phase SII: 11,600-11,400 ybp; a brief glacial re-advance occurred along with a climatic cooling.
> Phase SIII: 10,980-10,250 ybp; another brief glacier re-advance followed by glacier retreat.
> Phase SIV: 10,250-10,000 ybp; another glacier re-advance followed by glacier retreat.

Data further indicates that during the last stages of deglaciation (12,500-10,000 ybp), the Cordilleran Ice Sheet thinned rapidly and retreated northward. When ice water vacated the Strait of Juan de Fuca, marine waters entered the Puget Lowland that led to a rapid retreat of the ice sheet by 12,500 ybp (Easterbrook, 1963, 1992; Kovanen & Easterbrook, 2002).

Further out, on the Olympic Peninsula, data indicates that large glaciers descended western valleys of the Olympic Mountains six times during the last (Wisconsin) glaciation, terminating in the Pacific coastal lowlands. The early Wisconsin Lyman Rapids advance, which terminated prior to 54,000 ybp, represented the most extensive ice cover of the Wisconsin period. Subsequent glacier expansions included the Hoh Oxbow 1 advance, which commenced between 42,000 and 35,000 ybp; the Hoh Oxbow 2 advance between 30,800 and 26,300 ybp; the Hoh Oxbow 3 advance between 22,000 and 19,300 ybp; the Twin Creeks 1 advance between 19,100 and 18,300 ybp; and the subsequent, undated Twin Creeks 2 advance. The Hoh Oxbow 2 advance represents the greatest ice extent of the last 50,000 years, with the glacier extending 22 km further down valley than during the Twin Creeks 1 advance, which is correlated with the last glacial maximum. Local pollen data also indicate intensified summer cooling during successive stadial events. Because ice extent was diminished during colder stadial events, precipitation – and not summer temperature – influenced the magnitude of glaciation most strongly. Furthermore, regional aridity, independently documented by extensive pollen evidence, limited ice extent during the last glacial maximum (Thackray, 2001).

In western Washington beyond the limit of the Fraser Glaciation between 22,000-18,500 ybp (Porter, Pierce, & Hamilton, 1983) a different environment dominated the landscape. Vegetation graded from tundra, through parkland of spruce and other conifers, to pine woodland. Between 17,000-14,000 ybp (Waitt & Thornson, 1983), parklands of pine, spruce, while mountain hemlock prevailed, and tundra was limited to the colder valleys in the mountains.

Data further indicates that unglaciated western Washington was a Pleistocene refugium and important locus for late-glacial and Holocene plant migrations northward into British Columbia. This is similar to the Queen Charlotte Islands, that also were unglaciated in part during the Late Wisconsin and supported another locus that supplied disseminules, enabling the spread of plants in British Columbia and southeast Alaska (Heusser, 1965, 1985). It is interesting to note that though many of these refugia areas are currently underwater as a result of Holocene sea level changes, the oldest archaeological sites found in the Northwest Coast area are located along the edges of these refugias (Fladmark, 1985; Hester & Nelson, 1978; Hobler, 1982).

Climatic trends over the Pleistocene indicate relatively warm and wet intervals at 47,000 and around 30,000 ybp with the coldest and driest conditions in effect between 28,000 and 13,000 ybp for western Washington. After 13,000 ybp, annual temperature increased three degrees Celsius to a maximum at about 8,000 ybp, while an initial increase of 1,100 mm of precipitation by about 10,000 ybp was followed by a decrease amounting to some 900 mm when maximum temperature was reached. After 8,000 ybp, the climate has been in general colder and wetter with annual lowest temperature and heaviest precipitation between about 5,000-2,000 ybp (Heusser, 1965, 1985).

Further south in western Oregon, detailed data on late-glacial variations in vegetation and climate, as well as on the extent and character of Younger Dryas cooling in the Pacific Northwest, suggest that a subalpine forest was present at Little Lake, central Coast Range, between 15,700 and 14,850 ybp. A brief warm period between 14,850 and 14,500 ybp is suggested by an increase in *Pseudotsuga* pollen and charcoal, with the recurrence of subalpine forest at 14,500 ybp indicating a return to cool conditions. A subsequent warming trend is evidenced by the reestablishment of *Pseudotsuga* forest by 14,250 ybp followed by increased *haploxylon Pinus* pollen between 12,400 and 11,000 ybp indicating cooler winters than before, followed by warm dry conditions and the expansion of *Pseudotsuga*. Nearby, subalpine parkland occupied Gordon Lake, western Cascade Range, until 14,500 ybp, when it was replaced during a warming trend by a montane forest. A rise in *Pinus* pollen from 12,800-11,000 ybp indicates an increased summer aridity, while *Pseudotsuga* dominated the vegetation after 11,000 ybp. Other records from the Pacific Northwest also show an expansion of *Pinus* from around 13,000 to 11,000 ybp. This expansion may be a response either to submillennial climate changes of Younger Dryas age or to millennial-scale climatic variations (Grigg & Whitlock, 1998). This indicates that Oregon experienced a fluctuating climate during the Younger Dryas, but was predominately unglaciated by this time.

Thus, to summarize this region, it appears that much of the Northwest Coastal region was heavily submerged under the Cordilleran Ice Sheet throughout large parts of the Pleistocene. However, similar to the Alaskan coast, refugia areas remained ice-free throughout the Pleistocene providing biotically rich areas for flora, fauna, and possibly humans. Furthermore, many of the larger river valleys remained ice-free, disgorging large amounts of glacial moisture. These areas, along the glacial edge, are some of the richest biotic communities for both flora and fauna, providing ample resources for humans during the Pleistocene (Barrie & Conway, 1999; Beget, Keskinen, & Severin, 1997; Mehringer, 1985b). Likewise, as the archaeological record for the Northwest Coast indicates, the earliest sites presently known in the region are found within these coastal refugias, and seem to indicate movement north-south from refugia to refugia as well as west-east from refugia up through coastal valley floors.

Canada

Canada is an enormously large country that has several diverse and complex environments, both presently and prehistorically. Furthermore, Canada lies outside the scope of this book. However, it is important to briefly comment on the connection between the Laurentide Ice Sheet and the Cordilleran Ice Sheet and the "ice-free corridor" that is considered one of the ways the ancestors of today's American Indians came to the continental United States (Adams, 1997; Bonatto & Salzano, 1997b; Bonnichsen & Schneider, 1999; Bonnichsen & Steele, 1994; Bonnichsen & Turnmire, 1999; Pielou, 1991).

Most geologists now believe that there either was an ice-free corridor during the entire Wisconsin glaciation, or that, if Laurentide and Cordilleran ice did come into contact, the contact lasted only a few thousand years. In either view, there would have been a corridor running between the ice sheets from at least 75,000 years ago to the end of the Pleistocene, with the possible exception of a single, relatively brief, interval (Pielou, 1991). Furthermore, the exact location of that corridor would have shifted as the ice masses themselves shifted, but that would not alter the fact that such a corridor seems to have existed (Grayson, 1993; Holloway & Bryant, 1985; Ritchie, 1985; Williams, Webb, Richard, & Newby, 2000).

At the end of the Pleistocene, the climate warmed considerably and the Cordilleran and Laurentide Ice Sheets began to recede. This was a rapid process that began as early as 13,000 ybp and may have been achieved everywhere in the south by about 8,000 to 6,000 ybp. However, ice persisted in the Nouveau-Quebec-western Labrador region until about 6,000 ybp, which delayed warming air from reaching the northern regions of Canada. Afer 6,000 ybp influx values at sites in central Quebec, Nouveau-Quebec, and Labrador increased gradually to maximum proportions by about 4,000 ybp reflecting the northward migration of forests, notably composed of spruce, in response to the warmer conditions (Anderson, 1985). On the other side, the Cordilleran Ice Sheet receded into the Rocky Mountains at about 13,000 ybp, leaving much of the present-day province of Alberta ice-free by the beginning of the Late Pleistocene.

Thus, though the paleoenvironment of Canada is not specifically covered in this book, it is clear that an "ice free corridor" existed partially or wholly during the Pleistocene. Furthermore, because of the constant shifting of both the Laurentide and Cordilleran Ice Sheets, no clear archaeological "trail" should be expected. Instead, because of the constant dynamic nature of these two ice sheets, flora and fauna communities would have been highly variable, changing from valley to valley, forcing humans during this time to have been highly adaptable and "ephemeral" in their technologies, similar to what we see in the archaeological record of the Early Holocene for the region. Finally, the ice free corridor appears to be a possible migration route into the continental United States, which would allow for the possibility that American Indians reached the Plains and Plateau regions by the Late Pleistocene.

Plateau

The Plateau area, as discussed in chapter five, is a large cultural region that does not fit within any particular geographic, geologic, or hydrologic region, encompassing parts of the Columbia Plateau, Fraser River Valley, Fraser Plateau, Western Rocky Mountains, Eastern Cordilleran Mountains, and the Southern British Columbian Subarctic (Chatters, 1998; Driver & Massey, 1957; Walker, 1998). Therefore, the present paleoenvironmental review focuses on the "southern" Plateau region, primarily covering the Columbia Plateau, Eastern Cordilleran Mountains, and the Western Rocky Mountains within the contiguous United States. The reason that I focus on this region is that this is the area in which the Kennewick Man skeleton was recovered (see Figure 2). As I discussed above concerning Canada and the Northwest Coast, the Cordilleran Ice Sheet was a massive glacial complex stretching from the Coastal Mountains of British Columbia to the Rocky Mountains, effectively covering much of the northern Plateau during most of the glacial periods of the Quaternary. Data indicates that the Cordilleran Ice Sheet covered most of the Rocky Mountains west of the Continental Divide during each major Quaternary glacial advance. Similarly, it extended southward onto the Columbia Plateau, but only west of Grand Coulee. Furthermore, data indicastes that the Cordilleran Ice Sheet blocked the Clark Fork River at Lake Pend Oreille at least five times, forming Glacial Lake Missoula. The Cordillera Ice Sheet also blocked the Columbia River at Grand Coulee at least three times, impounding Glacial Lake Columbia. The ice dam impounding Glacial Lake Missoula collapsed at least three times, releasing catastrophic floods of enormous magnitude across the Columbia Plateau: once before and once during the Bull Lake Glaciation (160,000-130,000 ybp), and once just after the early Pinedale glacial maximum (25,000-16,000 ybp) (Richmond, 1965; Richmond, Fryxell, Neff, & Weis, 1965), with numerous, minor jokulhlaups occurring throughout this time.

More specifically, the Cordilleran Ice Sheet extended farthest south along the major south-trending valleys and lowlands, such as along the Okanagan Valley. As a result, the Columbia River and its tributaries east of the Grand Coulee is stratigraphically complex because several ice lobes from the Fraser Glaciation built outwash trains that aggraded into glacial lakes, which periodically overflowed causing the jokulhlaups. For example, the Purcell Trench lobe formed Glacial Lake Missoula and caused these floods by blocking the upper Clark Fork valley. This lake periodically emptied based on the thickness of the ice dam caused by the Purcell Trench lobe as great jokulhlaups that discharged down the Columbia River valley and the Channeled Scabland. There is evidence of at least 40 of these jokulhlaups occurring during the end of the Pleistocene (Waitt, 1980, 1983, 1984).

As noted, Pleistocene glaciers in Washington and Oregon consisted of the Cordilleran Ice Sheet, which originated in western British Columbia and invaded northern Washington on both sides of the Cascade Range. Glacial episodes of Early to Middle Pleistocene age are best known in the Puget Sound lowland of western Washington (discussed above), where two major glaciations are recorded, each consisting of two or more advances of the Puget lobe of the Cordilleran glacier into the area south of Seattle, Washington. In the mountains of western British Columbia, continued growth of alpine glaciers during the Fraser Glaciation formed the Cordilleran ice sheet, which expanded into northern Washington after 22,000 years ago and reached its maximum stand 50 miles south of Yakama, Washington between 15,000 and 13,500 years ago. Retreat of the glacier was accompanied and followed by glacio-marine conditions in the Puget Sound lowland from 13,500 to about 11,000 years ago. A subsequent re-advance of the Cordilleran glacier in the Fraser Lowland of northern Washington about 11,000 years ago was followed by a final disappearance of the ice sheet (Crandell, 1965), during which time, the Cordilleran Ice Sheet thinned rapidly and retreated northward (Easterbrook, 1963, 1992). Along with the glacial data, there is also extensive palynological data for the Plateau.

Pollen records provide information on late-glacial variations in vegetation and climate, as well as on the extent and character of Younger Dryas cooling for the southwestern Plateau. For example, data indicate that a rise in *Pinus* pollen from 12,800 to 11,000 ybp suggests increased summer aridity, while *Pseudotsuga* dominated the vegetation after 11,000 ybp. Other records from the Pacific Northwest (which encompasses the Plateau region in climatological frameworks) show a similar expansion of *Pinus* from around 13,000 to 11,000 ybp. This expansion may be a response either to submillennial climate changes of Younger Dryas age or to millennial-scale climatic variations (Grigg & Whitlock, 1998).

Not only did the climate of the Plateau change often and rapidly, but during the Holocene, several extensive ash-fall layers provide evidence of disruptive volcanic activity in the Plateau area. The Mazama ash, erupted from Crater Lake, Oregon, about 6,600 years ago, covered much of the northwestern United States and adjacent parts of Canada. Earlier, the ash fall that had its source at Glacier Peak Volcano, Washington is about 12,000 years old, and covered a broad zone to the east and southeast. The Pearlette ash fall (or ash falls) of late Kansan age spread over the Great Plains, and very similar ash has been found in middle Quaternary deposits in the Rocky Mountains and as far as Nevada (Wilcox, 1965).

It is interesting to note that an ash layer that appears geochemically correlative with Mt. St. Helens tephra set S (a stratigraphic soil layer) occurs in a sequence of Pleistocene lake sediments in the Ohop Valley of the southern Puget Lowland, below Vashon till deposited during the maximum Late Pleistocene advance (Fraser Glaciation) of the Puget Lobe of the Cordilleran Ice Sheet. As mentioned, the Puget Lobe reached its maximum southern extent around 14,000-14,500 ybp, and at least part of set S is evidently somewhat older. Geochemically correlative deposits of set S tephra occur in slackwater sediments coeval with the above mentioned Missoula Floods in eastern Washington, produced by jokulhlaups through the Purcell Trench Lobe of the Cordilleran Ice Sheet. These relationships suggest that advances of glacier lobes on the southern margin of the Cordilleran Ice Sheet were nonsynchronous, as the Purcell Trench lobe east of the Cascade Range advanced to its maximum southern extent prior to the time of the eruption of set S, before the

Puget Lobe west of the Cascades reached its maximum southern extent (Beget, Keskinen, & Severin, 1997).

Along with the nonsynchronous glacial lobes affecting the Plateau, Holocene deposits of Mahoney Lake, located in a closed basin in the semi-arid Okanagan Valley, contain evidence of frequent and marked changes in lake depth (up to >12 meters per 100 years), probably caused by short-term changes in effective precipitation in the region. Meromixis properties (chemical stratification in the water) developed around 9,000 ybp, and the lake has been episodically meromictic for about half the time since. Because of close linkages between sediments and depositional environments in meromictic and saline lakes, this evidence has been used to infer that laminated sediments indicate meromictic conditions and high lake levels, whereas thick marl layers and nonlaminated sediments indicate nonmeromictic conditions and thus low lake levels. This data indicate that during the Holocene this part of the Plateau area, as well as other areas based on similar evidence, experienced very short-term climatic changes in precipitation and temperature (Lowe, Green, Northcote, & Hall, 1997).

Slightly further south, along the Snake River plain of the Southern Plateau, oxygen-18 and carbon-13 values from *M. falcata* shell carbonate samples collected from three archaeological sites located along the Lower Salmon River Canyon of Idaho show several periods of increased and decreased rainfall over the last 12,000 ybp. Three notable periods of aridity are seen, with the first at 11,400 ybp and the second event developing after 11,000 ybp, culminating immediately before 10,000 ybp and the third at 9,000 ybp. Greater aridity is evidenced during the Late Pleistocene and Early Holocene, while after around 4,000 ybp precipitation rates increased relative to modern conditions. After around 1,800 ybp, precipitation levels trend toward modern values (Davis & Muehlenbachs, 2001). These same paleoenvironmental patterns are also recorded just north, at Mahoney Lake in the Okanagan Valley (Chatters, 1998; Davis & Muehlenbachs, 2001), and straddle the area where the Kennewick Man skeleton was found.

On the eastern edge of the Plateau glaciers were developed in most of the ranges of the Rocky Mountains as far south as latitude 33⁰22' (southern New Mexico) during the Pleistocene, and as far as latitude 35⁰40' (northern New Mexico) during the recent times. Early Pleistocene glaciers appear to have been broad shallow lobate masses, but after canyon erosion in mid-Pleistocene time, subsequent glaciers formed thick tongues in the canyons. Five distinct glaciations are recognized for the Rocky Mountains bordering the Plateau; from oldest to youngest they are named Washakie Point, Cedar Ridge, Sacagawea Ridge, Bull Lake, and Pinedale. Deposits of the three oldest glaciations are deeply weathered and their deposition was separated by major interglaciations. Bull Lake Glaciation includes two and perhaps three glacial advances separated by deglaciation intervals of lesser duration than preceding interglaciations. The Pinedale Glaciation includes at least three stades, or minor advances, and perhaps more, separated by brief interstades, which was followed by the Altithermal interval (Richmond, 1965; Richmond, Fryxell, Neff, & Weis, 1965). These glaciations indicate that any movement between the Plains and the Plateau would have been extremely difficult, if not impossible, until the Late

Holocene.

To summarize, therefore, although the paleoenvironment of the Plateau region is not as well understood as some areas, it appears to have been highly influenced by the southern ends of both the Cordillera and Laurentide Ice Sheets. However, the Columbia River Plateau and the Snake River Plain both were never covered by glacial ice, and much of the southern British Columbia Fraser lowlands, as well as the Okanagan Valley appear to have been ice-free for periods of time. Furthermore, the Plateau, similar to the Great Basin (as discussed below), appears to have received more moisture and to have had a milder climate at the end of the Pleistocene and Early Holocene than today. Therefore, the "southern" Plateau appears to have been habitable for humans throughout the Pleistocene, but that much of the evidence of early human occupation may have been buried or erased by the jokulhlaups released from Glacial Lake Missoula. Likewise, it also appears that it was not possible for humans to have entered the Plateau region during the Pleistocene by way of the Rocky Mountains until the Late Pleistocene. However, it does appear that humans could have moved into the Plateau by way of the Columbia River during the Pleistocene, which is in accord with some of the linguistic evidence (Ruhlen, 1994; Shipley, 1980)

California

Although California lies directly outside of the areas discussed in this book, it is important to briefly review the area because it borders both the Plateau and Great Basin regions to the east (see Figure 6). Furthermore, there appears to be extensive archaeological evidence of trade between the Great Basin, Plateau, and California regions, primarily for shells, dating back to the beginning of the Holocene (Connolly, 1999; Elston, 1986; Erickson, 1990; Galm, 1994). Similarly, as discussed in chapter five, California was originally included as part of the "California-Great Basin" area of general culture by Kroeber (1920).

Unlike the Northwest Coast and the northern Plateau, outside of the Sierra Nevada, California did not experience large glacial coverage during the Quaternary period. However, various glacial complexes in the Sierra Nevada, through seasonal and cyclical melt water, affected much of the region. For example, Pleistocene fluvial landforms and riparian ecosystems in central California were effected by climate changes in the Sierra Nevada. Contrary to the eastern Sierra, the specific glacial history of the western Sierra remains largely unknown (James, Harbor, Fabel, Dahms, & Elmore, 2002).

In Bear Valley, southcentral California, data from erratic boulders evidence three distinct glacial stages: 76,400+/-3800 ybp; 48,800+/-3200 ybp; and 18,600+/-1180 ybp (James, Harbor, Fabel, Dahms, & Elmore, 2002). To the south and east, pollen and algae from Owens Lake in eastern California provide evidence for a series of climatic oscillations late in the last glaciation. For example, juniper woodland, which dominated the Owens Valley from 16,200 to 15,500 ybp, suggests much wetter conditions than today. Although still wetter and cooler than today, the area then

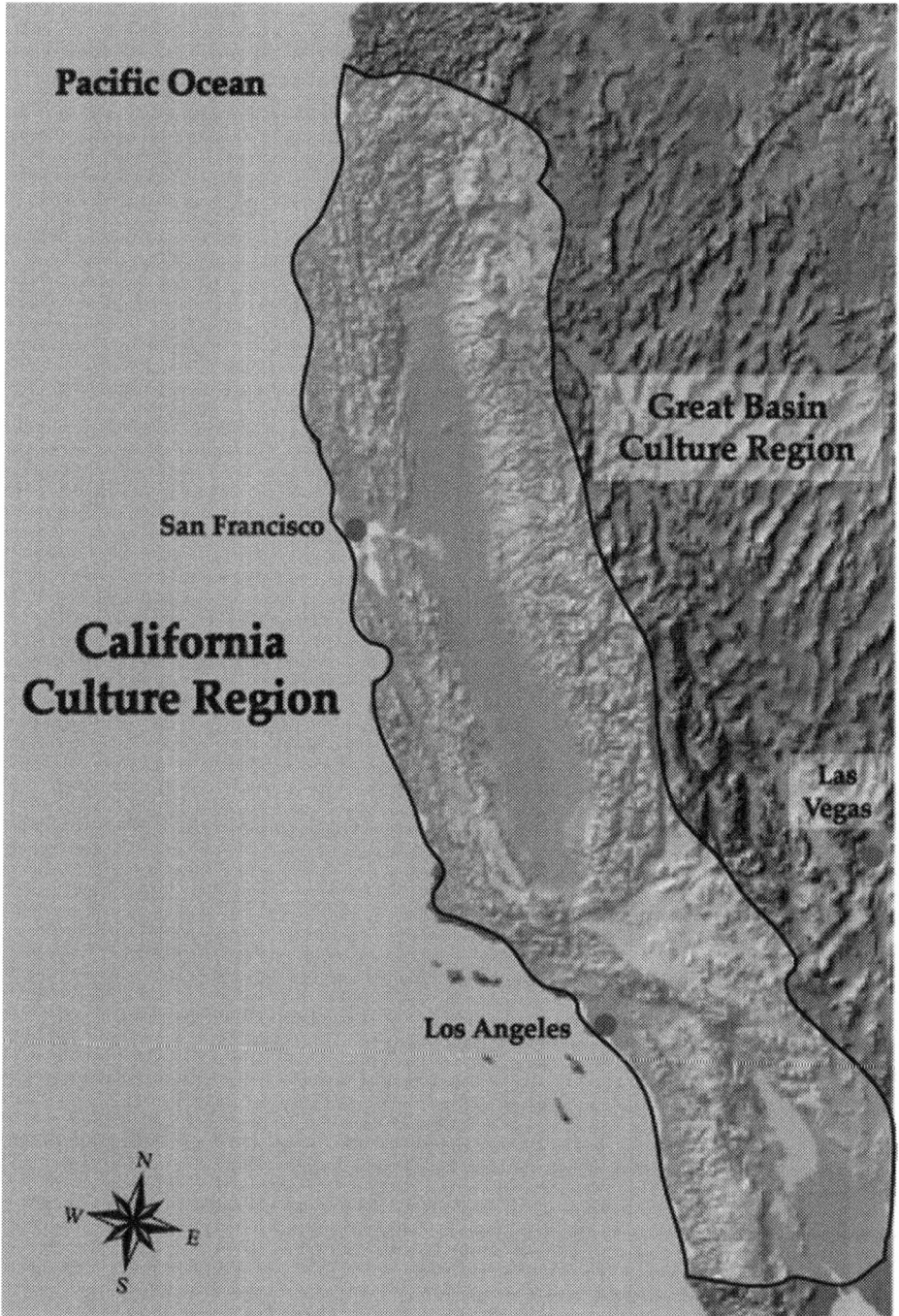

Pacific Ocean

Great Basin
Culture Region

San Francisco

California
Culture Region

Las
Vegas

Los Angeles

N
W   E
S

Figure 6. Map showing the California Culture Region, which lies directly adjacent to the Plateau and Great Basin Culture Regions.

became fairly warm and dry, with woodland being replaced by shrubs (mainly sage brush) from 15,500 to 13,100 ybp. Next, *Chenopodiaceae* (shadscale) increased, woody species declined, and lake levels fell – all evidence for a brief (circa 100-200 year) drought around 13,000 ybp. Subsequently, the climate continued to oscillate in eastern California between wet and dry from 13,000 to 11,000 ybp. After 11,000 ybp, low lake levels and the increased dominance of desert shrubs indicate the beginning of warm, dry Holocene conditions. Therefore, comparison of the Owens Lake record with data from the Sierra Nevada and Great Basin suggest that the climate was generally wetter between 13,000 and 11,000 ybp, with warmer summers then today, although no long-term consistent pattern of climate change emerges (Mensing, 2001).

The paleoenvironment of California is highly complex and grades from west to east and south to north. During the Pleistocene and Holocene, the paleoenvironment of the region was influenced by Pacific Ocean currents, the southern extreme of the Cordilleran Ice Sheet, the Sierra Nevada, and by the relative temperate climate of the Southwest region. However, as discussed above with the Plateau, it appears that precipitation levels fell in the Late Pleistocene accompanied by a general warming trend in the Early Holocene, with brief periods of either increasing or decreasing precipitation. During the Pleistocene, only the Sierra Nevada was glaciated, with the rest of the region experiencing climatic conditions similar to today, except generally cooler and moister (Davis, 1982; Heusser, 1985; Menking, 1997; Wahrhaftig & Birman, 1965). Thus, most of California would have been habitable throughout the Pleistocene and trade routes between the California coast and the Great Basin, as well as the Plateau, appear to have been possible during the Late Pleistocene and Early Holocene, primarily south and north of the Sierra Nevada Range, as the archaeological record indicates (Baugh & Nelson, 1987; Erickson, 1990; Galm, 1994).

Great Basin

The Great Basin is the other region that is of central importance for the purposes of this book, and the Spirit Cave Mummy was recovered from the western area of this region. As noted in chapter five, the Great Basin is a large area that covers the southern parts of Idaho and Oregon, all of Nevada and Utah, and small sections of California's eastern side, along with fragments of northern Arizona and western Colorado (see Figure 2). This area has the unique characteristics that all of the hydrographic features within the region drain internally like a basin. By this it is meant that all rivers and water features drain into sinks, lakes, or other features inside the Great Basin, and the water never makes it outside of this region. Today the Great Basin is a diverse ecological area that encompasses deserts, marshes, mountains with alpine tundra, and most environments in between. However, the predominant environment is that of a very dry desert, and it is because of this predominant environment that many early anthropologists considered the Great Basin to be an inhospitable place to live that only supported the most primitive of cultures throughout prehistory (e.g., Steward, 1955, 1970). Recent studies have shown that this is neither true for today's Great Basin, nor for the Great Basin of prehistory

(Aikens, 1978; Clemmer, Myers, & Rudden, 1999; D'Azevedo, 1986; Johnson, 1975).

The Great Basin's paleoenvironmental record is very complex, partly as a result of the numerous pluvial lakes that arose throughout prehistory. The two largest of these pluvial lakes were Lake Bonneville, which the Great Salt Lake is a remnant of today, and Lake Lahotan, a remnant of which can be seen in today's Pyramid Lake. Throughout prehistory, these lakes, as well as many others such as Lake Malheur in Oregon, supported a large diversity of flora and fauna (see Figure 7).

Lake Bonneville, the largest of the prehistoric pluvial lakes, experienced numerous highs and desiccations throughout the Pleistocene and Early Holocene. For example, some evidence suggests that Lake Bonneville experienced an extreme desiccation between 13,000 and 12,000 ybp. However, these low points appear not to have lasted long, and some evidence suggests that the Great Salt Lake, which was a part of Pleistocene Lake Bonneville, had high stands at around 3,400 and 1,000 ybp (Broughton, Madsen, & Quade, 2000). Furthermore, new sedimentological, geochronological, and paleontological data indicate that only four deep-lake cycles occurred during the Pleistocene. This interpretation suggests that large lakes formed in the Bonneville basin only during the most extensive of the Northern Hemisphere Wisconsin glaciations (Oviatt, Thompson, Kaufman, Bright, & Forester, 1999).

In southern Idaho, just to the north of the Lake Bonneville area, the paleoenvironmental record is similar for much of the Pleistocene. Before 9,000 ybp pollen records reflect Holocene vegetation and rising temperatures over the entire region. This was followed by 7,000 ybp shadscale and sagebrush communities had expanded at the expense of grass, and conifers lost ground to grass and sagebrush. By 5,400 ybp this trend had slowed and by 4,000 ybp it had reversed with the return of climatic patterns resulting in apparently more effective moisture. The moist maritime forests of northern Idaho and adjacent states appear to date no earlier than 2,500 ybp (Mehringer, 1985a).

To the east, in southern Oregon, evidence suggests that the earliest Quaternary record for Lake Malheur consists of occurrences of water-deposited tephra dated to around 70,000-80,000 ybp. Shells with ages of around 32,000 and 29,500 ybp date the next identified lake interval. However, no dates are presently available for the terminal-Pleistocene though lake(s) were present between around 9,600 and 7,400 ybp, indicating more moisture during this time with a brief dry period around 8,000 ybp. The lake system probably dried further after 7,400 ybp, although dates are lacking for the period between 7,400 and 5,000 ybp. Dune deposits on the lake floor are around 5,000 years old and indicate generally dry conditions and fluctuating shallow lakes have probably characterized the last 2,000 years (Dugas, 1998).

Nearby, in the Harney Basin, moderate-size lakes existed around 80,000-70,000 years ago, at 32,000 to 29,500 ybp, and 9,500 ybp. Shallower paleolakes were present approximately at 8,400, 7,800, and 7,400 ybp. These lakes are significant in that they are possibly equivalent to proposed post-10,000 ybp lakes in the Fort Rock, Alkali, and Chewaucan basins (Gehr, 1980; Willig, 1988, 1991; Willig & Aikens,

1988). Beginning approximately at 5,000 ybp, based on shells in the Malheur Lake dune islands, the Malheur Lake system's environmental history is marked by fluctuating water levels, a pattern apparently characterizing the remainder of Holocene time (Dugas, 1998).

Thus, data indicate that the northern Great Basin experienced a rapid wasting of glaciers, a shrinking of vast lakes followed by a final catastrophic flooding that attended the onset of post-glacial conditions. Diverse pollen spectra of this age retain aspects of full-glacial vegetation and reflect initial successes of pioneer floral invaders on newly available terrain. These data share several characteristics separating this time from later Holocene samples from the same sites, including:

> an initial treeless interlude indicated by an importance of non-arboreal pollen dominated by *Artemisia* and often accompanied by abundant grass pollen;
> a common occurrence of *Shepherdia canadensis*, *Juniperus* (probably *J. communis*), and small percentages of *Picea* pollen sometimes accompanied or followed by *Abies*;
> combinations of pollen types such as *Rumex-Oxyria*, *Bistorta*, *Polemonium*, *Eriogonum*, and *Koenegia*; and
> an unusual abundance of *Selaginella densa* — type along with other species such as *Selaginella selaginoides*, *Botrychium* and *Lycopodium annotinum*.

Furthermore, the alpine and subalpine character of these assemblages is similar over much of the Plateau at this time, including mountains of the northern Great Basin and adjacent Snake River Plain (Mehringer, 1985a).

In the south, around today's Mojave Desert of southern Nevada and California, mammal and lizard bones have been used to shed light on the local prehistoric fauna, since no lakes appear to have formed during the Pleistocene. Between 32,000 and 10,100 ybp the local fauna consisted of a mix of xeric- and mesic-adapted species. *Ochotona princeps* (American Pica) and *Thomomys talpoides* (Northern Pocket Gopher) then occupied the region, although these animals were extripated by the onset of the Middle Holocene. Data further indicates that *Sauromalus obesus* (Western Chuckwalla) and *Dipodomys deserti* (Desert Kangaroo Rat) probably migrated to the region during the late Pleistocene and *Dipsosaurus dorsalis* (Desert Iguana) entered the area after 8,000 ybp. This data is consistent with climatic interpretations for the northern Great Basin, as noted above, and which suggest a cool and moist Late Pleistocene climate for the northern Mojave Desert. In contrast to the northern Great Basin, however, this region appears to have experienced predictable summer precipitation coupled with increasingly warmer winters by 10,100 ybp, whereas the northern Great Basin probably experienced warm and dry conditions at that time. Furthermore, the modern northern Mojave Desert biota probably was not established until after 8,300 ybp (Hockett, 2000).

A little further north, in Long Valley, Nevada, data reveal a history of environmental change at the last glacial-interglacial transition. The data contain a suite of lacustrine, alluvial, and eolian deposits associated with pluvially reworked faunal remains and Paleoindian artifacts. Radiocarbon-dated stratigraphy indicates a history of receding pluvial lake levels followed by alluvial down cutting and subsequent valley filling with marsh-like conditions becoming prevalent at the end of the Pleistocene. A period of alluvial deposition and shallow water tables (circa 11,000 to 9,800 ybp) correlates to the Younger Dryas. Subsequent drier conditions and reduced surface runoff mark the Early Holocene with sand dunes replacing wetlands by 8,000 ybp. Additionally, the stratigraphy at Long Valley is similar to sites located 400 km south and supports the idea of regional climatic synchronicity in the central and southern Great Basin during the Late Pleistocene to Early Holocene transition (Huckleberry et al., 2001).

This paleoenvironmental reconstruction is further supported by data coming from black mats. Black mats are prominent features of the Late Pleistocene and Holocene stratigraphic record in the southern Great Basin, and have been used to reconstruct the paleoenvironmental record. Faunal, geochemical, and sedimento-logical evidence shows that the black mats formed in several microenvironments related to spring discharge, ranging from wet meadows to shallow ponds. Data indicate that sedges, shrubs, and trees were present around these areas, as well as salt-bush and saltgrass. Most of these black mats fall between 11,800 to 6,300 and 2,300 ybp to modern times. The total absence of black mats between 6,300 and 2,300 ybp likely reflects increased aridity associated with the mid-Holocene Altithermal. However, it must be pointed out that the Altithermal was a period of aridity, but not total desiccation and in-hospitability. The oldest black mats date to 11,800-11,600 ybp, and the peak in the black mat distribution falls around 10,000 ybp. As the formation of black mats is spring related, their abundance reflects refilling of valley aquifers starting no later than 11,800 and peaking after 11,000 ybp for the southern Great Basin. Reactivation of spring-fed channels shortly before 11,200 ybp is also apparent in the stratigraphic records from the Las Vegas and Pahrump Valleys. This age distribution suggests that black mats and related spring-fed channels in part may have formed in response to Younger Dryas age recharge in the region (Quade, Forester, Pratt, & Carter, 1998).

These data are similar to those found in other parts of the Great Basin that record successively smaller lakes from the Early to the Late Pleistocene. This decrease in lake size indicates a long-term drying trend in the regional climate that is not seen in global marine oxygen-isotope records. For example, Lake Lahontan in the early Middle Pleistocene submerged some basins previously thought to have been isolated. Other basins known to contain records of older pluvial lakes that exceeded Late Pleistocene levels include Columbus-Fish Lake (Lake Columbus-Rennie), Kobeh-Diamond (Lakes Jonathan and Diamond), Neward, Long (Lake Hubbs), and Clover. Very high stands of some of these lakes probably triggered overflows of previously internally drained basins, adding to the size of Lake Lahontan (see Figure 7). Simple calculations based on differences in lake area suggest that the highest levels of these pluvial lakes required a regional increase in effective moisture by a factor of 1.2 to 3 relative to Late Pleistocene pluvial amounts (assuming that effective moisture is directly proportional to the hydrologic index, or lake area/tributary basin area). These previously unknown lake levels reflect significant changes in climate, tectonics, and (or) drainage-basin configurations, and could have facilitated migration of aquatic, floristic, and faunal species in the Great Basin (Reheis, 1999).

A similar trend is seen in the eastern Great Basin at Lake Bonneville, as has been previously discussed. Deposits of a transgressive-phase Lake Bonneville stillstand or oscillation are found just below the elevation of the regressive-phase Provo shoreline at numerous exposures throughout the Bonneville basin. Existence of these sub-Provo shoreline deposits provides a new explanation for the massive size of Provo depositional and erosional landforms, which can no longer be explained by a long stillstand at the Provo shoreline. Instead, data indicate that Provo coastal landforms are large because they are superimposed on sub-Provo landforms. These data also help to clarify divergent interpretations regarding the relative age of the Provo shoreline and the number of times it was occupied by the water plane. Occupation of approximately the same level during both the transgressive and the regressive phase of Lake Bonneville may be coincidental, or it may indicate that a bedrock sill controlled outflow at sub-Provo as well as Provo time. Rise to the Bonneville level, therefore, most likely occurred after massive slope failure plugged the outlet pass preventing water from draining out of the basin (Sack, 1999).

Thus, as has been discussed, during "pluvial" periods of the late Quaternary, when the amount of effective moisture was greater than at present, many of the closed depressions of the Great Basin contained lakes. Data indicate that changes in the levels of these lakes, and the consequent impacts on prehistoric American Indians, occurred more-or-less simultaneously over much of the region. As I will discuss in chapter nine, many of these lakes were favored sites for the camps of prehistoric American Indians because they provided water and were the focus of several types of food-gathering activities. Those with stable levels and extensively developed marshes along the shores may have been the most attractive. Lake salinity, however, probably became a factor during climatic change; half or more of the lakes in the Great Basin were apparently fresh during their deeper stages, but the salinities of all but those adjacent to high mountains probably increased to unacceptable levels as they shrank. Even before reaching overall salinities that were unacceptable, though, some lakes may have developed concentrations of individual dissolved components that were harmful. However, probably only the magnesium-sulfate and sodium-sulfate lake waters produced their harmful effects rapidly enough to be identified as their cause. During temporary dry periods, or in areas of marked seasonal precipitation, lakes may also have provided the only year-round source of water in many areas of the Great Basin region (Smith, 1985).

Further data, from about 22,000 to 12,000 ybp, indicate that lake levels in the Great Basin were either at "high" or "intermediate" stands. Between 12,000 and 8,000 ybp, though, most lakes contracted, and by about 4,000 ybp, all had dried or shrunk to their present levels. There were some periods, however, when regional differences appeared, most notably around 10,000 ybp, when some lakes in the western part of the Great Basin underwent one or more brief expansions while those in the remaining basins apparently did not (Grayson, 1993). Between about 4,000 ybp and the present, about a third of the lakes in the Great Basin again underwent modest expansion that culminated between about 2,000 and 1,000 ybp.

Specific data, as was discussed, indicate that not all of these lakes were of freshwater quality, and some were actually quite brackish even during their deepest stages. Data from Searles Lake indicate that the salinity of the lake during its prior high stand (about 9,000 ybp) was a little more than one percent saline (Smith, 1979); this is only about a third the salinity of seawater, which some have used to support the idea that it is too brackish to be attractive to humans or to support most land plants. It is true that both springs and other water bodies in the Searles Lake region probably were far more attractive sources of drinking water, but the brackish water was ideal for brine shrimp and certain insect larvae, similar to present-day Mono Lake conditions (Smith, 1985), which have been historically utilized food resources.

If we look at the vegetational changes that were taking place during this time, it appears that though the Great Basin experienced wide changes in its floral characteristics, at no time was there ever a dearth of flora or vast expanses of sandy desert. For example, data from the White Mountains of the western Great Basin indicate that from approximately 34,000 to 27,000 ybp, Utah juniper grew with subalpine conifers, including bristlecone pine (*Pinus longaeva*) and limber pine (*P. flexilis*) in what is now pinyon-juniper woodland. Subalpine conifers became dominant during the full glacial period (around 18,000 ybp) and Utah juniper and other woodland plants were rare or absent during this period. Subsequently, between 13,500 and 11,000 ybp bristlecone pines remained as much as 1,000 meters below their general modern elevational limits. Some of the vegetational evidence suggests that there may have been a general drying trend during the period from between 13,500 to 11,000 ybp (Thompson, 1984). By 10,450 ybp bristlecone pine and other subalpine plants had all but disappeared from the many slopes, and modern desert scrub plants became common. In more moist, protected areas, subalpine conifers remained well below their modern elevational limits into the early Holocene (Thompson, 1984; Wells, 1983). Utah juniper and Rocky Mountain juniper (*Juniperus scopulorum*) formed woodlands with limber pine on the lower mountain slopes in east-central Nevada during the Early Holocene. Single-needle pinyon pine joined this assemblage between 6,500 and 6,000 ybp, and Rocky Mountain juniper and limber pine declined in importance after this time. Finally, little vegetational change is discernible from 6,000 ybp to the present for much of the Great Basin (Thompson, 1985).

To summarize, evidence indicates that around 11,000 ybp a mosaic of desert scrubs and juniper woodland existed and probably supported a fauna that was not much different than that of today. Pinyon pine was not available, however, since it had not yet arrived from its Pleistocene distribution in the southwestern deserts (Thompson, 1984; Thompson, 1985; Thompson & Hattori, 1983). Likewise, the Great Basin experienced dramatic environmental changes during the Late Pleistocene and into throughout the Holocene. As the Pleistocene pluvial lakes slowly dried up, marsh/lacustrine environments also shifted. The Middle Holocene desiccated most of the pluvial lakes, though temporary lakes continue to form in basins depending on precipitation levels. Thus, people living in the Great Basin during the Late Pleistocene and Holocene would have most likely followed a cyclical subsistence lifeway that allowed them to adapt to the diverse and dynamic environments present throughout this time.

Southwest

As with the Northwest, Canada, and California, the Southwest region (see Figure 8) lies outside of the direct areas of study in this book. However, it is still important to briefly review the regions paleoenvironmental record because many of the species that are now found in the Great Basin appear to have their prehistoric origin in the Southwest, such as Pinyon pine. Briefly, data indicate that during early- and full-glacial time, vegetation zones were lowered 1,400 to 900 meters and that the transition from glacial to post-glacial vegetation and climate occurred between 14,000 to 12,000 years ago. Early Holocene vegetation was characterized by decreasing woodlands, culminating in a marked shrinkage of woodland vegetation in the Middle Holocene during an episode of extremely warm and dry climate dated to about 7,000 to 5,000 ybp. The Late Holocene vegetation was characterized in general by increased abundance of woodlands. Incompleteness and uncertainty in the Late Pleistocene and Middle Holocene pollen records stem from changes in sedimentation rates, lowering of lake levels, drying of bogs, erosion, and soil formation. As a result, pollen sequences typically begin or end during the Late Pleistocene or Middle Holocene (Hall, 1985b).

Overall, the majority of the records for the Southwest are dominated by *Artemisia* and *Pinus* with minor amounts of *Picea* and *Abies* pollen that is generally interpreted as representing a cool sagebrush steppe or sagebrush-pine woodland vegetation; a vegetation type that is not widespread in the Southwest today. This sagebrush vegetation occupied lower elevation areas, which during much of the Holocene and today are dry shrub grasslands that produce assemblages dominated by *Gramineae*, *Chenopodiineae*, and *Compositae* pollen.

More specifically, during the Late Pleistocene a 1,000 meter lowering of upper forest limits was accompanied by a compression of the ponderosa pine zone, resulting in the San Juan Basin of the Four Corners region becoming occupied by a sagebrush and pinyon-juniper woodland vegetation and accounting for the large amount of *Artemisia* pollen and differentiated *Pinus edulis* grains that wind-drifted upslope to the Chuska Mountain lake sites. A decrease in *Abies, Quercus, Juniperus, Compositae,* and *Chenopodiineae* abundance frequencies and an increase in *Pinus* ponderosa percentages during the last part of the Pleistocene, about 18,500 to 13,500 ybp, has been interpreted as representing a 100 meter rise in the upper treeline for the region (Hall, 1985a, 1985b).

Further south, around the Gila River of Arizona it appears that prior to 18,000 ybp, the Gila River cut into its floodplain and created a deep, wide channel. Sand and gravel accumulated within this channel until 4,400-4,250 ybp, by which time the channel of the Gila River was narrow and deep. Around 5,000 ybp, fine-grained sediments began to accumulate on the floodplain though at 950-800 ybp there was a major period of channel widening. After this erosional episode, the channel again narrowed as it filled with sand and gravel until around 200 ybp. On the floodplain,

deposition continued from about 5,000 ybp to 500 ybp followed by a period of stability and soil formation between 500 and 200 ybp, after which overbank deposition
resumed and buried the soil.   Channel widening again occurred in the late 19th
century.   These changes observed in the sedimentologic history of the Gila River
show that during the Late Pleistocene, the Gila River was a competent stream capable of carrying and depositing coarse sediment loads.   Later deposition of sand and
gravel during the first half of the Holocene implies an increase in sediment yield
from upstream watersheds (i.e., increased precipitation).   Changes during the last
4,000 years reflect the response of the river to climatic perturbations, the timing of
large floods, internal landscape thresholds, and human impacts (Waters &
Ravesloot, 2001).

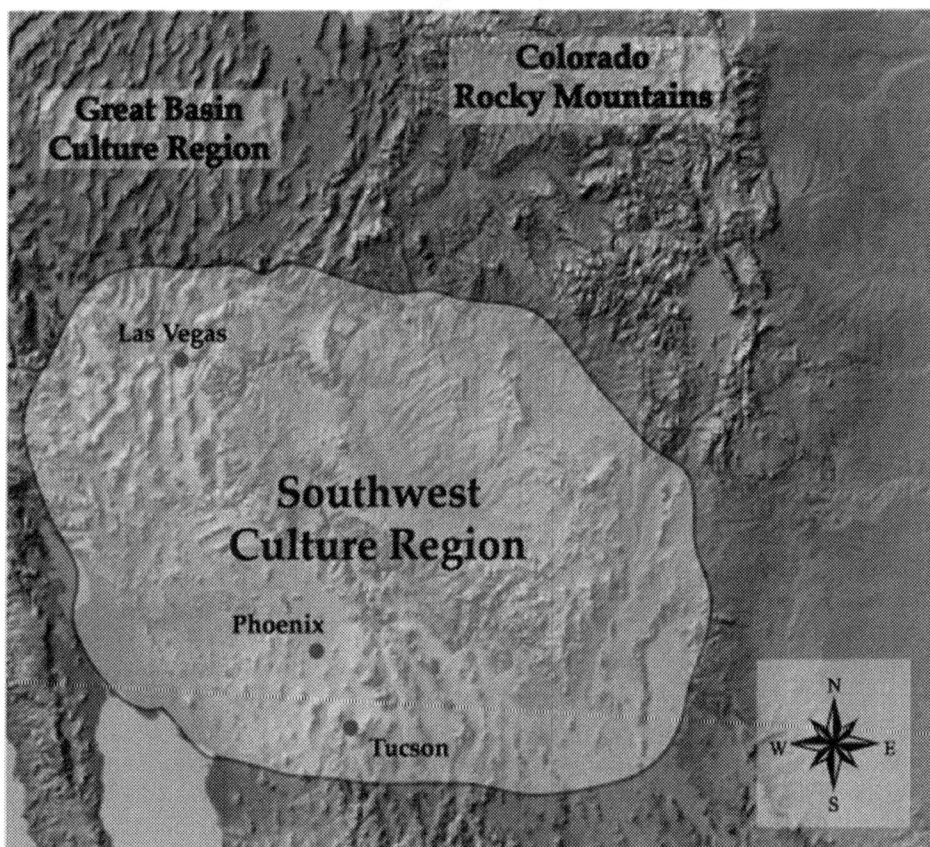

Figure 7. This map shows the location of the Southwest Culture Region in relation
to the Great Basin Culture Region to the north.

In New Mexico, to the east, a similar hydrographic record is observed.   Late
Pleistocene Lake Estancia in the 5000 km² Estancia basin of central New Mexico
rose and fell at least nine times during the 12,000 years that preceded the glacial termination (Allen & Anderson, 2000).   Data indicate that the lake reached an eleva-

tion of 1890 meters and a surface area of ~1100 km² at least five times during the last glacial maximum (LGM) and again shortly after 14,000 ybp. Furthermore, age relations and stratigraphic evidence indicate that the lake rose and fell rapidly, in some cases within several decades (Allen & Anderson, 1993), suggesting that climate was punctuated by rapid increases and decreases in the supply of atmospheric moisture reaching the western interior of North America. Lake Estancia disappeared completely after around 12,000 ybp, leaving a single 400 km² playa on the floor of the basin though some time after the episode of drying, a perennial lake reappeared in the Estancia basin. Indirect and limited evidence for the age of the final lake stand suggests that the last highstand in the Estancia basin could correspond to the Younger Dryas (12,500 to 11,300 ybp) climatic episode (Anderson, Lozhkin, & Brubaker, 2002; Anderson, Allen, & Menking, 2002).

Floral evidence for the region during this time indicates that in the Chuska Mountains vegetation was lowered by a minimum of 900 meters composed of spruce-fir and ponderosa pine communities, while a sagebrush and pinyon-juniper vegetation occupied the floor of the San Juan Basin (Hall, 1985a, 1985b).

The greatest reduction in pine forests occurred from at least 6,000 to 2,400 ybp, though there was an increase in pines at 2,400 ybp and again at about 600 ybp. By 2,200 ybp, *Pinus* pollen frequencies increased, indicating expanded pine forests and moister climate. Alpine sites in southwestern Colorado (e.g., Lake Emma, Hurrican Basin, Twin Lakes) show a general pattern of high *Picea/Pinus* pollen ratios during Midddle Holocene time followed by lower ratios beginning about 3,000 ybp, indicating lowered forest vegetation zones and a slightly cooler and moister climate. At lower elevations, a sharp decrease in *Pinus* pollen and an increase in *Artemisia* percentages about 4,000 ybp (Markgraf & Scott, 1981), indicate that the sagebrush grassland vegetation that characterizes the area today was established.

To the west, along the Utah border, from about 8,000 to 6,000 ybp, pollen ratios indicate a warmer and drier climate (relative to the Holocene average) that resulted in expansion of conifers into former sagebrush areas at high elevation sites. From about 6,000 to 3,000 ybp pollen ratios indicate generally warm and wet conditions with the post-3,000 ybp climate comparatively cool and dry (Hall, 1985a, 1985b). The landforms, stratigraphy, radiocarbon ages, and soils of the lacustrine and alluvial deposits indicate that Lake Cloverdale (in northern New Mexico) had a relatively long highstand during the last glacial maximum. Lower lake levels and incision of Animas Creek and its tributaries from Late Pleistocene time through the Early Holocene followed this highstand. Subsequently, during the Middle to Late Holocene, Lake Cloverdale experienced three lake stands as Animas Creek and its tributaries underwent a significant period of aggradation. The earliest lake highstand for which there is stratigraphic evidence is dated to approximately 20,000 to 18,000 ybp and created the topographically highest lake shoreline features at an elevation of 1578 meters (Krider, 1998).

To summarize, the Southwest appears to have experienced similar general climatic patterns as the rest of the American West. The Late Pleistocene was characterized by a cooler and moister climate over the region followed by a general warming trend into the Holocene. The Middle Holocene experienced a short cooling trend, followed by another period of warming to the present. Similarly, the present floral communities appear to have been established in the region by the end of the Middle Holocene, though some areas experienced dramatic floral changes due to human impacts. Finally, data indicates that the Southwest served as a floral, and perhaps faunal, source area for establishment and dispersal of various ecological communities into the Great Basin beginning in the Early Holocene.

Plains

The final region that is covered in this book is that of the Plains. Like other regions that border the Plateau and Great Basin, the Plains region is not directly pertinent to the questions being asked in this book. However, the Plains region is very relevant in that the "ice-free corridor" between the Cordilleran and Laurentide ice sheets would have opened up to the Plains region, allowing prehistoric American Indians to first occupy this area prior to eventually migrating to either the Plateau or Great Basin regions. Thus, it is necessary to include a brief overview of the paleoenvironmental record for the region.

Briefly, data indicates that by Early Pleistocene time, the southern Plains probably supported extensive grasslands, accompanied by gallery forests along the rivers. Early Pleistocene climates became more continental, and distinct fluctuations in the biota suggest alternating glacial and interglacial conditions. Interstadial conditions on the plains about 25,000 years ago resulted in grasslands on the central Plains and *Pinus*-parklands on the eastern Plains. As Wisconsin ice advanced to cover the northern Plains, tundra existed in Minnesota and Iowa, but conditions elsewhere on the Plains are unknown. When Wisconsin ice began to retreat in the Late Pleistocene, *Picea* forests and parklands spread across the northern Plains, but grasslands persisted in the central Plains. Conifer forests may have expanded on the western Plains in Early Holocene time, whereas the eastern Plains border was covered with a transitional deciduous forest. Most of the Great Plains probably became prairie-covered in the Early Holocene and remained that way to the present-day (Baker & Waln, 1985; DeMallie, 2001; Frison, 1999; Frye & Leonard, 1965; Lemke, Laird, Tipton, & Lindvall, 1965; Valero-Garces et al., 1997).

Drifts of all four major glacial and interglacial stages of the Pleistocene occur in the Plains region. Nebraskan drift and Aftonian paleosols and sediments are found buried by Kansan drift in southern Iowa. Kansan drift and Yarmouth paleosol and sediments are common under younger loess in south-central Iowa. Illinoian till is found only close to the Mississippi River in southeastern Iowa, but its correlative Loveland loess is widespread near the Missouri River in western Iowa, with well-developed Sangamon paleosol on top (Wright & Ruhe, 1965). In the eastern Plains loess was extensively deposited in Iowa between 29,000 to 20,000 years ago, when it was interrupted by the ice advance of the Tazewell phase of Wisconsin glaciation. Loess deposition continued in Iowa until about 14,000 years ago (Jacobs, Knox, & Mason, 1997). Wisconsin glaciation in Minnesota involved the interactions of four major ice lobes, from west to east the Des Moines, Wadena, Rainy, and Superior, localized by bedrock lowlands and characterized by distinctive rock types that reflect the bedrock geology of northern Minnesota and adjacent Canada. Only the Des Moines Lobe affected Iowa, reaching a maximum there about 14,000 years ago (Wright & Ruhe, 1965).

For the southern Plains pollen records for the Late Pleistocene (22,500-14,000 ybp) reveal evidence of mesic vegetation, and by inference, a cooler and perhaps wetter climate than today. In west Texas the grassland steppe conditions of the previous period were replaced in some areas by conifer forests. In southwest Texas there was an expansion of pinyon and juniper parklands while in nearby central Texas a mixed deciduous forest with some conifer elements dominated. In south Texas rich grasslands and oak scrublands formed a mosaic and in north Texas a mixed deciduous forest containing spruce formed the region's main vegetation (Bryant & Holloway, 1985a).

The Late Pleistocene (14,000-10,000 ybp) in Texas represents a transitional period characterized by a slow climatic deterioration which is noted in the fossil pollen record by the gradual loss of woodland and parkland areas in many regions of the state. In west Texas and in regions of the Llano Estacado in northwest Texas the Late Pleistocene is characterized as a period when existing areas of conifers at the lower elevations were replaced by open grasslands while conifer forests at higher elevations remained more or less stable. In southwest Texas the existing vegetation developed a broad mosaic pattern during the late-glacial period with scrub grasslands beginning to cover the larger areas of the landscape at the expense of the remaining pinyon-juniper woodland and parkland regions. In central Texas the deciduous woodland regions began to disappear and were replaced by grasslands and oak savannas. Finally, in east Texas the existing deciduous woodlands probably lost certain key taxa such as *Picea* and *Corylus*, yet the region remained forested with a wide variety of deciduous tree taxa (Bryant & Holloway, 1985a).

Moving west, and north, the paleoenvironments of Late Pleistocene and Early Holocene time on the southern High Plains have been studied for decades, but regionally extensive or long-term, proxy climate indicators have not been located. The stratigraphy of valley fill and upland eolian deposits along with stable-carbon isotope data, and geographically limited paleontological data provide clues to the environment during this time, which includes the Late Pleistocene and Early Holocene (~11,200-8,000 ybp). Between 11,200-10,900 ybp, data indicate that valleys contained perennial streams, which was followed by an abrupt change to lakes, ponds (with water levels fluctuating between several meters in depth), and marshes along with accumulation of sheet sands on uplands, starting the earliest phase of construction of the regional dune fields (10,900-10,200 ybp). These changing conditions indicate a shift from relatively wetter to relatively drier conditions accompanied with episodic droughts. During the rest of the Early Holocene the environment was relatively cool but fluctuated between wetter and drier conditions with an overall trend toward drying that resulted in further enlargement of the dune fields and culminated in the warm, dry Altithermal beginning ~8,000 ybp. The wettest time in terms of runoff and spring discharge appears to have occurred between 11,200-10,900 ybp. The subsequent period was drier and was the earliest episode of

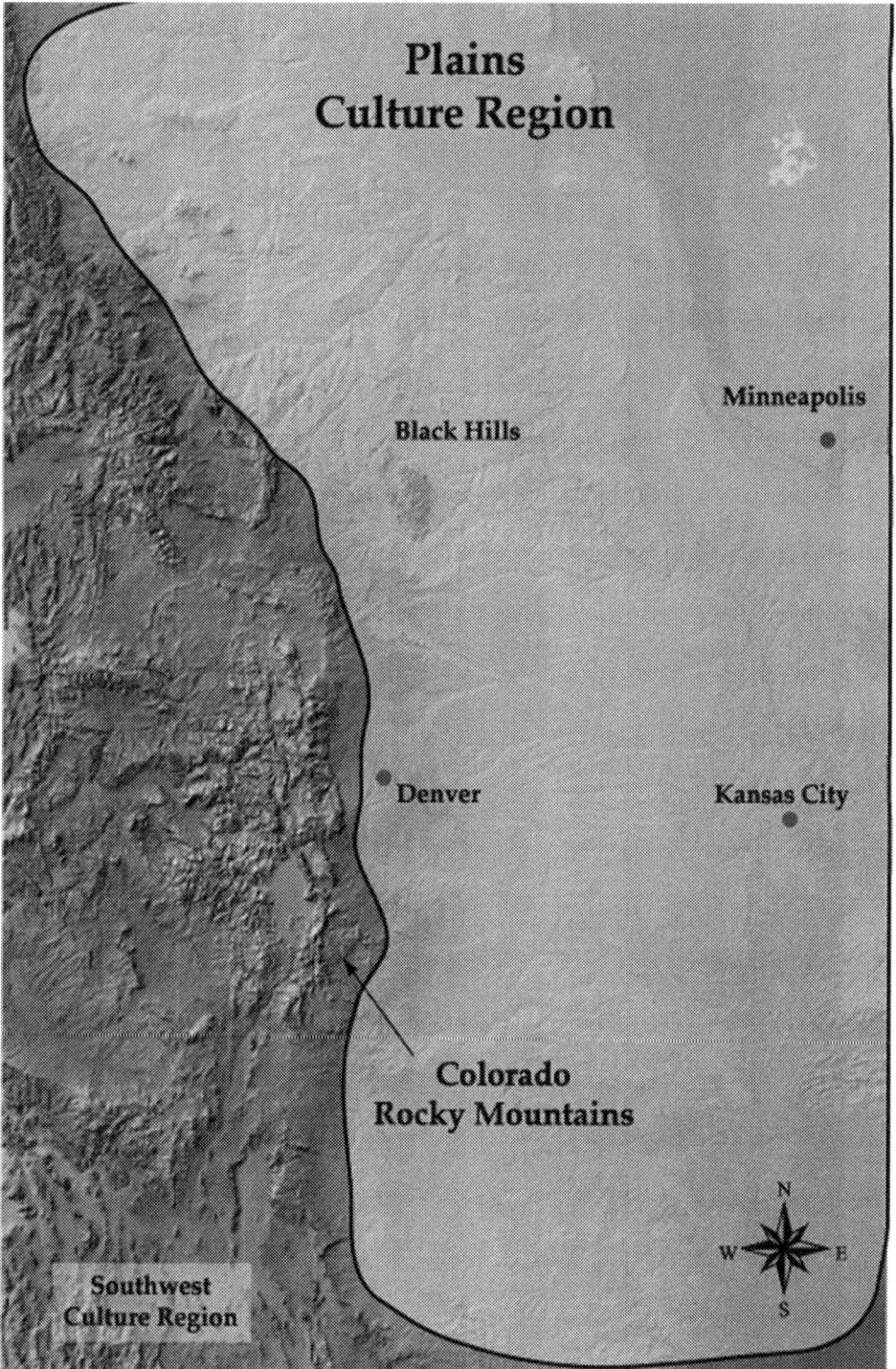

Figure 8. This map illustrates the Plains Culture region.

regional wind erosion and eolian deposition (Holliday, 2000).

The aridity characteristic of the Middle and Late Holocene first appeared as episodes of drought in the last millennia of the Pleistocene and earliest millennia of the Holocene. The stratigraphic record from dune fields and draws, and to a lesser extent from lunettes, indicates that the region was subjected to several periods of wind erosion and eolian sedimentation between 11,000 and 8,000 ybp, and evidence for drought during 11,200-10,900 ybp is sparse but evident. Data from ^{14}C isotopes show that the grass communities shifted between dominantly cool-season to dominantly warm-season species beginning around 11,200 ybp and continuing until around 9,000 ybp, with a very strong influence from warm-season grasses during 10,900-10,200 ybp and no evidence of boreal forest environments as took place further east. The drying, probably linked to warming, destabilized the landscape and resulted in wind erosion, eolian sedimentation, the beginning of construction of the dune fields of the region. The earliest and best-documented phase of marked regional drying and widespread eolian sedimentation occurred between 10,900 and 10,200 ybp and was largely coincident with what archaeologists have called the "Folsom" period of the region. Further evidence indicates that water was flowing in most draws until 11,000 ybp. At that time the hydrology of the draws began to change with lakes, ponds, and marshes abruptly replacing streams. At least twice during 10,900-10,200 ybp lakes with water several meters deep disappeared from the draws and were temporarily replaced with shallow ponds or marshes. Beginning around 10,000 ybp, the lakes and ponds began to fall permanently, leaving marshes, while on the uplands, sand sheets began to form beginning 10,900 ybp and spreading episodically until the Early Holocene, when they evolved into dune fields (Baker & Waln, 1985; Holliday, 2000; Valero-Garces, Laird, Fritz, Kelts, Ito, & Grimm, 1997).

Closer to the Plateau and Great Basin regions, glaciers were developed in most of the ranges of the Rocky Mountains as far south as New Mexico during the Pleistocene, and as far south as Colorado during recent times. Early Pleistocene glaciers appear to have been broad shallow lobate masses, but after canyon erosion in Midddle Pleistocene time, subsequent glaciers formed thick tongues in the canyons. Late Pleistocene ice occurred about as far south as central Colorado (Richmond, Fryxell, Neff, & Weis, 1965; Scott, 1965).

A sediment core recovered from Lost Park provides palynological evidence for postglacial vegetational and environmental change in the central Front Range of Colorado. It appears that pine-spruce woodland was the dominant vegetation type throughout the 12,000-year long record, although non-arboreal taxa showed substantial changes. From 11,800 to 9,100 ybp, high *Artemisia* levels suggest steppe vegetation indicative of a climate cooler than at present with an annual precipitation regime dominated by winter moisture. Lower *Artemisia* levels, coupled with increases in *Poaceae* pollen, suggest a shift to warmer conditions dominated by summer (monsoon) precipitation around 9,100 ybp. Increased charcoal occurrences between 6,000 and 4,000 ybp suggest the onset of drier summer conditions that would be expected with a waning summer monsoon circulation at that time. Since

1,800 ybp, a resurgence in *Artemisia* pollen suggests a return to relatively cool and/or dry conditions similar to the present climate (Vierling, 1998).

Data for the eastern Northern Great Plains just north of Colorado show a congruent Holocene record of effective moisture. Between 11,700 and 9,500 ybp, the climate was cool and moist with a gradual decrease in effective moisture between 9,500 and 7,100 ybp. A change at about 7,100 ybp inaugurated the most arid period during the Holocene though between 7,100 and 4,000 ybp, three arid phases occurred at 6,600-6,200 ybp, 5,400-5,200 ybp, and 4,800-4,600 ybp. Subsequently, effective moisture generally increased after 4,000 ybp, but periods of low effective moisture occurred between 2,900-2,800 ybp and 1,200-800 ybp (Valero-Garces, Laird, Fritz, Kelts, Ito, & Grimm, 1997).

Thus, as has been briefly discussed, the Cordilleran and Laurentide Ice Sheets affected the paleoenvironment of the Plains to a large extent in the north, as well as the various glacial coverages of the Rocky Mountains affecting parts of the western Plains. During the Late Pleistocene and continuing into the Early Holocene the Plains appear to have received more moisture, both in terms of stream and river flow as well as through rain and snow. Grasslands and prarie environments were present throughout this period, though these environments shifted their areas of coverage and sometimes replaced by pine and spruce forests in the north. Occupation of the Plains during this time would have been possible by humans, as much of the Plains were never covered by glacial ice sheets. Finally, the biota appears to have been slightly more mosaic than it is today, allowing for a greater diversity in resources for early peoples to utilize.

Summary of Paleoenvironmental Record

As this brief review of the paleoenvironmental record has attempted to illustrate, the Americas, and parts of Northeastern Asia have experienced drastic changes in environmental conditions throughout the Pleistocene and Holocene. However, despite times of great glacial ice cover there appears to be ample evidence that parts of Alaska and the Northwest Coast remained ice-free throughout the Pleistocene, acting as refugia for plants, animals, and possibly humans during times of greatest glacial coverage. Likewise, the Plateau and Great Basin were very different than they are today, and that these two regions, as well as the rest of the American West, has been in a constant dynamic of changing moisture levels, flora and fauna abundance and distribution, and resource potential. These latter points are very important when attempting to understand how early American peoples both arrived in the Americas and subsisted in these diverse and changing environments through time. Finally, as will be discussed below, it is important to keep the paleoenvironmental record in mind when attempting to understand various types of data and in looking at the question of cultural affiliation in the Plateau and Great Basin. The paleoenvironmental data argues for the understanding that the early people who arrived and began to subsist in the Plateau and Great Basin would have needed to have been highly adaptable not only in their technologies, but also in their subsistence and cultural economies. These later points will be addressed in further detail in the following chapters, especially the chapter on archaeology (chapter nine), though as I discuss in the next chapter, the ethnographic evidence demonstrates that American Indians practiced such a cultural pattern up until the arrival of the horse and Euroamerican contact.

SPECIES (LATIN NAME)	COMMON NAME
Abies amabilis	Pacific silver fir
Abies balsamea	Balsam fir
Abies bracteata	Bristlecone fir
Abies concolor	White fir
Abies fraseri	Fraser fir
Abies grandis	Grand fir
Abies lasiocarpa	Subalpine fir
Abies magnifica	California red fir
Abies procera	Noble fir
Alnus incana ssp. tenuifolia	Thinleaf alder
Alnus rhombifolia	White alder
Alnus rubra	Red alder
Alnus rugosa	Speckled alder
Alnus viridis ssp. sinuata	Sitka alder
Betula alleghaniensis	Yellow birch
Betula nigra	River birch
Betula occidentalis	Water birch
Betula papyrifera	Paper birch
Betula populifolia	Gray birch
Juniperus communis	Common juniper
Juniperus occidentalis	Western juniper
Juniperus osteosperma	Utah juniper
Juniperus scopulorum	Rocky Mountain juniper
Larix decidua	European larch
Larix laricina	Tamarack
Larix lyallii	Alpine larch
Larix occidentalis	Western larch
Picea abies	Norway spruce
Picea breweriana	Brewer spruce
Picea engelmannii	Engelmann spruce
Picea glauca	White spruce
Picea pungens	Blue spruce
Picea rubens	Red spruce
Picea sitchensis	Sitka spruce
Pinus albicaulis	Whitebark pine
Pinus aristata	Rocky Mountain bristlecone pine
Pinus attenuata	Knobcone pine
Pinus cembroides	Mexican pinyon
Pinus contorta var. latifolia	Rocky Mountain lodgepole pine
Pinus contorta var. murrayana	Sierra lodgepole pine
Pinus edulis	Colorado pinyon

Pinus flexilis	Limber pine
Pinus glabra	Spruce pine
Pinus jeffreyi	Jeffrey pine
Pinus longaeva	Great Basin bristlecone pine
Pinus monophylla	Singleleaf pinyon
Pinus monticola	Western white pine
Pinus muricata	Bishop pine
Pinus ponderosa var. ponderosa	Pacific ponderosa pine
Pinus ponderosa var. scopulorum	Interior ponderosa pine
Pinus pungens	Table Mountain pine
Pinus resinosa	Red pine
Pinus rigida	Pitch pine
Pinus sabiniana	Gray pine
Pinus strobiformis	Southwestern white pine
Pinus washoensis	Washoe pine
Populus angustifolia	Narrowleaf cottonwood
Populus balsamifera ssp. balsamifera	Balsam poplar
Populus balsamifera ssp. trichocarpa	Black cottonwood
Populus fremontii	Fremont cottonwood
Populus grandidentata	Bigtooth aspen
Populus tremuloides	Quaking aspen
Pseudotsuga macrocarpa	Bigcone Douglas-fir
Pseudotsuga menziesii var. glauca	Rocky Mountain Douglas-fir
Pseudotsuga menziesii var. menziesii	Coast Douglas-fir
Quercus agrifolia	Coast live oak
Quercus alba	White oak
Quercus ellipsoidalis	Northern pin oak
Quercus gambelii	Gambel oak
Quercus garryana	Oregon white oak
Quercus grisea	Gray oak
Quercus kelloggii	California black oak
Quercus laevis	Turkey oak
Quercus laurifolia	Laurel oak
Quercus lobata	Valley oak
Quercus lyrata	Overcup oak
Quercus macrocarpa	Bur oak
Quercus marilandica	Blackjack oak
Quercus phellos	Willow oak
Quercus rubra	Northern red oak
Quercus shumardii	Shumard oak
Quercus stellata	Post oak

Quercus turbinella	Shrub live oak
Quercus velutina	Black oak
Quercus virginiana	Live oak
Quercus wislizenii	Interior live oak
Salix alaxensis	Alaska willow
Salix amygdaloides	Peachleaf willow
Salix arbusculoides	Littletree willow
Salix bebbiana	Bebb willow
Salix exigua	Sandbar willow
Salix geyeriana	Geyer willow
Salix glauca	Grayleaf willow
Salix gooddingii	Goodding willow
Salix lasiandra	Pacific willow
Salix lutea	Yellow willow
Salix nigra	Black willow
Salix scouleriana	Scouler willow
Tsuga heterophylla	Western hemlock
Tsuga mertensiana	Mountain hemlock

Table 2. Tree species mentioned in the paleoenvironmental section with Latin and common names.

SPECIES (LATIN NAME)	COMMON NAME
Artemisia cana	Silver sagebrush
Artemisia filifolia	Sand sagebrush
Artemisia frigida	Fringed sagebrush
Artemisia nova	Black sagebrush
Artemisia papposa	Fuzzy sagebrush
Artemisia pedatifida	Birdfoot sagebrush
Artemisia pygmaea	Pygmy sagebrush
Artemisia rigida	Stiff sagebrush
Artemisia spinescens	Budsage
Artemisia tridentata ssp. tridentata	Basin big sagebrush
Artemisia tridentata ssp. vaseyana	Mountain big sagebrush
Artemisia tridentata ssp. Wyomingensis	Wyoming big sagebrush
Botrychium montanum	Mountain moonwort
Corylus Americana	American hazel
Lycopodium alpinum	Alpine clubmoss
Lycopodium obscurum	Ground-pine
Selaginella densa	Little clubmoss
Shepherdia canadensis	Russet buffaloberry

Table 3. Other flora species mentioned in the paleoenvironmental section with Latin and common names.

CHAPTER 7
ETHNOGRAPHIC EVIDENCE

As I discussed in chapters two and three, I review in this book several lines of anthropological evidence in accord with an epistemological praxis of epoché that is further guided by the methodological framework outlined in NAGPRA. Accordingly, in this chapter I begin this analysis by reviewing the ethnographic evidence concerning cultural affiliation in the Plateau and Great Basin. Because the topic of this book is the question of whether contemporary American Indian peoples are culturally affiliated with the peoples of the Late Pleistocene and Early Holocene, and specifically, the Kennewick Man and Spirit Cave Mummy, the ethnographic evidence is unable to provide information beyond the last couple hundred years. However, this evidence is still highly enlightening because it informs us on the lifeway pattern of the ethnographic period. This lifeway pattern, if it proves to be similar to the lifeway pattern revealed by the other forms of data reviewed in chapters eight thru eleven, would then provide a corroborating link arguing in favor of cultural affiliation. Therefore, in the rest of this chapter I cover the ethnographic evidence for the Plateau and Great Basin respectively.

Plateau

Non-professionals, namely interested explorers, traders, missionaries, and settlers, first recorded ethnographic data on Plateau American Indian peoples in the early nineteenth century. Trained anthropologists didn't begin work in the region until the late nineteenth century. Specifically, Europeans first came into direct contact with Plateau American Indians as fur trapping companies and exploring expeditions traveled the drainages of the Fraser and Columbia river systems in search of various resources. The first official U.S. contact was with the Meriwether Lewis and William Clark expedition of 1804-1806, which traveled down the Clearwater River to the lower Snake River and along the lower Columbia River to its mouth on the Pacific Ocean at Astoria in present-day Oregon. Captains Lewis and Clark, along with other members of the expedition, left reports, letters, and diaries that provide important data concerning the lifeway patterns of the American Indians they met (Coues, 1965; Jackson, 1978; Moulton, 1991; Sappington, 1989). Other references to Plateau American Indians occur in the accounts of other explorers, fur trappers, and fur trading company administrators from the end of the eighteenth century until the middle of the nineteenth. For example, fur traders like David Thompson (1914, 1916, 1917, 1920), Simon Fraser (1889, 1960), John Work (1909, 1912a, 1912b, 1914a, 1914b, 1914c, 1915, 1920), Alexander Ross (1904, 1913, 1956), David Douglas (1914, 1959), Peter Skene Ogden (1909, 1910, 1950), and George Simpson (1931) offer descriptions of Plateau American Indians in the precontact setting, as well as in the earliest stages of colonial contact. Likewise, the journals of Fathers Pierre-Jean de Smet (1843, 1847, 1859, 1863), and Nicolas Point (1967) are good sources on the Flathead, Coeur d'Alene, and Colville tribes in the middle nineteenth century, as dislocation and colonization intensified. Accounts by Washington Irving (1836) describing the Nez Perce, John K. Townsend (1970) on the Cayuse, Joel Palmer (1847), Daniel Lee and J.H. Frost (1844), and Samuel J. Parker (1846) on the Nez Perce and Klikitat, along with Meredith Gairdner (1841), Horatio Emmons Hale (1846), John Scouler (1848), Henry Warre (1848), and Paul Kane (1856, 1859) who provide information on several tribes each, have left invaluable accounts of American Indians as traditional lifeway patterns began to change.

This fairly large dataset indicates that until the adoption of the horse in the 1700s, Plateau American Indians maintained close connections with the Northwest Coast and the northern Great Basin, and that once the horse was introduced relations with the Plains were developed as well (Haines, 1938a, 1938b). Further, hostile relationships tended to occur with Shoshone and Paiute groups to the south, although there were substantial trade, exchange, and intermarriage relationships between Sahaptian groups and Northern Shoshone and Northern Paiute peoples. After adoption of the horse, composite band political organizations emerged in response to growing conflict with both Plains and northern Great Basin peoples, especially in the eastern and southern Plateau. This dynamic lifeway pattern based on a seasonal round focused on salmon and other riverine resources, as well as camas and other natural resources of the plateaus began to be radically altered in the nineteenth century.

In 1845 over 3,000 United States immigrants traveled what came to be called the Oregon Trail, passing through the Columbia Plateau (Ruby & Brown, 1972). An additional 1,350 immigrants entered the Oregon Territory in the following year (Fuller, 1931) with over 5,000 arriving in 1847 (Fuller, 1931; Harper, 1971; Johansen & Gates, 1957; Ruby & Brown, 1972) and by 1850 more than 11,500 emigrants had passed over the southern Plateau on the Oregon Trail. These emigrants brought goods, diseases, and prejudices in far greater magnitude than introduced by the previous four decades of the fur trade. Likewise, land speculation and the prospect of securing land claims and ownership in the lush and fertile valleys west of the

Cascades spurred on the pioneers (Unruh, 1979). These pioneers encountered and severely disrupted the various American Indian peoples and their lifeways, affecting some groups more rapidly and severely than others.

The following discussion outlines the basic territories and lifeway patterns of the American Indian peoples just prior to contact with these emigrating pioneers, beginning in the northern part of the Plateau and working south. The Lillooet peoples of southwestern British Columbia speak a language belonging to the northern branch of Interior Salish (see chapter ten). Lillooet territory in the early nineteenth century extended along the Fraser River from Leon Creek down and included the Bridge River drainage. The Seton Lake and Anderson Lake region was within this territory, as were the Birkenhead River and Green River drainages, along with the entire Lillooet River drainage south to Harrison Lake. Just to the south, the Thompson people occupied portions of the territory drained by the Fraser, Thompson, and Nicola rivers in British Columbia and are also Interior Salish speakers. Thompson territory was well defined along the rivers, primarily because families passed on rights to salmon fishing spots that required others to seek permission prior to there use. Upland territory was shared more freely with other Thompson groups and other peoples, although deer fences were inherited and hunters from one band could not build them in the hunting territory of another. The daily organization of life was local, but the Thompson were a people because they shared a common identity. They spoke a common language, used a common name, recalled their common origin (Teit, 1909/1975, 1912, 1914), and had ties of custom and kinship.

Nearby, the Shuswap peoples are speakers of the Interior Salish language and historically encompassed some 180,000 square kilometers in British Columbia (Dawson, 1892; Ignace, 1992; Palmer, 1975; Teit, 1909/1975). Their homeland was traversed by the Fraser and Thompson rivers, with most Shuswap communities located along the valleys of these rivers and their main tributaries. Peaceful relations with the neighboring people were maintained through marital alliances, especially with settlements located at the edges of Shuswap territory. Next to the Shuswap are the Nicola, an Athapaskan speaking people who lived in the midst of Interior Salish people in the Nicola and Similkameen valleys of interior British Columbia. Little is known about the Nicola, though ethnographic data indicates that they were similar to Thompsons in culture, but not in language.

To the east, along the Kootenay River is located the Kootenai. Their language classification is uncertain, as will be discussed in chapter ten. Briefly, Sapir (1917) included Kootenai in his highly speculative Algonkin-Wakashan grouping, thus positing a possible linguistic affinity to the neighboring Algonquian and Interior Salishan languages. This opinion was echoed by Haas (1965), though most anthropologists position the Kootenai as a language isolate (Boas, 1911a; Powell, 1891a; Voegelin & Voegelin, 1966). The Kootenai territory was defined in terms of the course of the Kootenay River, and the river was basic to their culture. The river and its environs provided the Kootenai with most of their subsistence needs, and was the means of both summer canoe and winter snowshoe travel and transportation. It was also the location of their more permanent camp and village sites.

The Northern Okanagan, Lakes, and Colville are the northerly components of an Interior Salish grouping that also comprises the Methow, Southern Okanogan, Nespelem, and Sanpoil. This larger group has been called by some (Kennedy & Bouchard, 1998) Okanagan-Colville, and they speak a single language simply called Okanagan. The distinction of a northern and southern division of Okanagan was introduced by Sapir (1917), though it is probable that such a distinction did not exist prehistorically or culturally. Their territory covered the area around Okanagan Lake south to the present-day U.S. border, as well as Upper and Lower Arrow Lake and south across the U.S. border along the Columbia River to just below Kettle Falls.

To the south, the Middle Columbia River Salishans lived along the middle Columbia River in northwestern Washington. These people were settled along the Columbia River and its western and northern tributaries, which drain the eastern slopes of the Cascades and the area north of the Big Bend of the Columbia River. Two closely related Interior Salish languages are spoken in several dialects by the Middle Columbia River Salishans. Columbian is the language of the downriver bands, and Okanagan is the language of the upriver groups. The Middle Columbia River Salishan social and trade network was extensive, having involvement with Flathead and Sahaptian peoples to the west. The neighbors of the Middle Columbia River Salishans were the Spokane of northeastern Washington who spoke an Interior Salishan language shared, in different dialects, with the Kalispel, Pend d'Oreille, and Flathead, though their language was probably a lingua franca in the northeastern Plateau (Walker, 1998). The Kalispel spoke an Interior Salish lan- guage and occupied the territory along the Pend Oreille River below Lake Pend Oreille in Idaho to the confluence of the Salmon River in British Columbia, as well as along the Clark Fork River east into Montana and Flathead territory.

The Flathead and the Pend d'Oreille are two groups of Salishan-speaking people with dialects that were mutually understood by each other, and had separate but somewhat overlapping geographic locations. Prehistorically, the Flathead occupied an area north of Yellowstone National Park extending to where the Missouri River emerges from the northern Rocky Mountains (Chalfant, 1974). They ranged east to Billings, Montana, and the Pryor Mountains, and west to the continental divide. The Pend d'Oreille inhabited the area west of the divide, extending down the Clark Fork River in Montana.

Just south, the prehistoric Coeur d'Alene territory extended over the drainage and headwaters of the Spokane River. Villages and some nearby resource sites were held by individual bands, but places between population centers, such as the Rathdrum Prairies, the camas prairie on Hangman Creek, and portions of the Clearwater and Clark Fork may have been regarded by more than one group as lying within their territories. The Yakama, Kittitas, Klikitat, Taitnapam, and Wanapam peoples were closely related but independent bands and villages of families who occupied con- tiguous territories in the south-central part of the state of Washington. The Yakama and other groups in prehistoric times did not have the formal political unity under a permanent central authority that is characteristic of today's tribes. Rather, they were small, politically autonomous groups, joined together by bonds of territorial contiguity, linguistic affinity, a common culture, and a high level of recurring social interaction.

To the south are the Sahaptian speaking Palouse first recognized by Hale (1846). The Palouse territory was centered at Palus on the Columbia River with dominance through the Fishhook Bend or Page area to the mouth of the Snake River. Down river were located the Wasco and Wishram who are Chinookan peoples who spoke Upper Chinook dialects and lived just east of the Cascade Mountains in Oregon and Washington. They wintered close to the Columbia River, but during the summer would utilize the abundant resources present on the eastern slopes of the Cascades and on the plateaus above the river bottoms.

Neighboring the Chinook peoples were the Western Columbia River Sahaptins, known as the Tenino and Warm Springs Indians, who identify themselves as members of village communities located on the Columbia River or its tributaries from just above The Dalles, Oregon, to above Alder Creek. The Cayuse, Umatilla, and Walla Walla are peoples who have long associated amongst themselves, with the Walla Walla and Umatilla speaking a dialect of Sahaptin, and the Cayuse a distinct language of uncertain affinities. In prehistoric times, intermarriage among the three peoples and the Nez Perce was accompanied by bilingualism. Their prehistoric territory centered on the confluence of the Snake, Yakima, Walla Walla, and Columbia rivers, as well as including the Umatilla River and various tributaries.

To the east, the Nez Perce, who spoke a dialect of Sahaptin, prehistorically lived on the middle Snake and Clearwater rivers and the northern portion of the Salmon River basin in central Idaho and adjacent Oregon and Washington. Finally, the Molala peoples spoke an isolated language not related to other Plateau languages, and lived in the greater part of the Cascade Range in west-central Oregon. South, on the Oregon and California border prehistorically lived the Klamath and Modoc who are closely related in language and culture.

Based on the ethnographic evidence it is apparent that a major criterion for the delineation of a Plateau culture area is linguistic distribution in early historic times. With the exception of some language isolates, the people of the Plateau spoke dialects of either Sahaptin or Salish languages. Around the entire periphery are the historic territories of peoples who speak quite different or very distantly related languages. However, the general cultural situation is not so easily bounded. All the peoples of the Plateau share significant traits with contiguous groups in surrounding regions and have for centuries intermarried with them, establishing many areas of joint use of lands, intermarriage, and multi-lingualism. Moreover, evidence for long-distance trade reveals that Plateau peoples were far from insular, maintaining extensive prehistoric and early historic connections with other regions. Any attempt to depict bounded limits for the culture area or its internal groupings must be perceived, therefore, as largely heuristic and requiring qualification in terms of historical events, mobility, and the record of self-identification of the groups involved. Despite this, however, it is clear based on the ethnographic evidence that the Plateau peoples all practiced a seasonal lifeway pattern focused on riverine resources, especially salmon, as well as various other plants, berries, and roots. Furthermore, the data indicates that although the Plateau peoples had specific group identities, they also shared a larger cultural identity as a result of intergroup marriages, trace and exchange practices, and the common pursuit of various subsistence resources.

Great Basin

The first reports to give some glimpse of the Great Basin and its people were made in the late eighteenth century by Spanish explorers seeking routes between their colonized territory in New Mexico on the southern fringes of the Great Basin and California. Later, both British and American troops penetrated the northern periphery early in the nineteenth century providing sketchy but important information about the environment and the American Indian peoples they encountered along the route that became the Oregon Trail. However, the vast interior of the Great Basin remained unknown, referred to on early maps as the "Mysterious Land" or "Unknown Land" until the first parties of trappers, explorers, and immigrants attempted to traverse the region in search of furs and a direct overland route to California. Some of these early explorers, such as Jedediah Strong Smith in 1827, Peter Skene Ogden in 1829, Joseph Walker in 1833, and John Bidwell in 1841, actually succeeded in crossing the basins and ranges of the central Great Basin to California. The first crossing of this area by Jedediah Smith went from California across what is now northern Nevada to the Great Salt Lake (Bancroft, 1890).

However, it was not until after the widely heralded explorations of John C. Fremont (1845) that the American public became convinced that the difficult passage could be made safely. It had been part of the lore of this unknown area that a great river, often referred to as the Buenaventura, emerged in the Rocky Mountains and flowed westward over the deserts to empty in San Francisco Bay. Fremont was among those who held to this view and his explorations searched for this river in order to make an easy passage to California. On his second expedition in 1844 he was led at last to the conclusion that the legendary waterway did not exist, and he noted on the map of the expedition that the area between the Wasatch Mountains in Utah and the Sierra Nevada was "surrounded by lofty mountains: contents almost unknown, but believed to be filled with rivers and lakes which have no connection with the sea." Having affirmed that this enormous and largely uncharted territory was one of interior drainage, he gave it the name "great basin" (Fremont, 1845, map).

After 1845 and the publicity of the Fremont expeditions, an increasing number of immigrant parties began to follow the Humboldt or Overland Trail, across the central Great Basin to California rather than taking either the Oregon Trail to the north in the Plateau or the Old Spanish Trails in the south, even though it continued to be known as a perilous route. As a result of the remoteness and the apparent inaccessibility of much of the region, the Mormons ventured into it in 1847, choosing the valley of the Great Salt Lake as a place of refuge from religious persecution, thus becoming its first Euroamerican settlers. They dreamed of building a new society, remote from Euroamerican pioneers to the north and east and from the distant Spanish claimants to the territory in the south and west, where the deserts would bloom with their labors and the Indians would join in defense of the land. Within a year they had proclaimed the state of Deseret, which included all of the region now known as the Great Basin, as well as other areas in the Southwest and southern California acquired by the United States in the Treaty of Guadalupe Hidalgo in 1848.

In 1849 with the discovery of gold in California a rush of thousands of new immigrants crossed the corridors of the Great Basin to the Pacific Coast. During the following decade, thousands more were attracted to the Comstock mines of western Nevada, many of whom remained to settle as ranchers and townspeople after the mining boom collapsed. The tide of immigration transformed the region into new territories and states with networks of American enterprise and settlement and a transcontinental railroad was completed in 1869 stretching across the Great Basin.

In many areas the original environment of the Great Basin was altered drastically by this large influx of people. Grasslands along the rivers were destroyed by livestock grazing, springs in arid sections were fenced by ranchers, some timbered areas were all but denuded by the needs of mines and towns, and large game became scarce. The conquest of the new territory was complete, but the impact upon the way of life of the American Indian peoples, who had at first cautiously welcomed the intruders and later attempted sporadic resistance, was devastating. Starvation and diseases brought by Euroamericans decimated large numbers, and those that survived were forced onto reservations containing lands least desirable to the new settlers. Furthermore, the access to the wide range of natural resources that had sustained traditional economy and culture became exceedingly difficult. Some became dependents and laborers on ranches or in mines, as well as on the fringes of the new Euroamerican communities. So desperate was the American Indian condition that Euroamerican observers in the latter part of the nineteenth century predicted their imminent extinction, and some even welcomed the possibility as a solution to "the Indian problem." Despite the near destruction of the American Indian peoples traditional lifeway patterns, numerous ethnographic accounts captured many aspects of this lifeway, and it is possible to reconstruct the basic territory and lifeway pattern of the Great Basin American Indian peoples.

In the far west of the Great Basin, the Washoe's range extended westward over the crest of the Sierra Nevada, and many of their cultural traits were shared with California American Indian peoples, although their major habitat and relations were along the eastern slope of the mountains in close proximity to the Northern Paiute. Because of their Hokan language (see chapter ten) and their location straddling state boundaries, they frequently were dealt with as a part of the California culture area by anthropologists, but their position as a Great Basin people has been generally acknowledged (Barrett, 1917; Kroeber, 1925a). In California, speakers of the Mono language in the Western branch of Numic are divided into two sections by the Sierra Nevada and they differ in dialect and cultural affinities. The Owens Valley Paiute (also referred to as the Eastern Mono) are the larger group and are culturally and linguistically related to the Northern Paiute, while the mountain or western group (Monache) are mainly oriented to neighbors in the California foothills and valleys. The Owens Valley Paiute are often delineated because of their relatively high degree of sociopolitical integration, their sedentary village pattern, and their unique irrigation practices, which are unique among the western Great Basin American Indian peoples.

At the southwestern extremity of the Great Basin are the Panamint-speaking Western Shoshone people in and around Death Valley whom establish the limit of distribution of the Central Numic languages. Their western neighbors, the Tubatulabal, speak a distinct language distantly related to Numic but are culturally associated with peoples of the westerly California foothills and valleys. The Panamint Shoshone, however, are clearly connected with Great Basin cultures such as those of the Owens Valley Paiute, the Southern Paiute, and other Western Shoshone not only linguistically but also culturally (Kroeber, 1925a; Steward, 1938). The small section inhabited by the Kawaiisu presents something of an anomaly. Their language is distinct enough to be considered separate from the larger Southern Numic division to the east that includes related peoples such as the Southern Paiute and Ute. Culturally, however, their affinities appear to be with California, though their early connections with the Chemehuevi have been noted (Kroeber, 1925b). Few identifiable Kawaiisu people remained in the mid-twentieth century, and these were scattered throughout southern California, further obscuring their exact cultural affiliation.

The well-defined Southern Paiute bands along the Colorado River constitute a firm boundary between speakers of the Southern Numic languages and the Yuman and Hopi-speaking peoples of the Southwest. South of the San Juan River, the Navajo began to expand into their territory in the nineteenth century. Although there is evidence of cultural trait diffusions across the river divides, including the adoption of some horticultural practices, the Southern Paiute maintained an essentially Great Basin lifeway pattern of subsistence and general culture. Along with the Ute peoples to the east, they are speakers of the Ute language, the most extensively distributed language of the Southern Numic branch of the Uto-Aztecan family. The separation between the Southern Paiute and Ute peoples is, therefore, not linguistic but based principally on cultural traits. As O.C. Stewart (1982) points out, the major distinction between them was brought about by historic events and cultural changes in the eighteenth and nineteenth centuries. The Ute, particularly those east of the Colorado and Green Rivers, were among the first groups to adopt the horse from the Spanish and were instrumental in the spread of equestrian practices from the Spanish settlements in the south to the north into the Plateau. In this process they were able to hunt buffalo on the western Plains and soon acquired many new elements of culture that led early anthropologists to mistakenly classify them ethnologically in the Plains culture area (Wissler, 1917). However, the western groups retained their central Great Basin cultural orientation.

The Eastern Shoshone peoples ranged over most of the Wyoming Basin along the upper reaches of the Green, Sweetwater, and Big Horn rivers east of the central Rocky Mountains. However, since historic times, they also ranged far out into the Northern Plains, and, like the Ute, were among the first peoples to adopt the horse and to transmit elements of Plains culture to the northern Great Basin (Kroeber,

1939). A group of these peoples known as the Comanche split off in the eighteenth century and slowly moved into their present location in the southern Plains in search of buffalo (Shimkin, 1980). Together with the Northern and Western Shoshone, the Eastern Shoshone and Comanche are speakers of Central Numic languages.

The Eastern and Northern Shoshone, along with the Bannock, are closely linked, and their combined ranges have been referred to as a "Northeastern subarea" of the Great Basin (Butler, 1981). In this area, several physiographic provinces come together: the Basin and Range, the Columbia Plateau and Snake River Plain, the middle Rocky Mountains, and the Wyoming Basin. The Northern Shoshone inhabited the area of the Snake and Salmon river drainages, and their culture, like that of the Eastern Shoshone and the Utes, was deeply influenced by the Plains, especially after their acquisition of the horse. Despite these influences their language and early cultural lifeway patterns were those of the other Shoshone of the Great Basin. Moreover, their general range of habitation and land use was in a section of the southern Columbia Plateau where the sagebrush and juniper plant cover was similar to that of the Great Basin floristic province. Except for their partial reliance on salmon, their subsistence practices were essentially like those of their Shoshone and Northern Paiute neighbors.

The Northern Paiute or Oregon and northern Nevada, speakers of a Western Numic language, also represent a Great Basin people whose range extends beyond the physiographic province and in the eighteenth century was even farther north (Ray et al., 1938; Stewart, 1966). There was also a large area of joint use with the Northern Shoshone on the border of Oregon and Idaho that was mutually utilized by both groups. In eastern Idaho, a small but often politically dominant minority of Northern Paiute people, known in the literature as the Bannock, have lived among the Northern Shoshone for hundreds of years (Liljeblad, 1957; Stewart, 1966). They were speakers of a dialect of the Western Numic Northern Paiute language, but were bilingual in Shoshone from which considerable linguistic borrowing took place.

As I have discussed here, and as will be covered further in chapter ten, the major criterion for the delineation of the Great Basin culture area is linguistic distribution. With the exception of the Washoe, the picture presented is one of a wide fanlike extension of the three branches of Numic languages. Around the entire periphery are the historic territories of peoples who speak quite different or very distantly related languages. However, the general cultural situation is not so easily bounded. All the peoples of the Great Basin share significant traits with contiguous groups in surrounding regions and have for centuries intermingled with them, establishing many areas of joint use of lands, intermarriage, and multi-lingualism. Moreover, evidence for long-distance trade reveals that Great Basin peoples were far from insular, maintaining extensive prehistoric and early historic connections with other regions. Any attempt to depict bounded limits for the culture area or its internal groupings must be perceived, therefore, as largely heuristic and requiring qualification in terms of historical events, mobility, and the record of self-identification of the groups involved. However, the subsistence lifeway patterns discussed in the ethnographic literature present a picture consisting of a seasonal subsistence round based on seasonal and precipitation factors. Furthermore, the ethnographic evidence indicates that this lifeway pattern was focused on a few primary resource areas that were visited seasonally for hundreds of years, reinforcing each group's cultural identity and affiliation with previous generations. Finally, like that of the Plateau, the American Indian peoples of the Great Basin shared a larger cultural identity as a result of intergroup marriages, trade and exchange practices, and the common pursuit of various subsistence resources.

Summary of Ethnographic Evidence

As was briefly discussed, the ethnographic evidence, as directed under the guidelines of inquiry established under NAGPRA, indicates that the present-day tribes of the Plateau and Great Basin have occupied their prospective areas since well before the beginning of the historic period (ca. 1800). Thus, the ethnographic data favors cultural affiliation and cultural continuity within the Plateau and Great Basin as far back as the beginning of the historic record. However, attempting to answer this question beyond the recent past is not possible when solely relying on ethnographic evidence. Instead, as the next several chapters will discuss, the ethnographic evidence must be synthesized with the biological, archaeological, linguistic, and oral tradition evidence when attempting to determine whether cultural affiliation exists between the peoples of the Late Pleistocene and Early Holocene and the present-day American Indians of the Plateau and Great Basin.

CHAPTER 8
BIOLOGICAL EVIDENCE

As discussed in chapters two and three, looking at cultural affiliation from an epistemological praxis of epoché, as well as through the guidelines established by NAGPRA, requires the review of the biological and physical evidence. In this chapter I spend some time review this evidence for both the Plateau and the Great Basin, as well as the evidence concerning the peopling of the Americas and the original populations from whom American Indians are theoretically derived. This extensive review is necessary because there is little contention within the biological/physical literature that historic or late prehistoric (~3,000-200 ybp) data (derived primarily from skeletal remains) is of American Indian ancestry. However, as one goes further back in time, such as with the Kennewick Man or Spirit Cave Mummy examples, it becomes more and more difficult to establish either biological affiliation or non-affiliation. Within this large body of data, it is possible to delineate four subcategories to help organize the discussion and review: 1) dental data; 2) craniometric data (morphological analyses); 3) genetic data; and 4) trichological data. It is important to note that though biological/physical data cannot reveal cultural affiliation, it can reveal biological/physical affiliation, which will help to answer questions concerning whether various population displacements or migrations have taken place in the Plateau and Great Basin during the prehistoric past.

Dental Evidence

Dental studies have been sporadically conducted on American Indian remains in an attempt to correlate their dental traits with those of southeast and northeast Asians (Kelley, 1991; Milner, 1991; Shields, 1996; Shields & Jones, 1996; Turner,

Nichol, & Scott, 1991; Turner, 1974; Turner II, 1967, 1985, 1989, 1994). These studies have revealed that there are two basic, discrete dental types within Asia, which have been labeled the Sundadont and the Sinodont (Turner II, 1985, 1989, 1994). The Sundadont traits are believed to have developed sometime between 30,000-17,000 years ago in south Asian populations. A branch group of people with the Sundadont traits is further hypothesized to have migrated to Northeastern Asia, at which point the Sindodont traits developed. Comparison between these two dentail trait groups and the dental traits of American Indians has led to the conclusion that American Indians are closer to the Sindodont dental trait characteristics. Furthermore, statistical analyses of twenty-nine dental traits in more than 15,000 American Indians, Old World, and Pacific Basin individuals evidences that teeth of American Indians are more like those of Northeast Asians than of other major world populations. The data indicates that American Indians and Northeast Asians appear to form one of two major world clusters, i.e., those people with Sindodont dental traits. The second cluster labeled Sundadont contains Africans, Europeans, Southeast Asians, and Oceanic peoples. This conclusion of two world clusters has not been supported, however, by some of the genetic studies (see Cavalli-Sforza, Piazza, Menozzi, & Mountain, 1988) based on many monogenic traits of living peoples. A strength, however, of the dental data is that it largely is from prehistoric samples, collected by a single observer (i.e., does not suffer from inter-observer errors), along with the fact that most dental traits seem to have a polygenic mode of inheritance. Thus, it has been proposed that the dental data provide better estimates of European-Asian-American relationships than do monogenic traits as much of the genetic data is composed of (see below). Furthermore, it has also been argued that there is a much less chance for dental admixture or the opportunity for selection or drift to cause evolutionary convergence in the dental data. Finally, diachronic dental studies of northern Eurasians seem to support these conclusions by showing marked dissimilarities between Europeans and Asians until about Late Pleistocene times, when admixture appears to have become prevalent (Turner II, 1994). Because it is believed that the first American Indians left Asia during Late Pleistocene, it is presumed that they would not carry any evidence of this admixture, a hypothesis born out by the data.

Another line of evidence that has been used to argue for the strength of the dental data over that of genetic data has to do with the data source. For example, as Turner noted "Although Cavalli-Sforza et al. (1988, p. 6003) assert that little or no admixture is present in their samples, one has to ask, how can they be certain? What is their prehistoric baseline? The answer, of course, is that there is none. This is the fundamental weakness of studies tethered to living populations where their biological prehistory cannot be directly checked" (Turner II, 1994, pp. 136-137). As this argument implies, and as the prehistoric Siberian archaeological and physical anthropological record seems to indicate, Europeans and Asians were meeting in western Siberia and interbreeding during and shortly before Neolithic times (Alexseev & Gokhman, 1984; Martynov, 1981). Thus, prehistoric admixture would be the underlying cause of the European-Asian linkage in the genetic tree, and not phylogeny. Thus, any hypothesized baseline used to reconstruct genetic relationships will be skewed as a result of admixture unless it is calibrated using dental data. This line of argument, along with several others, will be discussed in the section dealing with genetic data. First, however, it is important to note that there are also several problems inherent in the dental dataset.

For example, in attempting to use dental data in the Kennewick Man case, Powell and Rose (1999) found that,

> Although it is tempting to try to assign Kennewick to either the Sinodont or Sundadont (Turner 1990) patterns, it is simply not possible to attribute the Kennewick individual's dental discrete traits to either the Sinodont or Sundadont groups based on gross morphological observations. (1999, p. 6)

This is because Turner's dental patterns are based on relative frequencies of eight key traits based on a large Asian sample, and selecting any one individual drawn at random from either the Sinodont or Sundadont groups may exhibit none, some, or all of the characteristics associated with one of these groups. Furthermore, Powell and Rose (1999) also conducted a discrete trait analysis on Kennewick Man's dentition, demonstrating that "Kennewick had a probability of 0.48460 for membership in the Sinodont group, 0.93769 for membership in the Sundadont group" (p. 18). This is in theoretical congruence with most of the genetic studies (see below), as well as Turner's general conclusions that suggest that American Indians began migrating to the Americas between 40,000 and 25,000 years ago, though at first it would appear to contradict the dental evidence. The reconciliation between the Kennewick Man dental traits and those of Turner's data is possible when one understands that as the various peoples with Sundadont traits moved to Northeastern Asia and slowly either developed or gave rise to individuals with Sinodont traits, it is very likely that many of these individuals with mixed Sundadont/Sinodont traits were some of the groups that made their way to the Americas at this time. Thus, the dental evidence, though somewhat inconclusive as to Kennewick Man's biological affiliation, does support the hypothesis that he is American Indian. Furthermore, this is also the conclusion reached by specialists looking at the gross dental morphology of the Spirit Cave Mummy. As Goodman and Martin (1999) noted for the Spirit Cave individual, "The presence of severe shoveling on lateral incisors and shoveling on a canine strongly suggests affiliation with contemporary Native Americans" (p. 10), who exhibit a mixture of Sundadont and Sinodont dental characteristics.

To summarize, therefore, dental morphology, though somewhat controversial and lacking strong statistical power, indicates that the Americas were colonized by individuals whose genetic ancestry was with the evolving Late Pleistocene Northeast Asian population that culturally adapted to the Arctic and Subarctic frontier north of China and Southeastern Siberia around 30,000 ybp (Ameriks, 1985; Shields, 1996; Shields & Jones, 1996; Turner II, 1985, 1994). Furthermore, the dental evidence indicates that Early Holocene skeletal remains found in the Plateau and Great Basin such as the Kennewick Man and Spirit Cave Mummy are American Indian, and not related to any other population based on dentral traits. A similar conclusion can be reached, as will be discussed next, concerning the skeletal morphological data.

Craniometric Evidence

Physical anthropologists use various aspects of cranial morphology to measure similarities across crania in a corresponding statistical fashion to that of the previously discussed dental trait analyses. That is, by measuring aspects of a skeletal cranium and comparing it to other skeletal cranium from a known population, it is possible to say with some statistical power how closely the two craniums are morphologically related. This method has proven useful and informative in many cases, especially when the populations under comparison are known and contemporary with each other. However, as I will discuss below, several problems arise when this method is employed using either limited, unknown, or non-contemporary populations. These latter problems plague carniometric studies in the Americas that attempt to determine cranial morphological relatedness between contemporary American Indian populations and those of the prehistoric past. Because of the limited sample size (n= ~25) of skeletons found in the Americas prior to 8,500 ybp, craniometric morphological measurements of this dataset as a population are of very limited statistical value. Although most of the studies claim that Late Pleistocene and Early Holocene skeletons are "most similar" to South Asian and Polynesian populations (Jantz & Owsley, 1997, 1998, 2001; Owsley & Jantz, 1999, 2001; Powell & Neves, 1999; Steele & Powell, 1992, 1994, 1999), these studies also note some of their statistical limitations. However, these limitations are rarely recognized by individuals outside the physical anthropological field because of the field's specific methodologies and implicit assumptions. As Gould (1981) clearly stated:

> Science is rooted in creative interpretation. Numbers suggest, constrain, and refute; they do not, by themselves, specify the content of scientific theories. Theories are built upon the interpretation of numbers, and interpreters are often trapped by their own rhetoric. They believe in their own objectivity, and fail to discern the prejudice that leads them to one interpretation among many consistent with their numbers. (p. 74)

Steele and Powell (1992, pp. 319-320; see also Weidenreich, 1945), for example, note "that braincase shape alone cannot be used as a diagnostic character to differentiate all world populations and that dolichocrancy can occur in all geographic populations." This was clearly demonstrated by Newman (1962) who noted, "cranial samples from all known parts of the New World show a consistent trend toward brachycrany. This widespread and continuing trend is such that a truly dolichocephalic sample of living Indians... would be difficult to find" (p. 243). Furthermore, as Steele and Powell (1992) also state,

> we still face the most difficult task of all. Are these distinctive structural features a reflection of subtle differences in the genomes of these earlier populations, or do the differences reflect an adaptational difference, an adaptation accomplished by the plasticity of human growth and development? At present, we cannot accurately answer this question. (pp. 312-313)

This last limitation is very important when attempting to compare prehistoric skeletons with those of modern-day individuals to answer questions of cultural affiliation and cultural continuity. The human skeleton, including the crania, is one of the most "plastic" morphological skeletal features of our species. The human skeleton responds to a wide array of environmental, dietetic, genetic, life course, and cultural forces to which it is exposed. As Swedlund and Anderson (2003) have stated, "we have volumes of data on how the cranium responds to nutritional, dietary (they are not the same), and environmental forces within the life span, particularly during growth and development" (p. 163). However, these extraneous factors are rarely taken into account when comparing ancient to modern crania and inferring biological affiliation between the two crania or two cranial populations. Further, limitations are also found in the assumptions built into the methodological theory of these studys. Perhaps the most recent example of this disregard for the potential of cranial plasticity, especially when dealing with a time period of thousands of years, is the work of Gonzalez-Jose and colleagues (Gonzalez-Jose, Dahinten, Luis, Hernandez, & Pucciarelli, 2001; Gonzalez-Jose et al., 2003). Instead of allowing for various environmental, nutritional, dietic, cultural, and other processes to explain the difference found in skulls from Baja California to those of the present inhabitants of the Americas, they concluded that a "different origin for for Palaeoamericans and Amerindians is invoked to explain such a phenomenon" (2003, p. 62).

In 1912, Franz Boas, one of the founders of American anthropology published a study demonstrating the plastic nature of the human body in response to changes in the environment. The results of this study have been cited for the past 90 years as evidence of cranial plasticity without a serious look at the studies' statistical and biological validity. Recently, however, two studies have been published that have taken a close look at both Boas' dataset as well as the statistical methods used within his classic study. One study concluded that results point to very small and insignificant differences between European- and American-born offspring, with no effect of exposure to the American environment on the cranial index in children. These results contradict Boas' original findings and demonstrate that they may no longer be used to support arguments of plasticity in cranial morphology (Sparks & Jantz, 2002). The other study, however, came to the opposite conclusion, stating that Boas' methods may have been a little weak, but that the results are the same, and that there is a significant amount of effect on crania and skeletons from environmental factors (Swedlund & Anderson, 2003). Similarly, a third study also came to the same conclusions as those of Swedlund and Anderson (2003), that Sparks and Jantz (2002) actually support one of Boas's fundamental conclusions, that the cephalic index is subject to change, even within a single generation (Gravlee, Bernard, & Leonard, 2003). These two studies point out the inchoate nature of craniometric studies, which have been refined and strengthened over the years since Boas' time, but that still have numerous limitations, especially when dealing with issues central to this book. Below I discuss a couple other limitations concerning the use of craniometric data in determining biological continuity between populations of the distant past, such as those of the Kennewick Man and Spirit Cave Mummy, and contemporary American Indian populations.

The first limitation inherent in the present use of craniometric data for inferring biological affiliation stems from dating and excavation problems associated with many of the skeletons originally found prior to the 1980s. Many of the skeletons currently used in these analyses were found prior to accurate dating methods and now cannot be properly dated without destructive sampling. One of the better known examples of this type of limitation involves the crania found in California in the early 1970s (Bada, Gillespie, Gowlett, & Hedges, 1984; Bada & Helfman, 1975; Bada & Masters, 1982; Bada, Schroeder, & Carter, 1974). In 1974 (Bada, Schroeder, & Carter, 1974) and 1975 (Bada & Helfman, 1975), several skeletons from California were dated as being 40,000 to 50,000 years old, using a new technique called amino-acid racemization dating.

These early racemization dates were thought to provide important new evidence that people migrated into the Americas much earlier than the more generally accepted time of entry of 10,000 to 15,000 years ago. However, the early racemization dates were viewed with skepticism by some, who either consider the racemization dating technique itself to be of questionable validity or believed that the radiocarbon age of the skeleton used to "calibrate" the amino-acid racemization reaction (i.e., the Laguna skull) was unreliable.

For example, in 1971, ^{14}C dates were obtained on the Laguna (17,150+/-1470 ybp) and Los Angeles (>23,000 ybp) human fossils (Berger, Protsch, Reynolds, Rozaire, & Sackett, 1971). Using the Laguna fossil to calibrate aspartic acid racemization (AAR) dating of human bone, AAR ages were determined on several other human skeletons giving the following dates: Los Angeles Man dated as 26,000 ybp (Bada & Helfman, 1975); the Del Mar skeletons dated as 41,000-48,000 ybp (Bada & Helfman, 1975; Bada, Schroeder, & Carter, 1974); La Jolla Shores Man (W-2) dated as 44,000 ybp (Bada & Helfman, 1975); and the Sunnyvale fossil dated as 70,000 ybp (Bada & Helfman, 1975).

However, as it turned out, these early amino-acid racemization dates were inaccurate. Several of these human fossils were redated in the 1980s by a more accurate method of ^{14}C, which revised the ages from 20,000-70,000 ybp to within the Holocene epoch (<11,000 ybp). Similarly, radiocarbon dating by Taylor et al. (1983) yielded ages of 8,000-1,800 ybp on human fossils dated originally as 28,000-70,000 ybp. Furthermore, the advent of accelerator mass spectrometer (AMS) ^{14}C dating and its ability to date 1 mg of carbon enabled additional human fossils to be measured for ^{14}C: the Sunnyvale fossil's age changed from 70,000 to <5,000 ybp (Taylor, Payen, Gerow, Donahue, Zabel, Jull, & Damon, 1983), and that on Yuha from 23,600 to <4,000 ybp (Stafford et al., 1984). Five additional human skeletons previously assigned Pleistocene ages also subsequently changed to <8,470+/-140 ybp (Bada, Gillespie, Gowlett, & Hedges, 1984).

Furthermore, accelerator dating was used on the same specimens and all were dated younger than 6,500 years old. The oldest, one of the Scripps specimens, has been dated to 6,300 years. The Los Angeles skull dated to 3,560 years; Laguna Beach, the one that was originally used to calibrate the racemization curve, dated to

5,100 years. All of this redating has resulted in the fact that at the moment, there are no well-dated human bones from the Americas that are over 11,500 years old (Grayson, 1993). Though none of these crania turned out to be excessively old, this example demonstrates some of the problems with dating previously excavated crania. Today, however, it is possible to get highly accurate dates with minimal consumptive amounts (<1mg), though consumptive testing of any kind is highly opposed by most American Indians for spiritual, religious, and epistemological reasons. Furthermore, once a crania is dated, it still does not help in determining whether the skull is biologically affiliated with a particular American Indian tribe or not. Other forms of knowledge must be sought, which usually falls under craniometric statistical forms of knowledge, ignoring any other form of epistemologically based knowledge that American Indians may have concerning who the skeleton may be related to.

Because cranial morphological knowledge is consulted in questions of biological affiliation, it is important to further review this subject. A common approach to comparing skeletal material has been through the use of Mean Measures of Divergence (MMDs), which are based on 25 nonmetric cranial traits. This method yields patterns of affinity among these skeletons that are interpreted to reflect differences in timing and amount of gene flow between: 1) groups derived from a 10,000-8,000 ybp population stratum (usually named Paleoindians); and 2) those of a more recent time, usually dating to 4,500-2,000 ybp.

This statistical methodology has found that Aleuts, contrary to the prevailing view of their monophyletic origin with Eskimos, are both on a trait-by-trait basis as well as in multivariate comparisons intermediate between Athapaskans and Eskimos. This pattern suggests that Athapaskan ancestry involved mixture between "Paleoindians" and contemporary American Indian people, leading to the conclusion that Aleut, somewhat isolated in their archipelago, contain craniometric features linking them to Early Holocene populations. Likewise, historic tribes of the northern Plains and their Late Woodland ancestors appeared to also have traits associated with Early Holocene populations. This has led researchers to conclude that the MMD data indicate that Early Holocene populations were derived more directly from the "Arctic Mongoloid" stock that evolved in Northeast Asia during the Late Pleistocene (whose Asian descendants are thought to be represented by Chukchi and Siberian Eskimo peoples) than from the classic Mongoloid stock (represented by Japanese and Tungus peoples) (Ossenberg, 1994). Furthermore, there appears to be no break in continuity between the Early Holocene American Indians and contemporary Eskimo, Aluet, and Athapaskan speaking American Indians.

Ossenberg, who through previous studies indicates that MMDs yield valid taxonomical information, has conducted much of this work, demonstrating that population distance estimates significantly correlate with known historical relationships (Ossenberg, 1976), with rankings of Eskimo samples based on linguistic and geographic criteria (Ossenberg, 1977), with craniometric distance measures in East Asians (Ossenberg, 1986), and with genetic distances based on serological data in North Americans and Siberians (Szathmary & Ossenberg, 1978).

Furthermore, some of this MMD data is in agreement with the archaeological evidence arguing for an uninterrupted occupation of the Aleutian islands by Aleuts and only Aleuts, for at least four millennia (Dumond, 1984, 1987; McCartney, 1984). However, these data do not support Hrdlicka's theory of racial discontinuity whereby late prehistoric people with a brachycephalis cranium replaced an earlier long-headed population. However, dental trait frequencies in these skeletal samples show an east-west gradient, but no significant differences between prehistoric American Indians and contemporary Arctic crania, indicating population continuity in the Northwest Coast and Arctic culture regions (Ossenberg, 1994; Turner II, 1967).

Much of the craniometric data has also been used to support the idea that nonmetric cranial traits are not subject to environmental forces. For example, some have used the fact that the Tlingit and Haida data is similar to that of the Apache and Navajo, tribes that live in extremely different environmental areas to support this idea (Szathmary, 1979, 1984, 1985, 1994; Szathmary & Ossenberg, 1978). However, what is forgotten is that these tribes are all part of the same language family (Athapaskan), and that the Navajo and Apache only recently moved out of the Northwest Coast/Subarctic region and into the Southwest region (around 1000-500 ybp) (see Helm, 1981; Ortiz, 1983), thus, possibly not allowing enough time to have influenced nonmetric cranial traits.

Furthermore, as Szathmary (1979, pp. 24-27) concludes, it is not possible to objectively distinguish between craniometric similarity caused by admixture or by phylogeny. Likewise, it is not possible to distinguish between similarity produced either by common ancestry or by adaptive evolutionary convergence. This last point, the possibility of adaptive evolutionary convergence has recently been emphasized by several researchers who compared craniofacial data of New World and Old World samples finding that, "The first entrants to the Western Hemisphere of maybe 15,000 years ago gave rise to the continuing native inhabitants south of the U.S.-Canada border" (Brace et al., 2001, p. 10017), emphasizing that common ancestry seems to be the more accurate conclusion in this case.

As has been discussed, there are several opposing views and limitations in the present use of craniometric data. However, of particular importance to the question of biological affiliation, as well as the affiliation of Kennewick Man and Spirit Cave Mummy specifically, is the fact that comparing crania from a single (or even from a limited sample of 25) 8,000+ year old individual(s) with modern populations is inherently misleading.

> This is problematic, because a specimen that might date approximately 8,000 years older than its closest reference sample is not only separated by geographic distance but also by considerable temporal distance. We can translate this into very approximate generation times (e.g., 8,000 years/20) and quickly discover that we are talking about a "distance" of approximately 400 generations in which gene flow, drift, mutation, and natural selection have had an opportunity to operate between the specimen and its referents.

Add to this environmental plasticity and it is not at all surprising to us that some early Archaic American specimens might plot more closely to Asian, Eurasian, and even European samples. (Swedlund & Anderson, 2003, p. 163)

This point has been emphasized in the case of Gordon Creek Woman, an Early Holocene skeleton found in the Plateau, in which Owsley and Jantz disregarded the many problems raised with the measurement of Gordon Creek Woman, and statistically rejected her from any of the population samples used to infer biological affiliation between ancient populations and contemporary American Indian populations. Not only does it seem flawed to reject Gordon Creek Woman's cranial measurements from the Early Holocene population database, but as Swedlund and Anderson (2003) have noted, the sample selection and statistical interpretation of the results is also flawed, allowing the conclusions to go well beyond the restrictive limits of the method, not just in this individual case, but for similar comparisons as well. Likewise, the neglect of Gordon Creek Woman from the overall Early Holocene population sample will also skew the results when this "population" is statistically compared to single individuals such as the Kennewick Man and the Spirit Cave Mummy. Furthermore, as Hackenberger (2000) has noted, "All of these studies are severely limited by problems of sample sizes and are subject to qualification on the basis of assumptions about grouping of sub-samples by geographic and linguistic areas" (p. 13).

A further limitation in the present use of craniometric data can be seen in the usual conclusion that many Early Holocene crania do not fit into recent modern-day samples. Most of the studies discussed above use Howells' statistical methods developed in the 1970s. One of Howells' criteria for validating his samples is similarity by sex. However, these studies combine both male and female crania, which contradicts Howells' basic criteria and weakens the statistical power of any study. This can lead to faulty conclusions, such as that reached by Jantz and Owsley (2001), where they conclude that Wet Gravel Male fits well into as many as five American Indian samples (p. 151), whereas Wet Gravel Female's first five probabilities are completely out of the Western hemisphere altogether (p. 151). This conclusion would imply that Wet Gravel Male is an American Indian ancestor, whereas Wet Gravel Female is not, even though these two skeletons were recovered from the same site! If one goes back to the founders of Boas and Kroeber, it should be recognized that "race" (biological affinity), language, and culture are independent, and that American Indian "identity" in this context is primarily a cultural category, not a biological one (Swedlund & Anderson, 2003).

This basic misunderstanding of ancestry and a lack of awareness of many of these limitations can be seen in the Kennewick Man and Spirit Cave Mummy repatriation cases. For example, although the reports cited by the Department of Interior's original decision conclude that Early Holocene skeletons are more similar to those of the Polynesian and South Asian populations, some found that Early Holocene skeletons, "both male and female samples, did not differ significantly from the majority of the samples with which they were compared" (Steele & Powell, 1999, p. 110), while others found that their skulls "fall outside the range of any modern population represented by currently available samples" (Jantz & Owsley, 1997, p. 79). These two contradicting results demonstrate the divergent conclusions one can reach depending on how the data is interpreted and manipulated within statistical functions. Finally, as Hackenberger (2000, p. 4) notes concerning the Kennewick Man, "however, as of yet, no other comparisons with early Northwest specimens have been published with similar statistical techniques." Thus, it is really impossible to tell based on the available dataset and methodological techniques where the Kennewick Man's skeleton fits with both other Early Holocene skeletons or with present-day American Indians.

The situation in the Great Basin with the Spirit Cave Mummy is similar. For example, Barker, Ellis, and Damadio (2000) rely on the numerous craniometric studies that have been conducted in recent years to support their conclusion that the Spirit Cave remains are not culturally affiliated with the Fallon Paiute Tribe. Like the Kennewick Man studies, these studies examined Early Holocene skeletons and compared them to present-day American Indian populations, as well as other populations throughout the world. These studies conclude that no Early Holocene cranium is significantly similar to present-day American Indians and that they predominately "agree in being most similar to European, Native American, Polynesian, or East Asian populations" (Owsely & Jantz, 1999, p. 89). Likewise, Brace et al. (2001) concluded that Early Holocene craniofacial data showed ties to Ainu and Polynesian populations. However, as has been noted, these studies should only be considered preliminary since they are based on samples sizes ranging from 4 to 28 individuals, a population size lacking statistical power. Furthermore, "The skeletal remains recovered from archaeological sites are considered a limited representative sample of the actual population who might have lived in the area prehistorically" (Brooks & Brooks, 1990, p. 69), thus potentially skewing the dataset, which calculates means across the population. Similarly,

> The use of the craniometric data force an assumption of both "pure" and "stationary" biological lineages through time, and the data simply does not support that these hypothetical populations exist now or ever have existed at any time in any region. Craniometry cannot take into account individuals of mixed biological lineages. These individuals will always introduce variation into the measurements. (Goodman & Martin, 1999, p. 8)

Along with methodological limitations, relatively few studies have looked at the homogeneity of a Plateau or Great Basin population through time; instead most use individual cranial samples from disparate locations to create a "universal" Early Holocene population. However, in a relatively unique study using 250 human remains from Stillwater Marsh, western Nevada, it was concluded,

> Their similarity and comparability with other Great Basin skeletal remains, especially from the northern and central areas of Nevada, indicate that a relatively homogenous, robust people occupied this region of the Nevada Great Basin from perhaps 3,000 BP to the time of EuroAmerican contact, with no evidence of replacement by

other peoples or migration. (Brooks & Brooks, 1990, p. 71)

This continuity would link Middle Holocene peoples to the Numic speaking peoples, and overlaps the time of the hypothesized Numic expansion (see below), arguing for biological affiliation.

In an earlier analysis of Great Basin craniometric data, Brooks and Brooks (1977) analyzed data from three geographic areas in Nevada: Pyramid Lake, Humboldt Sink, and Lost City. These researchers found that,

> When the absolute and derived measurements or the morphological analyses on a continuum scale were evaluated, there were no marked differences between the three groups. On the contrary, when the whole crania for each of these groups were lined up together, there was a marked physical resemblance between the crania or each area that was not reflected in the anthropometric or morphological continuum data. (Brooks & Brooks, 1977, p. 176)

This would imply, that along with the limitations to using the current craniometric methods already mentioned, various resemblances do not show up in purely craniometric analyses, and that these methods may overly stress differences without noting similarities between populations.

Furthermore, it is important to understand how these methods can potentially bias results if there are differences in population substructure within regions, since increased variation among local populations could inflate regional diversity. For example, Relethford (2001) computed the mean diversity within local populations and found that sub-Saharan Africa has the highest levels of phenotypic variation, consistent with many genetic studies (see below). Polynesia and the Americas, however, both show high levels of regional diversity when regional aggregates are used, but the lowest mean local population diversity when compared to world populations. Regional estimates computing scores made using quantitative genetic methods show that both Polynesia and the Americas also have the highest levels of differentiation among local populations, which inflates regional diversity (Relethford, 2001). These results demonstrate that geographic sampling can affect results, as noted above, and suggest caution in making inferences regarding regional diversity when population substructure is ignored, such as has been discussed concerning the comparison of an Early Holocene "populations" and contemporary American Indian populations.

The Department of Interior took these limitations into account when they noted that "the analyses are not particularly robust," and that "Although the Kennewick remains do not have a close affinity to any modern group, metric data do suggest an association with the small number of early Holocene human remains" (Interior, 2000). Therefore, though the evidence is inconclusive as to Kennewick Man's morphological heritage, it is reasonable to conclude that Kennewick Man and the other similar Early Holocene human remains such as the Spirit Cave mummy, Gordon Creek woman, the Buhl skull, the Marmes burials, and others, as has been discussed, are of American Indian ancestry. "Based on our understanding of how biocultural processes work on a micro-evolutionary scale, we assume that all of the 9000-year-old individuals would not look like or be measurably similar to indigenous people during the last thousand years or so" (Goodman & Martin, 1999, p. 7). This understanding is further supported by the large volume of literature documenting the fact that as people shift to a sedentary, agriculturally based lifestyle, significant dental and cranial morphological changes occur (Larsen, 1997), and because these processes have taken place in the Americas, American Indian crania should reflect these changes.

It should be noted here that the original report on the Marmes burial by G. S. Krantz (1979) concluded that the skeletons from this site did not differ in any determinable way from modern American Indians. This assertion has never been questioned and the Marmes skeletons have not been used in any of the biological studies that claim Early Holocene populations are not related to modern American Indians. Similarly, as Chatters (2000) notes in his "official" report on the Kennewick Man skeleton, the Kennewick Man is comparable to other Early Holocene remains and that, "Ideally, if we are hoping to identify places and populations of post-diaspora origin, we should compare ancient people with their contemporaries and predecessors in various parts of the world, not with their successors" (p. 306), the latter of which is what the standard craniometric methods have done. As has been noted, the human skeleton is highly plastic, responding to environmental, nutritional, and cultural pressures, and therefore it is not surprising that craniometric data from Early Holocene populations is consistent within itself, but does not resemble any present world population. This last fact has even been noted by some of the social scientists that are currently conducting these types of analyses. "The heterogeneity among early American crania makes it inadvisable to pool them for purposes of morphometric analysis" (Jantz & Owsley, 2001, p. 291).

Finally, it is interesting to note a quote by the famed archaeologist Jesse D. Jennings (1978). He begins the discussion talking about how the earliest humans found in the Americas were long-headed people and goes through various American Indian origin theories of the time and then concludes,

> Lacking better data, it is therefore taken as a given that the founding New World population was, in fact, Asiatic Homo Sapiens of Caucasoid-Mongoloid mixture and that the American Indian evolved in the New World in response to a variety of environmental and evolutionary processes. (p. 18)

It is easy to understand, based on the paleoenviormental review discussed in chapter six, how the diverse and changing environments of the Late Pleistocene and Early Holocene could have played such a role in the change of cranial morphological features.

To summarize the craniometric evidence, it would appear that contemporary American Indians do not directly fit into any of the current Early Holocene "population" samples based on craniometric measurements. However, neither does any other modern population across the world. The reasons for this most likely reside in the various limitations discussed above with the statistical methods, as well as the fact that current craniometric studies do not take into account skeletal plasticity nor the effects of the radically changing paleoenvironment. However, despite these limitations, there is no evidence that a population arrived in the Americas at some point in the last 10,000 years and displaced the American Indians of the Plateau and Great Basin based on craniometric evidence. Furthermore, even if other peoples arrived in the Americas through a series of migrations as opposed to one migration, they would still be considered American Indian and biologically/physically affiliated to the present-day American Indian tribes. It would seem, therefore, that the most parsimonious conclusion to be drawn from the data is that American Indians have over the last 10,000 plus years evolved, both physically and culturally, to the diverse and varied environments that they inhabited in the Americas, and that Early Holocene skeletons are biologically affiliated with contemporary American Indian populations.

Genetic Evidence

Genetic studies within biological/physical anthropology are a relatively new line of inquiry, becoming established a little over 20 years ago (by genetic studies, it is meant those involving mtDNA or Y-chromosomes). This field promises to greatly facilitate the field of anthropology in numerous areas, including issues of biological affiliation. However, based on an extensive review of the published literature, it appears that there are still many limitations within the field, which will be discussed in some detail below. It is necessary to discuss these limitations in such detail because of the weight genetic studies are given by most anthropologists as well as by lay people, lawyers, and government officials. The reason for this weight is that genetic studies are seen to be highly objective, accurate, and "scientific" because they are based on DNA and are presumed to not be influenced by subjective researcher biases. However, as will be discussed in this section, this perceived strength is ill-founded, and genetic data should be approached with the same caution one approaches archaeological, linguistic, or other biological/physical data. Briefly, it can be summarized that most genetic studies done to date locate the ancestral population of American Indians somewhere in Northern Asia or Siberia and that they came to the Americas in either a single wave of migration (Altheide & Hammer, 1997; Ballinger et al., 1992; Bianchi et al., 1997; Bianchi et al., 1998; Bonatto & Salzano, 1997a; Easton, Merriwether, Crews, & Ferrell, 1996; Merriwether, Hell, Vahlne, & Ferrell, 1996; Merriwether, Rothhammer, & Ferrell, 1995) or several waves of migration (Brown et al., 1998; Cavalli-Sforza, Menozzi, & Piazza, 1994; Forster, Harding, Torroni, & Bandelt, 1996; Karafet et al., 2001; Karafet et al., 1997; Karafet et al., 1999; Santos et al., 1999; Schurr et al., 1990; Schurr & Wallace, 1999; Wallace & Torroni, 1992) 40,000 to 20,000 ybp. There is nothing contradictory about these general findings, for as has been noted with the dental and craniometric data, as well as will be discussed with the archaeological data, it is generally believed by anthropologists that this general conclusion is valid though perhaps a little older than originally thought. However, what is controversial and highly contested are how the genetic studies are used when discussing

American Indian demographic history, biological affiliation, and biological continuity.

These genetic studies rely either on mtDNA (mitochondrial deoxyribonucleic
acid) or Y-chromosome data that is primarily obtained through convenience sampling. Furthermore, majority of these studies have looked at the timing and possible Asian ancestral populations of these migrations (Jones, 2004b). Few, however,
have attempted to address possible prehistoric migrations within the Americas or
questions of biological affiliation. The few exceptions to this are the Kaestle and
Smith studies (Kaestle, 1995, 1997, 1998, 2000; Kaestle & Smith, 2001). These studies directly address the hypothesized Numic Expansion (discussed in chapter nine),
concluding that the ancient Stillwater Marsh "population" is more genetically related to Californian peoples than Great Basin peoples. There are several flaws apparent in the current methodological assumptions of genetic anthropological studies,
which I discuss below under the following subsections: the assumption of coalescent
times as times of origin; the current use of haplogroups to infer biological affiliation; limited sample sizes (i.e., population sizes) ranging between 25 and 40 individuals; the use of linguistic categories to construct quantifiable groups; and the use of
contemporary American Indian reservations as identifiable populations to infer prehistoric demographic history.

Coalescent Times as Times of Origin

One of the primary problems confounding the uses of mtDNA and Y-chromosomes to infer American Indian demographic histories, biological affiliation, and
biological continuity is in interpreting the coalescent times of genes as times of origin for specific populations. Although tracing the genealogy of mtDNA or Y-chromosomes theoretically can lead to a single common ancestor, this is not evidence
that the human population went through a period when only one breeding population was alive and reproducing. Tracing the coalescent times leads to one ancestor of a unilineally transmitted set of markers, but the descendents of the original
mtDNA or Y-chromosome population most likely will have had haplotype frequencies that differed among themselves, resulting in a biased sample of the total historic
population when using coalescent times. This is because working back in time does
not allow one to take into account the various branches of diversity that the historic
population had, but only the lineal history of the specific marker being coalesced.
Three primary *a priori* assumptions arising from the use of coalescent times
(Hoelzer, Wallman, & Melnick, 1998; Hudson, 1990; Templeton, 1993, 2002;
Wolpoff, 1999) that have been employed in understanding American Indian biological affiliation:

   • that gene coalescence is a regular process of mutation accumulation in a
   neutral system, and therefore can be timed like a regularly ticking clock
   with an acceptable range of error;
   • that American Indian populations were isolated from each other after
   they originated or migrated to the Americas; and
   • that the history of particular gene systems is the history of the specific

populations in which they are found.

Prior to the historic period, and especially before the formation of reservations beginning in the 1850s, many American Indian groups were highly mobile autonomous entities, covering large areas of land in a cyclical lifeway pattern. Similarly, many American Indians practiced a high degree of spousal exchange and intergroup marriage with other groups in order to solidify trade arrangements and political alliances. Some of these exchanges took place well over 500 miles from where the group has been historically recorded to inhabit. Examples of these trade centers are the large Native fisheries of the Northwest Coast such as The Dalles, Celilo Falls, and the Lillooet River Fishery (Hayden, 1992; Hayden & Schulting, 1997; Schuster, 1998; Stern, 1998) where groups from the Northwest Coast, Plateau, Northern Plains, and Great Basin culture regions gathered for short periods of time. Other examples can be found from the archaeological record that show similar large regional centers that may have acted as gathering and/or redistribution centers such as Chaco Canyon in the Southwest culture region (Lekson, 2000) and Monte Alban, San Jose Mogote, Tlapacoya, and Tlatilco in central Mexico (Flannery & Marcus, 1994). In fact, as Walker (1998) has noted for the Plateau peoples,

> It is clear that Plateau peoples were and remain highly inter-active maintaining extensive intergroup connections as well as extensive linkages with the Plains, Northwest Coast, and Great Basin groups. Connections with Subarctic groups are evident in the northern reaches of the Plateau of Canada. (pp. 5-6)

One important requirement in the coalescence theory is the use of random samples of genes from the population under study. However, most studies have not used random samples, but instead have used convenience samples obtained from diabetic, rheumatic, and AIDS studies, as well as other medical studies (Jones, 2002). As Donnelly and Tavare (1995) point out,

> In practice, genetic data are typically obtained from convenience samples rather than proper random samples. There is an obvious danger that such data may contain individuals who share relatively too much ancestry on the relevant timescales. The extent to which application of coalescent (or traditional) methods to such convenience samples may be misleading remains an open, and potentially serious, question. (p. 418)

Furthermore, most studies rely on the idea that American Indians came over in small groups (usually thought to have occurred as part of one to three migration waves; see Dillehay, 2000 to cite one recent work) across the Bering Land Bridge in prehistoric times. If this is the case, coalescence times will be shorter because smaller populations in the past are more likely to share ancestors (Donnelly & Tavare, 1995, p. 410), and thus lead to an accelerated time of origin for American Indians, not truthfully demonstrating the occupational time depth American Indians have in the Americas.

For example, the 121 base pair (bp) product from the intergenic spacer region located between the genes coding for lysyl tRNA and cytochrome oxidase II is a small region containing two interesting features: the first being a 9-bp repeat that is usually present in most human lineages but has been eliminated in a certain proportion of ethnic groups that originated from Asian ancestors (Horai & Matsunaga, 1986; Wrischnik et al., 1987); these groups include American Indians (Wallace & Torroni, 1992) and other groups (Demarchi, Panzetta-Dutari, Motran, Lopez de Basualdo, & Marcellino, 2001; Watkins et al., 1999; Yao, Watkins, & Zhang, 2000). Also in this sequence is an A-to-G transition that causes the elimination of one restriction site (Hae III) and the creation of another (Ave II). This change has been shown to occur in 3 out of 241 individuals representing diverse locations throughout the world (Cann, Stoneking, & Wilson, 1987). The transition occurs at base 8251 and the restriction site replacement occurs in 5 mtDNA variants comprising one clade in the phylogeny of the 62 total mitochondrial varieties of the Japanese people (Knight et al., 1996; Roy-Engel et al., 2001). Interestingly, an identical transition and restriction site change is evident in other populations, including American Indians. Another important diagnostic site (Hinc II) begins at nucleotide 13259, and this site is not present in 2 out of 5 American Indians and is missing in 1 of 55 Asians surveyed (Andrews, 1994). These nuances within a particular area of the genetic data can be misinterpreted when coalescence times based on convenience samples are solely relied upon.

Furthermore, departures from random mating due to inbreeding, assortative mating, or population stratification can lead to non-random association between genotypes and further complicate the interpretation of the data and coalescent times. One such example is the well-documented moiety and clan system among the Tlingit peoples of southern Alaska. Among the Tlingit, marriage was always with a member of one's opposite moiety, and preferably with a member of the father's clan and house (De Laguna, 1975). This means that the Tlingit as well as many other American Indian groups of the Northwest Coast and other regions practiced a highly selective, non-random form of mating that could influence the genetic data (for more examples, see the *Handbook of North American Indian* series published by the Smithsonian Institution). There is also a growing body of evidence suggesting that there could have been various forms of admixture between American Indians, Japanese, and Russians during the last 500 years (Boyd, 1999; Jones, 2002, 2003; Quimby, 1985; Van Stone, 1984), not to mention known examples of admixture during the historic period with trappers, fur traders, explorers, and other Europeans. Likewise, and more specifically, Karafet et al. (1997) concluded that because of the presence of the 1T haplotype (a Y-chromosome combination haplotype [see next section for a discussion of haplotypes]) in both Northeastern Siberia and the Americas, the possibility of historic and prehistoric back-migration is extremely likely. Similar studies have also noted the possibility of gene transfer or the "hitch-hiking theory" among American Indian and Asian populations (Bianchi, Bailliet, Bravi, Carnese, Rothhammer, Martinez-Marignac, & Pena, 1997; Bradman & Thomas, 1998; Hudson, 1990). Because population-coalescence times are frequently a result of the fusion of several of the ancient phylogenetic clusters and not the age of individual populations (Watson, Forster, Richards, & Bandelt, 1997), faulty results may be reported. It is evident that neither American Indians nor specific American

Indian groups were ever isolated populations and that the history of a contemporary group's genes are not a specific history of that American Indian population. Therefore, using gene coalescent times as possible times of origin for American Indian populations can lead to spurious conclusions, for there is no evidence that American Indians were ever: 1) part of a neutral system that can be timed like a regularly clicking clock, 2) were isolated from each other or from Asian populations, and 3) that the current gene systems found in a particular population fully represent the diversity and history of that population.

Current Uses of Haplogroups

The second major limitation I will discuss in genetic studies concerning biological affiliation is the current use of what are called haplogroups. Although it has been noted that limitations exist when studying only one gene (Chen et al., 2000; Karafet, Zegura, Vuturo-Brady, Posukh, Osipova, Wiebe, Romero, Long, Harihara, Jin, Dashnyam, Gerelsaikhan, Keiichi, & Hammer, 1997; Mountain & Cavalli-Sforza, 1997), most studies still rely on only one gene and its alleles because of the ease in identifying differences in a restricted location on that gene, especially in non-recombining genes such as mtDNA. The allele sequences that are studied are called haplotypes, which for American Indians presently fall into five recognized haplogroups (A, B, C, D, and X), and have been used in most studies concerning American Indian population genetics.

One of the current limitations with the uses of haplogroups for inferring American Indian biological affiliation is that there is the possibility of discovering new haplotypes as more tribes are studied and techniques develop (Easton, Merriwether, Crews, & Ferrell, 1996; Karafet, Zegura, Vuturo-Brady, Posukh, Osipova, Wiebe, Romero, Long, Harihara, Jin, Dashnyam, Gerelsaikhan, Keiichi, & Hammer, 1997; Schurr, Ballinger, Gan, Hodge, Weiss, & Wallace, 1990; Smith, Malhi, Eshleman, Lorenz, & Kaestle, 1999). By testing only for known haplogroup frequencies, it is likely that other haplotypes will go undetected, resulting in spurious conclusions from simplified haplogroup frequencies. Along with the possibility of new haplotypes being discovered, it is known that many prehistoric American Indian groups were not stationary and that the use of within-local-population frequencies for the genetic sequences may have been highly affected by each population's specific recent demographic history. Therefore, when relying on the use of haplogroups, scientists will probably underestimate the nucleotide diversity of American Indians as a whole (Bonatto & Salzano, 1997a). As a result, the differing analyses between CR (control region) sequences and RFLP (restriction fragment length polymorphism) data cannot be explained either by sample size or attributed to the different ways in which the haplotype frequencies were treated, but are more probably due to the different populations or regions of the mtDNA studied. Furthermore, it is well known that the only changes introduced in genes are point mutations, insertions, and deletions (with insertions and deletions being rare in comparison to point mutations). In fact, this is the means by which haplotypes are identified. This means, however, that each of the five possible founding lineage clusters (i.e., haplogroups) can be thought of as containing the founding lineage haplotype plus a collection of that lineage's descendants. However, as has been noted for the Y-chromosome, the original Y-chromosome can eventually die out, shifting time, haplotype frequency, or relationships (Bradman & Thomas, 1998), and can result in faulty inferences when comparing present American Indian tribal frequencies to those of ancient American Indian haplotype frequencies. As Bradman and Thomas (1998) pointed out using the insertion of the YAP (Y-chromosome alu polymorphism) indel (insert) on the Y-chromosome, descendents of individuals after only one generation may not carry the same Y-chromosome alleles. It is possible that a descendent of the individual who first acquired the YAP indel may lose that indel, yet still remain a biological descendent of that individual. This is also possible with mtDNA, where a father's son or daughter will not carry the genetic information of that person's father's mother. By only looking at specific alleles, the data concerning mutations, insertions, and deletions can be viewed as coming from discontinuous populations.

Likewise, "the combination of a decrease in the effective population size and genetic hitch-hiking may have been the cause producing a single variety of Y-chromosomes in the earliest ancestors of extant Amerindians," (Bianchi, Bailliet, Bravi, Carnese, Rothhammer, Martinez-Marignac, & Pena, 1997, p. 87), which would result in faulty results in determining affiliation between American Indian groups when cross comparing two non-synchronous populations. Similarly, because the mitochondrial genome undergoes no recombination, all 16,569 base pairs of the genome behave evolutionarily as a single locus. As MacEachern (2000) notes,

> In particular, it appears that there may be significant variability in selection mechanisms on the genome itself and in the mitochondria and in rates of phylogenetic versus intergenerational mtDNA mutation that are only now being appreciated (Gibbons 1998; Parsons, Muniec, and Sullivan 1997). (p. 358)

Therefore, inferences from any one such locus lack biological robustness (Pamilo & Nei, 1998). As noted above, because of the potential inaccuracy in using a constant molecular clock, estimates of mutation rates are going to be biologically imprecise (Donnelly & Tavare, 1995; Hoelzer, Wallman, & Melnick, 1998). Because of the high mobility of American Indian groups in the prehistoric, partically because of the radically changing environment (as discussed in chapter six), along with examples of intergroup marriage and non-random mating (as discussed in chapter seven), there is ample reason to believe that the genetic history of American Indians is much more complex then the current five haplogroups lead us to believe.

Sample Size

Many of the discrepancies and much of the unreliability of the data employed in American Indian genetic studies to date rests in the sample sizes of the populations used. Variations in biological population size are commonly attributed to bottlenecks and the so-called founder principle in which a population encounters a severe reduction in size or a few individuals colonize a new area. This new, founding biological population has a smaller, derivative selection of gene frequencies compared with the original population. However, an important complication that makes it impossible to determine biological census size of a prehistoric human group as a direct estimate of the effective population size is that human populations have overlapping generations. Rogers and Jorde (1995) have shown that the only method in which genetic sequence diversity (i.e., haplotypes) can be employed as a measure of the population age is as an estimation of the time during which a particular population has expanded after experiencing a severe bottleneck or founding. This is because we are dealing with alleles (haplotypes), and not with distinct populations that actually existed in history. In fact, the error variance increases with time and the earliest observations (the most recent chronologically) are the most precise. Computer simulations that suggest that the five major haplogroups found among American Indians underwent a bottleneck followed by a large population expansion may be questioned. These simulations are based primarily on the analysis of CR sequences from haplogroup A and do not take into account haplogroups B, C, D, and X (as well as the possibility of future haplogroups being defined). Similarly, although most studies on the problem of dating the original occupation of the Americas have used sequence diversity as a measure of age, few have investigated whether their samples met the very stringent assumptions required by this practice (Bonatto & Salzano, 1997a). Furthermore, Bonatto and Salzano (1997, p. 1417) have also noted that data using RFLPs indicates that haplogroup B has a much lower diversity than the other three (A, C, D), which will lead to inaccurate computer simulations if not taken into account.

Based on this, the current dates from mtDNA and Y-chromosome studies contending that American Indians arrived in the Americas around 35,000 years ago can be questioned (Bonatto & Salzano, 1997a; Brown, Hosseini, Torroni, Bandelt, Allen, Schurr, Scozzari, Cruciani, & Wallace, 1998). Instead, this number is actually the time during which American Indians theoretically experienced an expansion after a bottleneck. However, it is unknown if this bottleneck took place in Asia, the generally accepted origin of American Indians, or in the Americas after their arrival, nor is it known what effects subsequent migrations and bottlenecks from disease and other factors have on this time estimation. Therefore, the date of 35,000 years ago could be the time one group of American Indians entered the Americas or when a group experienced a bottleneck in Asia and subsequently entered the Americas, or any number of other possible scenarios.

Another problem with the current genetic sample sizes being used is in the actual numbers of individuals tested to infer the genetic makeup of the entire population (i.e., number of individuals used to infer genetic population of the entire biological population). Typically, sample sizes range between 4 and 30 individuals per tribal population; this is insufficient to detect little more than the most common haplotypes in each population. Although it is necessary to have genetic samples from 50 males or 50 females of an individual population to accurately infer genetic demographic history, no study has done this to date. The largest study to date on American Indians dealt with 2,198 males from 60 global populations, including 20 American Indian groups (Karafet et al., 1999; this study relied on large amounts of data gathered from previously published reports, and thus could not correct for those sample sizes). Within these 20 American Indian populations, however, only the Inuit Eskimo and Navajo samples were over the necessary 50 individuals, at 62 males and 56 males respectively. All others ranged from as high as 44 to as low as two individuals per tribal (population) group. It is unrealistic to assume that one can get an accurate picture of a tribe's genetic frequencies using only two males. In fact, Weiss (1994, p. 834) suggests that we may not be able to distinguish loss of lineages after one migration or from separate migrations from a common source population, thus further stressing the critical need for adequate biological population sample sizes. A clear example of the importance of sample size is seen in Easton et al.'s (1996) study and Torroni et al.'s (1993) study on the Yanomamo. In Easton et al.'s sample they detected both haplotypes X6 and X7, but in Torroni et al.'s sample from a neighboring village they did not detect any of these two haplotypes even though the samples were from the same biological population. As Ward et al. (1993) have noted, a sample size of 25 will detect around 63 percent of the lineages in a tribe with normal diversity. In tribes with extensive diversity a sample size of 25 individuals will only detect around 40 percent of the lineages and sample sizes of 70 or above are required to detect two-thirds of the lineages. The fact that the majority of studies lack the required sample sizes necessary to detect even 63 percent of the lineages in a normally diverse tribe brings into question many of the results of these studies, especially when it has been noted that most American Indian tribes are believed to have a high level of diversity (Ward, Alan Redd, Valencia, Frazier, & Paabo, 1993).

In the past, as now, geographic, socioeconomic, religious, ethnic, and other constraints largely dictate choice of mates. This has the effect of subdividing and stratifying the gene pool of a population in very complex ways, some of which were briefly mentioned in chapter seven. Likewise, migration is also difficult to reconstruct from mtDNA and Y-chromosomes. The most meaningful measure of migration from a genetic point of view is obtained by taking the individual biological generation as the time unit. Measuring the distribution between birthplaces of parent and offspring theoretically can yield a statistical measure of migration. However, this method works only for a continuous model in which the biological population size is constant, and is not entirely satisfactory when the population is highly clustered as is believed most prehistoric American Indian populations were (Cavalli-Sforza & Bodmer, 1971, p. 433). A similar limitation in using such data to infer migrations is that exchange between non-neighboring clusters is frequent enough among American Indians to violate the rules of the simplest stepping-stone models (Cavalli-Sforza & Bodmer, 1971, p. 433).

Another aspect of human DNA confounding many of the current uses of these data to reconstruct hypothetical populations and their demographic histories is that human mtDNA variation is high. This means that genetic variation within populations is much greater than between populations (Walpoff, 1999, p. 551), resulting in the fact that mtDNA evolution, and possibly the evolution of other genetic systems, is not the same as the evolution of particular populations. As Scozzari et al. (1999) have noted, groups or tribes thought to have descended from a common ancestor more than 10,000 years ago may have lost even their shared-by-descent portion of their gene pool and can no longer be thought of as biologically affiliated through genetic analyses. Furthermore, because genetic differentiation of human populations does not fit all of the assumptions of the evolutionary models (e.g., gene flow does occur between daughter populations), it is not possible to be certain that the branchings of a tree reflect the actual paths of evolution. Although there is disagreement among population geneticists on this issue (e.g., Cavalli-Sforza, Piazza, Menozzi, & Mountain, 1988), it is inappropriate to refer to dendrograms derived for human groups as phylogenetic trees (Szathmary, 1994).

Page and Charleston (1990) have identified a method for visualizing and quantifying the relationship between a pair of gene and species trees that constructs a third, reconciled tree. Reconciled trees use a more critically optimal method for mapping the combined history of genes and populations. However, even this more accurate method of depicting gene and population trees has limitations such as allele phylogenies and horizontal transfer, neither of which has been addressed in studies concerning American Indians. In fact, many of the polymorphisms observed for mtDNA probably predates population separations (Mountain & Cavalli-Sforza, 1997) and would not be useful in constructing genetic, population, or reconciled trees.

In order to estimate the significance of variation of gene frequencies between groups, it is necessary to estimate how large a genetic sample must be in order to be representative of the biological group. This can only be accomplished, however, if an accurate estimate of the real variation to be expected in the gene frequencies is possible. On a local level, roughly 10 percent of total genetic variation exists among major geographic regions, 5 percent exists among local populations within regions, and the remaining 85 percent exists within local populations (Barbujani, 1997). This is similar to values that have been found from craniometric analysis (Relethford, 2001), as discussed in the previous section. It is clear that by taking geographic regions as the unit of analysis we include a small but significant component of variation due to genetic differences among local populations, and regional diversity estimated by pooling individuals from different local groups could inflate regional genetic diversity. Furthermore, if there are differences in the level of variation among local populations from one region to the next, then comparison of regional genetic diversity can result in statistical biases.

This estimation is valid only for genes without dominance, in which case genes can be counted. However, if people in the sample from a given tribal village or town are closely related, a single source of variation may greatly inflate the estimate of genetic variance between biological populations (Cavalli-Sforza & Bodmer, 1971, p. 422). Multivariate analysis, or the use of more than one trait or gene, which is presently the strongest method of analysis, poses more difficult problems in that one must determine the maximum number of genes possible for each biological population in order to be accurate when cross-comparing populations. Unfortunately, many authors have tested only a small set of markers on one gene (univariate) for their studies (Cavalli-Sforza, Menozzi, & Piazza, 1994, p. 22), combining their data with those of others to result in several sets of markers to arrive at their multivariate analysis. Presently we don't have the necessary database size to accurately model the between population variations and biological affiliations.

Language

Although linguistic groupings of American Indians will be discussed in much greater detail in chapter ten, I will spend some time here discussing some of the limitations inherent in using language groups as the basis of biological populations. That is, most studies have relied on the use of controversial linguistic phyla in order to place their genetic data into objective, quantifiable biological groups. However, as several studies have pointed out, not only do the correspondences between languages and biological populations differ (Barbujani, 1997; Karafet, Zegura, Posukh, Osipova, Bergen, Long, Goldman, Klitz, Harihara, de Knijff, Wiebe, Griffiths, Templeton, & Hammer, 1999; Schurr, Sukernik, Starikovskaya, & Wallace, 1999; Scozzari, Cruciani, Santolamazza, Malaspina, Torroni, Sellitto, Arredi, Destro-Bisol, De Stefano, Rickards, Martinez-Labarga, Modiano, Biondi, Moral, Olckers, Wallace, & Novelletto, 1999), but there is no agreed upon set of linguistic phyla for American Indians of which to rely on for genetic studies (Bateman et al., 1990; Greenberg, 1987; Greenberg, Turner, & Zegura, 1986; O'Grady et al., 1989; Ruhlen, 1986, 1994). Most studies use several linguistic phyla that are subject to serious criticism, such as Altaic, Austric, Indo-Pacific, Amerind, and Na-Dene (e.g., Greenberg, 1987), which are in turn awarded equal status as more accepted phyla from other parts of the world such as Sino-Tibetan, Indo-European, and Dravidian (Bateman, Goddard, O'Grady, Funk, Mooi, Kress, & Cannell, 1990). Furthermore, it has been noted that "given 56% correspondence between linguistic phyla and population aggregates at the coarse level of resolution, 11% correspondence at the fine level, and the poor integrity of both superphyla, the parallelism between the genetic and linguistic entities does not strike us as especially 'remarkable'" (Bateman, Goddard, O'Grady, Funk, Mooi, Kress, & Cannell, 1990, p. 7). Likewise, the use of linguistic phyla and genetic populations suffer from a disjunct in chronological datasets. For example, "there is an important problem of time scales involved in this work, since at this point neither genetic nor linguistic research can lay claim to chronometric techniques comparable in precision to those used by archaeologists and historians" (Pluciennik, 1995, pp. 44-45). Languages do not change at specific rates and using contemporary linguistic phyla to extrapolate prehistoric population groups will result in low confidence rates. For example, in 1995 there were approximately 209 native North American languages still spoken, close to only half the estimated number that existed 500 years earlier (Goddard, 1996a). More specifically, of the Eastern Algonquian languages, only seven were spoken in 1970 out of a total of 20 from 200 years earlier (Goddard, 1978).

As a result, Scozzari et al. (1999) concluded that geography is a better method for identifying biological affiliation then linguistics. Likewise, Poloni et al. (1997) concluded that genetic data is more accurate and useful for distinguishing between linguistic phyla than between populations within the same language family. Finally, Schurr et al. (1999) noted that populations on the Kamchatka peninsula were genetically similar based on geography but quite divergent when compared to linguistically related groups. Therefore, the use of linguistic phyla may be useful when studying the differences between language phylas (e.g., between Na-Dene and Eskimo-Aluet), but not as useful when studying groups within the same language phyla (e.g., Yakama and Nez Perce). Furthermore, not taking into account the current discrepancies between American Indian language phylas can lead to several different conclusions depending on how the linguistic and genetic data are combined. For example, Karafet et al. (1997) found that Y-chromosome markers did not agree with the linguistic phyla proposed by Greenberg et al. (1986) for the peopling of the Americas. However, in a later study using different Y-chromosome markers Karafet et al. (1999) did agree with the linguistic phyla proposed by Greenberg et al. (1986). Other studies have arrived at similarly contradictory conclusions (see Schurr et al., 1999; Poloni et al., 1997). To use current American Indian languages as the basis for prehistoric American Indian genetic populations and thus biological affiliations seems presumptuous. Until linguistic specialists agree upon the classifications of American Indian languages, linguistic phyla should be used with caution and in conjunction with other types of data such as oral history, archaeology, and ethnology as a means of inferring and objectifying prehistoric biological population groups.

Contemporary American Indian Reservations and Demographic History

As previously discussed, the current sample sizes of most studies fall far short of a reasonable database size to be considered an accurate genetic dataset of the population. However, besides the limitations arising from the small sample sizes, as well as those discussed concerning the present use of linguistic phyla, there are even greater problems lying in what the studies consider populations. Presently, studies concerning American Indian biological affiliation test several individuals from a reservation and combine their allele frequencies with other individuals from the reservation to arrive at the haplotype makeup of that population. Therefore, the researchers are using contemporary American Indian reservation demographics to arrive at a population that they then infer back into prehistory. However, one of the primary problems with this method is that most contemporary American Indian reservations are not made up of a single group, but consist of several different groups of American Indians that prior to being forced onto reservations were autonomous groups (see also chapter seven). For example, Merriwether et al. (1995) used samples from Haida, Dogrib, and other contemporary American Indian reservation groups which they considered as individual biological populations. However, the Dogrib as a whole tribe were prehistorically made up of several different bands that occupied a large area in the Northwest Territories, Canada, between the Great Slave Lake in the south to the Great Bear Lake in the north and from the lowlands on the east side of the Mackenzie River to Contwoyto, Aylmer, and Artillery Lakes (Helm, 1981). The Dogrib are known to have had regular contact with the Bearlake Indians, the Slaveys, Chipewyans, and occasionally Eskimos (Helm, Rogers, & Smith, 1981, p. 291). Similarly, the Haida, along with other Northwest Coast tribes were known to have traded slaves up and down the coast (Blackman, 1990).

Other such examples can be found in the studies by Smith et al. (1999), Karafet et al. (1999), Lorenz et al. (1996), and Brown et al. (1998) that use contemporary reservation populations as prehistoric biological populations. Such contemporary groups as the Yakama and Apache are good examples to further illustrate this point. The present Yakama reservation in Washington is made up of at least five different

TRIBAL AFFILIATION BASED ON BLOOD SAMPLES	GEOGRAPHIC PROXIMITY	GEOGRAPHIC LOCATION
Alaskan	Distant	Arctic
Arikara	Distant	Plains
Assiniboin	Distant	Plains
Bannock	Distant	Great Basin
Blackfoot	Distant	Plains
Canadian	Distant	Subarctic
Cascade	Neighboring	Plateau
Cayuse	Official Blood Line	Plateau
Cherokee	Distant	Plains
Cheyenne	Distant	Plains
Chippewa	Distant	Plains/Subarctic
Chocktaw	Distant	Southeast
Cochiti	Distant	Southwest
Coeur d'Alene	Neighboring	Plateau
Colville	Neighboring	Plateau
Cowichen	Distant	Coast
Cowlitz	Neighboring	Plateau
Cree	Distant	Plains/Subarctic
Crow	Distant	Plains
Flathead	Neighboring	Plateau
Grande Ronde	Distant	Coast
Hopi	Distant	Southwest
Klamath	Neighboring	Plateau
Klickitat	Neighboring	Plateau
Kootenai	Neighboring	Plateau
Laguna	Distant	Southwest
Lummi	Distant	Coast
Makah	Distant	Coast
Modoc	Distant	Coast
Muckleshoot	Distant	Coast
Navajo	Distant	Southwest
Nez Perce	Neighboring	Plateau
Ottawa	Distant	Northeast

groups that were prehistorically independent bands (Schuster, 1998). Similarly, there is still much disagreement among American Indian specialists as to how many different Apache groups there were prior to the arrival of Euroamericans. Currently there are seven recognized Southern Apachean speaking groups: Chiricahua, Jicarilla, Kiowa-Apache, Lipan, Mescalero, Navajo, and Western Apache. However, depending on "how much more extensive their territories are conceived to have been in the past depends upon one's view of claims that the Querechos, Vaqueros, Teyas, Janos, Jocomes, Mansos, Sumas, Cholomes, Jumanos, Cibolos, Pelones, Padoucas, and various other groups named in early Spanish and French records were Apacheans" (Opler, 1983, p. 368). Finally, over the last hundred years

Paiute	Distant	Great Basin
Palus	Neighboring	Plateau
Pawnee	Distant	Plains
Puyallup	Distant	Coast
Quinault	Distant	Coast
Sac and Fox	Distant	Plains
Seminole	Distant	Southeast
Shoshone	Distant	Great Basin
Siletz	Distant	Coast
Sioux	Distant	Plains
Snohomish	Distant	Coast
Spokane	Neighboring	Plateau
Tulalip	Distant	Coast
Walla Walla	Official Blood Line	Plateau
Warm Springs	Neighboring	Plateau
Wasco	Neighboring	Plateau
White Mountain Apache	Distant	Southwest
Winnebago	Distant	Plains
Wishram	Neighboring	Plateau
Yakama	Neighboring	Plateau

Table 4. Tribal affiliation blood samples found in members of the Confederated Tribes of the Umatilla Indian Reservation.

it should be pointed out that reservation populations have been greatly affected by outmarriage with other tribal groups and marriage with non-Indians. An example

of this change can be seen in a study done by Walker (1990; see also Walker, 1972) for the Confederated Tribes of the Umatilla Indian Reservation (CTUIR). This study showed that in 1990 54 different tribes were represented in the blood of CTUIR individuals (see Table 4). Furthermore, one CTUIR individual had various amounts of Cayuse, Walla Walla, Umatilla, Nez Perce, Snohomis, and non-Indian blood, while another individual had Umatilla, Cayuse, Walla Walla, Yakama, Nez Perce, Quinault, Snoqualmie, Cascade, and non-Indian blood. It is evident that the tribal populations current studies are using to infer American Indian biological affiliation are not acceptable. One cannot use contemporary allele frequencies from a few individuals of a contemporary American Indian reservation to arrive at an unequivocal haplogroup for that population, either presently or prehistorically.

A further problem in the use of contemporary American Indian reservation based populations can be found in the use of ancient DNA (aDNA). Several reports have used aDNA to construct ancient populations that are then compared to present American Indian reservation populations. For example, Kaestle (1997) attempted to compare an ancient population from western Nevada to those of contemporary reservation populations in the region through haplotype frequencies. However, Kaestle's ancient "population" spanned 5000 years in time. A genetic sample dating to 5,905+/-125 ybp cannot be considered part of the same biological population as a genetic sample dating to 860+/-75 ybp without also automatically designating contemporary American Indians as part of that population. Furthermore, ancient DNA samples are not populations in the traditional sense of the term. The individual specimens that constitute aDNA samples may span several centuries and even geographic space, and are the equivalent of sampling an individual every few generations to characterize a continuous biological population (O'Rourke, Hayes, & Carlyle, 2000). A similar methodological limitation was also noted when discussing craniometric comparisons of Early Holocene "populations" and contemporary American Indian populations.

Likewise, the use of aDNA models to reconstruct a biological population assume (or cannot accurately model) that these ancient populations were somewhat isolated (both spatially and geographically), and that these populations did not practice forms of intergroup, outgroup, or non-random marriage. However, as previously noted in chapter seven, highly complex forms of intergroup, outgroup, and non-random marriage have been practiced for centuries (see also D'Azevedo, 1986; Suttles, 1990; Walker, 1998).

Genetics and American Indian Biological Affiliation

The fact that most studies have not addressed the above concerns is only part of the present problem with applying genetic anthropological data to American Indian biological affiliation. In fact, no studies concerning American Indians have seriously taken into account the demographic history of the last 500 years when Euroamericans arrived in the "New World." Almost every contemporary American Indian tribe or group in the Americas has experienced severe epidemic diseases, depopulation, acculturation, and displacement from their native lands. These factors have caused some tribes to disappear, others have experienced population fluctuations greater than 80 percent, and some have been displaced from their homeland by hundreds of miles (Boyd, 1990, 1999; Dobyns, 1983, 1992; Ehle, 1988; Jones, 2002, 2003). For example, the American Indians of California numbered upwards of 310,000 during the 18th century, but by the turn of the 20th century the native population had dropped to 20,000 (Cook, 1978). Similar population declines are known for the Plateau with a loss of approximately 20,000 American Indians between 1805 and 1860 (Boyd, 1990), the Northwest with a population decline from approximately 200,000 American Indians in 1774 to 40,000 in 1874 (Boyd, 1990, 1999), as well as other regions. Furthermore, admixture with historic Europeans and Euroamericans such as fur trappers, explorers, African Americans, and earlier settlers must be accounted for; it is well known, though not well documented, that many of these non-indigenous peoples married or mixed with American Indians. These recent demographic facts and large population declines most likely greatly reduced the number and frequency of haplotypes in the Americas, and bring into question any present conclusion about biological affiliation between contemporary American Indian tribes and skeletal remains of individuals from the ancient past, such as the Kennewick Man or Spirit Cave Mummy.

These limitations, however, do not mean that all of the data from genetic anthropological studies is spurious. On the contrary, mtDNA and Y-chromosome studies can provide great insights into American Indian origins and prehistoric relation-ships, although caution should be used when drawing conclusions of biological affil-iation. Mitochondrial DNA and Y-chromosome studies are in their infancy. Because of the various limitations listed above, as well as a lack of correlation between genet-ic anthropological data, archaeological data, ethnographic data, and oral tradition data, these studies should be viewed as inchoate and requiring further investigation and support from the other fields of anthropology.

To summarize, the mtDNA and Y-chromosome data indicate that the ancestors of present-day American Indians arrived in the Americas between 35,000-25,000 years ago. Furthermore, there appears to be no evidence of admixture between American Indians and Europeans or other ethnic groups within the last 20,000 years, except for the instances that can be traced within the historical record, i.e., between early European and Euroamericans and various American Indian groups. Furthermore, the genetic data indicate, though inconclusively, continuous biologi-cal affiliation between Early Holocene individuals such as the Kennewick Man and Spirit Cave Mummy and present-day American Indians.

Trichological Analysis

The final line of data that falls into this chapter is that of trichological data, or the study and comparison of hair. Trichological analysis is a relatively small field within biological/physical anthropological studies concerning American Indians. The pri-mary reason for this is that hair, like skin, has a poor preservation ratio when com-pared to bones, and thus very limited hair samples have been recovered from pre-historic skeletons of any time depth. Furthermore, hair analyses are relatively imprecise, only allowing the researcher to place the samples within broad categories of ethnic relations, and not within more specific categories of American Indian bio-logical affiliation on a tribal or group level (Hicks, 1977). For the purposes of this book and the question of biological affiliation in the Plateau and Great Basin, tri-chological data provides little information. No hair has been recovered or analyzed from any known skeletons within the Plateau area, and only one analysis has been conducted within the Great Basin of which the author is aware.

Hair was recovered with the Spirit Cave Mummy and analyzed. It was concluded that the hair was similar in color, structure, and grain size to other prehistoric American Indian populations as well as contemporary American Indian populations (Goodman & Martin, 1999; Lahren, 1997), though it was noted by the original recovering archaeologist that the hair color changed upon exposure to light and air (Wheeler & Wheeler, 1969). The hair analysis also concluded that the hair was dif-ferent than present-day Caucasian hair (Goodman & Martin, 1999).

To summarize, therefore, trichological data are currently of very limited value in attempting to answer questions of biological affiliation. Hair has only rarely been recovered from sites in the Plateau and Great Basin, and the evidence indicates that presently the hair recovered from these areas is different than contemporary Caucasian hair and is similar to contemporary American Indian hair. Thus, the trichological data indicate, though with no real evidentiary weight, that American Indians have been in residence in the Plateau and Great Basin since the Early Holocene.

Summary of Biological Evidence

As I have discussed at some length in this chapter, the current biological anthropological data indicates that the origins of Early Holocene peoples are attributed to one of three geographic locations in Asia. Dental characteristics show that Early Holocene peoples arose in Northern Asia sometime around 20,000 years ago (Turner II, 1967, 1985, 1989, 1994). Craniometric analyses tend to indicate that Early Holocene populations are most similar to Polynesian and South Asian populations morphologically, although some Early Holocene skulls either reside on the extreme end of the present-day American Indian range or are not similar to any modern world population (Jantz & Owsley, 1997, 1998, 2001; Owsley, 1992, 1996; Owsley & Jantz, 1999, 2001; Powell & Rose, 1999; Powell & Neves, 1999; Steele & Powell, 1992, 1994, 1999). Finally, genetic studies presently conclude that the ancestors of modern American Indians were from Northern Asia or Siberia (Alves-Silva et al., 2000; Bonatto & Salzano, 1997a; Brown, Hosseini, Torroni, Bandelt, Allen, Schurr, Scozzari, Cruciani, & Wallace, 1998; Easton, Merriwether, Crews, & Ferrell, 1996; Forster, Harding, Torroni, & Bandelt, 1996; Karafet, Zegura, Vuturo-Brady, Posukh, Osipova, Wiebe, Romero, Long, Harihara, Jin, Dashnyam, Gerelsaikhan, Keiichi, & Hammer, 1997; Karafet, Zegura, Posukh, Osipova, Bergen, Long, Goldman, Klitz, Harihara, de Knijff, Wiebe, Griffiths, Templeton, & Hammer, 1999; Lorenz & Smith, 1996; Merriwether, Hell, Vahlne, & Ferrell, 1996; Merriwether, Rothhammer, & Ferrell, 1995; Merriwether et al., 1997; O'Rourke, Hayes, & Carlyle, 2000; Schurr & Wallace, 1999; Smith et al., 2000; Smith, Malhi, Eshleman, Lorenz, & Kaestle, 1999; Torroni, Schurr, Cabell, Brown, Neel, Larson, Smith, Vullo, & Wallace, 1993; Torroni et al., 1992). Thus, the current biological database indicates that Early Holocene peoples, and therefore the ancestors (or possibly relatives) of Kennewick Man and the Spirit Cave Mummy, as well as present-day American Indians, arose in Asia between 35,000-20,000 years ago. Furthermore, these people eventually made their way to the Americas either in one migration (which could have consisted of many groups) or through a series of migrations (also potentially consisting of numerous groups). There is little evidence, however, within this dataset demonstrating how these Early Holocene peoples arrived and populated the Americas beyond the basic assumption that they came across the Bering land bridge either through the "ice-free corridor" or by the Northwest Coast route. Most importantly concerning the topic of this book, there is no convincing evidence that would support the idea that Kennewick Man, the Spirit Cave Mummy, and other Late Pleistocene to Early Holocene remains found in the Americas are not biologically affiliated to contemporary American Indians. In fact, the "preponderance of the evidence" would seem to support the long held idea that Early Holocene peoples are the direct ancestors of present-day American Indians. This last aspect was also noted by Goodman and Martin (1999),

We conclude that there is no support for the position that Spirit

Cave Mummy is not culturally connected to contemporary Native Americans based on biology. Furthermore, similarities in hair color and tooth form are highly suggestive of biological continuities and cultural affiliation with contemporary Native Americans (p., 35).

Likewise, this is the same conclusion that Dixon (1999), Dillehay (2000), and others have have arrived at, as well as some of the original thinkers in the field (see Bryan, 1986; Cressman, 1977). What the biological dataset does not tell us is tribal cultural affiliation (i.e., ethnic affiliation); instead, the biological data evidences biological affiliation. Furthermore, as is well known, culture is not solely transmitted through biological mechanisms, indicating that although Early Holocene peoples such as Kennewick Man and Spirit Cave Mummy may be biologically affiliated with present-day American Indians, it is still unclear whether they are culturally affiliated on a tribal/group level. Finally, the biological dataset is also silent on the question of biological affiliation within and between contemporary American Indian groups and the peoples of the Early Holocene. Currently, based on the available data, it is impossible to accurately conclude which group or tribe Early Holocene skeletons are most biologically affiliated with. In order to answer this, and the more complex question of cultural affiliation, the biological data must be correlated with the archaeological, linguistic, ethnographic, and oral tradition evidence, which is the focus of the next three chapters.

CHAPTER 9
ARCHAEOLOGICAL EVIDENCE

As I have discussed in the last two chapters dealing with ethnographic and biological data, the question of cultural affiliation between today's American Indian tribes and the people of the Late Pleistocene and Early Holocene is still quite murky and ill formed. The ethnographic evidence indicates that the contemporary American Indian tries of the Plateau and Great Basin have resided in their homelands for at least the last several hundred years. The biological data, on the other hand, indicate that the people from the Late Pleistocene and Early Holocene are American Indian, but it is silent as to which contemporary tribe these peoples are most closely affiliated with. In this chapter, most of this opaqueness is cleared away as I spend some time discussing the archaeological evidence. As should be obvious, the archaeological data deals with cultural affiliation, and not solely biological affiliation, as was the case in the previous chapter. However, like the biological database there are also numerous limitations and "gaps" within the archaeological database, despite the fact that the archaeological database is more extensive and better known. Furthermore, these "gaps" in the database reflect a lack of knowledge on the archaeologist's part, and not necessarily evidence of displacement or migration.

To better contextualize why there are numerous "gaps" in the archaeological record, a brief overview of the archaeological fieldwork process conducted in the Plateau and Great Basin regions is helpful. Though some archaeological investigations were done prior to the 1950s, much of the archaeological research in the Plateau and Great Basin did not begin until after World War II.

While fieldwork on the Plateau began well before World War II, its real impetus was post-war dam construction, and the resulting River Basin Surveys of the 1950s. The great majority of projects since the 1950s have been related to dams and reservoirs. Within the last 25 years work has expanded out of the canyons and river bottoms. Virtually all of this work is also CRM [Cultural Resource Management] related in the form of Forest Service projects, pipeline projects, etc. An impressive body of evidence has built up, but it has significant limitations. Excavations in the canyons, for example, focus on pithouse sites, and on the house pits themselves. We have, therefore, far more information about the contents of the structures than we do for exterior activity areas. (Ames, 2000, p. 2)

Likewise, in the Plateau over 1000 miles of river bottomland were submerged under the numerous reservoirs created on the Columbia River and its tributaries. This land, as was discussed in chapter seven, was the primary location of most American Indian settlements. Thus, it is not surprising that the archaeological database has so many "gaps" for the Late Pleistocene and Early Holocene, since most sites that people during this time period would have utilized and left evidence for archaeologists to discover are now under water. A very similar historical process is also seen in the Great Basin, with a fair amount of archaeological work (again predominantly CRM) having taken place after World War II in the areas of greatest development, namely along the eastern Wasatch Range in Utah and areas around Las Vegas and Reno/Tahoe in Nevada. Other work has been conducted sporadically throughout the Great Basin and Plateau in the form of BLM archaeological surveys and selective cave deposit excavations. However, because of the rapid assessment nature of CRM work, we have extensive archaeological surveys with little depth in data and analysis resulting in the various "gaps" found in the record. Furthermore, many smaller, less structurally based sites such as lithic scatters, pit houses, and temporary campsites that we would expect to find associated with Early and Middle Holocene time periods are not usually recorded or excavated by CRM work.

A similar reason that many "gaps" appear in the archaeological database is that the primary models utilized by Great Basin, and to a lesser extent Plateau, archaeologists are based on Plains-correlated evidence.

> A primary reason for reluctance to consider certain dated evidence is that [Great] Basin archaeologists, working before many radiocarbon dates were locally available, had extrapolated a model from the better-dated projectile point sequence of the Great Plains and applied it to the Great Basin. (Bryan & Tuohy, 1999, p. 250)

This extrapolation of sequences has led many Great Basin and Plateau archaeologists to attempt to relate Great Basin and Plateau sequences and subsistence economies to those of the Plains sequence. This is highly problematic, primarily because the Plains sequence has a clearer "Paleoindian" period of subsistence economy based somewhat on big game hunting, which has never been shown to be true for the Great Basin or Plateau (Aikens, 1978, 1982; Ames, 2000; Bryan & Tuohy, 1999; Cressman, 1977; D'Azevedo, 1986; Elston, 1986; Grayson, 1993; Jennings,

1978; Tuohy & Dansie, 1997; Walker, 1998). Likewise, the Plateau and Great Basin areas had extensively different flora and fauna during Late Pleistocene to historic times as noted in chapter six, such as the famous salmon runs of the Columbia River system, large herds of antelope, extensive rabbit populations, large camas fields, and more recently (i.e., after about 5,000 ybp) extensive Pint Nut groves that allowed American Indians through time to maintain a very different subsistence economy than that of the Plains, which was more focused on large game such as the buffalo, elk, and deer.

A clear example of how these "gaps" are present in the archaeological database, and how the nature of most CRM studies results in less than desirable knowledge of particular areas, can be illustrated in the recent findings from the Carson Sink of western Nevada. The archaeological record from the Carson Sink area underwent a dramatic transformation resulting from extensive flooding of the basin during the period between 1982-1984. Subsiding floodwaters exposed numerous pithouse features, burials, and dense artifact scatters and provided, at least for some researchers, compelling evidence for intensive and residential use of the marsh for multiple seasons, if not during the entire year (Raven & Elston, 1988, 1991; Raymond & Parks, 1990). The Carson Sink area, prior to this recent flooding, had been the site of numerous archaeological surveys over the years, but it was not until the flooding occurred that hundreds of new sites that had previously been overlooked were discovered.

Despite a relative lack of thorough, in-depth, scientific excavations in the Plateau and Great Basin, regional archaeologists have been able to establish an agreed upon cultural chronology that is relatively consistent within specific micro-regions, and to some extent, the larger marco-region. However, this has been complicated by the use of specific sequences on a micro-regional basis that can be very confusing and sometimes contradictory to the larger macro-regional sequence. In this chapter I review the archaeological data for each macro-region (i.e., the Plateau and Great Basin). First, however, I briefly review the Late Pleistocene data that has been found in Northeast Asia, as well as the Late Pleistocene and Early Holocene subsistence lifeways hypothesized to have existed in the Plateau and Great Basin. As noted above, one of the primary reasons for the numerous "gaps" within the archaeological record is the lack of knowledge for each area, specifically knowledge that comes from a more diachronic, macro-regional perspective. Thus, by covering both what the archaeological record demonstrates for Northeast Asia (the theoretical point of departure for the ancestors of American Indians), and for early subsistence lifeways within the Plateau and Great Basin, one is better able to understand cultural developmental factors that have taken place within the Plateau and Great Basin. Subsequently, after this review, the two most recent and prominent macro-regional sequences for the Plateau and Great Basin, respectively, will be covered. Finally, an overall synthesized sequence will be discussed for the regions as a whole based on the archaeological database. As discussed in chapter three NAGPRA mandates that the "preponderance of the evidence" must either favor or not favor cultural affiliation, therefore it is necessary to take such a broad, and comprehensive view of the archaeological data to properly answer and understand whether cultural affiliation can be demonstrated.

Northeast Asia

In this section I briefly review the northeast Asian paleolithic record to provide a contextual background for the next section, which discusses the Late Pleistocene and Early Holocene data and the controversial issue of a "megafauna killoff." In short recent excavation data shows a long series of paleolithic materials dated from about 200,000 to 10,000 years ago for northeast Asia (Akazawa, 1999), and that most of the northeast Asian area had some inhabitants throughout the this time span, including the Japanese archipelago by the Middle Pleistocene (Akazawa, 1999; Goebel & Slobodin, 1999; Goebel, Waters, & Dikova, 2003; Grosswald, 1999; Hoffecker, Powers, & Goebel, 1993; Kuzmin & Tankersley, 1996; Shields & Jones, 1998).

Furthermore, the data indicates that humans penetrated into far northern Siberia above latitude 60⁰ N during the Pleistocene. During this time, as discussed in chapter six occupation would have been easier during times when woodland was more widespread, than later, during glacial conditions, when woodland was more restricted (Martin, 1982). However, continuous occupation would have been possible throughout the Pleistocene in various regions. Under these circumstances, people appear to have developed a specialized subsistence system, heavily dependent upon megafauna such as *Mammuthus spp.* and equipped with distinctive tool kits dominated by microblade assemblages. The extremely cold climatic conditions that occurred during the last glacial maximum around 20,000 to 18,000 years ago seem to have forced certain groups to migrate south to China, the Korean Peninsula, and the Japanese archipelago, and northeast into Alaska, though it is unlikely that the region was completely depopulated during this time (Akazawa, 1999; Pitulko, Nikolsky, Girya, Basilyan, Tumskoy, Koulakov, Astakhov, Pavlova, & Anisimov, 2004).

The archaeological data for this time period has been called the Asian Initial Upper Paleolithic (45,000-30,000 ybp) tradition and can briefly be characterized by the elaboration of blade technologies showing both Middle and Upper Paleolithic characteristics. The best-known of the northeast Asian Initial Upper Paleolithic sites, Kara Bom, in the Altai region of southern Siberia, has been dated as early as 43,000 years ago (Brantingham, Krivoshapkin, Jinzeng, & Tserendagva, 2001).

These archaeological assemblages, however, do not conform to western Eurasian typological expectations of the Initial Upper Paleolithic, nor do they directly conform to the first lithic assemblages found in the Americas. The high frequencies of side scrapers and notched-denticulate tools are more consistent with Middle Paleolithic typological definitions, though end scrapers and burins are present but in relatively low frequencies. Such typological distinctions – including those emphasizing the presence or absence of lithic "types" such as Emireh points – may at best have regional chrono-stratigraphic relevance, and they probably have little to do with the behavioral and evolutionary processes underlying the origin and elaboration of the Initial Upper Paleolithic. In fact, the only substantive difference between the Middle and the Initial Upper Paleolithic in northeast Asia is a shift in emphasis toward the production and use of lithic blades. Current archaeological evidence suggests that Initial Upper Paleolithic industries first appeared in southern Siberia around 43,000 years ago, in the Mongolian Gobi (Tsagaan Agui and Chikhen Agui, respectively) between 33,000 and 27,000 years ago, and in northwestern China at Shuidonggou by 25,000 years ago. Taken together, it appears that the expansion of the Initial Upper Paleolithic was gradual, lasting more than 10,000 years (Brantingham, Krivoshapkin, Jinzeng, & Tserendagva, 2001).

Thus, the primary technological features of the northeast Asian Initial Upper Paleolithic include: 1) expanded patterns of raw-material exploitation and transport, 2) emphasis on blade production from Levallois-like prepared cores, 3) high frequencies of retouched blades, 4) occasional classic and elongate Levallois points, and 5) Middle Paleolithic retouched tool types, especially side scrapers, notches, and denticulates (Brantingham, Krivoshapkin, Jinzeng, & Tserendagva, 2001; Goebel, Waters, & Dikova, 2003; Pitulko, Nikolsky, Girya, Basilyan, Tumskoy, Koulakov, Astakhov, Pavlova, & Anisimov, 2004). The people who created and used the Initial Upper Paleolithic assemblages most likely are the same people who inhabited Beringia shortly after this time period, and possibly migrated into the Americas.

Currently in western Beringia there are 35 archaeological occupations that are considered to date to the Late Pleistocene or Early Holocene (the end of the Initial Upper Paleolithic). Only 15 of these, however, have been chronometrically dated to before 7,000 ybp, while the rest are dated solely on typological or stratigraphic grounds. Of the radiocarbon-dated occupations, three are assigned to the Late Pleistocene (>10,000 ybp) and 12 to the Early Holocene (9000-7000 ybp). The majority of these sites are located in the upper Kolyma basin in southwestern Beringia and in the Chukotka Peninsula opposite Alaska, two areas that appear to have not been covered by glacial ice during the Late Pleistocene.

The earliest evidence for humans in western Beringia dates to about 14,000 ybp, as documented by the blade-and-biface assemblage (Layer VII) at the stratified Ushki-I site, located in central Kamchatka (Goebel & Slobodin, 1999). Similar assemblages have been identified at Berelekh, an Upper Paleolithic campsite in the lower Indigirka Basin radiocarbon dated to about 12,200 ybp, and El'gakhchan, a site that occurs in a stratified context but has not yet been dated. The Uptar-I site also contains a bifacial industry that may date to Late Pleistocene times, but this site has only an upper-limiting date of 8,260 ybp. Together these sites suggest the presence in western Beringia of a pre-11,000 ybp lithic complex characterized by blade and biface technologies, which may be related to similar industries found in the Americas (e.g., the Nenana complex of central Alaska), though this correlation is tenuous (Goebel & Slobodin, 1999; Hamilton & Goebel, 1999).

The Early Holocene of western Beringia has a probable age of 9,000-7,000 ybp. During this interval, conical core and blade/microblade industries lacking ceramics and polished stone tools dominate the archaeological record. Most of the known Early Holocene sites occur in the upper Kolyma region, but they also have been identified on Zhokhov Island, located far to the north in the East Siberian Sea, and possibly at Lake Tytyl' (interior Chukotka) and Puturak Pass (Chukotka Peninsula). These industries may be tied to the Sumnagin Early Holocene complex of the Lena River basin west of Beringia (Goebel & Slobodin, 1999).

The data indicates, therefore, colonization of western Beringia after the Last Glacial Maximum (about 22,000-18,000 ybp) and is further supported by archaeological evidence in the Lena River basin, west of Beringia, where the earliest unequivocal sites date to around 18,000-17,000 ybp (Goebel & Slobodin, 1999; Goebel, Waters, & Dikova, 2003; Hamilton & Goebel, 1999).

To summarize, the archaeological evidence is indicative, to some extent, of a movement of people at least as early as 40-30,000 ybp towards Beringia and the east. The significance of all of this seems to be that people traveled north, probably along the Pacific coast and its immediate inland environments, by at least 50,000 years ago (if not earlier), and crossed the Bering land bridge or, using boats, hopped from refugia to refugia. Some of these people most likely found their way into the Americas and gradually worked their way eastward and southward so that by 20,000+ years ago (though these data are still very controversial, see Dillehay, 2000) they were on the Atlantic coast of North America and at least as far south as Ayacucho, Peru (Smith & Smith, 1982). There is not the space, nor the necessity for the purposes of this book, to discuss the various theories behind how American Indians first arrived in the Americas beyond merely stating that the vast majority of the evidence supports the conclusion that the ancestors of today's American Indians made their way from northeast Asia to the Americas (see, for example, Alsozatai-Petheo, 1986; Anderson & Gillam, 2000; Bonatto & Salzano, 1997a; Bonnichsen & Turnmire, 1999; Brace, Nelson, Seguchi, Oe, Sering, Qifeng, Yongyi, & Tumen, 2001; Dixon, 1999; Gruhn, 1994; Merriwether, Hell, Vahlne, & Ferrell, 1996; Schurr, Ballinger, Gan, Hodge, Weiss, & Wallace, 1990; Schurr & Wallace, 1999; Surovell, 2003; Wright, 1999).

Pleistocene Megafauna and the First Americans

Once the first peoples made their way into the Americas, the next question that must be addressed for the purposes of this book is the one concerning subsistence regimes and mobility patterns. That is, to establish cultural continuity it must be shown that contemporary American Indians of the Plateau and Great Basin have resided in their known ethnographic territories since the time of either Kennewick Man or Spirit Cave Mummy, i.e., the Early Holocene. If the archaeological record demonstrates that the people who first came to the Americas followed a similar subsistence regime as the contemporary American Indians did in the recent past, then there is a parallel between the two cultures that may be affiliated. Furthermore, as I will discuss below, the data indicates that the first people to the Americas practiced a subsistence regime similar to that of their relatives of northeast Asia, which as was just covered, consisted of a diverse use of natural resources in a cyclical, seasonal lifeway pattern. If this is the case, it implies that the first Americans stayed in their local natural resource environments in prehistory rather than constantly move from environment to environment, which would give evidence towards continued occupation in these areas unless the archaeological data can evidence migration or abandonment.

A problem arises in this subsistence regime reconstruction, however, because as discussed above, many of the hypothesized subsistence regimes for the Plateau and Great Basin stem from Plains region derived reconstructions. This "Plains dominance" has further resulted in the hypothesis called the "blitzkrieg" hypothesis, whereby the first Americans are hypothesized to have killed to the point of extinction the Late Pleistocene megafauna of the Americas. As a result of this "Plains dominance," many archaeologists (e.g., Martin, Rogers, & Neuner, 1985; Martin, 1982; Martin, Thompson, & Long, 1985) have claimed that all of the first Americans were "big game hunters," including the peoples of the Plateau and Great Basin, who killed off all of the large Pleistocene mammalian fauna. This conceptualization of early Americans as "big game hunters" has further added to the confusion surrounding issues of cultural affiliation because shortly after the Early Holocene, the archaeological data appears not to reflect a big game hunting subsistence regime, but more of a broad scale, dynamic subsistence regime that utilized a wide variety of flora and fauna in a cyclical, seasonal round. Thus, it is necessary to examine to some degree what is known of the early American's subsistence regime, and to briefly summarize the evidence concerning the "overkill" or "blitzkrieg" hypothesis.

The "blitzkrieg" hypothesis is based on the fact that during a thousand-year period, more than 40 Late Pleistocene mammalian genera disappeared, resulting in an extinction rate of 77 percent prorated throughout the stratigraphic interval. Thirty-nine of the 40 genera were large mammals. In geologic terms, this extinction, occurring in thousands rather than millions of years, was extraordinarily fast. By way of contrast, the second fastest mammalian extinction took place in the Late Hemiphillian (12-8 million ybp). It extended over 1.5 million years and involved 62 genera, 35 of which were large mammals (Whitney-Smith, 2001). However, not all of the Pleistocene mammalian fauna became extinct (i.e., *Bison spp.*), and those that did become extinct did not die off at the same time. For example, it appears that nine of the genera became extinct after 12,000 years ago, and that the extinctions were largely over by 10,000 years ago (Grayson, 1993). This fact has been one of the major stumbling blocks to Martin's overkill Hypothesis (Martin & Mehringer, 1965; Martin & Szuter, 1999; Martin, Thompson, & Long, 1985). This is because only nine of the genera that became extinct can be securely shown to have been contemporaneous with lithic points associated with the first Americans (i.e., Clovis style fluted points). Furthermore, if it could be proven that all of the mammals survived until the end of the Pleistocene, attributing the extinctions to human predation would require the major assumption that the first Americans relied heavily enough on these large mammals that they became extinct.

Studies that have compiled paleontological sites of the United States have shown that horses and camels are the first and third most frequently reported Late Pleistocene megafauna mammals in sites, while mammoths and mastodon are second and fourth, respectively. Horses and camels, however, have never been reported in secure "kill" sites associated with fluted points. Indeed, although a few kill associations are known for mastodon, the only extinct mammal that shows up in such a context in any number is the mammoth. Furthermore, as was covered in the paleoenvironmental chapter, the climatic models demonstrate that the Americas underwent enormous environmental change during this period and may possibly account not only for part of the extinction of the large mammals, but also for huge changes in the ranges of many small mammals that occurred at the same time (Barnes, Matheus, Shapiro, Jensen, & Cooper, 2002; Grayson, 1993, 2000b).

Not only have some of the most abundant extinct Late Pleistocene mammals (horses and camels, for instance) never been found in a convincing human-kill context, but it has not been demonstrated that the majority of the extinct mammals actually overlapped in time with the Late Pleistocene and Early Holocene peoples, (usually thought of as the Clovis "people" by archaeologists), thought by some to have been the major cause of the extinctions. This is especially true for the Plateau and Great Basin regions, two areas that contain only a few Late Pleistocene mammal sites. As Grayson noted in his review of the Great Basin, "There are no convincing associations between fluted points and the remains of extinct Pleistocene mammals in the Great Basin" (1993, p. 238).

There is, however, an interesting correlation between the first archaeological evidence of humans and the extinction of the Pleistocene megafauna. For example, the median extinction occurs 1,229 years after the initial archaeological evidence of humans in North America. The earliest was at 801 years after, and most extinctions took place by 1,640 years after the initial arrival of people in the Americas based on archaeological data, though not genetic data as discussed in the previous chapter. These time spans translate to dozens of human generations, and because it takes 260 years for a founding human population to exceed 1,000 individuals, and 410 to exceed 10,000, some researchers have argued that we might not expect the archaeological record to show evidence of humans before those times in accord with the genetic data. Furthermore, a 1,200 to 1,000-year overlap of humans and Pleistocene megafuana might be expected. The earliest appearance of Clovis artifacts (i.e., Early Holocene lithic points) in the United States is at about 13,400 ybp, and the very youngest calibrated ^{14}C dates on extinct megafauna are around 12,260 ybp. The known overlap from the current dataset is therefore around 1,200 years, leading some researchers to conclude that it is possible for those Early Holocene peoples to have caused the Late Pleistocene megafauna extinctions (Alroy, 2001; Martin, Rogers, & Neuner, 1985; Martin, 1982; Martin, Thompson, & Long, 1985; Miller, 1982). The only problem is that as noted above, this overlap does not empirically demonstrate that Early Holocene peoples hunted the now extinct megafauna to the extent necessary to cause large-scale extinction.

A useful analogy that can be used to shed some light on the paradox is to look at present-day U.S. Fish and Wildlife statistical hunting figures. In 2001 nearly 13.0 million people aged 16 and older partook in hunting activities in the U.S. Of these 13.0 million, 10.9 million were so-called "big game" hunters. This is an overall increase of 31 percent from 1955. Furthermore, on average the U.S. Fish and Wildlife estimates that 700,000 people pursued elk as their big game of choice. However, despite this large number of increasing hunters, there is still generally considered an elk overpopulation in the U.S. (see U.S. Fish and Wildlife website, www.fws.gov and the Rocky Mountain Elk Foundation website www.rmef.org). These numbers are much higher than the hypothesized population of Early Holocene "big game hunters." Thus, it would seem highly unlikely that Early Holocene peoples could have caused the extinction of the Late Pleistocene megafauna if today's hunters, exceeding the hypothesized Early Holocene population, have not caused detrimental population pressure on today's "megafauna."

It is also interesting to recognize that the Pleistocene extinction was a "process" and not an "event." As even staunch advocates of a blitzkrieg overkill model admit (e.g., Martin, Thompson, & Long, 1985) the phenomenon likely lasted at least a few hundred and perhaps a few thousand years. To further complicate the interpretation of the data, for a specific taxon the youngest reliable radiocarbon date marks its last recognizable appearance and thus the termination of the extinction process of that taxon. It is common practice to compile data lists for the last appearance of specific taxa (e.g. Kurten & Anderson, 1980, Table 19.6) and to attempt to correlate this with various archaeological lithic scatters representing early American sites. There are, however, several points of caution that must be raised with regard to the use of such tables. First, there is little reason to suppose the extinction process was synchronous across space (Kurten & Anderson, 1980). Furthermore, the use of a single date to mark the extinction of an entire taxon masks potential regional variability in the extinction process (Meltzer & Mead, 1985).

Likewise, as Meltzer and Mead (1985) have pointed out, the Late Pleistocene megafauna overkill Hypothesis can be falsified if:

- individual genera or species of Pleistocene megafauna survived into the Holocene prior to becoming extinct;
- extinctions are not time-transgressive north to south;
- megafauna and prehistoric groups co-existed over a long period of time, demonstrated by • archaeological occupations predating 12,000 ybp; or
- extinctions are non-synchronous across taxa in the same region.

It is interesting to note here that reptiles experienced a very different outcome during the Late Pleistocene to Early Holocene boundary. For example, the main effects of the Quaternary on North American reptiles appears to be changes in their range resulting from a fluctuating ecology, along with some speciation, principally at the subspecies level, and some extinction (Auffenberg & Milstead, 1965). The effects of the temperature changes on reptiles were probably the least important of the Pleistocene changes. Colder climates contributed to the extinction of some species and had some slight influence in the speciation of a few forms, but the major effect was in modifying the northern range of the reptiles as a group. Throughout the entire span of the Pleistocene the reptiles as a group were pushed farther south with each succeeding glacial age, and they reinvaded less far northward with each interglacial. This effect was felt primarily in the periglacial zones, however, and relatively few species were involved (Geist, 1999). Thus, changes in environment appear to have had similarly "drastic" consequences for reptiles.

Other changes in environmental conditions have also been linked to species range change. With each glacial age the level of the sea was lowered, while with each inter-glacial it rose. These fluctuations had considerable influence on the geographic ranges of species living in coastal areas. The main effect of high sea-level stages was in providing a physical mechanism for isolation and subsequent speciation. Low sea levels made available certain types of dispersal routes unavailable during high levels. Similarly, throughout the Quaternary there were significant changes in precipita-tion and humidity that modified, for example, the mammalian and reptilian faunas across the entire United States (Auffenberg & Milstead, 1965). Conditions were at times more mesic and at other times more arid than those of today. Such fluctua-tions were important in opening and closing certain east-west and north-south dis-persal routes (Auffenberg & Milstead, 1965).

Thus, although the Quaternary was a period of relatively "little" change for rep-tiles in species context, extensive speciation and extinction took place in the mam-mals. This can be expected because mammals are usually considered more sensitive to environmental changes than other species. Furthermore, during the Pleistocene many northern species of fauna were found south of their present day ranges and southern forms were found north of their present day ranges. The most widely accepted Hypothesis to explain this phenomena has been the "climatic equability model" (e.g. Hibbard, 1960; Holman, 1976; Slaughter, 1975): mild winters account for the presence of southern extralimital species and cooler summers account for the presence of northern extralimital species (Brewer, 1985). Thus, there is a strong correlative link between the various environmental fluctuations and changes that took place during the Late Pleistocene to Early Holocene (see chapter six) and the simultaneous extinction of several Pleistocene megafauna.

However, these facts do not mean that Early Holocene peoples did not hunt nd kill Late Pleistocene megafauna, as some sites clearly demonstrate (Alroy, 2001; Beltrao, de Moura, de Vasconcelos, & Neme, 1986; Borrero, 1986; Caviglia, Yacobaccio, & Borrero, 1986; Fidalgo, Guzman, Politis, Salemme, & Tonni, 1986). At the end of the Pleistocene, there were significant climate changes and, following the appearance of humans on each inhabited continent, significant megafaunal extinctions (Whitney-Smith, 2001). Thus, facts point out the inadequacies of both the climate change and overkill hypotheses. Neither explains why of the mam-malian fauna: 1) browsers, mixed feeders, and non-ruminant grazer species suffered most, while ruminant grazers generally survived; 2) why many surviving mammal species were sharply diminished in size; and 3) why vegetative environments in many areas shifted from a patch-based pattern to a more striped-based one (Guthrie, 1980; Whitney-Smith, 2001).

As noted earlier, the simplistic idea of the Early Holocene peoples equaling big game hunter analogy fails on several lines of evidence, and it is more parsimonious to assume a broad-spectrum subsistence diet (hunters and foragers) analogy. For example, early American lithic toolkits initially suggest greater investments in oppo-site ends of the diet spectrum. Early Holocene assemblages are rich in formal, hafted flaked stone tools (points, bifaces, and scrapers), which are good for hunting and processing large animals, but there is also ample evidence that these early Americans were exploiting fish, various flora, and small mammals (Aigner & Del Bene, 1982; Butler, 1996; Chartkoff, 1985; Collins & Dillehay, 1986; Cressman, 1977; Dillehay, 1986, 2000; Erlandson & Moss, 2001; Tuohy & Dansie, 1997; Tuohy, 1988a, 1988b, 1990; Tuohy, Dansie, & Haldeman, 1987). However, presently most sites have only yielded one type of artifact assemblage. Much of this discrepancy can be explained by the fact that lithic tools have a much higher preservation rate than bone, wood, and fiber; all resources that Early Holocene peoples most likely utilized.

Thus, when archaeologists look at the subsequent period (usually termed the Archaic period, spanning the Middle Holocene), many have claimed there is evidence of a discontinuity in the record because of the apparent increase in complexity of site artifact assemblages. However, the seasonal Archaic pattern (also observed ethnographically) of living in winter camps on stored food (especially seeds) and utilizing a broader spectrum of resources, while becoming more mobile during the remainder of the year, can more parsimoniously be seen as subsistence adaptation to the changing environment and ecosystem.

Not only are there many misconceptions about early American subsistence regimes, but there has also been an over exaggeration of Late Pleistocene to Early Holocene faunal populations. For example, there very likely were never 100 million or even 60 million bison on the Plains just prior to the arrival of Euroamericans because the carrying capacity of the grasslands was not high enough to sustain such a population. Flores (1991) has shown that the best technique for determining bison carrying capacity on the southern Plains, for example, is to extrapolate from United States census data for livestock, and the best census for the extrapolation is that of 1910, after the beef industry crashes of the 1880s had reduced animal numbers, but before the breakup of ranches and the Enlarged Homestead Act of 1909 resulted in considerable sections of the southern Plains becoming fragmented by farmers. Additionally, dendrochronological data seem to show that at the turn of the century rainfall on the southern Plains was at median, between-droughts levels, rendering the census of 1910 particularly suitable as a base line for reconstructing carrying capacity and prehistoric animal populations (Flores, 1991).

The 1910 agricultural census indicates that in the 201 counties on the southern Plains (which covered 240,000 square miles), the 19th century carrying capacity during periods of median rainfall was about 7,000,000 cattle-equivalent grazers — specifically for 1910, about 5,150,000 cattle and 1,890,000 horses and mules. The prehistoric megafauna population, such as the bison was almost certainly larger, since migratory grazing patterns and co-evolution with the native grasses made bison as a wild species about 18 percent more efficient on the Great Plains than domestic cattle. The ecological reality was a dynamic cycle in which carrying capacity could swing considerably from decade to decade, but if the Plains bovine carrying capacity of 1910 expresses a median reality, then during pre-horse times the southern Plains might have supported an average of about 8.2 million bison, and the entire Plains perhaps 30-28 million (Flores, 1991).

Furthermore, ecological studies on Pleistocene mammals show that they differ considerably from post-glacial species by possessing "plastic" food habits, adaptable to seasonal variations. The large-scale variations in seasonal temperature from winter to summer, as well as the frequent fluctuations in environmental habitats, required Pleistocene mammals to possess what is called a multithermic ecological competence. That is, the Pleistocene mammals were capable of changing the morphology of their digestive systems to suite seasonal and ecological needs (Hofmann, 1983), and they rarely developed extremely specialized food-related adaptations, such as hypsodont dentition, which is very common in tropical ruminants. As they were specifically adapted to diverse environments, and not to environmental constancy, they were not able to succeed against their specialist relatives in more southerly latitudes. Therefore, the Pleistocene mammals also could not successfully populate ecosystems with more benign climates, except where ecological specialists were absent, such as those that emerged during the Early Holocene after the glaciers receded (Geist, 1999).

Finally, as has been discussed, not only are there numerous problems with the Early Holocene peoples equals big game hunters analogy concerning the archaeological evidence for the "overkill" or "blitzkrieg" hypothesis, but there is also evidence from various regions that indicate intensification of hunting large mammals actually increased from the Late Pleistocene through the Early Holocene and onwards. For example, sites along the California coast indicate that sustained resource intensification and population increases that began during the Middle Holocene continued until at least 1000 ybp, and that there is a variety of archaeological evidence indicating that hunting of highly ranked large mammals actually increased during this time (Hildebrandt & McGuire, 2002).

Therefore, as can be seen, the Late Pleistocene to Early Holocene interval is extremely complex, both paleoenvironmentally (as previously reviewed in chapter six) and faunistically as dealing with the Late Pleistocene megafauna extinctions. The evidence points to a multivariate explanation for the Late Pleistocene megafauna extinction with human, climatic, and ecological factors all contributing to the process. Finally, it is important to stress that humans are distinctly aware of their environment, especially if they must subsist upon it in the same way as early American Indian hunters and gatherers had to. It is highly unlikely that these Early Holocene peoples and their descendants would exploit a resource that they are either partially or wholly dependent on until it is completely gone. This type of exploitation is only a recent phenomenon caused by people who are disconnected, either physically or mentally, from the resources they are utilizing. Thus, it seems myopic to project the same mental consciousness of present-day Westerners (and in most cases, Western trained scholars) onto the consciousness of Early Holocene hunters and gatherers.

Early First American Subsistence Lifeways

As was discussed in the previous section of this chapter, the "overkill" Hypothesis is circumscribed on many lines of evidence. However, what is more important for the purposes of this book is to look at basic subsistence patterns and methods that Early Holocene American peoples practiced. The reason that this is important is that subsistence practices not only allow us to understand basic aspects of lifeway patterns, but they are also directly related to forms of ethnoscience. It is this last aspect that is important to investigate for the purposes of coming to understand issues surrounding cultural affiliation and cultural continuity, for by coming to understand as completely as possible these ancient peoples' ethnoscience, we can begin to arrive at a closer understanding of their epistemology. As I will discuss in chapter thirteen, in order to demonstrate cultural affiliation it is necessary to show that a similar epistemology unites the two cultural units of analysis, for it is epistemology that forms the ontology and subsequently the culture. Therefore, this section will take a close look at what the archaeological evidence reveals concerning Early Holocene peoples subsistence practices in several diverse environments. I will begin the discussion on the Pacific Coast and work my way inland, relying on a wide array of archaeological evidence.

Quebrada Tacahuay, a site located on the south coast of Peru, gives evidence to one of the oldest expressions of maritime adaptations in the Western Hemisphere, and the evidence indicates that humans focused their activities on the collection and butchering of marine birds, particularly cormorants and boobies, along with other marine resources more than 10,290 years ago. The abundant use of seafood indicates that Quebrada Tacahuay represents a specialized coastal extraction station used by Late Pleistocene and Early Holocene populations with a well-developed littoral adaptation (deFrance, Keefer, Richardson, & Alvarez, 2001).

Furthermore, evidence from Quebrada Tacahuay, as well as numerous other sites located along the Peurvian and Californian coasts indicate that Early Holocene peoples hunted large quantities of marine birds, possibly with "flight nets" or while they were feeding in shallow waters, along with large amounts of shellfish, fish, and marine mammals (deFrance, Keefer, Richardson, & Alvarez, 2001; Erlandson & Moss, 2001; Moss & Erlandson, 1995; Rick & Erlandson, 2000; Rick, Erlandson, & Vellanoweth, 2001). This evidence has led some researchers to conclude that although the population may have returned to this locale at different times of the year, the absence of shell midden debris, stratified refuse, and other residential features (e.g., postmolds, prepared living floors) as compared to either Quebrada Jaguay (Sandweiss et al., 1998) or the Ring Site (Sandweiss, Rothhammer, Reitz, & Feldman, 1989), two south coast Peruvian sites with contexts dating to the Late Pleistocene, indicates that some of these sites were utilized more as temporary encampments than permanent settlements (deFrance, Keefer, Richardson, & Alvarez, 2001). This evidence lends support to the idea of a cyclical perennial or semi-perennial subsistence lifeway.

Further north, along the central coast of California, recent excavations at the Cross Creek site (CA-SLO-1797) have revealed a stratigraphically discrete midden component dating between 10,350 and 9,700 ybp, making it the oldest mainland shell midden on the west coast of North America (Jones et al., 2002). A large recovery volume revealed an assemblage dominated by grinding implements (handstones and milling slabs) and crude core and flake tools typical of what has been called California's Milling Stone horizon. However, the Cross Creek findings extend the antiquity of the Milling Stone horizon back to the Late Pleistocene, when previously it was thought to date to only the Middle Holocene. Furthermore, the tools and associated faunal remains suggest a gathering economy, that as will be discussed, was similar to the Late Pleistocene "big-game" hunting economy in parts of the interior of North America (Jones, Fitzgerald, Kennett, Miksicek, Fagan, Sharp, & Erlandson, 2002). Similarly, shell and charcoal dates from Daisy Cave located in the Channel Islands off the coast of California indicate that foraging populations were using boats, collecting shellfish, and fishing as early as 11,700 years ago. At Cross Creek, charred seed and shellfish remains and abundant milling tools (outnumbering projectile points by a ratio of 6:1) possibly indicate a sedentary or more likely cyclically based economy focused heavily on gathering, and not exclusively hunting (Jones, Fitzgerald, Kennett, Miksicek, Fagan, Sharp, & Erlandson, 2002).

Furthermore, the data from sites SBA-2057, SDI-9649, Quebrada Jaguay, Lake Mungo, and other Late Pleistocene and Early Holocene sites suggest that systematic reliance on net fishing for relatively large yields of small fish has a greater antiquity than previously recognized. This indicates adaptations to a wide variety of marine habitats among the earliest people to arrive on the Pacific coast of the Americas. Further, while the intensity of net fishing may have increased during the Late Holocene, much of the data suggest that systematic net fishing for small schooling fish was present along the southern California Coast by at least 8,300 years ago. Fish continued to be a supplemental dietary resource at many sites during the Middle Holocene, but the ability to engage in a wide variety of subsistence strategies was also in place. For example, the use of boats, cooperative net fishing, line fishing, sea mammal hunting, shellfish collecting, land mammal hunting, and plant collecting are all aspects of Early and Middle Holocene subsistence lifeways (Erlandson, 1994; Erlandson & Moss, 2001; Moss & Erlandson, 1995; Rick & Erlandson, 2000; Rick, Erlandson, & Vellanoweth, 2001). These data indicate an eclectic and diversified economy, which varied in intensity both geographically and temporally throughout the Holocene (Rick & Erlandson, 2000; Rick, Erlandson, & Vellanoweth, 2001).

Similar evidence comes from the Eel Point Site on San Clemente Island located in the Channel Islands of California. Occupied from around 9,040 to 600 ybp, the Eel Point Site represents one of the longest sequences of near-continuous marine resource exploitation on the west coast of North America (Porcasi, Jones, & Raab, 2000). Faunal remains suggest transitions from a heavy exploitation of fur seals and sea lions during the Early Holocene, to increased hunting of cetaceans (dolphins) by the Middle Holocene, to a focus on sea otters and fish during the Late Holocene. These trends are consistent with patterns of increasing exploitation and economic intensification on the California and Oregon mainland, but they also suggest watercraft-based hunting earlier on the island than elsewhere (Porcasi, Jones, & Raab, 2000).

This site, as well as the other ones discussed above, along with the overall archaeological evidence from the coasts of both North and South America indicate that marine mammals were exploited from the Late Pleistocene throughout the Holocene. Likewise, California sea lions, Guadalupe fur seals, sea otters, and several species of small cetaceans (dolphins) were also exploited, along with various forms of fish, fowl, and other marine-based resources (deFrance, Keefer, Richardson, & Alvarez, 2001; Erlandson & Moss, 2001; Jones, Fitzgerald, Kennett, Miksicek, Fagan, Sharp, & Erlandson, 2002; Moss & Erlandson, 1995; Porcasi, Jones, & Raab, 2000; Rick & Erlandson, 2000; Rick, Erlandson, & Vellanoweth, 2001). Finally, it should also be noted that in California, wetlands may have become an especially important buffer zone during the Middle Holocene, when warmer ocean temperatures apparently reduced the extent of offshore kelp beds and subsequently the productivity of the entire maritime resource base (Glassow, Wilcoxon, & Erlandson, 1988), adding further complexity to the picture. Thus, Early and Middle Holocene coastal peoples seemed to have had an eclectic subsistence economy based on a cyclical or semi-sedentary lifeway.

Turning inland towards the Great Basin we find a very different natural resource base that was exploited, but a similar lifeway pattern. Here, it appears that rabbits, antelope, fish, fowl, various types of insects, as well as other species were regularly exploited from Late Pleistocene times through to the present (Adovasio, 1986b; Aikens, 1978, 1982; Arkush, 1999; Bettinger & Baumhoff, 1983; Butler, 1996; Coltrain, 2002; Connolly, 1999; Cressman, 1977; Delacorte, 1994; Elston, 1982, 1986; Follett, 1977; Grayson, 1993; Janetski, 1990; Jones, Beck, Jones, & Hughes, 2003; Jones & Madsen, 1989; Kelly, 1995; Madsen, 1982; Madsen & Schmitt, 1998; Tuohy, 1990). In a study looking at both subsistence "zones" and lithic procurement areas, occurrences of extralocal obsidian can be used as the basis for describing lithic conveyance zones (i.e., Seeman, 1994) that appear to geographically delimit the foraging territories of Early Holocene peoples and later populations in the central Great Basin. Data indicate for the central Great Basin that obsidian was conveyed from sources within a zone measuring over 450 km in a north-south direction and 150 km in a west-east direction. The corresponding foraging territory may have been larger, but it appears not to have extended beyond the Nevada-Idaho border to the north and the eastern edges of the Bonneville Basin in Utah to the east (Jones, Beck, Jones, & Hughes, 2003). As I covered in chapter six, as warming and drying proceeded in the Early Holocene, there were commensurate reorganizations of biota and the loss of mesic habitats in many Great Basin valleys. One apparent consequence of these changes was a decline in resource abundance within favored subsistence patches like wetlands, and many of the Pleistocene marshes began to dry up. Much of the evidence suggests that Early Holocene peoples and later American Indians responded to these conditions by incorporating seeds, using a wider range of animal prey, and generally increasing diet breadth (Jones, Beck, Jones, & Hughes, 2003). However, what is particularly interesting about much of this data for the purposes of this book is that although diet breadth and subsistence regimes adapted to these new conditions, the American Indians of the Early and Middle Holocene, as well as later periods did not move out of their general lithic conveyance zone, thus their cyclical lifeway zone.

Every eastern Nevada assemblage of any size contains the same suite of [obsidian] sources – Brown's Bench, Panaca Summit, and source B. From this we conclude that, with rare exception (e.g., Sunshine Well), Paleoarchaic foragers did not transport stone tools made from these sources to other sections of the Great Basin. (Jones, Beck, Jones, & Hughes, 2003 p. 32)

These results have allowed researchers to construct a set of lithic conveyance zones that have been interpreted as coterminous with the foraging territories of Early, Middle, and Late Holocene peoples. The patterns of obsidian source representation suggest that the principle axes of movement were north-south, paralleling the orientation of mountain ranges and valleys throughout the Great Basin. Furthermore, it has been tentatively concluded that three north-south territories once existed across the middle of the Great Basin, with separate territories conforming to the northern Great Basin and Mojave Desert (Jones, Beck, Jones, & Hughes, 2003). It is interesting to note that these Early Holocene through Late Holocene lithic conveyance zones correspond to the tripartite linguistic organization of present-day Great Basin tribes, and would seem to lend support to their occupation of the Great Basin far back into time.

Recently, with the rise in popularity of optimal foraging theory, many archaeologists have argued that Great Basin peoples did not exploit many of the smaller animal and plant resources found in the region, reminiscent of Steward's (1955) early cultural ecology theory. These optimal foraging theorists argue that the energetic return rates of many small animal and plant resources are often density dependent, meaning that unless the resource occurs in great abundance, it is not calorically worth harvesting these resources. However, change in abundance can dramatically affect diet rank, which challenges the general assumption that caloric return rates are generally correlated with resource body size. Thus, when mass collecting is employed, as a result of either natural events (e.g., windrows) or technological developments (e.g., nets), population density may largely determine the overall return rate for a resource. Since a food or resource type can be many prey types, an increase in the abundance of a food resource can change its diet rank. An example of this can be seen in Madsen and Schmitt's (1998) work in which they examined this relationship at Lakeside Cave in northwestern Utah, and discovered that when the abundance of grasshoppers is high, and mass collecting is productive, the hunting of bighorn sheep and other large animal resources may have been greatly reduced, contradicting commonly held assumptions about prey size and hunting strategy. Therefore, in archaeological situations it may be necessary to determine what foraging technique was used before assuming that the presence of small animals and fish in the diet is a result of reduced foraging efficiency or that change in subsistence regime implies change in peoples (Madsen & Schmitt, 1998).

One problem that has been encountered by many researchers in attempting to reconstruct subsistence regimes of Early, Middle, and Late Holocene American Indians is that because of the extensive climatic change that has taken place throughout the Holocene, many of the resources utilized by these peoples can no longer be found. For example, many traditionally used plants are now difficult to find because of wetland loss and the impact of cattle. A similar situation exists for waterfowl, animal, and plant resources in the Great Basin (Fowler, 1986b), boreal

Canada (Merculieff, 1994), Arnhem Land in Australia (Isaacs, 1980), and other areas (Nicholas, 1998). Likewise, recent studies of early American Indian activity at Stillwater Marsh, in the Great Basin, attests to extensive evidence of human settlement, including shallow pithouses, storage pits, and burials, along with indicators of wetland and terrestrial resource exploitation.

Looking at this data diachronically, it appears to indicate that often the same wetlands were used in different ways over time. This further indicates that Early and Middle Holocene, as well as later peoples of the Great Basin, were not static entities but groups of people that responded to social, demographic, and environmental pressures or opportunities in a remarkable variety of ways, all the while remaining in their general lifeway zone. As a result of this dynamic nature, it is more parsimonious to conclude that Great Basin peoples changed their subsistence economies but kept their general lifeway cycle as opposed to assuming that they maintained their subsistence economy and migrated from location to location (i.e., abandonment of their lifeway cycles).

If we turn now to the Plains region, we encounter the classic Clovis/Folsom "big game" hunting complex. Here it has been argued for many years that large herds of bison were likely the major source of fat and protein in the "Clovis" and "Folsom" diet[7]. Of the 20 Folsom sites in the central and northern Plains that have yielded any faunal remains, 19 contained bison, while only nine, or 45 percent contained non-bison ungulate remains (MacDonald, 1998). Furthermore, it has been noted that much of the evidence indicates that certain landforms were used to aid in the procurement of mammals. In Early Holocene times, the best evidence of this is associated with the extinct subspecies of bison (*Bison antiquus*). For example, parabolic sand dunes, such as those at the Casper site (Frison, 1974), as well as head cuts in arroyos, such as at the Agate Basin, Hawken, and Carter/Kerr-McGee sites (Frison, 1976, 1984), appear to have been used advantageously to hunt these animals. The deep arroyo present at the Colby Mammoth site in northern Wyoming (Frison & Todd, 1987) may also have been an important factor in regular and systematic mammoth procurement there (Frison, 1999).

Thus, for Clovis and Folsom producing peoples, as well as the later Agate, Plano, and other Plains lithic "cultures," the optimal subsistence strategy appears to have focused to a large extent on bison procurement. Bison provided an unlimited supply of goods for foragers (Bamforth, 1988), including necessary fats and lipids that are difficult to obtain in other forms of food (Speth, 1983). While other food items were likely procured as secondary resources, bison procurement appears to have been the optimal solution to the dietary needs of these lithic producing peoples (MacDonald, 1998). However, there is also a large amount of archaeological subsistence evidence that supports the notion that Early Holocene peoples exploited a wider range of both floral and faunal resources than just bison. Not only did these people hunt large game animals, they also took smaller mammals, fish, fowl, reptiles, and a wide variety of flora. For example, analyses from Cougar Cave in Montana indicate that marmot (*Marmota flaviventris*), rabbit (*Lepus sp., Sylvilagus sp.),* and blue grouse (*Dendragapus obscurus*) were favored taxa. Bison (*Bison bison*) and mountain sheep (*Ovis canadensis*), however, were also taken to some extent (Bonnichsen & Bolen, 1985).

As has been briefly reviewed, a growing body of evidence furthermore suggests that Early Holocene hunters were generalists who probably exercised a preference for large game, but frequently exploited smaller animals as well. Early Holocene sites have yielded, in addition to mammoth, the remains of horse, camel, peccary, sloth, bison (*Bison antiquus*), caribou, and wolf, (all extinct or largely extirpated from Late Pleistocene and Early Holocene ranges), and deer, bear, pronghorn, rabbit, marmot and other rodents, turtle, fish, bird, and mollusk (Bryan, 1969, 1986, 1991; Stanford, 1991, 1999; Willig, 1991; Willig & Aikens, 1988). Evidence has also accumulated from many areas of North America suggesting that the Early Holocene diet commonly included collected plants (Willig, 1991; Willig & Aikens, 1988; Zier & Kalasz, 1999). Furthermore, sites tend to be located near water sources, particularly marshes, ponds, streams, and rivers but they also occur in waterless hinterlands (Greiser, 1985). Site types include kill and/or butchering sites, campsites both with and without connections to kill sites, and isolated artifacts. Early Holocene campsites and kill locations are suggestive of band-level organization, with little evidence for the type of large-group communal activity found at Middle and Late Holocene sites.

To summarize, for the Pacific Coast, Great Basin, and Plains regions, the Late Pleistocene through Holocene subsistence lifeways was very diverse, exploiting the full range of available flora and fauna from large ungulates to small fowl species, as well as a wide variety of fish, mollusks, insects, seeds, nuts, and other vegetal resources. This subsistence economy also seems to have been based on a cyclical pattern that was tied to both climatic and seasonal variations, as well as resource availability. Furthermore, although I did not specifically review the Plateau in this section (though I will cover it later in this chapter), it is reasonable to assume that the Late Pleistocene and Early Holocene peoples of this region practiced a similar lifeway pattern, though exploiting different resources such as salmon and camas. The evidence does not support the idea that Early and Middle Holocene, as well as later American Indian peoples wandered the landscape in a haphazard fashion migrating from one resource area to the next. Instead, the evidence argues for a more long-term familiarity with both the environment, as well as its resources, in an increasingly sophisticated fashion as cyclical subsistence lifeway time-depth increased. With this cyclical lifeway pattern in mind, we can now look at the question of cultural continuity in the Plateau and Great Basin in more detail.

Plateau and Great Basin Archaeological Synthesis

As has been briefly reviewed in the previous sections of this chapter, there are still many "gaps" in the archaeological record concerning how American Indians came to the Americas and subsequently made their way down to the Plateau and Great Basin. Likewise, the various technologies and subsistence practices employed by these early American Indians appears to have been highly complex and adaptive, both to macro-regional environmental situations, as well as micro-regional ecological situations. In the rest of this chapter I review in some depth the archaeological database for the Plateau and Great Basin regions beginning at the Late Pleistocene to Early Holocene boundary and carrying through to the beginning of the ethnographic period, which was covered in chapter seven. This archaeological data review and synthesis is based largely on the most recent macro-regional sequences for each region.

The Plateau

For the Plateau region, the general chronological time periods used in Ames (2000), Ames, Dummond, Galm, and Minor (1998), and the U.S. Department of the Interior (2000) are the most recent and comprehensive in offering a macro-regional sequence. The time periods begin with Period IA (13,500-7,000/6,400 ybp) and chronologically descend through Periods II (7,000/6,400-3,900 ybp), Period III (3,900-380 ybp), and the Modern Period (380 ybp- present). Along with these four macro periods, Period IA is also synchronous with Period IB, which only slightly differs from IA as I will discuss below.

Period IA (13,500-7,000/6,400 ybp) is the first period and includes "Clovis" type lithic points, which many archaeologists have termed Western Fluted (Beck & Jones, 1997; Dixon, 1999; Grayson, 1993). These lithic style points are weakly represented, but enough have been found to distinguish Period IA from Period IB. However, subsistence and mobility patterns are considered to have been the same between Period IA and IB. Furthermore, it is believed that during this initial period, there were very low population densities, coupled with relatively high levels of mobility, and a subsistence orientation that emphasized mesic environments. Early artifact assemblages (pre-9,000 ybp) are marked by the presence of stemmed and shouldered lanceolate projectile points, with later archaeological assemblages becoming dominated by foliate, or leaf shaped points (known as the classic Cascade point). However, these lithic forms overlap in time, with Cascade points appearing in small numbers earlier than stemmed or shouldered lanceolate points (Ames, 2000; Ames, Dummond, Galm, & Minor, 1998). Finally, like Period IB, the subsistence economy appears to have included a range of large and medium mammals (such as bison, deer, and rabbits), along with salmon and riverine exploitation. There is presently little evidence that any form of subsistence resource storage was utilized by these early peoples (Ames, 1988, 1991, 2000; Ames, Dummond, Galm, & Minor, 1998; Dixon, 1999; Interior, 2000; Uebelacker, 2000), and Galm (1994) and Sprague (2000a; 2000b) have noted that during the end of this period (both IA and IB; around 6,000-4,000 ybp), there is evidence for a "burial complex" in the northeastern and northcentral Washington area of the region.

Synchronous with Period IA was Period IB (13,500-7,000/6,400 ybp), which is differentiated only by the occurrence of Windust and Cascade type lithic points. These are the type of points found at a majority of archaeological sites during this time, and one was found embedded in the Kennewick Man individual's hip bone. Subsistence orientation during this period appears to emphasize riverine environments with the exploitation of salmon, other fish species, large mammals (including bison), medium mammals (e.g., rabbits), and a wide variety of plant life including camas bulbs and berries (Ames, 2000; Ames, Dummond, Galm, & Minor, 1998;

Campbell, 1985a, 1985b; Cressman, 1977; Dixon, 1999; Erickson, 1990; Galm, 1994; Hicks, 2000a, 2000b; Jaehnig, 1984, 2000; Uebelacker, 2000). The differences in material culture between the Windust (13,000-9,000 ybp) archaeological assemblages and the early Cascade/Vantage (9,000-7,700 ybp) archaeological assemblages are limited. As noted, the major differences are between projectile point forms, although the presence of burins in Windust assemblages and the relative frequencies of edge-ground cobbles, along with a greater reliance on basalt for stone tools during the latter portion of this period have been noted (Ames, 2000). Furthermore, Ames (2000) noted that towards the end of Period IB (which includes Cascade/Vantage type lithic points) subsistence economies shared a mixture of characteristics similar to both Period IA and the subsequent Period II, except that it appears that medium sized mammals became less important. Atwell (1989), Schalk and Cleveland (1983), and others see this time as being characterized by a very diffuse, broad-spectrum subsistence economy, while Chatters (1995) argues that it appears to be somewhat narrower than the subsequent Period II (also called the Pithouse I period) subsistence economies.

The subsequent Period II (7,000/6,400-3,900 ybp) includes what has come to be known as the Tucannon phase. There are no major differences between Period II and Period I (A and B) archaeological assemblages. Instead, the differences that can be seen in the archaeological record are the result more of cultural adaptation and technological changes than of cultural population displacement, migration, or abandonment (Ames, Dummond, Galm, & Minor, 1998; Cressman, 1977; Dixon, 1999; Erickson, 1990; Hess, 1997; Jaehnig, 1984, 2000; Sprague, 2000b; Uebelacker, 2000). In fact, the conclusion that the archaeological evidence indicates cultural adaptation and technological change was first recognized by Leonhardy and Rice (1970), who developed the original cultural typology for the Lower Snake River: "The continuity of cultural material between pre-ash and post-ash [Mount Mazama ash, dated to 6,850 ybp] does not indicate abandonment and then later resettlement by a different population, as Mallory supposes" (Leonhardy & Rice, 1970, p. 11). Instead, the data indicates that subsistence orientation continues with an intensification of salmon and other anadromous fish, though as noted above medium size mammals (e.g., rabbits) appear to lose importance. Ames (2000, p. 6) construes this as evidence for subsistence patterns being "significantly different than during previous periods," although in an earlier work (Ames, Dummond, Galm, & Minor, 1998) he sees little change between Period I and Period II. Furthermore, pithouses appear in the southeastern and south-central areas of the Columbia Plateau by 5,000 ybp, and some areas exhibit archaeological evidence of long periods of occupation. It should be noted that these pithouses occur in both riverine canyons and on the southern uplands (Lohse & Sammons-Lohse, 1986), an occupation pattern that is similar to the ethnographic record as noted in chapter seven. As Ames et al. (1998) note,

> if there is a cultural manifestation represented during this interval, then, it is clearly transitional in its stylistic elements between the better represented Period IB, and the vastly better represented Period IIIA. Any such entity must also have continued the subsistence orientation of the earlier time and continued a pattern of liv-

ing that involved ephemeral and shifting, rather than stable, settlements. (p. 111)

Likewise, Boxberger (2000, p. 24) also sees a transition, not a discontinuity, between
Period I, Period II, and the subsequent Period III.

Period III (3,900-380 ybp), according to Ames (2000), demonstrates the most
change between preceding Periods I and II. There is evidence of an intensification
of camas and other root resources, as well as evidence of more exploitation of fish,
increased population, use of storage pits, and an increase in number and sizes of pithouses (Ames 2000). Many archaeologists (Hicks, 2000a, 2000b; Jaehnig, 1984,
2000) attribute most of these changes to the changing climatic patterns during this
time when there were cooler, wetter springs and summers early in the period and
then warmer, more modern climatic environments towards the end of this period
(see also the discussion for this region in chapter six). Though Period II showed
some signs of the modern Plateau cultural lifeway such as long periods of occupation of particular riverine and upland sites as reviewed in chapter seven, this is the
period during which most archaeologists believe that the modern Plateau cultural
lifeway fully emerged. The last period in this macro-regional archaeological
sequence is the Modern Period (380 ybp-present). This period is covered by the
ethnographic literature in chapter seven and continues the patterns established in
Period III.

As the majority of archaeologists have noted, as well as Ames himself (1998, 2000),
there is no evidence in the archaeological record of displacement or migration of
any Columbia Basin peoples throughout prehistory, and for the larger Plateau
region in general. Furthermore, Ames (2000) notes that the Plateau has been continuously inhabited since the Early Holocene, and that there are only a few "gaps"
in the record:

> There are very few sites on the Columbia Plateau which contain the
> full temporal sequence; the sequence is stitched together from bits
> and pieces from all over. Therefore, some gaps are to be expected.
> The entire Plateau has a record of continuous occupation through
> the entire Holocene, but the central Basin appears to have been vir-
> tually unused for a few millennia, the Upper Columbia in the area
> of the Wells and Chief Joseph Reservoirs have no appreciable
> record for Period I, and there are gaps after that (between the
> Kartar 4500-1500 BC, and Hudnut 1500 BC-AD 1 phases). (p. 14,
> section 3, chapter 2)

These "gaps" present a difficult situation, for there is no other evidence to support
the idea that the peoples of the Plateau abandoned or moved away from these locations during the time of these "gaps." However, this leaves the questions of what
happened in these areas during these "gaps." As will be discussed in the conclusion,
many of these "gaps" are simply the result of archaeological categorization, and are
not necessarily reflective of the data themselves. For example, Cressman (1977)
used a much broader system of chronological sequences, designated the Early

Period (12,000-7,500 ybp), the Transitional Period (7,500-5,000 ybp), and the Late Period (6,000-historic times). As a result of this broader system, Cressman noted that there were marked changes throughout these periods in climate, technology, and subsistence economies, but that overall the archaeological record supported the conclusion of continuous cultural continuity of Plateau peoples (Cressman, 1977; see also Rudolph, 1995). Furthermore, Cressman (1977) sees similar continuous cultural adaptation and continuity for the Great Basin and Fraser Canyon areas.

Likewise, it may be useful to look at similar situations outside the Plateau to shed light on this question. For example, the oldest pit houses in western North America are found in southwestern and south-central Wyoming (Larson, 1997), where 28 sites have produced some 45 structures. One structure has a date of 8,400-7,700 ybp, with the majority of dates falling between 6,800-5,000 ybp. For the Plateau, Chatters (1989; 1995) and Ames (1988; 1991) have argued that pit house construction stopped around 3,800 ybp. However, in a recent analysis Ames (2000) noted that this conclusion may be misleading because some of the apparent "gaps" may be due to shifts in settlement patterns into or away from river canyons, and not evidence of prehistoric migrations or abandonment of areas. As can be seen with the Wyoming pithouse data, if the one pithouse dating to 8,400 ybp had not been found, archaeologists would argue that pithouse use did not start in Wyoming (or perhaps the northwestern Plains) for another 2,000 years. Furthermore, Lohse and Sammons-Lohse (1986) note that, "Traditional explicators — intensified salmon fishing, root collection, or development of storage facilities — cannot account for these early settlements" (p. 115), and thus our current explanations for these "gaps" fail to provide any conclusive arguments either way.

Furthermore, because of the nature of CRM work itself, and the lack of scholarly publications resulting from this CRM work, it is difficult to locate Plateau research reports to fill in these "gaps" (Lyman, 1985, 1997). Because of the relative lack of deeply stratified sites that span all time periods, none of these "gaps" can be looked at as evidence of cultural displacement or as evidence of migration either into or out of the Columbia Plateau. In fact, there is a large body of evidence to support the standard anthropological theory of continuing cultural adaptation and technological change by Plateau peoples from the Late Pleistocene to the present. This indication of continuity includes several lines of archaeological evidence, which I will cover below.

The first line of evidence for continued cultural development in the Plateau is the exploitation of salmon and other fish species dating back 11,000 ybp and extending to the present (Roll & Hackenberger, 1998; Rudolph, 1995; Schalk & Cleveland, 1983; Schalk et al., 1998). For example, "The available evidence is that fishing, including salmon fishing, occurred continuously on the Plateau from its earliest occupation" (Ames, 2000, p. 25, section 6, chapter 2). Furthermore, isotopic analysis of the Buhl skeleton revealed that her diet consisted of meat and anadromous fish similar to the ethnographically recorded Plateau American Indian diet. AMS dating indicated that this skeleton has an age of 10,675+/-95 ybp, which would indicate the continued exploitation of salmon and other anadromous fish beginning in the Late Pleistocene and Early Holocene (Green et al., 1998) and continuing through to the present.

The second line of evidence is also based on subsistence use data. The archaeological database indicates continued exploitation of camas bulbs, berries, and other plant species dating back 11,000 ybp and extending to the present (Chatters, 1989, 1995; Chatters & Pokotylo, 1998; Green, Pavesic, Woods, & Titmus, 1986; Green, Fenton, Woods, Titmus, Tiezen, & Miller, 1998; Gustafson, 1972; Rudolph, 1995). Furthermore, Hunn (1999; 2000) has done some recent work dealing with the ethnobiology of Plateau peoples and linguistic analysis. Based on an extensive investigation of Sahaptin ethnobiological language uses, he has concluded that, "The contemporary Sahaptin ethnobiological vocabulary gives no suggestion whatsoever that the Sahaptin-speaking peoples ever lived elsewhere than in their historic homeland" (Hunn, 2000, p. 19).

Similarly, the archaeological data indicates occupation of a central locality (i.e., a cyclical subsistence lifeway) around which various groups or bands would move throughout the seasons exploiting various subsistence resources dating back to the Early Holocene (Chatters, 1989, 1995; Chatters & Pokotylo, 1998; Cressman, 1977; Dixon, 1999; Green, Pavesic, Woods, & Titmus, 1986; Green, Fenton, Woods, Titmus, Tiezen, & Miller, 1998; Gustafson, 1972; Hicks, 2000a, 2000b; Jaehnig, 2000; Lohse & Sammons-Lohse, 1986; Roll & Hackenberger, 1998; Rudolph, 1995; Uebelacker, 2000). A clear example of this cyclical lifeway pattern has been discussed by Connolly (1999) in his in depth study of the Newberry Volcano area of southern Oregon in which evidence suggests that people used the caldera as a home base that they continued to revisit every year during the summer months, moving to more hospitable locations during the winter months. Furthermore, as Rudolph has discussed for the Hetrick Site in Idaho, "It is more likely that the site represents a seasonal occupation by a small group, just as it was during all previous occupations" (1995, p. 85).

A fourth archaeological line of evidence for continuous cultural occupation of the Plateau is a progression in lithic technology from stemmed and shouldered lanceolate and notched projectile points during Period IB; to stemmed, cornered, and side-notched projectile points during Period II; to Period III containing smaller notched projectile points, although stemmed and corner varieties continue (Hicks, 2000a, 2000b; Jaehnig, 2000; Leonhardy & Rice, 1970; Uebelacker, 2000). This progression can be seen as a logical development of projectile points used with atlatls and spears during Period I and Period II to the development and adaptation of the bow and arrow at the end of Period II and the beginning of Period III (Dixon, 1999). It should also be noted that all projectile point types overlap in time for the Plateau area (Hicks, 2000a, 2000b; Jaehnig, 2000). "These changes follow broader patterns of replacement of projectile point styles in western North America (e.g., Lohse 1995), including the appearance of a range of small points around AD 1, although larger forms persist for a few hundred years" (Ames, 2000, p. 10, section 6, chapter 2). Hicks (2000a) has also arrived at the conclusion that the evidence supports lithic technological progression through time:

First, thrusting spears, bearing points similar to Cascade points, were used until post-contact times on the Plateau. ... Side-notched projectiles are found throughout the chronological sequence after the Cold Springs points, declining in size as the delivery system transitioned from atlatl-dart technology to bow-and-arrow technology. (p. 2)

Finally, it is important to stress that many of the "gaps" in the lithic and archaeological database for the Plateau can be argued to be archaeological lithic "type" reductions, and not necessarily reflecting artifact "gaps" in the record (see chapter fourteen for a further discussion of this point).

The final line of evidence demonstrated by the archaeological record is the continuing indication of trade and exchange from 11,000 ybp to the present (Carlson, 1994; Connolly, 1999; Erickson, 1990; Galm, 1994; Hayden & Schulting, 1997). For example, there is also extensive evidence of obsidian trade between Plateau peoples and those of the Great Basin, Northwest Coast, and Plains that dates back to the Early Holocene (Jones, 2003). Specifically, there is evidence of trade and exchange of obsidian from southern Oregon, central Idaho, and British Columbia around Mt. Edziza and Anahim (Fladmark, 1985; Galm, 1994) and the Newberry Crater (Connolly, 1999), along with the use of saltwater shells including *Olivella biplicata*, *Dentalium pretiosum*, and 14 other genera by Plateau peoples (Erickson, 1990). Similarly, the Marmes burials (Breschini, 1979, p. 153) contained evidence of olivella beads, red ochre, and other artifacts that would suggest ancient trade systems with Northwest Coast, and possibly Great Basin peoples. Furthermore, Galm has noted that, "The presence of Olivella beads at Marmes during the Windust phase (D. Rice 1969, 1972) implies that marine shell was an item of trade in the Dalles-Deschutes area at least as early as 8000 BP" (1994, p. 296). There is also evidence of trade in southern Idaho obsidians between the Great Basin and Columbia Plateau during this time and expanding about 6,000 ybp, confirming the long history of trade and exchange relationships between the Plateau and Great Basin regions (Galm, 1994). Finally, the DeMoss Site, which dates to around 6,000 ybp, revealed obsidian points and Olivella shell beads, both of which had been traded into the Plateau from distant sources (Green, Pavesic, Woods, & Titmus, 1986). This pattern of trade and exchange increases through time, culminating in the famous trading centers described in the ethnographic literature at such places as The Dalles and Celilo Falls (Hayden & Schulting, 1997; Stern, 1998).

Finally, it is interesting to note that Collier, Hudson, and Ford (1942) conducted an extensive survey of the Upper Columbia region prior to much of the river damming that has taken place in the last fifty years, which as mentioned above flooded numerous archaeological sites and is a result of many of the "gaps" in the archaeological record. They concluded that, "No significant cultural differences were noted for our region, either horizontally or vertically" (p. 110). This means that these researchers could not find a significant difference between the present-day American Indian peoples of the Upper Columbia region and those of the prehistoric past dating back to the Early Holocene. This would imply that the archaeological evidence for continuity is stronger than for discontinuity, a conclusion that will be discussed in further detail later.

The Great Basin

Although the Great Basin lies directly south of the Plateau region, as has been reviewed in chapters five, six, and seven, the natural resources and lifeway patterns of the ancient and ethnographic Great Basin peoples are very different than those of the Plateau peoples. As a result, the archaeological database is also different, both in types of artifacts recovered, but also in the spatial and temporal occurrence of "gaps." Despite these limitations, I will review the archaeological database for the region as I did for the Plateau, following the most recent and comprehensive macro-regional chronology developed by the U.S. Bureau of Land Management (Barker, Ellis, & Damadio, 2000) and Grayson (1993). This macro-regional archaeological chronology consists of four periods similar to the Plateau archaeological chronology, except that the temporal dates for each period are different: Period I (10,000-7,500 ybp), Period II (7,500-4,500 ybp), Period III (4,500-500 ybp), and the Modern Period (500 ybp- present).

Period I (10,000-7,500 ybp) covers the Early Holocene and includes "Clovis" type lithic points (i.e., both stemmed and fluted points). This period is weakly represented in the Great Basin, evidenced only by several cave sites from the western Great Basin, including the Spirit Cave Mummy site, along with a few surface quarry sites, lithic sites, and shallow cave deposits located throughout the larger Great Basin region. Because of this relatively sparse dataset, some archaeologists (Barker, Ellis, & Damadio, 2000) have noted that, "There is no evidence from the early Holocene that one can use to identify a human group that is distinct from other human groups that may have lived in the area" (p.15). However, others have countered that it now seems reasonable, "to postulate a direct historical relationship between the Clovis culture and the Desert Culture which it appears to precede" (Aikens, 1978, p. 72). As noted earlier in this chapter, the "Clovis culture" is an archaeologically derived characteristic thought to be representative of Early Holocene big-game hunters, while the "Desert culture" is archaeologically defined as a broad-spectrum hunting and gathering pattern. Further complicating the distinction between these archaeological characteristics is the fact that actual Clovis points have not been recovered from deep, stratified deposits in the Great Basin that can be accurately dated (Aikens, 1978, 1982; Elston, 1986; Grayson, 1993). As a result, the data indicates that the people who made the Clovis lithic points are the direct ancestors to the people who made the Desert culture lithic points and later peoples of the Great Basin. This was also the conclusion supported by the data in the discussion concerning cyclical subsistence lifeways earlier in this chapter. Finally, as Bryan and Tuohy (1999) note, "Actual dates indicate that fluted points were used in the 'greater Great Basin' between 11,000 and 8500 yr BP, so they do not make a good period marker" (p. 255), arguing that both the Fluted Point tradition and the Stemmed Point traditions must be viewed as technological traditions, and not as cultural traditions. Thus, the data indicates technological adaptation and change, not cultural migration or displacement.

This technological change is further evidenced in Period II (7,500-4,500 ybp) when stemmed and fluted type lithic points slowly become replaced by smaller notched "dart" points. Subsistence orientation also appears to shift away from the streams and marshes to more of an upland, dry seed and hunting orientation during this period. This most likely is the result of the overall drying of the Late Pleistocene and Early Holocene pluvial remnants as I discussed in chapter six. Grayson (1993) has claimed that this 1,000 year plus period of drying, coupled with the fact that eight cave sites from the Spirit Cave Mummy area that date to this period lack data is evidence for population decline or abandonment. However, Cressman (1977), Elston (1982, 1986), Thomas (1981, 1994, 1999), and others have also noted the lack of sites that date to this period, and have argued that the current view of discontinuity could be a result of our understanding due to the limited archaeological dataset during this time.

> It has been thought by some archaeologists that the Great Basin was depopulated during the dry Altithermal period, even though convincing evidence has been available for more than twenty-five years that this was not the case. There is evidence for a reduction of population density, but not depopulation. (Cressman, 1977, p. 123)

Furthermore, there are no technological or subsistence breaks within this period. Instead there is only archaeological evidence for continued usage of natural resources along with an increase in technological and resource diversity.

The next archaeological period is Period III (4,500-500 ybp), during which time the environment again shifts to a moister and cooler climate. Marshes, meadows, and shallow lakes reform in valley bottoms similar to Period I. Archaeological data indicates that settlement and subsistence patterns continue to focus on upland resources, but with an increase in exploitation of riverine resources with the recover of tule duck decoys and twill/twined water bottles dating to this period, along with cave sites that are oriented towards lake resources (Aikens, 1982; Bard, Busby, & Findlay, 1981; D'Azevedo, 1986; Elston, 1986; Grosscup, 1974; Jennings, 1978; Thomas, 1981). Thrown darts are replaced by the bow and arrow during this time, and rabbit hunting and other small game are increasingly exploited, though large game exploitation continues though the period. Finally, pottery appears around 600 ybp at the very end of the period, replacing basketry in some areas. "Between 5,000 and 4,000 years BP the archaeological record begins to look very much as if it could have been created by people living much the way some Great Basin native people lived when Europeans first encountered them" (Grayson, 1993). However, some conclude that only in the last 1,000 years are there artifacts that clearly represent the ethnographic period (Elston, 1982, 1986; Thomas, 1981, 1994, 1999). The final period is the Modern period (500 ybp-Present), which continues the patterns established in the Late Holocene, and which I covered in chapter seven.

Like that for the Plateau, there is no direct evidence in the archaeological record of displacement or migration of any Great Basin peoples throughout prehistory (although see the discussion concerning the Numic expansion hypothesis later in this chapter). Similarly, there are various "gaps" in the archaeological database as there were for the Plateau, but these can easily be attributed to the nature of CRM work, a lack of scholarly publications resulting from CRM based investigations, and simply because of the relative lack of deeply stratified sites that span all time periods. However, despite these limitations there is a large body of evidence supporting the theory of continuing cultural adaptation and technological change by Great Basin peoples from the Early Holocene to the present.

The first line of evidence demonstrating continuity is the continued exploitation of fish species and other riverine resources dating back 10,000 ybp and extending to the present (Butler, 1996; Raven & Elston, 1988; Tuohy, 1990). Furthermore, Greenspan (1998) has recently conducted an analysis in order to determine whether many Great Basin archaeological sites are the result of natural or cultural processes that reflect exploitation of fishing.

> Taken together, the cultural context and burned condition of the bones, the quantities of fish remains in some features, the relatively large size and narrow size range of the fish remains from each feature and the presence of net weights and bone gorges are fairly compelling evidence that tui chubs were an important, deliberately fished resource for the inhabitants of the Harney Dune site. (pp. 982-983)

There is also evidence of continued exploitation of marsh plants, upland seeds, and other plant species dating back 10,000 ybp and extending to the present (Jorgensen, 1994). This use of natural resources for subsistence purposes is reflective of a cyclical subsistence lifeway pattern. This cyclical lifeway pattern, or "restricted pattern" as Elston (1982) has termed it, "is characteristic of much of the western Great Basin where winter camps and base camps tended to be located in optimal situations..." (p. 189). Likewise, the continued use of lacustrine-marsh resources, as well as seeds (bulrush, pickleweed, pine nut, or other small seeds), suggests both familiarity with Great Basin environments and subsistence continuity within the area (Elston, 1982, 1986; Elston & Zeanah, 2002; Ferguson, 1996; Raven & Elston, 1988, 1991; Rhode & Madsen, 1998). Furthermore, Eerkens (2003) has suggested that the evidence from pottery use in the Western Great Basin demonstrates that pots are located in particular areas that appear to have been used as cache sites that people returned to year after year in a cyclical fashion. This continued cyclic lifeway pattern can be seen to span through time to the ethnographic present for much of the Great Basin. "A comparison of artifacts recovered from Lovelock Cave and other sites of the same period with Northern Paiute ethnographic traits shows a great similarity between the two lots" (Grosscup, 1974, p. 20). Similarly, as Nials (1999) noted for site distributions throughout the northern Great Basin, the majority are located: 1) on or adjacent to late shorelines of pluvial lakes, 2) in alleviated areas, 3) along upland valley bottoms, 4) near springs, and 5) in rockshelters and caves. These are all areas that are reported in the ethnographic literature to have been exploited by contemporary American Indian Great Basin peoples.

A second archaeological line of evidence demonstrating continuity is a progression in lithic technology from stemmed and fluted projectile points during the Early Holocene to a gradual replacement with smaller, side-notched projectile points during the Middle Holocene, followed by the Late Holocene that contained small projectile points used on arrows, although side-notched varieties continued. This progression can be seen as a logical development of projectile points that began with the use of atlatls and spears during the Early Holocene to the development and adaptation of smaller spears and darts during the Middle Holocene, and culminating in the development of the bow and arrow during the Late Holocene. Furthermore, it should be noted that all lithic point types overlap in time, and there is no evidence of a technological break (Grayson, 1993, 2000a; Pendleton, McLane, & Thomas, 1982; Tuohy, 1988b; Tuohy & Clark, 1979; Tuohy, Dansie, & Haldeman, 1987). The Elephant Mountain Cave archaeological site located in the Winnemucca area of the western Great Basin demonstrates an example of this continued lithic technological progression. The earliest lithics recovered from this site are those of the Western Pluvial Lake tradition of stemmed points (10,000-7,000 ybp). These were found below Pinto Series Points (7,000-3,500 ybp), along with Elko Series Points (4,000-1,500 ybp), Rose Springs and Eastgate Series Points (1,500-800 ybp), and Desert Series Points (post-800 ybp).

> Based on these data, the cave appears to have been initially occupied during the Pre-Archaic (Stemmed Points) and then during the Early Archaic (Pinto Series Points). It was reoccupied [this language may be misleading] during the Middle Archaic Period (Elko Series Points) and then again during the Late Archaic (Rosegate Series Points). Finally, the presence of Desert Series Points suggests that the cave was last used during the Late Prehistoric Period. As represented by the number of points in each period, the cave was most intensively occupied during the Rosegate and Elko times, i.e., from about 4,000 years BP through 800 years BP. (Barker, 1994, pp. 3-4)

This continuous progression of lithic points it would seem, if one takes a more parsimonious perspective, to indicate that instead of being "reoccupied" as Barker states, the cave was continuously used by the peoples of the area, and that based on the lithic progression consistency, it would appear that they were the same peoples throughout time. Furthermore, it should be noted that the time of "highest" occupancy was during the supposed "Numic expansion," which would seem to contradict the idea that the Numic peoples pushed out the original inhabitants of the area. I will discuss the Numic expansion hypothesis shortly, but first there are two more lines of archaeological evidence demonstrating cultural adaptation and continuity over time.

As with the Plateau, there is continuing evidence of trade and exchange from 10,000 ybp to the present in the Great Basin. This includes the trade and exchange of obsidian from southern Oregon and California, along with the use of saltwater shells including *Olivella biplicata, Dentalium pretiosum*, and other genera from California (Elston, 1986; Erickson, 1990; Galm, 1994). This pattern of trade and exchange continues through time, fluctuating between periods of greater and lesser activity throughout the Holocene. Furthermore, many of these Early and Middle Holocene trade routes still existed in the Late Holocene as documented in the ethnographic record (Clemmer, Myers, & Rudden, 1999). However, this system of trade and exchange does not appear to have reached the extent that it did in the Plateau.

Finally, the data demonstrates continuing evidence that the peoples of the Great Basin practiced a cyclical subsistence lifeway focused on marsh and lacustrine environments, with seasonal exploitation of upland areas for various resource needs (Aikens, 1998; Bard, Busby, & Findlay, 1981; Brooks & Brooks, 1990; Connolly, 1999; D'Azevedo, 1986; Follett, 1977; Janetski, 1990; Jennings, 1978; Raven & Elston, 1988; Thomas, 1981; Tuohy, 1990; Tuohy, Dansie, & Haldeman, 1987). This cyclical subsistence lifeway pattern is established in the Late Pleistocene and Early Holocene around the numerous pluvial lakes of the period and continues through the Holocene with some areas experiencing more modification in the pattern than others based on pluvial lake desiccation and specific local environmental variables. Thus, there appears to be a deep-time knowledge and relationship to Great Basin resources that can be explained by continuous and deep-time habitation within the area by American Indian peoples.

As I have discussed, there are many "gaps" in the present understanding of the archaeological record for the Great Basin. For example, there are only a few sites that date to the Early Holocene, the same time as the Spirit Cave Mummy (10,000-7,000 ybp), and these tend to be either surface quarry sites, lithic scatters, or similarly shallow cave deposits. Likewise, from 7,500-5,000 ybp (most of Period II) few sites have presently been located, and those that have are widely scattered across the Great Basin. This makes it extremely hard to infer subsistence, settlement, population movement, and social patterns for the prehistoric peoples of the Great Basin. Furthermore, there are several "gaps" in the dataset concerning the caves of the western Great Basin. Many caves appear to have been used sporadically for various amounts of time, with intervals of several hundred to a couple thousand of years between uses when no activity seems to have taken place. Some archaeologists, including Barker, Ellis, and Damadio (2000, p. 18) note this specific lack of continuity within these particular sites and interpret it to mean discontinuity in population presence or evidence for the migration of peoples. However, these conclusions are highly problematic because they not only fail to correlate changing subsistence patterns with paleoenvironmental changes, but they also misunderstand basic characteristics of semi-nomadic, hunter-gatherer people's lifeways. As Thomas (1981) has noted, "The gaps, however, are more a reflection of the archaeologists than the archaeology" (p. 163). One example of archaeologists interpreting a lack of evidence as evidence for discontinuity as opposed to reflecting site use is the interpretation of caves as primary sites. However, these caves and rockshelters were rarely, if ever, used as residential base camps (i.e., primary sites), but instead were used for burials and as caches for equipment and goods to be used during the cyclical seasonal lifeway pattern (Elston, 1986, p. 140). Therefore, by interpreting the data from these caves and rockshelters as "typical" evidence of Great Basin people's subsistence economies, highly problematic and misleading conclusions may be reached. As Aikens (1998) notes, not only was the subsistence lifeways of these people highly complex and resourceful, but it can be traced back far into prehistory:

> The subsistence economics of this lifeway [hunter-gatherer] entailed that these Northern Uto-Aztecans routinely gathered, transported, and stored plant foods, relying on species, and on milling and other technology, that can be followed back some 10,000 years in the archaeological record of the Great Basin desert culture. (p. 4)

Finally, it is necessary for me to spend some time discussing the so-called Numic expansion hypothesis as it pertains to cultural continuity in the Great Basin. The Numic expansion hypothesis was originally proposed by Lamb (1958, 1964a, 1964b) proposed in which he claimed the Numic speaking peoples expanded across the Great Basin in recent times (around 1,000 ybp). This hypothesis has been accepted by many archaeologists as a proven theory into which they attempt to fit their data, rather than as a propositional hypothesis that is to be scientifically tested. As has been briefly discussed in previous chapters, this hypothesis fails on several levels of analyses. Not only does the biological, archaeological, and as will be discussed below the linguistic and oral tradition literature fail to support this hypothesis, but there are several inconsistencies within the hypothesis itself. Lamb (1958, 1964a, 1964b), and many others (see, for example Adovasio & Pedler, 1994; Bettinger, 1994; Bettinger & Baumhoff, 1982; Jorgensen, 1994; Simms, 1994; Young & Bettinger, 1992), have claimed that the Numic speaking peoples spread across the Great Basin approximately 1,000 ybp from an original homeland centered around the southwest corner of the Great Basin, close to the Mojave Desert.

Contrary to this hypothesis, Lyneis (1982) argued that there are many changes that took place within the supposed Numic homeland that would argue against any reason to suppose that the Numic peoples expanded into the Great Basin in recent times from such an area. Furthermore, as Thomas (1994) has pointed out concerning the Numic expansion hypothesis,

> This paper makes two simple points about the relationship of the Numic expansion linguistic model to Great Basin archaeology: 1) archaeologists using the Numic spread model have overemphasized the magic date of 1000 BP; 2) the Numic spread model has no demonstrable relevance to high-elevation archaeology of the central and western Great Basin. (p. 56)

Much of the support for the hypothetical Numic expansion hypothesis relies on either linguistic evidence (see chapter ten for a discussion of the linguistic evidence) or specific aspects of the archaeological database. As I just covered, however, the lithic and subsistence archaeological database seems to evidence a continuous progression of technological sophistication based primarily on a hunter and gatherer cyclical subsistence lifeway. Further, it is very hard to imagine how one group of people could move into an area and eventually displace the previous inhabitants with no set of superior technological or cultural advantages over those of the people being displaced, which would be required under the Numic expansion hypothesis. Likewise, it is similarly hard to imagine that peoples coming into an environment could subsist in the environment in a more "optimal" fashion than people who had been living in the environment for hundreds or thousands of years, especially with no specific technological advantages, a process which the Numic expansion hypothesis supports.

Not only is there no evidence demonstrating how the Numic peoples supposedly displaced the previous inhabitants of the Great Basin, but there is no evidence that entire lifeway areas were "abandoned" (though there is limited evidence to infer that a particular archaeological site may have been), nor that another group of people "migrated" into an area displacing the previous inhabitants. As Raven and Elston note concerning the apparent disappearance of archaeological sites in pluvial areas, "A 'sudden' appearance or disappearance of sites in the marsh could be indicative of large scale changes in the organization of prehistoric systems, but it also could be a function of changes in the location or productivity of the marsh" (Raven & Elston, 1988, p. 15). This interpretation is supported by the evidence indicating that the basin in which the Spirit Cave is located has seen continuous use from 10,000 ybp to the present (Tuohy, 1990), though at different locations within the basin. Similarly, Hogup Cave and Danger Cave in Utah show continuous use throughout the Holocene (Aikens, 1978, 1982; Jennings, 1978). These cyclical subsistence lifeway patterns were also highly diverse and complex across the Great Basin, changing as needed based on population, resource availability, and environment. To further complicate this picture, it is important to note that, "During most, if not all, time periods, groups in the Basin have ranged from almost fully sedentary to fully mobile" (Madsen, 1982, p. 207), adding to the complexity of the picture.

Unlike the Plateau, which lacks any of the usual diagnostic representations of cultural or group membership dating far back into the Holocene such as clothing, pottery, or weaving, the same is not true for the Great Basin, where woven artifacts have been recovered dating back to 9,000 ybp. This evidence has been used to support the conclusion of cultural discontinuity in the Great Basin by some archaeologists (Adovasio, 1974, 1986a, 1986b; Adovasio & Pedler, 1994; Barker, Ellis, & Damadio, 2000; Bettinger & Baumhoff, 1982), primarily based on weaving and basketry evidence. Adovasio (1986a) divides the Great Basin into three major regions: the Eastern region which includes Utah and the eastern part of Nevada; the Western region which includes western Nevada and parts of California; and the Northern region which encompasses southern Oregon and adjacent areas in Idaho and Nevada. In each of these regions Adovasio claims that there are unique basketry styles and weaving techniques that can be distinguished from the other regions, and that each of these unique basketry styles are diagnostic of a unique cultural group of people. In particular, Adovasio states, "around AD 900-1200 or slightly later, major changes occurred in the textile inventories of all three Great Basin basketry regions. These changes reflect population or ethnic discontinuities that seem to be related to the dispersion of Numic-speaking peoples" (1986a, p. 204). First, it is important to note that these three regions do not correspond to linguistic divisions, usually considered a stronger identifier of population or cultural affiliation than basketry styles. This is countered, however, by a later statement declaring that "nearly

all these groups produced textiles and most of the prehistoric textile techniques discussed here are found somewhere among historic Numic-speaking groups" (1986a,
p. 204).

Like the use of lithic point styles, there are numerous problems associated with
using weaving techniques to differentiate between population or cultural groups.
As Simms (1990) has described for ceramics, "the old distinctions between Fremont,
Promontory, and Late Prehistoric may be overstated, or at least better seen as variations in the frequency of specific morphological attributes, rather than completely
different ceramic industries" (p. 2). This same conclusion can also be reached when
looking at basketry in the Great Basin. Furthermore, basketry is considered a highly artistic skill in which innovation and individuality in *design* can be expected
between individuals, groups, and generations, but not necessarily *architectural* or
foundational techniques that are fundamentally basic to weaving and basketry formation itself. An example of this can be seen in the fact that "at least 13 different
basket wall-construction techniques are known, including at least seven basic twining variations and six coiling types" for the Northern Great Basin area (Adovasio
1986a, p. 195), and "at least 16 basketry wall techniques or types are represented in
the Western Basin region" (Adovasio 1986a, p. 197). These are all foundational
techniques necessary in constructing useful, functional baskets, and are not necessarily indicative of design techniques representing different cultural groups. As
Connolly (1999) has noted for the northern Great Basin, "The twined basketry from
the northern Great Basin exhibits continuity from Early Holocene to historic
times..." (p. 11). Finally, as Grayson (2000a) reiterates,

> Second, it is asserted that differences in textile technologies
> between two populations necessarily imply differences in ethnicity,
> such that ancestral-descendant relationships are excluded (see, for
> instance, Adovasio and Pedler, 1994). It is the second assertion that
> is extremely problematic, and it is problematic because it has never
> been shown that ancestral-descendant relationships have not and
> cannot exist if two peoples possess different textile technologies.
> (p. 4)

A modern-day example of these fundamental facts can be seen in the curio trade of
the early 1900s that created several new artistic variations and styles of basketry
among the Washoe, Mono, Paiute, and Pomo Indians of eastern California and western Nevada (Cohodas, 1999; Gigli, 1974). Recent work by some archaeologists have
taken these fundamental facts concerning the distinction between artistic variation
and actual evidence of cultural affiliation into consideration. For example, Horting
(2000), who used the same evidence as Adovasio, concluded that many of the basketry techniques used by Adovasio as markers of cultural identity, are in fact more
parsimoniously reconciled to be reflections of,

> broad environmentally-related adaptive strategies to climatically
> changing and geographically restricted floral resources.
> Specifically, coiling techniques and associated basketry forms can
> be interpreted as related to subsistence strategy, rather than the

defining criteria of population movement, which has been the accepted raison d'etre for the rise and demise of the Prehistoric Fremont in the eastern Great Basin. (p. 18)

Furthermore, it is important to note that Adovasio (1974) himself recognizes that much of the technique-based traits he uses as diagnostic indicators of "cultures" are in fact part of the general evolution of basketry throughout the Americas. "Despite some contradictory data from Mexico, the earliest technique in all areas where long sequences are available would appear to be twining which may prove to be part and parcel of the Paleo-Indian craft milieu" (Adovasio, 1974, p. 124). Furthermore, Adovasio also notes for Great Basin basketry, that "The similarities in the basketry of each region represent instead shared technologies rooted in broad, environmentally related adaptive strategies that cut across many different ethnic groups" (Adovasio, 1986a, p. 194). This would seem to indicate that using basketry as a diagnostic trait to distinguish cultural groups is seriously limited beyond merely noting the general progression of the development of basketry techniques within an area. If this were true, then it would appear that the people who made the first twining baskets within the Great Basin are descendents of the American Indians of the Great Basin today.

> Scholars who grapple with the question of tracing cultural identi-
> ties or ethnic continuities in the archaeological record never tire of
> reminding each other that artifacts do not speak and cannot reveal
> the linguistic and ethnic identity of their makers. Those who are
> willing to argue that elements of style could serve as markers of eth-
> nic identity, nevertheless have to concede that ultimately we have
> no way to be sure which elements of style mean what, in the
> absence of testimony from informants who know the meanings.
> (Aikens, 1998, p. 5)

O'Connell, Jones, and Simms also reached a similar conclusion concerning the use of basketry and cultural identity:

> Basin archaeologists commonly assume that where variation in arti-
> fact form and assemblage composition is not readily accountable in
> functional terms, it is best attributed to cultural preference. Where
> similar sets of types are found, they are often seen as a mark of eth-
> nic identity. There is good reason to doubt this inference, especial-
> ly when it is presented as an unsupported operating assumption.
> (O'Connell, Jones, & Simms, 1982, p. 228)

Finally, Earl H. Swanson, Jr., in 1972 addressed the very same question of cultural continuity and affiliation for the northern Great Basin and the Northern Shoshoni. He concluded that "The evidence at hand indicates that the ancestors of the Northern Shoshoni were in the region by 8,500-8,000 years ago..." (Swanson, 1972, p. 187). Thus, the attempt by some archaeologists to use basketry design indicators as evidence of cultural groups that are then used to support the so-called Numic expansion hypothesis would seem to be a highly dubious and unscientific methodology. If basketry evidence cannot be used to support the Numic expansion hypothesis, which is the only theory cited to evidence cultural discontinuity in the Great Basin, then the only other evidence supporting such a theory is that of linguistic data. The linguistic data, as I will discuss in the next chapter, is also highly dubious, and it seems to be more parsimonious to place the burden of proof on discontinuity and the Numic expansion hypothesis rather than the other way around.

Summary of Archaeological Evidence

During this chapter I have focused on the question of whether the archaeological evidence indicates cultural continuity or discontinuity within the Plateau and Great Basin regions. In order to adequately address this question, I reviewed several lines of archaeological evidence, beginning in Northeast Asia and discussing what the data indicated concerning technological and subsistence practices. This evidence indicated that the people of Northeast Asia practiced a cyclical subsistence lifeway pattern utilizing a wide array of natural resources. I then reviewed the evidence for Late Pleistocene and Early Holocene subsistence lifeways in the Americas, where a strong correlation was found between the peoples of Northeast Asia, their technology and subsistence practices, and those of the first peoples of the Americas. This correlation, adjusted for various ecological differences, indicates an affiliation between these two regions, though the peoples of the Americas demonstrate a continuous adaptation and technological development as one moves through the Holocene to the modern period. Furthermore, this correlational link and the discussion challenging the so-called "blitzkrieg" hypothesis demonstrates that as the first peoples occupied the Americas, they maintained their cyclical subsistence lifeway patterns, and did not continually migrate across the landscape hunting big game to the point of extinction. After these archaeological data were discussed, I then reviewed the evidence for the Plateau and Great Basin. The archaeological data for the Plateau supports cultural continuity and continuous adaptation to the changing environment throughout the Holocene, and not discontinuity or displacement. As Ames et al. (1998) concluded,

> If there is a cultural manifestation represented during this interval
> [Period II], then, it is clearly transitional in its stylistic elements
> between the better represented Period IB, and the vastly better represented Period IIIA. Any such entity must also have continued the
> subsistence orientation of the earlier time and continued a pattern
> of living that involved ephemeral and shifting, rather than stable,
> settlements. (p. 111)

Furthermore, there appears to be a consistent progression in the development of lithic tools on the Plateau, along with continued long-term trade and exchange and subsistence patterns that would all lend support to the idea of cultural continuity and adaptation.

Similarly, the preponderance of the evidence for the archaeological record of the Great Basin indicates continuous occupation of the area by Numic speaking peoples. As Brooks et al. (1988) have noted in the only report to date studying a population from one location through time, "The skeletal pathologies and anomalies add support to the suggestion that there was no marked change of occupants of the Stillwater Marsh area over time, since there was no grouping of a particular pathology or anomaly through archaeological association" (Brooks et al., 1988, p. 153). Likewise, as Cressman (1977) notes, "Great Basin culture was essentially an indigenous growth, and its remarkable conservatism is perhaps unique in the field of culture history. This continuity in material culture and exploitative activity is presumptive evidence of continuity also in social organization" (p. 124). Furthermore, there is no evidence for migration or cultural discontinuity when all of the archaeological record is reviewed, as was concluded for the Plateau. Although there are numerous "gaps" in the archaeological database for both the Plateau and Great Basin, these must be considered as gaps in our archaeological knowledge, and not necessarily as evidence of regional abandonment or migration. Certainly these processes took place in prehistory, but all of the archaeological evidence reviewed indicates that the most parsimonious interpretation of the current database is one of continuous occupation of these regions through time, along with continued technological adaptation and development.

CHAPTER 10
LINGUISTIC EVIDENCE

T he penultimate line of inquiry that NAGPRA mandates in determining cultural affiliation as covered in chapter three, and that I review in this book, is that of linguistic evidence. Unlike the other lines of evidence thus far reviewed, linguistic evidence proves to be highly troublesome beyond the historic period. This is because linguistic evidence leaves no object behind from which linguistic data can be arrived at (except for in the form of written texts or hieroglyphics, neither of which occurred in North America). Further complicating this line of inquiry is the fact that there is no agreed upon method of reconstructing proto-languages or language phylogenies. That is, there is no agreed upon method of determining when various languages and language families diverged from each other. This is particularly evident when attempting to reconstruct languages beyond a few thousand years, as is the case for the Plateau and Great Basin. For example, Forster and Toth (2003) demonstrate that even within linguistic studies of Indo-European, the largest and best-documented language family in the world, "the reconstruction of the Indo-European [phylogenetic] tree, first proposed in 1863, has remained controversial" (p. 9079).

Two primary methods have been used when investigating the question of linguistic affiliation in the Americas, that of historical linguistics or multilateral comparison. The method of historical linguistics is widely used and has been stringently developed for the past hundred plus years when it was originally proposed by August Schleicher. Contrary to this, the method of multilateral comparison was developed by Greenberg (1987), and has been rarely used by other linguists. In either case, extreme caution should be exercised in using linguistic classifications, and conclusions derived from them, especially those that are based on the comparison of super-

ficially similar words and grammatical elements. The linguistic evidence as presently known is compatible with a wide range of possible scenarios for the earliest peopling of the Americas and the affiliation of contemporary American Indian peoples
with these earliest colonizers. In exploring the best fit between linguistic evidence
and nonlinguistic evidence concerning cultural affiliation, only historically and
empirically grounded hypotheses will prove to be of value (Campbell, 1997;
Goddard & Campbell, 1994). This is because the relationship between linguistic history and other aspects of history is highly complex, and simple assumptions about
this relationship are risky. People can learn and pass on new languages or reinter-
pret languages, symbols, and other related linguistic items. Likewise, languages can
become extinct in populations that can survive culturally or biologically. As a consequence, attempts to correlate language groupings with cultural populations or
cultural movements at deep time levels face major obstacles. For example, it is well
known that the language spoken by a group of people may come and go and it is
likely that language replacement and extinction have been, over time, relatively
common phenomena.

   In the present survey, various linguistic terminologies are used to help clarify the
various complexities surrounding linguistic analyses. "Dialect" is used here to mean
only a variety (regional or social) of a language that is mutually intelligible (however difficult this concept may be to define or apply in practice) with other dialects of
the same language. It does not mean, as it does in the usage of some historical linguists (especially in the past), a daughter language in a language family. "Language"
means any distinct linguistic entity that is mutually unintelligible with other languages. A language "family" is a group of *genetically* related languages, ones that
share a linguistic kinship by virtue of having developed from a common earlier
ancestor. Thus, it is common to find linguistic families being designated with the
suffix -an (e.g., Algonquian, Athapaskan, Uto-Aztecan). In addition, the term
"genetic unit," less commonly encountered in the literature, is used to designate
independent (or otherwise of unknown relation) families and isolates, i.e., Washoe
(*sensu* Campbell, 1997). Furthermore, it is important to note that language families can be of different magnitudes. That is, they can have different time depths,
with some larger-scale families including smaller-scale families as their members or
branches (e.g., Celtic is a language family that has a shallower time depth than the
larger language family of Indo-European, of which Celtic is part). However, linguists use a wide array of confusing terms to distinguish more inclusive from less
inclusive family groupings. For example, the term subgroup (also termed subfamily or branch) means a group of languages within a well-defined language family that
are more closely related to each other than to other languages of that family; they
constitute a branch of that family (i.e., Numic is a subfamily of Uto-Aztecan).

   Terms that have been used for postulated but undemonstrated higher order, more
inclusive families (i.e., proposed distant genetic relationships) include "stock," "phylum," and the compounding element "macro-" (as in macro-family, macro-stock,
and macro-phylum). These terms have become confusing and controversial, as
might be expected when proposed names for entities that are not fully agreed to
exist are at stake (such as Greenberg's Amerind). Stock is ambiguous in that in
older linguistic usage it was equivalent to "language family" (a direct transfer of the

common German linguistic term *Stamm* [or *Sprachstamm*]). However, the term has often been used in America to indicate a postulated but unconfirmed larger long-range grouping that would include more than one established language family or genetic unit (Campbell, 1997; Goddard & Campbell, 1994; Ruhlen, 1986; Sherzer, 1976), such as Penutian in the Plateau. Finally, the terms phylum and macro have also been used to designate large-scale or long-range proposed but unestablished language families. To avoid as much confusion and controversy as possible I will not use these terms, and instead I solely use the term family which appears both sufficient and not as controversial. This is because if the entities called "stock," "phylum," or "macro-" were to be found to be correct, they would in fact be families, and therefore they can simply be referred to as "proposed distant genetic relationship," "postulated family," "hypothesized remote affinity," and so forth (Campbell, 1997).

As I noted at the beginning of this chapter, there are two dominant approaches to the study of the relationships among American Indian languages, which can be referred to as "multilateral word comparison" and "standard historical linguistics" (Aikens, 1998; Bateman, Goddard, O'Grady, Funk, Mooi, Kress, & Cannell, 1990; Campbell, 1997; Davidson, 1999; Forster & Toth, 2003; Foster, 1996; Goddard & Campbell, 1994; Goss, 1977; Greenberg, 1987; Greenberg, Turner, & Zegura, 1986; Hill, 2000; Krauss & Golla, 1981; Lamb, 1958, 1964a; Lamberg-Karlovsky, 2002; Mithun, 1990; Ruhlen, 1986, 1987, 1994). As I mentioned, The multilateral word comparison method has been employed predominately by Greenberg (1987, 1986) and Ruhlen (1986, 1987, 1994), who simply call it "multilateral comparison," an allusion to the large number of languages surveyed in the method. These scholars present their data in the form of lists containing numerous sets of words that are superficially "similar in sound and meaning" (Ruhlen, 1987, p. 6), along with discursive considerations of similarities in grammatical morphemes. The aim of the method is classification, but the classification that results from it is simply a codified statement of the judgments of similarity that have been made in assembling the sets of words.

On the other hand, the approach of standard historical linguistics employs techniques for formulating and testing hypotheses about the undocumented history of languages. These techniques have been developed and refined, over the last century and more, on the basis of the study of the historical changes undergone by a wide variety of languages. The goal of historical linguistics is to work out the linguistic history of languages and thereby to determine the principles and factors that govern language change (Campbell, 1997; Goddard & Campbell, 1994).

These two methods have also been called the "lumpers" or the "inspectional approach" and the "splitters" or the "assessment approach." The so-called lumpers seek to reduce the number of language families in the Americas by proposing more inclusive and more remote relationships among the language groups. On the other hand, the so-called splitters ask for explicit evidence for proposals of distant relationship, rejecting those proposals for which the evidence is not found to be compelling. Golla calls the former approach "the inspectional route to genetic classification" (1988, p. 434), while Watkins calls it "etymology by inspection" (1990, p.

293). The terms used by Golla and Watkins reflect the fact that Greenberg's method depends essentially on lexical similarities determined by visual inspection. The assessment approach, dubbed "the major alternative" by Greenberg et al. (1986, p. 477), employs standard techniques of historical linguistics to attempt to work out the linguistic history of the languages involved.

As with the biological and archaeological databases, there are several limitations that are inherent to either one of these linguistic methods. Of primary concern here is the fact that after related languages have been separated for only a few thousand years, the resemblances between them that are due to their historical connections decrease through normal linguistic changes. The longer languages have been separated, the harder it becomes to develop a proper phylogenetic tree demonstrating the history of the particular language and how it relates to other languages.

These limitations in reconstructing the phylogenetic tree of languages in the Americas is particularly evidence in the work of Greenberg, Turner, and Zegura (1986) and Greenberg (1987) who used multilateral word comparison to examine the rate of retention of a specific list of 200 words. They determined that slightly more than 80 percent of this list is retained over 1,000 years, and that it is possible to designated three primary language families (Amerind, Na-Dene, and Aleut-Eskimo) that are thought to be ancestral to all contemporary American Indian languages, a conclusion that has been highly contested.

This theoretical work has not generally met with success among specialists in the field, for example see discussions by Adelaar (1989), Campbell (1997), Chafe (1987), Goddard (1996a; see also, Goddard & Campbell, 1994), Golla (1988), and Matisoff (1990). As these authors demonstrate, both Greenberg's methodology and its application are severely limited and controversial. For example, the initial step in comparative work has always been a survey of languages for obvious similarities. The better one knows the languages, of course, the more similarities one can perceive. When superficial resemblances are detected among a set of languages, one can begin to determine whether these are due to chance, borrowing, or to common inheritance. Greenberg's methodology is essentially the first step without the second, more important step. As noted his method consists of what he terms "multilateral comparison," through which one can look "at the basic vocabulary and concrete grammatical markers of a large number of languages simultaneously" (Greenberg, 1987, p. 648).

It is through this "multilateral comparison" that Greenberg feels the genius of the method lies. It is certainly true that more similarities will be found among 15 languages considered simultaneously, for example, than between any two. Likewise, when the number of languages one compares is raised to 2,000, all the more similarities will become obvious. However, a primary critique of Greenberg's method is his failure to take into account the mounting role of chance in the comparison process. The more languages considered, the more likely resemblances would appear. Mohawk, for example, contains 8 consonants: t, k, s, n, r, y, h, ?. The root verb for "eat" is -k-. It is doubtful that one would have to look too far to find another language with a verb containing k, or perhaps a sound somewhat similar such as g or x, whose meaning is something like "consume," "eat," "bite," "chew," etc., which would be similarity through chance. Unfortunately, Greenberg's multilateral word comparison stops short of separating the role of chance from that of genetic relationship in producing these resemblances (Mithun, 1990). Likewise, on the basis of initial visual inspection (which is how Greenberg makes determinations concerning what he calls "etymologies"), English two (phonetically pronounced "tu") might appear to be more closely related to Lithuanian "du" or Latin "duo" than to German "zwei" (phonetically pronounced as "tsvai"), which in fact it is not (Campbell, 1997).

Similarly, many linguists have pointed out that the data Greenberg utilized in his study were of a poor quality. For example, his data were often drawn from brief early notes made by explorers passing through an area for the first time, such as those mentioned in chapter five, rather than the rich, linguistically superior dictionaries and grammars now available for many languages. Furthermore, in an attempt to increase the compatibility of the lists, Greenberg retranscribed them into his own phonetic system, apparently without knowledge of the actual phonetic systems of the languages (Mithun, 1990). Thus, many linguists have claimed that numerous errors have been introduced into Greenberg's dataset. The retranscription additionally renders it impossible to recover the original sources of the material, none of which are cited because "listing all these sources in a general bibliography would have added greatly to the length and cost of the work" (Greenberg, 1987, p. xv).

Finally, it has been noted that while basic vocabulary is on the whole more resistant to replacement than lexical items from other sectors of the vocabulary, such basic words are in fact also often replaced, so that even in clearly related languages, not all basic vocabulary reflects true cognates. This was one of the valid insights of Swadesh's glottochronology, generally discredited as a method of dating, but nevertheless based on the valid observation that even basic vocabulary can be and is replaced over time (Bright, 1970; Campbell, 1997; Forster & Toth, 2003; Lightner, 1971).

Thus, as has been discussed, multilateral word comparison has been rejected by most linguists, primarily since all of its basic assumptions have been challenged and demonstrated to be invalid (Campbell, 1997; Goddard, 1996a; Goddard & Campbell, 1994; Goss, 1977). As these linguists have pointed out, multilateral word comparison does not find or test relationships, but instead it assumes that the languages being compared are related and proceeds to attach a date based on the number of lexical similarities between the languages that are checked off. As a result of a priori assumptions in this methodology, some language groupings in Greenberg's analyses (1987) are now thought to be indisputably wrong.

Beyond these methodological problems associated with the multilateral word comparison method, it is important to point out some of the factual limitatinos in the data that Greenberg (1987) uses. This is because Greenberg's theoretical linguistic groupings have been used as evidence that biological and archaeological data have been accorded to. As I discussed in chapters eight and nine, the biological and archaeological data have been used to both support and as evidence for some of Greenberg's linguistic conclusions. However, if not only the methodology but also the data themselves can be seriously questioned, then so must the biological and archaeological conclusions that rest on this dataset and method. A primary problem with Greenberg's dataset is that some language names into the dataset are not languages at all. For example, Membreno, which Greenberg (1987, pp. 194, 293, 382, 425) classified as a Lencan language, "is actually the name of a person, a reference (Alberto Membreno 1897) which contains several Lenca word lists from different Honduran towns" (Campbell, 1997).

In several instances, Greenberg gave the names of towns where a certain language was spoken as names of distinct languages (1987:382 and elsewhere): for example, there are not six Lencan languages; there are only two, though Greenberg gives as languages such town names as Guajiquero [sic, Guajiquiro], Intibucat [sic, Intibuca], Opatoro, and Similaton. Papantla is not a separate Totonacan language but a town where Totonac is spoken (Greenberg 1987:380); Chiripo and Estrella, presented as Talamancan languages (Greenberg 1987:382) are names of towns where Cabecar is spoken. "Viceyta" (given by Greenberg 1987 as also Talamancan) is a colonial name which referred to both Bribri and Cabecar, and certainly not to a third independent language. Moreover, Terraba, tiribi, and Tirub are also not separate languages but rather refer to Tiribi. The christianized Tiribi brought by the Spanish from Panama to Costa Rica after 1700 are called Terraba; Tirub is merely the native version of the name of Tiribi that some scholars prefer to use (see Greenberg 1987:382).

> Corobisi is a language name found in Spanish sources from the sixteenth and early seventeenth centuries, but no word of this language is known to have been recorded and preserved, and therefore its colonial referent is unknown. Eduard Conzemius (1930) nevertheless equated a word list from Upala with the Corobisi language, though Upala is not in the area attributed to the Corobisi in colonial reports (but it is near it). This word list turned out to be Rama, but whether the colonial Corobisi may have been associated somehow with Rama remains unknown. In any case, the Corobisi of Conzemius and Rama are not distinct languages, though Greenberg (1987:111) grouped his version of Corobisi with Guatuso, Cabecar, and Rama on the basis of a single cited "Corobisi" form (see Campbell 1988b:610). (pp. 14-15)

Further problems abound in the dataset, and it becomes clear that many of the datasets Greenberg uses in his analysis are flawed.

At this point I breifly trace the history of American Indian linguistic classifications in order to better illustrate how present-day linguistic understandings have been arrived at, and how these linguistic classifications fit with the question of cultural affiliation in the Plateau and Great Basin. The first to classify American Indian languages in some fashion was that of John Wesley Powell. Powell's (1891a) classification of the American Indian languages north of Mexico, which included 58 families (or "stocks"), became the baseline for subsequent work in the classification of American Indian languages; "the cornerstone of the linguistic edifice in aboriginal

North America" (Sapir, 1917, p. 79).

In spite of his impact on most subsequent work, Powell's method was not very refined. Instead, it appears to have been a rather impressionistic inspection of rough word lists and vocabularies gathered from the field, "The evidence of cognation [that daughter languages are derived from a common ancestral family] is derived exclusively from the vocabulary" (Powell, 1891b, p. 11). Subsequently, Franz Boas took the lead from Powell in classifying American Indian languages (1911a). Boas, as has been well documented (Darnell, 1969; Orta, 2004), came to be associated with a cultural particularist approach to language and culture, in which he compared and contrasted the typological traits of languages in a particular geographical area to determine how they might have been reshaped as a result of mutual influence in that limited area. Darnell (1969) has suggested that it was Boas's work with the diffusion of folklore elements among Northwest Coast groups that convinced him of the difficulty of distinguishing linguistic traits that are due to a genetic linguistic relationship from those that are due to simple linguistic borrowing.

At about the same time as Boas, Paul Radin (1919) also published some influential work concerning American Indian languages. Radin argued that all American Indian languages are genetically related and belong to one large family. He saw in his colleagues' work (that of Alfred Kroeber, and Edward Sapir) only 12 remaining independent groups and felt that merging them into one was "hardly so revolutionary" (1919, p. 490). However, most of Radin's contemporaries did not accept his attempt to unite all these languages (Campbell, 1997).

Today, American Indian language classification has been greatly influenced by the opinions of these early linguists, especially that of Sapir and his followers, which Greenberg has claimed allegiance to more recently. As both Golla (1988, p. 435) and Rankin (1992) have independently pointed out, the methods of Greenberg and Sapir are fundamentally different, in spite of their shared interest in large-scale consolidation of linguistic groups in the Americas. A basic fact on which all linguists agree is that there historically was extensive linguistic diversity in the Americas. Greenberg claims that the Americas were settled by three separate population movements (the three wave migration theory), equated in his linguistic terms with Amerind, Na-Dene, and Aleut-Eskimo, in that chonological order (Greenberg, 1987; Greenberg, Turner, & Zegura, 1986, p. 477). However, those who advocate the historical linguistic approach count approximately 55 genetic units (families and isolates) in North America, 10 in Middle America, and more than 80 in South America, a total of approximately 150 distinct genetic units, and not the three of Greenberg (Campbell, 1997). Furthermore, it is important to keep in mind that supporters of the historical linguistic approach put little stock in these numbers, since it is anticipated (or at least hoped) that continued research will demonstrate additional legitimate connections, thus further reducing the total number of genetic units (a view that is frequently misrepresented by its detractors). Most of these supporters are sympathetic to the notion that many or perhaps all American Indian languages may be related, but historical linguistic scholars believe that this cannot be demonstrated at present because of the great time depth and the inadequacy of linguistic methods to recover history after so much change has taken place. Thus, according to this view, it cannot be demonstrated that two American Indian languages — or any two languages, for that matter — are not related, and the burden of proof falls on those who claim that closer affinity exists among some groups than among others (Bright, 1970; Campbell, 1997; Goddard & Campbell, 1994).

As I just noted, the tripartite classification of American Indian languages (that is, Eskimo-Aleut, Na-Dene, and all others) is not new, but reflects the opinion handed down since Sapir (1917). This tripartite view has also diffused widely into the thinking of many nonlinguists on the matter, especially the genetic anthropologists as discussed in chapter eight (Bonatto & Salzano, 1997a; Easton, Merriwether, Crews, & Ferrell, 1996; Forster, Harding, Torroni, & Bandelt, 1996; Jones, 2002; Karafet, Zegura, Vuturo-Brady, Posukh, Osipova, Wiebe, Romero, Long, Harihara, Jin, Dashnyam, Gerelsaikhan, Keiichi, & Hammer, 1997; Karafet, Zegura, Posukh, Osipova, Bergen, Long, Goldman, Klitz, Harihara, de Knijff, Wiebe, Griffiths, Templeton, & Hammer, 1999; Lorenz & Smith, 1996; Merriwether, Rothhammer, & Ferrell, 1995; Schurr & Wallace, 1999; Smith, Malhi, Eshleman, Lorenz, & Kaestle, 1999; Torroni, Theodore G. Schurr, Yang, Szathmary, Williams, Schanfield, Troup, Knowler, Lawrence, Weiss, & Wallace, 1992; Wallace & Torroni, 1992). Therefore, Greenberg's three groupings, though highly controversial, are not necessarily new, but instead clearly continue the tradition established by Sapir.

Finally, before I discuss the linguistic evidence for the Plateau and Great Basin specifically, it is important to note that all of these theories are compounded by the fact that American Indian linguistic classifications are highly complex and not straight forward. Moreover, as Lamb himself cautioned, "expansion and extinction of languages are not the same as expansion and extinction of people. Clearly, prehistorians must be very careful about using geographic distributions of linguistic families as evidence for past movements of people" (1964b, p. 461). Attempts to correlate language classifications with biological or archaeological "cultures" face grave difficulties. In fact, a single language can be spoken by a genetically diverse population (for example, Euroamericans, African Americans, American Indians, and Asian Americans, as well as many other people throughout the world speak American English), or a genetically homogeneous group may speak more than one language (many multilingual American Indian communities speak English or Spanish and their native language, or speak more than one American Indian language). That is, both multilingualism and language shift or loss are facts of linguistic life — genes neither cause these phenomena nor are correlated to them (Campbell, 1997; Goddard & Campbell, 1994).

There is also a fairly large body of evidence amongst the ethnographic literature documenting how language usage is not directly related to or corresponds to biological or archaeological "cultures." For example, in 1839 Duff found that 10 percent of the American Indian population of the lower Fraser region on the Plateau and Northwest Coast boundary were slaves, and figures from 1845 indicate that slaves then constituted 6 percent of the population of the whole Northwest Coast region (Amoss, 1993, pp. 10-11). When the numbers of refugees from other villages and intermarriages (where in this region polygyny was correlated with wealth) are added to this, it becomes quite evident that the amount of genetic flow across linguistic and cultural borders was not insignificant in the Northwest Coast culture area (see Suttles, 1990). Therefore, the Northwest Coast is precisely an area where we would not expect the extant linguistic diversity and human genetic traits to be correlated as a clear reflection of earlier history (particularly given the fact that a large number of different languages from several different language families are found in this area). Given this situation, it is no great surprise that Turner's Na-Dene dental cluster (Greater Northwest Coast group), as was discussed in chapter eight, turns out to be represented by members of all three of Greenberg's major linguistic groups, and that it does not correlate well with any one of them.

Many of these claimed biological-linguistic correlations have proven inaccurate, and in any case a close correspondence is not to be expected, since human populations easily can and frequently do lose their language, shift to the language of others, or become multilingual. Moreover, human biological and archaeological features easily flow across language borders by means of the cultural mechanisms of intermarriage, slavery, and various types of contact. A close biological-linguistic correlation is probably more the exception than the rule in some culture areas of the Americas (Campbell, 1997; Hill, 2000; Sherzer, 1976).

As has been discussed, American Indian language classifications are still very controversial when one attempts to reconstruct in deep time the larger families from which many of the present American Indian languages are hypothesized to have stemmed. However, there is some general consensus when examining specific families, such as Uto-Aztecan, Sahaptian, Algonquin, Salishan, and others. The two language families that are relevant for the purposes of this book are the hypothesized Penutian family of the Plateau, and the relatively agreed upon Uto-Aztecan family of the Great Basin, parts of the Southwest region, and areas of Mexico. I will now first discuss the Plateau, followed by the Great Basin

The Plateau culture region is dominated by two language families, the Sahaptian and the Salishan, which are hypothesized to be a part of the larger Penutian family. Sahaptian historically was, and still is in some places, spoken throughout the southern Plateau area, from the west of the Cascade divide in Washington and Oregon to the Rocky Mountains on the east. Within this large area of the southern Plateau, the several American Indian groups that inhabited this area, also historically spoke a wide array of languages. The languages commonly thought to make up the Plateau culture region are: the Sahaptian family (Nez Perce and Sahaptin); Upper Chinook (Kiksht); Nicola (Athabaskan); and Cayuse, Molala, Klamath, Kootenai (Kutenai), and Interior Salishan (a subgroup of the Salishan family with several members). As covered in chapters five and seven, the Plateau is a relatively clearly defined culture area, but whether it constitutes a legitimate linguistic area or whether it should be included in the Northwest Coast region (since most of the traits of its languages are also found in the Northwest Coast area) is an open question. Kinkade, Elmendorf, Rigsby, and Aoki (1998) are of the opinion that "there is no outstanding set of language traits that sets off the Plateau as a major linguistic diffusion area distinct from other regions; rather it is part of a larger area that includes the Northwest Coast culture area" (1998, p. 63). In the northern section of the southern Plateau such dialect groups include Klickitat, Yakama, Taitnapam (also known as Upper Cowlitz); Upper Nisqually (Mishalpam); Wanapum, Tygh, Palouse (Palus); Wallawalla (Waluulapam); and Lower Snake (Chamnapam, Wauyukma, and Naxiyampam). The Columbia River section includes Tygh Valley; Tenino; Celilo (Wayampam); John Day; Rock Creek; and Umatilla. Finally, on the east, the large Nez Perce dialect group was also part of the Sahaptian language family (Campbell, 1997; Goddard, 1996b; Kinkade, Elmendorf, Rigsby, & Aoki, 1998).

Sahaptian is often thought to be a principal member of the proposed Penutian family originally proposed by Kroeber (1939). However, in spite of Kroeber's role in launching the Penutian family hypothesis and his early use of methods that were less than precise in attempts to reduce the number of independent language families in North America, he came to have serious reservations about Sapir's broader conception of Penutian and about the methods upon which it was based (Campbell, 1997; Sapir, 1917). Though it remained controversial, Sapir's Penutian was initially widely accepted by other linguists. Since Sapir's work, more extensive descriptive materials on most of these languages have become available and much historical research has been undertaken, demonstrating that presently the Penutian family Hypothesis fails on several accounts (Campbell, 1997; Goddard, 1996b). However, there is considerable evidence that Sahaptian, Klamath, and Molala are related, though in what phylogenetic fashion remains unclear (Kinkade, Elmendorf, Rigsby, & Aoki, 1998).

Therefore, the prevailing attitude today among Plateau specialists is that the languages involved in the various versions of the Penutian hypothesis have not been successfully shown to be related. Therefore, one should not put much faith in the original Penutian family hypothesis and, by implication, certainly not in the broader Macro-Penutian proposals (see Shipley, 1980; Whistler, 1977). However, the evidence that at least some of these languages share broader genetic relationships is also mounting, and most scholars do not discount entirely the possibility that the near future will see more successful demonstrations of these family relations (Campbell, 1997; Goddard, 1996b; Kinkade et al., 1998). Therefore, although the Penutian language family is still contentious, it will be used in this book to designate the proto-family of Sahaptian, Interior Salishan, Klamath, and Molala. However, this does not mean that at a future date these languages may be not be related. Instead, it is simply a way to talk about the Plateau region in linguistic terms during the Late Pleistocene and the Early and Middle Holocene.

As has been discussed, Sahaptian (the modern language family of the Nez Perce, Yakama, and other Interior Columbia Basin tribes) is part of the hypothesized Penutian language family which Ruhlen (1994), Swadesh (1954), and Hunn (2000) all believe to be ancestral to southern Oregon and northern California. Likewise, Hunn (2000) and Rigsby (1969) believe that proto-Penutian was spoken in the Columbia Plateau dating back to as early as 8,000-9,000 years ago. One of the commonly used arguments against linguistic affiliation across such a long timespan is that the hypothesized proto-Penutian language of the Early Holocene was most likely not mutually intelligible with Plateau languages of today. However, what many fail to realize is that this is true for all languages over time, and this does not logically lead to the conclusion that modern American Indian peoples of the Plateau (Penutian speakers) are not linguistically affiliated or descended from these Early Holocene Penutian speakers. All languages evolve over time and it can only be reasonably concluded that two peoples are not linguistically affiliated if they speak languages from different languages phylums, such as Penutian and Indo-European. This is not the case in the Plateau as noted by Hunn (2000), Rigsby (1969), Swadesh (1954) and Ruhlen (1994). Furthermore, and perhaps more telling, is the fact that there is no linguistic evidence that any other language was spoken in the Plateau at some point in history other than Penutian or one of its daughter languages. Therefore, the preponderance of evidence suggests that the Plateau is the location where Penutian, and subsequently Sahaptian, developed, and it can be concluded that prehistoric American Indian peoples of the Columbia Basin spoke an earlier version of either Penutian (the larger language phylum) or Sahaptian (a language family within the Penutian phylum).

Turning to the Great Basin, it appears that a similar linguistic understanding has developed. As defined by Sherzer (1973, 1976) and Miller (1986), the languages of the Great Basin linguistic area are those of the Numic branch of Uto-Aztecan along with the linguistic isolate Washoe. The Numic branch of Uto-Aztecan can be further broken down into three general areas, the Western, Central, and Southern. The Western grouping of the Numic branch includes the Paviotso-Bannock-Snake (Northern Paiute) and Monache (Mono) dialects. The Central grouping includes the Shoshoni-Goshiute, Panamint, and Comanche dialects. Finally, the Southern grouping includes the Southern Paiute, Ute, Chemehuevi, and Kawaiisu dialects.

Though there are many similarities between the Numic branch of the Uto-Aztecan family, there is some reason to doubt that the Great Basin is a legitimately defined linguistic area as was also the case for the Plateau, primarily because the common traits in Washoe and Numic are also found in languages of adjacent areas. As Jacobsen (1986) points out:

> This approach [Sherzer's] of starting out from culture areas seems to introduce some distortions as applied to Washoe, in that it minimizes the comparably great similarities to the California stocks (some of which Sherzer 1976:128, 164, 167, 238-239, 246 indeed notes). For example, ... the two striking points of agreement, presence of i and n, are also shared with groups to the west, while the other features of Washoe- presence of glottalized stops, l, and a s/s contrast, and absence of Kw- separate it from Numic and unite it with one or more of its western neighbors. (p. 110)

Jacobsen (1986, p. 110) mentions other features that are common to Great Basin (Numic) and California languages. For example, similarities between Washoe and Northern Paiute systems of kinship terminology are shared with the Miwok and Yokuts, and the Washoe reduplication pattern is similar to that of Numic but also to that of Maiduan and less so also to that of Sierra Miwok. Likewise, instrumental verb prefixes are shared by Washoe and Numic (where they are unique among Uto-Aztecan languages) and are also found in Maiduan, Shasta, and Achumawi. Finally, the pronomial inclusive/exclusive distinction, innovative in both Washoe and Numic, is found also in Miwokan. Jacobsen (1980) further argues that this distinction diffused in a number of more or less contiguous languages of north-central California, the Great Basin, and their neighbors — in Numic (Uto-Aztecan), Washoe (an isolate), Tubatulabal (Uto-Aztecan), Yuki (Yukian), Palaihnihan (primarily in Achumawi), Wintu (Wintuan), Sahaptin (Sahapatian, in the Plateau area, bordering the Northern Paiute), Shuswap (Interior Salish, also located in the Plateau), Kwakiutl (Wakashan), and languages of the east: Algonquian, Siouan, Iroquoian, Kiowa, Pawnee, and Yuchi. Both the inclusive/exclusive contrast and switch-reference are also widely found in contiguous languages extending across a large area (Jacobsen, 1986). Thus, the whole concept of a Great Basin linguistic area may be questioned, and it may be merely an extension of the Northern California linguistic area. In any case, it demonstrates the difficulties that can be created by assuming, as Sherzer (1973, 1976) does, that culture areas and linguistic areas will coincide.

Furthermore, the Numic languages of the Great Basin also have some interesting enigmas. For example, Bettinger and Baumhoff (1982, p. 490) note that it is peculiar, "why the same Shoshone language spoken at Tonopah, Nevada was also spoken on the Snake River, Idaho, while it differed substantially from the Mono Lake Paiute language only a few miles west of Tonopah." They claim that the only realistic explanation for such a phenomenon is the Numic expansion hypothesis. However, based on the proposed expansion model and the "wedge-shaped distribution of the subbranches" (Bettinger & Baumhoff, 1982, p. 490), both the Tonopah and Mono Lake languages would fall under the Western sub-branch while the Snake River language would fall under the Central branch, which would seem to contradict the Numic expansion hypothesis, not support it.

As discussed above, although many linguists disagree with Greenberg's (1987; 1986) classification of three primary language families for all American Indian tribes, most agree on the designation of the Uto-Aztecan language family. Uto-Aztecan is one of the oldest language phylums in the Americas, stretching from central Mexico to southern Oregon and consists of many well-known modern American Indian languages such as Aztec to the south and Numic in the north. The hypothesized Numic expansion is based on the linguistic technique of multilateral word comparison discussed above, and hypothesizes that this language expansion took place around 1,000 years ago (Lamb, 1958, 1964a). However, as Aikens (1998) and others have noted, granting the superphylum relationship of Uto-Aztecan to Penutian could reasonably carry the thread of linguistic continuity argued in this book back into the earliest phase of Great Basin occupation in western North America. As Goss (1977) also pointed out, this is the most parsimonious hypothesis by which to link archaeological and linguistic prehistory in the desert west, and no factual evidence suggests a better conclusion. Finally, like that for the Plateau linguistic evidence, there is no data that would indicate that there was another language family in the Great Basin prior to the so-called Numic expansion. In fact, the linguistic data for the Great Basin evidences a deep time occupation in the region with no evidence of a linguistic break or disruption

Linguistic Evidence Summary

In this chapter I reviewed the evidence for linguistic affiliation in the Plateau and Great Basin, beginning with a discussion of the two primary methods used for reconstructing historic linguistic affiliations. Greenberg's method of multilateral word comparison was discussed, focusing on the method itself as well as the data used in his analyses. The possibility of reducing American Indian languages down to the tripartite divisions that Greenberg argues for is highly circumspect, even by the more accepted method of historical linguistics. I then briefly discussed the historic formation of the various language families that are accepted by anthropological linguists, focusing on the Plateau and Great Basin. Finally, the chapter concluded with a discussion of the linguistic evidence for linguistic affiliation in the Plateau, focusing on the possibility of a Penutian family that incorporates all Plateau languages, and on the Numic expansion hypothesis and the language family of Uto-Aztecan in the Great Basin. The linguistic evidence argues for linguistic affiliation in both the Plateau and Great Basin between the language of Early Holocene peoples and that of the present-day American Indians. Furthermore, there is no linguistic evidence that would support the conclusion of either language discontinuity or of the migration of people speaking a different language into either area, replacing a different language speaking people. The final line of evidence that I will review in this book is that of oral tradition evidence, which is related to linguistic evidence, although instead of focusing on the language spoken, the next chapter focuses on what is said with the language.

CHAPTER 11
ORAL TRADITION EVIDENCE

The final line of evidence I will review in this book is that of oral tradition evidence. Like linguistic evidence as discussed in the last chapter, there is no agreed upon method of reconstructing oral tradition evidence in deep time. Similarly, there is no agreed upon method of reconstructing changes in oral tradition evidence. However, that does not diminish the oral tradition evidence that is available, nor does it decrease its importance in accord with an epistemological praxis of epoché, as discussed in chapter two. In fact, there is a large body of evidence that shares common creation stories throughout the Plateau and Great Basin tribes. It should be noted, first, that oral traditions are different than myths, legends, fairytales, and the like for one primary reason. Oral traditions contain information that is highly valued by the society of whom they are part of, and they usually are based in some form of "truth" (cultural, physical, or social). Myths, legends, and fairytales may contain information that is useful in teaching morals and values to individuals of the social group, but they are usually not grounded in a sociocultural valid "truth," and thus are subject to change much more readily than oral traditions. Despite this, however, both theoretical considerations and empirical evidence indicates that usage of information drawn from oral traditions is a delicate exercise at best. Oral tradition evidence must be used with great care by linguists and folklorists who are intimately familiar with both the languages of the peoples whose oral traditions are being examined, as well as their highly symbolic and metaphorical content. Likewise, as will be discussed below, empirical proof of prehistoric migrations or claims that oral traditions do not date to deep time requires evidence in other areas of inquiry. For example, review of American Indian oral traditions from the Plateau and Great Basin, and more broadly from other parts of North America, indicates that giants, red headed beings, and other fantastic creatures reflect world wide patterns of psychological projections found in oral literature (Aoki & Walker, 1989; Bascom, 1965; Bath, 1977; Clark, 1953; Dangberg, 1968; Drews, 1988; Dundes, 1965a; Liljeblad, 1986; Olrik, 1965; Ramsey, 1977; Thompson, 1977; Thoms, 1965; Vansina, 1985). There is little reason to believe, therefore, that giants, red headed beings, little people, ogres, cannibal monsters, and other oral tradition creatures represent prehistoric "races" or "cultures" as some have concluded (see Barker, Ellis, & Damadio, 2000) Nor does the available evidence from oral traditions support the idea of migrations in which the ancestral Sahaptians and Uto-Aztecans moved into the Plateau and Great Basin, displacing previous populations. In fact, the available oral tradition evidence favors an *in-situ* origin and development for the Sahaptian and Uto-Aztecans who are part of a much larger prehistoric population extending throughout the Intermountain area (and into present Mexico) with an extremely ancient time depth in the same area.

Unlike the other chapters in which I followed a geo-centric framework for reviewing the evidence, oral tradition evidence does not lend itself to the same framework. There are literally thousands of oral traditions that have been recorded from Plateau and Great Basin American Indian peoples, and there is no possible way to review each tribe's vast body of oral traditions. Instead, I focus this review on a few central issues concerning the possibility of whether oral tradition evidence can demonstrate in-situ development and depth of deep time. Suffice it to say, in the large body of oral tradition data reviewed for this book, nowhere was there any oral tradition evidence indicating discontinuity or the migration of peoples into or out of either the Plateau or Great Basin

For example, the oral traditions for the Plateau all refer to a time in the distant past when Coyote killed the Monster and broke the fish dam which brought salmon to the American Indian peoples of the region (Clark, 1953; Ramsey, 1977; Walker & Matthews, 1994). These oral traditions describe a time when the Columbia River was dammed by Monster and how Coyote killed the Monster and broke the fish dam, subsequently allowing the salmon to swim up the Columbia River and its tributaries, providing subsistence for the people. Similarly, such oral traditions as "Blood Red Lake" (Clark, 1953, p. 72), "How Coyote made the Columbia River" (Clark, 1953, p. 88), "Legends of Steamboat Rock" (Clark, 1953, p. 112), "Origin of the Palouse Falls" (Clark, 1953, p. 117; Colville, 2000, Part 2c), "The Serpent Monster and Rock Lake" (Colville, 2000, Part 2c), and "The Animal People's Race and the Palouse Hills" (Colville, 2000, Part 2c) all have been interpreted as describing the immense glacial floods, lakes, and river channels that occurred in the region during the Late Pleistocene and Early Holocene. As was discussed in chapter six, the Late Pleistocene and Early Holocene was a time of immense climatic change. It was during this time that glacial Lake Missoula repeatedly collapsed, releasing thousands of tons of water down the Columbia River channel and creating such well-known geological features as the channel scablands of eastern Washington, Grand Coulee and Moses Coulee, and Palouse Falls, as well as numerous other features. As Boxberger (2000) notes,

> This past cannot necessarily be identified with a specific date in pre-
> history, but it is a past that was a time when the landscape was being

transformed, when there were glaciers, when river channels were being cut, when salmon were populating the Columbia River and its tributaries, when buffalo were found on the Plateau, and when the myth people were preparing the way for the coming of the people. (p. 11)

All of these oral traditions features are directly reminiscent of the Late Pleistocene and Early Holocene changing environment, and it would be hard to imagine that even the most creative individuals could have understood that Palouse Falls was formed by massive glacial flood waters without either being there at that time or possessing the knowledge of glacial actions, processes of erosion, paleoenvironments, and the like. Furthermore, "Most groups have an oral tradition describing a shift or adjustment in the climate on the Plateau personified through a battle between 'Warmweather and Coldweather,' or between Coyote and the Coldweather" (Boxberger, 2000, p. 41), which also seems to reference the Late Pleistocene and Early Holocene boundary.

Some scholars have used oral traditions that refer to "nomadic people" or "stick people" as evidence to support the idea of both migration and displacement of peoples in prehistory or the possibility of another cultural group having been in the area in prehistoric times. These somewhat controversial oral traditions do not, however, diminish the overall weight of the oral tradition evidence. In the large body of recorded oral traditions there is little or no mention of a nomadic people or another group of people coming into the Plateau, nor of any previous group of people prior to the modern-day Columbia Basin peoples. There is mention of "Stick people" or "Stick Indians" in the oral traditions, and these oral traditions have often been misinterpreted to show a lack of oral tradition continuity. For example, in *Coyote Was Going There: Indian Literature of the Oregon Country,* compiled by Jarold Ramsey (1977), there is a tale of "Stick Indians." As it is explained in this tale, the Stick Indians were not another group of people, but instead are "spirits who live in high gloomy places, like Grizzly Flats (south of Mt. Jefferson) and upper Shitike Creek (southwest of Warm Springs Agency)" (Ramsey, 1977, p. 85). Similarly, many take the often occurring theme of "rain" in these oral traditions to link the present-day tribes back to when the Plateau experienced a wetter, somewhat cooler climate around 3,900-3,000 ybp. However, this oral tradition evidence can be more parsimoniously linked to the Late Pleistocene and Early Holocene and the increased precipitation levels that took place during this time as covered in chapter six. A few oral traditions that may describe this time are "Coyote and the Swallowing Monster" (Ramsey, 1977), "Creation of the Animal People," "How Coyote made the Columbia River," and "The Origin of Palouse Falls" (Clark, 1953). Thus, it would seem more parsimonious to conclude that the oral traditions describing "rains," "flooding," or "dams" are also linked to this older time when the Plateau experienced cataclysmic flooding, a large amount of rain, and the creation of many of the natural features.

In the Great Basin various oral traditions have been interpreted to give evidence of discontinuity, such as those just reviewed for the Plateau. The most recent example is that of Barker, Ellis, and Damadio (2000), who concluded that oral traditions among the Northern Paiute describe an ancient population that was in the Fallon area prior to the Paiute. Barker et al. (2000) reason that this hypothetical population was driven out by the present-day Northern Paiutes through a series of battles, with the concluding confrontation taking place when the Northern Paiute trapped these people, the "Saidukah," in a cave and burned them. However, when looking at the oral tradition evidence in total for the region, several problems in this understanding become apparent. First, the Paiute origin myth is fairly standard from Owens Valley to Surprise Valley (Steward, 1970), which argues for deeper ancestry between Northern and Owens Valley Paiute than the supposed Numic expansion hypothesis would argue for, which is Barker et al.'s interpretation. Second, "The preponderance of evidence contained in the statements indicates that the legend of the original people is local, and its incorporation into the creation myth would indicate that it is of considerable antiquity" (Bath, 1977). Much of the misunderstanding of this particular oral tradition arises from the fact that "Saidukah" has been interpreted to mean "outsider or other peoples." Goss has discussed this in detail, noting that, "The best solution of the puzzle is that, probably the Saidukah were another Northern Paiute ancestral group that the Humboldt-Carson Paiute ancestors had difficulties with. In time the term 'Saidukah' was applied more generally to 'difficult' folks to the North. It was quickly interpreted to mean 'enemy' by outsiders" (Goss, 1999). This would lend support to the conclusion that the "Saidukah" were not another "cultural" group of peoples, but a clan or kinship lineage of Northern Paiutes who had confrontational contact with another clan or kinship lineage of Northern Paiutes. Furthermore, like that of the Plateau, there are no oral traditions which mention a migration of peoples into or out of the region, and all recorded oral traditions contain an *in situ* origin location (Sutton, 1993).

Along with examining the specific sub-region's body of oral tradition evidence, it is informative to take a broader perspective and to look at oral traditions in general. Various compilations of oral traditions in general are available (D'Azevedo, 1986; Dundes, 1965b; Ramsey, 1977; Thompson, 1977; Vansina, 1985; Walker, 1998) and indicate that the motifs listed in Table 5 are found broadly throughout Native North America, as well as among Plateau and Great Basin peoples.

Alan Dundes, one of the most influential contemporary scholars of American Indian oral tradition evidence has outlined a modern theoretical position relevant to the question of interpreting oral traditions in cases of cultural affiliation as follows, "In the nineteenth century and before, folklore was thought to be a dead survival from ages past rather than a live, functioning part of the present day world of man" (Dundes, 1980, p. 33). He further explains that many of the functions of oral traditions are projective and psychological and that the major points of an oral tradition may be factual, but the majority of the narrative has little to do with reality. Dundes affirms that oral traditions are a kind of projection of the tensions and anxieties experienced in particular cultures. For example, he states that, "Projections are to be found in all types of literature including comedies, television, and motion pictures…and that projection can involve placement in the far distant past or the far distant future" (Dundes, 1980, p. 50). Very relevant examples of this type of bizarre psychological projection concerning hunger and starvation with their attendant psychological anxiety can be seen in the Plateau and Great Basin oral traditions in many accounts. Sven Liljeblad (1986) notes this in depth with his study of Great

Basin oral traditions:

> There are legends about man-eating ogres of superhuman size, who also figure as frightening characters in the mythological tales. The Owens Valley Paiute called the dreadful giant roaming their valley *Ninimisi*. The Mono Lake Northern Paiute told of two such monsters, *Tsenahaha* and *Puwihi* (Steward 1936: 428); their names imitate the weird chanting the giants make when approaching their victims. The latter term, Northern Paiute *piwihi* or *pikwihi*, was apparently a loan word (cf. W.Z. Park 1933-1940, 1:32-33); the current expression, *paiza*, is a colloquialism from the generic term *pahico?o*, of unknown origin and etymology. The Shoshones envision this class of supernatural beings, still common in Great Basin folklore, as a solitary figure, named in the literature *Tsoavits*, a term etymologically related to Shoshone "ghost." They still call the Sawtooth Mountains in south-central Idaho *coapiccan kahni* "the giant's house," just as the Washoe call a peak overlooking Topaz Lake *hanawiywiy ?anal*, meaning the same thing (Dangberg 1968: 20). In Washoe folklore, the various manifestations of this cyclops, who is at home in the Sierras, differ in many details; he occurs as several different characters under a variety of names (William Jacobsen, personal communication 1984). Despite the variety of terms applied, the conceptions were largely the same throughout the common area; hence Lowie (1909: 234-235) defines a "Dzo'avits cycle" of stories. The theme is the abduction of people by the man-eating ogre (Motif G440), in Ute tradition represented by a fabulous race of humanlike creatures, living in a society of their own, and variously called *Si'ats* (Lowie 1924a: 74-76) or Saints (Smith 1940,2: 101-105, 193-195; Jorgensen 1960: 54-55, 110). Elsewhere in the area, the giant appears with only one eye or with large, glowing eyes (Motif G652), or his whistling as he enters (Motif D2071). The belief in these monsters, who could be killed only by fire (Motif G512.3), is firmly rooted in Great Basin mythology. They appear under different names both in the legends and the mythological tales as characters form a prehuman era or as cannibals once living in caves in the mountains but now extinct. Thus, the Northern Paiutes used to call these mythological giants "people-crushers" form their habit of pounding human victims in mortars. The Chemehuevis called them *tutusiwi* and considered them ancestors of the neighboring Mohaves (Laird 1976: 160, 256). This mysterious race was also known as Northern *Paiute saiduka?a* "under the tule." Originally this term was applied to the tribes on the Columbia River who lived in tule-covered long-houses and were often in conflict with the Oregon Northern Paiutes. Ultimately it came to mean "foreign enemy." In anthropological literature, this term has been confused with the group name *saidika?a* "tule-eaters" applied to certain local groups who have a marsh-culture economy (cf. O.C. Stewart 1941: 431, 440-441). (p. 655)

Similarly, Hultkrantz describes these bizarre projections further as follows (Hultkrantz, 1986):

> The Numic peoples dreaded most of all, besides ghosts, the little dwarf spirit with poisonous arrows. This little being lived every-where- in mountains, among bushes, in caves, around wells- and was mostly unseen. Its arrows caused pneumonia. The beliefs in the dwarf spirits were very uniform over the Numic area and, to judge from reminiscences and legends, attracted more attention than any other religious beliefs. Although ideas of similar pygmy spirits existed in surrounding culture areas- particularly the Plateau and the Plains- they were most typical of the Numic religions, espe-cially in the north. (p. 633)

and,

> The Western, Northern, and Eastern Shoshone tell stories of fights between huge serpents and eagles, dwarfs and eagles, witches and eagles, and even monster beings (cannibal or water giants) and mythical birds. Southern Paiutes relate that Rabbit, father of Wolf and Coyote, shoots arrows into the sea (Fowler and Fowler 1971: 78). A similar theme seems to underlie the legend of the Cannibal Bird, when it is said that water beings help the hero who has been carried away by this bird to return home. Often this cannibal bird is identified with the eagle, or thunderbird (S. Thompson 1929: 318). (p. 640)

Finally, Liljeblad correctly casts doubt on the empirical validity and the actual time depth that can be attributed to such oral traditions in the following (Liljeblad, 1986):

> There are no boundaries between verifiable historical memories and legendary fiction. Sometimes these stories are localized and regarded as the incorporeal property of people descended from the principal actor in the story; however, identical realistic stories with human characters do occur as migratory legends in places far apart. The ultimate horizon of personal history coincides with the time-depth of known genealogy. In most cases this is the grand-parental generation of the speaker. Most historical legends record-ed by 1900 would therefore refer to early postcontact time. There is an emotional keynote of privation and misfortune in many of these narratives. Typical examples are the often recurring almost identical stories about cannibalism sometimes told as having been committed by a relative of the victim, by early White travelers, or by man-eating shamans (witches) practicing ritual cannibalism (Kroeber 1901: 280-285; Lowie 1909: 290-292, 1939: 347; Steward 1938a: 190; Smith 1940: 109-118; Miller 1972: 33-37; Laird 1976:

32-33, 1977: 100; Zigmond 1980: 205).   That these stories of
anthopophagy, even when recorded in autobiographical accounts,
are legendary, is further borne our by their having been characterized as the act of a "cannibal witch" and as "unwitting," "occasional," or "deliberate cannibalism," motifs G11.3, G60, G70, (77 and
79) in S. Thompson's (1955-1958) motif index. The entire com-
plex- the realistic stories in their relation to legends about man-eat-
ing ogres (Motif G11.2)- is treated by Smith (1940: 60-75). (pp. 651-
652)

Thus, as scholars in the field have noted, oral traditions can be used to gain a general inclination as to the time depth of the various American Indian peoples in a
particular region, as was noted for the Plateau and the body of oral traditions dealing with "rains," the breaking of the fish dam, and similar traditions. However, oral
traditions can rarely be used to garner specific historic facts such as population displacement or migration.

However, the linguistic prehistorians who have had extensive training and experience can sometimes detect general evidence of prehistoric events such as major natural disasters or cataclysmic events in the oral traditions of particular peoples whose
languages and cultures they have intensively studied. Despite this, the use of oral
traditions to infer specific prehistoric events is highly problematic, such as the claim
that oral traditions referencing "giants" or "stick people" are evidence of population
displacement. For example, Sith Thompson (1977) has conducted an in depth
analysis of the occurrences of giants in the oral traditions of Europe and has concluded the following:

The term [giant] has become confused with that of the French
ogre and the German Teufel, so that mere size is only a small consideration in a tale like Jack the Giant Killer. Giants are even equated sometimes with the dragon concept, so that the dragon fighter
is said to go out and kill the seven-headed giant. They may, or
course, be thoroughly human, like Goliath. As far as the traditions
of northern Europe are concerned, however, neither of these concepts is valid. The giant there is thought of as being an enormous
person of human shape many times the size of a mortal. Such
giants live ordinary lives and have usual family relationships. A
huge number of stories are known about their activities, though
many of these parallel the stories of fairies or dwarfs.
Polyphemus was a typical giant in this sense, for he had one eye
in the middle of his forehead (Type 1137; F531.1.1.1). Other
giants are headless, and some have shaggy hair all over their bodies, and sometimes long beards. Some of them wade the ocean,
and nearly all of them throw great rocks around and produce
changes in the landscape. Two specific cycles of giant legends
deserving mention are those of Gargantua in France and of Paul
Bunyan in America. Readers of Rabelais are familiar with the satir-
ical use a great author can make of such popular traditions, but

they are perhaps not always aware of the extent to which such legends are actually a part of the folklore of France. Whether these French traditions were preserved by the colonists in New France, or whether stories of gigantic persons reached the French Canadians from other sources there seems little doubt that these people have had much to do with the spreading of the tradition of a purely American giant, Paul Bunyan, the enormous woodsman. In spite of all the discussion of Paul Bunyan during the last thirty years, much about the tradition of him and his enormous ox remains very dark. But the popularity of this legend among lumbermen today, whatever its origin may have been, shows that the stories of giants are perennially interesting.

The giant concept is so varied in its appearances that it is hard to be sure of the role which a giant will play in popular tradition. Frequently he is thought of as a kindly helper, benevolent if slightly stupid; sometimes he is the acme of stupidity; and very often he is an ogre quite as frightful as any monster conjured up by the folk imagination. The same double nature may be found in stories of dwarfs and trolls. (p. 249)

Thus, as Thompson has noted, the occurrences of giants in oral traditions, as well as "stick people," "nomadic people," or "red-headed giants" is far from concise, nor can it be used as a distinct entity to show discontinuity or the presence of other people in the area of study. In fact, occurrences of giants is such a numinous entity that no concise interpretation can be given other than the specific one from which the oral tradition arises. This fact was particularly misunderstood by Barker et al. (2000) and to a lesser extent by Magistrate Jelderks ("Robson bonnichsen et al. Vs. United states of america et al.," 2002) in the Spirit Cave Mummy and Kennewick Man cases, respectively. Furthermore, the occurrence of giants, ogres, monsters, dwarfs, cannibals, and even red headed beings is very widespread in the oral traditions of North American Indians. A few examples of which are given below.

Karok:
"The Cannibal Giant." This myth details the story of a giant who kills and eats people. He captures a girl and raises her, feeding her traditional food such as deer and salmon. One day the giant eats the girl's brother so she decides to kill him. She burns down his house with him in it. (Kroeber & Gifford, 1980, pp. 134-136)

"Yadubi'hi." This is the story of a giant and his son. The people trick the giant from leaving his house by making it snow. Soon the giant figures out the people's tricks. The giant becomes mad at his son for not telling him about the people's tricks, so he decides to sleep with his son's wife. The son becomes mad at this and takes all of the belongings from the giant's house. The giant chases his son and gets his things back and returns money, feather ornaments, white deerskins, and other things to the people. (Kroeber & Gifford, 1980, pp. 113-118)

"Story about Ixyarukbitsi." In this myth the giant is crazy for women. The people on the other side of the ocean try and trick the giant to come over to their land, for wherever he lives the people will be immortal. The giant goes over to the other side, but his wife dies. He gets married again, but his second wife also dies. The giant then goes back to Karok country where he falls in love with a girl. To please the girl he makes Scott Valley. Then he went up Yreka Mountain, faced toward Katimin and became a rock. (Kroeber & Gifford, 1980, pp. 118-121)

Klamath:
"Gilili." Mink and Weasel hunt the monster herbivore, Gilili. Weasel begs to take the first shot, misses, and runs off after Gilili pursuing him for two years. Mink, thinking him dead, goes into mourning. Weasel eventually slays Gilili and the nearby villagers give him food. Rattlesnake then claims the kill, but is vanquished by Weasel. The people skin Gilili, but cannot hang up his great hide. (Stern, 1963, p. 34).

"Thunderbird." Coyote goes along and enters the mouth of the giant. He stabs his heart, emerges, accompanied by all the people whom the giant had swallowed (Stern, 1963, p. 34).

"A Pit River Giant Story." The giant lives on an island, and puts all comers to a test, enslaving all who fail. The giant knows Aisis has power and sends for him. Aisis comes with Grey Eagle, Bluebird, and Beaver. The giant's bird-messenger, Rock-copulator, tells Aisis his mater's tricks and joins Aisis. The giant sends Aisis to retrieve "down" from underwater rocks. Aisis, however, sends Rock-copulator with instructions what to do, and the bird brings back the "down," which Aisis gives to the giant. The giant then tells Aisis to climb a pole and dislodge a bird sitting there. Aisis sends Bluebird, who climbs up, knocks down the giant's bird, and climbs back down the victor. The giant then sends Aisis for his daughter, who lives underwater. Aisis sends Beaver, with a rope tied fast to a tree. Beaver ties the rope around her waist, and retrieves the daughter. Finally, the giant proposes a race between Wind and Eagle. Aisis warns Eagle to stay on top and as Wind whirls trying to catch Eagle, Eagle wins. Aisis then sends back the people who were enslaved by the giant. The giant subsequently has Aisis and his daughter kneel by the fire, and as the smoke rises they go up into the air (Stern, 1963, p. 41).

Crow:
"The Giants and Their Buffalo." In this oral tradition a group of Crow follow the buffalo through a cave into another land where there are giants. The giants use the buffalo as horses and speak Crow. The giants are very vulnerable and die with the slightest scratch. (Lowie, 1993, pp. 216-220)

A. Cosmogony and Cosmology

    1. Gods and Culture Heros

    2. Establishment of Heavens and Earth

    3. Ordering of Earth and Human Life

    4. Vegetable and Animal Life

B. Animals

    1. Mythical Animals

    2. Helpful Animals

    3. Animal Marriages

    4. Other Animal Motifs

C. Tabu

    1. Various Explanatory Tales

D. Magic

    1. Transformation

    2. Magic Objects

    3. Magic Powers

E. Return from the Dead

    1. Resuscitation

    2. Ghosts

    3. Reincarnation

    4. The Soul

F. Marvels

    1. Other-world Journeys

    2. Marvelous Beings

    3. Marvelous Places and Things

    4. Remarkable Occurrences

G. Ogres and Cannibals

    1.Various Types

Cree:
"Chakabesh and the Giant Women." Chahkabesh is out hunting one day and hears a noise. It is two giants cleaning beaver skins, and he wants to

sleep with them. However, the giant's mother catches him and puts him in a pot. He overturns the pot and eats the stew. (Ellis, 1995, pp. 105-109 and 315-317)

H. Tests

    1. Identity Tests

    2. Marriage Tests

    3. Tests of Prowess

I. The Wise and The Foolish

J. Deceptions

    1. Contests Won by Deception

    2. Thefts and Cheats

    3. Deceptive Escapes and Captures

    4. Fatal or Disastrous Deceptions

    5. Seduction and Deceptive Marriages

    6. Deceiver Falls into Own Trap

    7. Other Deceptions

K. Victory of the Weak

    1. Unpromising Hero

    2. Modest Choice Best

    3. Pride Before Fall

L. Fortune

    1. Gambling

    2. Accidents

    3. Influential Helpers

M. Sex

    1. Chastity

    2. Illicit Sex Relations

    3. Conception and Birth

    4. Rearing of Children

Table 5. This table shows many of the common themes that can be found throughout American Indian oral traditions of the United States.

Lenape:
"Manabozho." This oral tradition is about when a great manitto visited earth and had four sons. These sons were giants. The first son was

Manabozho, who is a friend of the human race. The second, Chibiabos, is the caretaker of the dead. The third is Wabassa, a powerful spirit under the guise of a rabbit. The fourth is Chokanipok, or the Man of Flint, or Firestone. (Emerson, 1965, pp. 336-343)

As can be seen, not only are there occurrences of giants in the oral traditions of American Indians, but there are also oral traditions concerning "red heads" or people with red hair.

Sioux:
"Pah-Hah-Undootah or The Red Head." This oral tradition is about a boy who must kill the Red Head to prove his merit. The Red Head was the most powerful sorcerer and the terror of all the country, living upon a small island in the center of a lake. The Red Head had a son who was looking for a wife. The boy decided to dress as a woman and marry the Red Head's son in order to get close to the Red Head and kill her. In the end the boy kills the Red Head and swims safely back to his village with great fame, eventually becoming a chief. (Williams, 1991, pp. 151-154)

Crow:
"Red-woman." In this myth Red-woman adopts a boy who is really a water animal. She raises this child, but he is told that she is a witch and must die. The boy gets a tiger and a bear that attacked Red-woman and kills her. Then the boy burns Red-woman. (Lowie, 1993, pp. 204-205)

"Red-Hair's Hair." In this oral tradition a young man wants to marry a girl, but he must first bring some of Red-Hair's hair. The young man married Red-Hair and lived with her for a long time. One day he killed Red-Hair and cut off all of her hair. Red-Hair's brothers followed him, but he hid and escaped. In the end he married the woman because he brought back Red-Hair's hair. (Lowie, 1993, pp. 141-143)

Clackamas Chinook:
"Idya'bixwasxwas." In this myth a giant goes around to different villages and purchases women who he hears are beautiful. His favorite wife had red hair, though sometimes it was referred to as yellow-brown. One day she gave birth to a son, who later in the oral tradition rebels against his father the giant. The giant and the son fight and the son wins. The son then becomes the chief of the people and installs the woman with red hair (his mother) as his wife. (Jacobs, 1959, pp. 109-110)

Like that for "giants," there is a wide body of oral traditions that reference "red heads" and other creatures, only a few of which were reviewed here. As should be obvious, to use these oral traditions as evidence of actual specific historical events is highly circumspect, as Baker, Ellis, and Damadio (2000) did for the Spirit Cave Mummy case and Magistrate Jelderks ("Robson bonnichsen et al. Vs. United states of america et al.," 2002) did for the Kennewick Man case. Instead, oral tradition evidence should only be used as a general indicator of larger scale historical events, such as the oral traditions referencing coyote breaking the dam of monster as evidence of the collapse of glacial Lake Missoula.

Summary of Oral Tradition Evidence

As I have reviewed in this chapter, there is an enormous body of oral tradition evidence for the Plateau and Great Basin. Within this large body of data, there are oral traditions evidencing *in situ* self-creation of the present-day American Indian peoples of the region, and there are no oral traditions referencing migration into or displacement of peoples from these regions. Therefore, the oral tradition evidence indicates oral tradition continuity for the Plateau and Great Basin dating back to the Late Pleistocene and Early Holocene, when many oral traditions reference the radically changing environment of this period. However, like the linguistic evidence reviewed in the previous chapter, the oral tradition evidence can only be used as evidence for general historic events and processes, and not as evidence for hypothetically proposed specific events. Thus, the oral tradition evidence indicates that the present-day American Indian peoples of the Plateau and Great Basin have resided in their present regions back to the Late Pleistocene and Early Holocene, though information of specific events beyond this general picture is not possible. This lack of explanability will become more evident in the next chapter where I discuss the necessary requirements needed to empirically demonstrate discontinuity or the migration of peoples either into or out of a specific region.

CHAPTER 12
MIGRATIONS, DIFFUSIONS, AND SUBSISTENCE IN AMERICAN PREHISTORY

Over the last five chapters I have reviewed several lines of evidence that are used to establish whether cultural affiliation exists between the peoples of the Late Pleistocene and Early Holocene and the present-day American Indians of the Plateau and Great Basin. Not only were several lines of evidence covered, but several theories and different interpretations within each line of evidence were discussed. Prior to an overall synthesis and unified anthropological interpretation is given according to an epistemological praxis of epoché, I will spend the present chapter discussing one further theoretical premise that is central to establishing cultural affiliation or non-affiliation. This theoretical premise is the question of how to empirically establish the migration of peoples either into or out of a specific region in prehistory. As I discussed in chapters eight and nine, many scholars use the various "gaps" in our knowledge of the biological and archaeological databases to support their contention that a migration or population displacement has taken place within either the Plateau or Great Basin in prehistory. Others, as discussed in the previous chapter, use various oral traditions to hypothesize that references within the oral traditions also support migration or cultural displacement in prehistoric times. Furthermore, many link these various hypothesized migrations to contentious linguistic phylums and families to support their hypothesis as covered in chapter ten. For example, in the two most publicized and controversial NAGPRA cases for each area, these "gaps" in our knowledge of the archaeological and biological databases were used to either show a lack of cultural continuity and potentially prehistoric population displacement ("Robson Bonnichsen et al. vs. United States of America et al.," 2002), or to bolster the contentious Numic expansion hypothesis, and thus demonstrate a lack of cultural continuity dating back beyond the "Numic expansion" time barrier (Barker, Ellis, & Damadio, 2000). However, both of these examples I argue fail to understand what these "gaps" in the database represent and how one is able to empirically demonstrate that an actual migration has taken place. Therefore, in this chapter I briefly review the requirements necessary to empirically demonstrate such a movement of people has occurred and whether such a movement took place in the Plateau or Great Basin in the last ten thousand years or so.

In a now famous symposium held in 1958 on the problems associated with empirically establishing migration events or processes in prehistory various factual tests were established (Thompson, 1958). Two archaeologists, Emil Haury and Irving Rouse, each advanced several of the now widely accepted criteria. Haury noted that the following must be shown to allow for the possibility of a prehistoric migration:

> 1) if there suddenly appears in a cultural continuum a constellation of traits readily identifiable as new, and without local prototypes, and
> 2) if the products of the immigrant group not only reflect borrowed elements form the host group, but also, as a lingering effect, preserve unmistakable elements from their own pattern.
> The probability that the phenomena outlined above do indeed represent a migration, rather than some other force that induces culture change, is increased:
> 1) if identification of an area is possible in which this constellation of traits was the normal pattern, and
> 2) if a rough time equivalency between the "at home" and the displaced expressions of the similar complexes can be established. (Thompson, 1958, p. 1)

The Haury criteria for migration, as can be seen, indicate that no migration should be assumed only if there suddenly appears in a cultural continuum a constellation of traits readily identifiable as new and without local prototypes, but a migration could be assumed if the products of the immigrant group not only reflect borrowed elements from the host group, but also, as a lingering effect, preserve unmistakable elements from their own group. The probability that a migration has occurred is strengthened if an area can be identified in which this constellation of traits was the normal pattern, and further if a rough time equivalency between the "at home" and the displaced expressions of the similar complexes can be established.

Rouse, in the same symposium, advanced even more stringent standards as follows:

> 1) The first point can perhaps best be discussed in the terminology of the Society for American Archaeology culture-contact seminar. I think it is necessary for the archaeologist who wishes to infer a migration to demonstrate a site-unit intrusion, that is, to uncover the remains of one or more specific communities- components, foci, or phases in archaeological terminology- and to show that

these communities are probably intrusive in the region where they occur. Similarly, the ethnologist should be able to single out one or more communities, tribes, or other social units and to demonstrate that these have intruded into the local population.

2) Once intrusive social groups have been established, then the next logical step, it seem to me, is to trace these groups back to their homeland. This involves identification of the original social group from which each migrating group split off and discovery of traces of the group in the intervening areas through which the migration is presumed to have passed. In other words, one should ideally be able to point to a series of site-units or social groups marking the route of a presumed migration, although these units need not always have a continuous distribution, since it is theoretically possible for a migrating people to pass quickly through an area without leaving identifiable traces of their passage.

3) Both Haury and Meggers and Evans have recognized the necessity of establishing the contemporaneity of their site-units, since otherwise it would have been impossible for migration to have taken place. The other authors might perhaps have done more to satisfy this requirement than they have. This is another reason why it would have been advantageous for Newman and Voegelin to correlate their physical anthropological and linguistic evidence with specific site-units of archaeology, since the latter usually provide the best evidence of chronology.

4) In inferring migrations, as Collier implies, it is also important to note whether the proper environmental and cultural conditions for migration are present. For example, I am more inclined to accept the Meggers and Evans theory of migration, even though it assumes the crossing of almost the entire width of a continent, because the Amazon provides such a good waterway and the Indians of the area are known to have been experienced canoeists, so that it must have been relatively easy for them to travel long distances. Moreover, the historic Indians of the area are known to have had traditions of more favorable lands in the distance which would have provided an incentive for migration if these traditions were also present prehistorically. One would therefore expect more and longer-range migrations in Amazonia than, for example, in the Southwest, where neither the physical nor the cultural conditions for migration were so favorable. Even in the Southwest, though, one might cite the refugee groups of historic times, for example, the Rio Grande people at Hopi, to justify theories of prehistoric migration.

5) Finally, I would follow Haury and Childe (1950: 8-10) in suggesting that it is incumbent upon the person who wishes to demonstrate migration to consider and eliminate the possibility that some other Hypothesis may better fit the facts at his disposal. Specifically, an archaeologist is always faced with the question whether the similarities he finds between several different areas

may not be due to what our seminar called trait-unit intrusion rather than site-unit intrusion. Both of these processes would produce cultural similarities between areas, and it seems to me essential in all cases to weigh one possibility against the other. I submit that in any study of migrations the differences as well as the similarities in culture between areas need to be considered, for if these differences are great enough they would favor trait-unit diffusion over site-unit diffusion. (Thompson, 1958, pp. 65-66)

As the points raised in this now famous symposium demonstrate, it is necessary to have hard, empirical evidence in order to even begin to suggest that either population displacements or migrations have taken place in prehistory, otherwise continuity should be assumed. However, what appears to have happened in many cases, and especially with the Numic expansion hypothesis in the Great Basin, is that scholars have assumed migration events or processes are evidenced when in fact, diffusion processes accords more parsimoniously with the data. "As will be shown presently, migration and diffusion theories have quite different intellectual pedigrees, and their relationship in practice has often been antithetical" (Adams, Van Gerven, & Levy, 1978, p. 483). As Adams et al. (1978) further discuss, migration events or processes have never been formally articulated as a general principle of historical explanation. However, as noted several times throughout this book, various scholars have nevertheless utilized it as an ad hoc explanation for cultural, biological, linguistic, and other forms of culture change and evolution. Likewise, because migration events or processes have never been the subject of study in and of themself, the actual mechanisms of how migrations work has received even less attention. "Some culture historians seem deliberately to beg this issue by talking simply about 'expansion,' without specifying whether population expansion or only cultural dissemination is envisioned" (Adams, Van Gerven, & Levy, 1978 pp. 485-486).

Migration events or processes are the obvious explanations for anomalous site distributions (i.e., either the sudden abandonment of old sites or the appearance of new ones), while diffusion processes are preferred to explain actual trait distributions (i.e., abandonment of old traits and the appearance of new ones). As I reviewed in chapter nine, the archaeological data for both the Plateau and Great Basin regions indicates diffusion processes over migration ones. For example, there is no evidence of anomalous site distributions in either region, except for the small appearance of the Lovelock sites in the western Great Basin, which can be explained as a form of extreme trait diffusion accompanied with cultural innovation. A clear example of this a priori jump to the positing of migration processes being evidenced over those of diffusion can be seen in the work of Adovasio (1974, 1986a, 1986b, 1994) and his analyses of Great Basin basketry. For example, Adovasio claims, "The utter disappearance of Lovelock Wickerware, which is not known ethnographically among the Numic speakers or anyone else, signals one of those rare major 'turnovers' in a regional basketry sequence attributable to population replacement rather than to intragroup stylistic or technological change" (1986a p. 205). Because the Lovelock Wickerware has no antecedents within or outside of its place of origin, nor does it "migrate" to another region based on trait analyses, the phenomenon of its disappearance does not seem to support Adovasio's claim of migration.

Furthermore, the rest of the archaeological record during the appearance and disappearance of the Lovelock Wickerware remaines continuous, further supporting cultural innovation and diffusion rather than cultural migration as an explanation for the appearance of these basketry styles. Finally, it is important to note:

> In short, migrations based on site distributions are nearly always conceived as internal migrations within the same general area. On the other hand, migrations based on trait distributions must, almost by definition, bring in outsiders from far away to account for the presence of seemingly anomalous traits, since traits originating in the same general area would probably be explained on the basis of diffusion rather than migration. Thus, trait-based migration theories have a much lower inherent probability value than have site-based theories, and it is primarily the former which have been and are foci of controversy." (Adams, Van Gerven, & Levy, 1978, p. 488)

The foregoing discussions suggest once again that hypothesized prehistoric migrations require hard, empirical evidence and not mere theoretical speculation from linguistics, "gaps" in the biological or archaeological record, or from sloppily interpreted oral traditions. Until demonstrated otherwise, the most defensible scholarly position is that the people within the area of question, in this case the Sahaptian and Salishan (as well as perhaps the Nicola, Wasco-Wishram, Kootenai, Molala, Cayuse, and Klamath) of the Plateau and the Numic of the Great Basin are part of a much larger and ancient population long resident in the Intermountain (i.e., the Plateau and Great Basin) region of North America. Aikens, whose earlier work has been used by some to support the Numic expansion hypothesis, has recently voiced a stance consistent with this position based on his over 30 years of work in the Great Basin. In a recent personal communication based on a paper given at the Great Basin Anthropological Conference in Bend, Oregon he notes the following:

> My view is that the Great Basin has been the Numic/Ute-Aztecan homeland for a very long time, and that the idea of a "Numic expansion" (*sensu* Lamb) is greatly overdrawn. I theorize shifts in group ranges across environmental transition zones along the eastern and western edges of the Basin as part of a complex response to environmental changes. But look again, and you will see that I do not argue for Numic peoples "pushing" anyone out of anywhere. I do not believe that the range changes which I envision were conflict situations, but were instead obvious solutions to resource needs for people on both sides of the equation. I have a paper on Ute-Aztecan peoples in a Chacmool symposium volume that is due out any time now, and when it appears I will send you a copy. The basic argument there is that the Great Basin, and much of the western intermontane, deep into Mexico, has been a Ute-Aztecan homeland going back into deep time. To me the evidence clearly indicates that Ute-Aztecan peoples were supremely well-adapted to the western deserts, because of their very long experience there. Their thorough knowledge of the desert environment

and its vicissitudes, and their highly flexible and mobile way of life, were keys to their mastery of this realm. I am working on another paper with two colleagues wherein we review linguistic evidence suggesting old relationships among Ute-Aztecan and other peoples around the northwestern periphery of the Great Basin, but that is not yet fully thought out. (M. Aikens, personal communication, June 15, 2001)

Similarly, Goss (1977, 1999), Elston (1982, 1986), and others have also argued that there is no evidence of a linguistic spread from the southern Great Basin to the north and east.

The linguistic replacement model is at least based on the ethnographic distribution of language groups (Lamb 1958; Hattori 1980) but fails to state exactly how linguistic changes are related to changes in material culture, and how these should be manifest in the archaeological record. (Elston, 1982, p. 190)

Because of the apparent "fit" of Lamb's linguistic hypothesis, many archaeologists have taken an *a priori* stance in deriving their inferences from the archaeological data when looking at the possible Numic spread. This fact was noted by Lyneis (1982),

The theory of the late spread of Numic speakers across the Great Basin proposed by Lamb has served as a mold into which archaeological facts have been fitted rather than as a proposition for scrutiny and testing. Goss's model of long-term in situ development of the Numic languages is an equally plausible alternative. (p. 177)

Similarly, as O'Connell, Jones, and Simms (1982), point out,

Virtually every prehistorian concerned with this topic has assumed that Numic languages, which evidently spread into the Basin quite recently (Lamb 1958), reached their historic distribution by a process of migration.... If, however, the ethnographically documented patterns of settlement and subsistence antedate the arrival of Numic speakers throughout most of the western and central Basin (Thomas 1973; Jennings 1957), then a difficult problem presents itself: How and why does one hunter-gatherer population displace another where both evidently possess the same or very similar technologies and display the same or similar patterns of land and resource use? (p. 230)

Finally, as Barker (1994, p. 18) observed, and as I discussed in chapter nine, "it is impossible to separate Numic ceramics and projectile points from those supposedly made by non-Numic populations." Much of the evidence used to support the Numic expansion hypothesis comes from the analysis of a specific material remain, such as lithic projectile point styles, settlement patterns, or basketry traits and are taken out of the larger archaeological context. However, when all of the material artifacts are considered together, there is little evidence to support such a hypothesis.

> In the Carson Desert south of Lovelock Cave, for instance, Raven (1994) found that human use of the area changed little over thousands of years, and that "pre-Numic" foragers may have employed a "Numic-like" foraging strategy. Given this, the notion that Numic speakers had an adaptation to the environment that gave them a competitive edge seems doubtful. (Ferguson, 1996, p. 20)

Further, as Hughes (1994) notes, "Appeal to the time-honored principle that 'different groups often produce different styles of artifacts' (Holmer 1990a: 42) ignores evidence that the same group may produce, curate, and use different styles of artifacts depending on seasonal (e.g., Thomson 1939) or socioreligious consideration" (p. 68). Likewise, "Even if Numic speakers could be distinguished archaeologically, [which seems unlikely, see Madsen (1982; 1998; also see Madsen & Simms, 1998)], an appeal to migration... falls well short of an explanation" (O'Connell, Jones, & Simms, 1982, p. 230).

Along with the use of basketry traits by Adovasio to attempt to find evidence in support of the Numic expansion hypothesis, some archaeologists have used the so-called disappearance of the Fremont "culture" or theoretical implications steming from optimal foraging theory as potential support for the Numic expansion hypothesis. Some archaeologists have used the so-called "disappearance" of the Fremont "culture" in the eastern Great Basin as a "proof" of the Numic expansion. There are several reasons why such an assumption fails, but principally,

> The author notes that there is no one set of material remains that can be identified as "Fremont" but this has not stopped archaeologists from lumping together all evidence of people in the Utah area during that time to be part of the Fremont culture. (Simms, 1994, p. 82)

Simms (1994) goes on to state that, "The author views the Numic spread as being evolutionary and fluid, taking place over several thousands of years with no displacement" (p. 82). Thus, if anything, the archaeological evidence indicates diffusion as opposed to migration, and "Archaeologists have not critically examined alternative mechanisms for the proposed event" (Lyneis, 1982, p. 180). Furthermore, those archaeologists supporting the Numic expansion hypothesis usually argue that the Numic peoples possessed a clear technological advantage over the peoples who they displaced. However, this theory fails to account for two major factors: first, if the Numic displaced certain peoples, where did these displaced peoples go? There is no evidence to the north (Plateau), south (Southwest; other than the Athabaskans, who are believed to have come from Canada), and only scanty evidence to the east (the Rocky Mountains and Plains) that within the last 1,000 years a migration of people took place into one of these regions (i.e., the Comanche onto the Plains). Second, the population pressure idea has many inherent limitations,

In the recent past, Cowgill (63, 64) has reacted strongly against the population-pressure models of explanation, asserting that the tendency of population to expand to and beyond the limits of carrying capacity cannot be safely assumed, as Boserup and her followers have done. (Adams, Van Gerven, & Levy, 1978, p. 524)

There has never been an accepted model that would explain how or why hunters and gatherers would over-exploit their resources. In fact, as was discussed in chapter nine for the Great Basin, when the environment changed and many of the marsh and wetland resources disappeared, the people did not leave but simply adopted to a new subsistence regime based more on mammals, seeds, and other resources, and less so on fish and lacustrine resources. Furthermore, as was concluded in chapter eight the biological data appear to support the idea of culture change, and not cultural displacement:

> On these bases it is assumed that during the occupation period represented by the artifacts recovered and described in Tuohy, et al. (1987), the inhabitants of these site areas [the Stillwater Marsh area of western Nevada] remained relatively the same skeletally, although their artifact styles changed through time. (Brooks, Haldeman, & Brooks, 1988, pp. 157-158)

The last major explanation sometimes used in support of the Numic expansion hypothesis stems from notions of optimal foraging theory. Optimal foraging theory originally stems from the modeling of animal foraging behavior, and looks at basic factors such as search and handling times for locating resources and the energy content of those resources, in order to determine prey and resource choice by foraging animals. Based on these animal models, anthropologists have attempted to construct a model that maximizes the net energy intake rate of the human forager and that predicts the "optimal" diet of the human. More sophisticated models then modify and refine the original model to take into account factors such as prey recognition time, food patches, and central place foraging. Optimal foraging theory has been widely used in the Great Basin in an attempt to understand, based on Julian Steward's (1955) limited and largely discredited model of culture change, how Great Basin peoples have been able to survive and flourish in what has historically been perceived as a "hostile" environment.

Bettinger and Baumhoff (1982, 1983), Young and Bettinger (1992), Jorgensen (1994), Jones and Madsen (1989), along with many others have advanced the usage of optimal foraging theory in the Great Basin in order to lend support to the Numic expansion hypothesis. For example, Bettinger and Baumhoff (1982) suggest that,

> If we apply this logic to the Numic expansion [which they take as fact], where travelers and processors are in competition, it is clear that no matter how desirable it might be for the Prenumic travelers to adopt a processing strategy, and thereby blunt the competitive advantage of the advancing Numic processors, the time lag

required to make the necessary adjustment in sex ratios would mil-
itate against this solution; for the travelers, any more toward a processing strategy is hindered by an excess of males and a shortage of
females. (p. 492)

In this example, Bettinger and Baumhoff utilize optimal foraging theory to propose
that the "Prenumic" peoples of the Great Basin had a different hunting and gathering subsistence economy than those of the Numic peoples. As will be discussed
shortly, there are numerous problems with the use of optimal foraging theory in this
manner. However, first I shall point out a few logical flaws with Bettinger's and
Baumhoff's conclusions. First, it seems highly unlikely that the so-called Prenumic
peoples were unable to adapt their subsistence economy over time, allowing themselves to be displaced by these new (i.e., Numic) foragers. Humans and their cultures are highly adaptive, and it would make more sense to think that if there were
an invasion of Numic peoples into the area, the Prenumic would have adapted a
similar strategy based on the processes of diffusion. Second, it seems unlikely that
a group of peoples could have a better adaptive strategy to an environment that they
had never been in than those of the people living in the environment itself. To posit
that the Numic peoples had a better subsistence strategy than the Prenumic peoples
seems to be highly conjectural and illogical.

As mentioned above, there are several limitations in using optimal foraging theory
to explain human subsistence economies, which I will discuss here. Perhaps one of
the most recognized limitations is that optimal foraging theory assumes environmental heterogeneity, which does not account for the fact that since the environment differs across the land as well as over time, no single organism (e.g., humans)
can possibly hope to be optimally adapted (either physically or through technology)
to every place it might reasonably find itself, nor if it is adapted now should it be certain to remain so. This assumptive limitation further implies that since no organism
(e.g., humans) are optimally adapted to every place they encounter or reside, either
physical or technological change must occur. This is exactly what the archaeological record reveals, as discussed in chapter nine with the gradual technological progression of lithic tools over time and the emergence of various basketry styles, as the
paleoenvironments of the Plateau and Great Basin changed from the Late
Pleistocene through the Holocene.

A second limitation that optimal foraging theory does not directly take into
account is that of the idea of evolutionary lag, which simply points out that populations are most adapted to their previous environments (except under extremely for-
tuitous and rather rare circumstances). Thus, it should not be surprising nor should
it be expected for one to find that animals (or humans) are optimally adapted to the
present environment (or in cases more pertinent to this book, environments that
have recently changed or been encountered). This idea further supports the notion
that as humans either encounter new environments, or as environments change,
there will be a period of time when either human subsistence economies are not
optimally based, or it becomes necessary for a population to change its socioeconomic or technological patterns to fit the new environment. This, like the above-
mentioned limitation, would further support the idea that changes or "gaps" in the

archaeological record (and the biological record) reveal culture adaptation, cultural continuity, and cultural affiliation.

A third limitation with optimal foraging theory is that of panglossism. Panglossism refers to the tendency to see all structures that an animal has as the best possible. This is usually conceived of meaning that because natural selection occurs and is such a powerful force, resulting adaptations are optimal, even if they don't appear so. This idea has been used by optimal foraging theorists studying humans to imply that all technological progressions, such as developments in lithic point styles, are optimal. Thus, when a "new" technology appears in the archaeological record, it is claimed that either this is a logical, optimal development from the previous technology, or that a new group of peoples migrated into the area with this new "optimal" technology. An example of this in the Great Basin is the Lovelock "problem," where it is claimed that Lovelock Wickerware, because it is unique to all other forms of Great Basin basketry, must be the result of a migration and displacement of the previous population of the Lovelock area. However, this line of reasoning fails for several reasons, such as discussed above concerning how this idea denies the possibility of cultural innovation. Likewise, it also does not correspond with the archaeological data, which do not demonstrate any evidence of a new population migrating into the area, especially along the lines of the criteria noted above. Furthermore, it would seem presumptuous to claim that all developments that persist in the archaeological record are "optimal." There are numerous examples from recent history where some technological developments were not at all optimal, but occurred and persisted because of economic, political, or other reasons. Such diverse examples as collective farming, eight-track tapes, Air Buses, and toob tops readily come to mind.

The Spandrels of San Marcos, a fourth limitation, refers to an observation made by Gould and Lewontin (1979) based on the San Marco Cathedral in Venice. Spandrels are flat panels that are needed to help put a dome on supporting architecture. In San Marco they are highly decorated, yet they are obviously not the reason or goal of San Marco nor does the decoration represent an optimization of their actual function. Like the idea of panglossism, the existence of a trait does not prove its adaptive value. This idea points out the difficulty of applying optimal foraging theory to humans, because unlike some biological species in which optimal foraging theory was originally developed and tested, humans are not rational, linear, aconscious organisms. Instead, humans constantly act in ways that are not "optimal," such as through the construction of labor-intensive objects that are then ritually destroyed or by hunting and gathering various resources because they either taste good or perhaps provide some ritual need. Optimal foraging theory, as utilized in the Great Basin (and somewhat in the Plateau), fails to recognize that humans do not hunt "optimally" all the time, and will seek out resources for a number of reasons, optimality being only one.

Finally, it should be noted that optimal foraging theory usually applies the logic of "just so stories." This "technique" starts with the present (the current end point of evolution) and then makes a series of causal conjectures as to what happened to get things to where they are at the present. It is important to avoid the construction of reasonable stories that are nothing more than conjecture without having some way to test them, and short of a test, it is very important not to make much of these arguments no matter how pretty or pleasing they are, for they are little better than syllogisms (they have not been discredited while reasonable alternatives have been knocked down). This is especially a problem in social science because there is a tendency to generalize about behavior from animals to humans and vice versa without a lot of evidence, and although these speculations are very interesting, it is often forgotten that they are nothing more than speculations.

As just discussed, the Lovelock "culture" has been cited as an example of one group of peoples that was displaced by the Numic speakers. This is because many of the archaeological traits of the Lovelock artifacts are highly unique when compared to other areas of the Great Basin. However, as Grosscup (1974) has emphasized, correlates between the Lovelock "culture" and the contemporary Northern Paiute can be seen when one accounts for culture change.

> A comparison of artifacts recovered from Lovelock Cave and other sites of the same period with Northern Paiute ethnographic traits shows a great similarity between the two lots. Most of the traits which are considered to be highly distinctive of the Lovelock Culture do not occur ethnographically but a number of such traits do occur. Some traits seem to have been lost shortly before the contact period. (Grosscup, 1974, p. 20)

Similarly, and also just discussed, the Fremont "culture," is also often cited in support of the Numic expansion hypothesis. However, as with the Lovelock "culture," and perhaps even more clearly, new research indicates that the Fremont "culture" was neither as tightly constrained as archaeologists have portrayed (thus limiting the use of the term "culture"), nor were they as mono-economic in their subsistence regimes. For example, Barlow (2002) recently reported that, "In some cases, apparently contemporaneous sites within close proximity yield as much variation in assemblage composition as is common between Basketmaker and Pueblo sites in the Anasazi area, or even broadly between Fremont sites versus the Anasazi, Mogollon, or other culture regions" (p. 69). Barlow (2002) also notes that because the Fremont were heavily interactive with the Southwestern agricultural communities, but that their local ecology was much different than that of the Southwest, Fremont sites should be, "examined as a case representing extreme intersite variation in the economic importance of farming" (p. 65). As Madsen and Simms (1998) have also noted, the Fremont archaeological "culture" is better understood as representing a time of transition from foraging to farming, followed by a period of adaptive diversity, and culminating in the eventual abandonment of farming by people in the eastern Great Basin, rather than as the "disappearance" of a group of people and the "appearance" of another group of people.

Finally, as recent research in other regions outside of the Plateau and Great Basin indicates, prehistoric peoples were well aware of their environment and changes within it. For example, recent research has led to the idea that instead of abandonment within the Mimbres area of the Southwest, regional reorganization took place that allowed the people to continue subsisting in the area during poor social or environmental conditions, "maintaining regional occupational continuity" (Nelson & Hegmon, 2001, p. 213). This last example is also more in line with recent archaeological theory that recognizes that residential movement is not always equated with relinquishment of ownership and certainly not with the disappearance of a people (Nelson & Schachner, 2002).

To conclude, then, as I discussed in this chapter, in order to demonstrate that a migration has taken place within a particular place and time period, very stringent criteria of empirical evidence must be met. However, as has been noted in discussing the Numic expansion hypothesis, migrations in prehistory, and the use of optimal foraging theory, none of these criteria have been met. Instead, the Numic expansion hypothesis is closer to a syllogism in that the only evidence it is based upon stems from linguistic theoretical assumptions that are then taken as facts to support other assumptions. The Numic expansion hypothesis fails when one looks at the underlying assumptions upon which the linguistic model is based, as was covered in chapter ten. Furthermore, there is no other evidence for the Great Basin or for the Plateau that would lend support to the idea of a prehistoric migration or population displacement, let alone meet any of the criteria discussed above required to demonstrate that such an event took place in prehistory. Similarly, as I argued based on four fundamental limitations to optimal foraging theory, this theoretical line reasoning cannot be used to demonstrate a lack of cultural affiliation or as evidence for migration events. In the next chapter I will review all of the lines of evidence covered in chapters seven through eleven, arriving at a synthesis of the evidence in order to answer the question of cultural affiliation in the Plateau and Great Basin between the peoples of the Late Pleistocene and Early Holocene and the present-day American Indians.

CHAPTER 13
SYNTHESIS OF THE EVIDENCE

D uring the last six chapters I have reviewed in some depth the various lines of evidence that are mandated by NAGPRA for determining cultural affiliation. As discussed in chapter three, NAGPRA mandates that questions of cultural affiliation be resolved by looking at the "preponderance of the evidence" demonstrated by the geographic and kinship data (the ethnographic data), the biological data, the archaeological data, the linguistic data, and the oral tradition data. As this book has demonstrated, this process is very complex, and depending on how one "reads" the data, different interpretations of the evidence may result. However, this book has attempted to review the data from an epistemological praxis of epoché as discussed in chapter two, in an attempt to not let any presuppositions influence the data and how they are "read." By doing so, this analysis and the conclusions drawn in this book rest on the data themselves, and not on presumptive stances or biased theoretical orientations.

As a result of this process, the following synbook of the evidence is indicated by the data for each area of inquiry. The ethnographic data can only directly evidence events that have taken place either within the recent prehistoric or the historic period. Concerning the question of cultural affiliation within the Plateau and Great Basin, the ethnographic data strongly indicates cultural continuity and cultural affiliation between the present-day American Indian tribes of these regions and the peoples of the early prehistoric. The ethnographic evidence is unable to provide information concerning the Late Pleistocene and Early Holocene peoples of these regions. Although the ethnographic data is unable to lend direct support to the question of cultural affiliation between the Kennewick Man and Spirit Cave

Mummy, the data does provide direct evidence linking today's American Indians to those of the recent past for both regions. There is no evidence for migration or cultural displacement during the protohistoric or historic period in either the Plateau or Great Basin. Likewise, the ethnographic evidence does provide anecdotal evidence linking today's American Indians to the people of the Late Pleistocene and Early Holocene based on subsistence lifeway patterns as discussed in chapter seven.

As discussed in chapter eight, the biological data offers several separate lines of evidence, including dental, craniometric, genetic, and trichological. As discussed in this book, these lines of evidence have several limitations inherent within both their theoretical assumptions and their methodological analyses. Based on the current understanding of the biological data, the evidence supports the conclusion that during the Pleistocene, various peoples from northeastern Asia made their way across Beringia, either by land or by sea, and populated the Americas. These people then slowly diversified, adapting and evolving to the multitude of environments encountered throughout the Americas during the Late Pleistocene and Early Holocene. Furthermore, there is no biological evidence that lends support to the idea of a "break" in biological populations or biological population displacement between these Late Pleistocene and Early Holocene peoples and their Middle Holocene descendents. Furthermore, the biological data also evidences in some detail the plastic nature of human biological characteristics, demonstrating that peoples' biological nature can change dramatically over a period of several hundred or thousands of years. Specifically, dental morphology appears not to have changed demonstrably enough to distinguish between northeast Asians and American Indians, let alone between ethnic groups from within the same area (i.e., within the Americas). Furthermore, craniometric data can only offer basic measurements of cranial attributes that can distinguish between contemporaneous biological populations, but offers little in regard to comparisons between such deep-time questions like those addressed in this book. Likewise, craniometric analyses, like trichological analyses, are unable to provide insights concerning inter-group differences (i.e., cultural level differences). Finally, as was discussed in detail, though the promise of genetic data (both ancient and modern) is great, currently the database, methods, and theories surrounding this field are equivocal in addressing issues relevant to this book. The genetic evidence supports the conclusion that American Indians originally migrated from northeast Asia some 20,000-35,000 years ago, but offers little in distinguishing between cultural differences (i.e., between contemporary tribes), as well as between the present-day American Indians and the people of the Late Pleistocene and Early Holocene. Thus, although the biological data cannot directly support cultural affiliation dating back to the Late Pleistocene and Early Holocene, it does support biological continuity. Furthermore, the biological data indicates that the peoples of the Late Pleistocene and Early Holocene were American Indian, though the skeletal morphology of particular individuals may cover a wide statistical range. Therefore, the Kennewick Man and Spirit Cave Mummy, based on the biological data, are American Indian and are biologically affiliated with the present-day American Indians of the Plateau and Great Basin, respectively.

Chapter nine, which followed the discussion of the biological data, reviewed the archaeological data for the Plateau and Great Basin. As I discussed, the archaeological data is highly complex and dependent upon various subjective levels of analyses. Furthermore, the archaeological database contains numerous "gaps" within its record, primarily due to a lack of knowledge as opposed to a demonstration of migration or population displacement. In fact, from a diachronic, macro-regional perspective, the archaeological record for both the Plateau and the Great Basin evidences continuous technological adaptation and sophistication from the Late Pleistocene and Early Holocene until the historic period. Likewise, there is no hard data to support the theoretical premise of either population displacement or migration within either of these two regions. There is some subjective interpretation of various "types" of archaeological data from specific micro-regions, but this level of analysis fails on a larger, macro-regional scale. Finally, the archaeological record for both regions demonstrates a large body of evidence in support of continued cultural exploitation, development, and evolution by the same peoples and their descendents from the Late Pleistocene and Early Holocene until the historic period. Thus, the archaeological record indicates cultural affiliation between today's Plateau and Great Basin American Indians and those people of the historic, protohistoric, and prehistoric record.   Furthermore, the archaeological context associated with Kennewick Man and the Spirit Cave Mummy does not appear to have experienced a "break."   In fact, as reviewed in chapter nine, the archaeological data evidences continued technological and cultural evolution from the Late Pleistocene and Early Holocene to the historic period, arguing for cultural affiliation between the present-day American Indians and the peoples of the Late Pleistocene and Early Holocene.

Following the chapter on archaeological data, I covered the linguistic data. As discussed, using linguistic evidence for analyses dating back beyond several hundred or thousand years is highly controversial and problematic, especially the multilateral word comparison method of Greenberg (1987). For the two regions under investigation in this book, there is only one linguistic theory proposed to support the idea of a migration or population displacement, which is known as the Numic expansion hypothesis. As has been discussed, this linguistic-based theory lacks any supporting evidence other than syllogistic assumptions based on the faulty methodology of multilateral word comparison.   Furthermore, when crosschecked with biological, archaeological, and oral tradition lines of evidence, the Numic expansion hypothesis loses all factual grounding.   Thus, the Numic expansion hypothesis cannot be considered a strong hypothesis in support of either migration or population displacement until further lines of evidence corroborate its basic theoretical assumptions.   For the Plateau and Great Basin, linguistic evidence indicates that the Sahaptian and Uto-Aztecan language families have been in place within these regions dating well back into the Holocene, and there is no evidence that another language was spoken within these areas at any point in prehistory. Therefore, the linguistic evidence supports linguistic affiliation between the peoples of the Late Pleistocene and Early Holocene and the present-day American Indians of the Plateau and Great Basin.   Further, the linguistic evidence indicates that the Kennewick Man and Spirit Cave Mummy spoke either an early version of Sahaptin and Uto-Aztecan, or a proto version of these languages such as Penutian.

Chapter eleven, the final line of evidence covered in this book, discussed oral tradition data. Though it is problematic to lend too much specific factual weight to
oral traditions, it is reasonable to allow for some general factual basis to be present
in oral traditions. As discussed, the oral traditions of the Plateau and Great Basin all
maintain *in situ* origin stories, as well as demonstrating a complete lack of references to either migration or population displacement. There is some limited reference to confrontations or disputes with other peoples having taken place within
some of the oral traditions, but these can parsimoniously be attributed to stories referencing earlier times when now peaceful kinship groups or intertribal groups had
been in dispute, and not as evidence of population displacement. Furthermore,
there are numerous oral traditions from these regions that appear to reference
major climatic events that took place during the Late Pleistocene and Early
Holocene boundary, lending evidence to the conclusion of a deep-time occupation
within the Plateau and Great Basin by today's American Indians. Thus, though not
perhaps as strong as some lines of inquiry, the oral tradition data all lend support to
the conclusion of cultural affiliation in the Plateau and Great Basin from the Late
Pleistocene and Early Holocene to the present day. Further, the oral tradition data
also references the time of the Kennewick Man and Spirit Cave Mummy, arguing
that the present-day American Indians are culturally affiliated with these individuals
and other peoples of the Late Pleistocene and Early Holocene.

To conclude, therefore, as this summary of the evidence demonstrates, based on
the NAGPRA mandated lines of inquiry and an epistemological praxis of epoché,
the present-day tribes of the Plateau and Great Basin can reasonably claim cultural
affiliation with the land, artifacts, skeletons, and other cultural patrimony of these
areas dating from the Late Pleistocene and Early Holocene through prehistory to
the present. This would mean that both the Kennewick Man and the Spirit Cave
Mummy are culturally affiliated with the contemporary American Indian tribes of
these regions. In the Kennewick Man's case, the five tribes that requested repatriation, the Umatilla, Colville, Yakama, Nez Perce, and Wanapum as a whole are culturally affiliated with the individual. Likewise, for the Spirit Cave Mummy, this
would mean that the Northern Paiute of the Fallon Reservation are culturally affiliated with the individual. Thus, as the "preponderance of the evidence" indicates for
these two NAGPRA cases, both the Kennewick Man and the Spirit Cave Mummy
should have been repatriated as mandated by the guiding legislative body of the
Native American Graves Protection and Repatriation Act. Furthermore, future dis-
coveries that are found within these regions should also be assumed to be culturally
affiliated with the present-day American Indians until conclusive evidence is found
to demonstrate otherwise. As I have discussed to some length in this book, there is
no evidence that would indicate that population displacement or migration events
have taken place within these regions during the last 10,000 years.

Though both of these cases are now closed, the larger implications of this book
and its findings should be noted. Until future evidence is discovered demonstrating conclusively that either migrations or population displacements took place in
the Plateau or the Great Basin regions during prehistory, future and present artifacts, skeletons, and other cultural patrimony should be considered affiliated with
the present-day American Indian tribes of these regions. Finally, this conclusion,

based on the "preponderance of the evidence," has larger implications for the field of anthropology as a whole as we move into the twenty-first century, which I will discuss in the next chapter.

	SUPPORTS CULTURAL AFFILIATION	DOES NOT SUPPORT CULTURAL AFFILIATION	AMBIGUOUS; DOES NOT SUPPORT OR DENY
Ethnographic Evidence	X		
Biological Evidence			X
Archaeological Evidence	X		X
Linguistic Evidence	X		X
Oral Tradition Evidence	X		

Table 6. This table shows the various lines of inquiry and whether the evidence supports cultural affiliation or not.

CHAPTER 14
ANTHROPOLOGY AND AMERICAN INDIANS

A s discussed in chapter two, this book has followed an epistemological praxis of epoché in an effort to understand the data for what they are, and not for what the anthropologist wants them to be. In order to begin from an epistemological praxis of epoché, I have attempted to drop any specific theoretical stances or *a priori* assumptions. Instead, this process has relied upon the guidelines of inquiry established by the Native American Graves Protection and Repatriation Act (NAGPRA), primarily because this is currently the guiding legislation concerning issues of American Indian cultural affiliation in the United States. Furthermore, as I discussed in chapters one and three, the guidelines of inquiry established by NAGPRA are in line with the foundational framework of American anthropology as originally developed by Franz Boas, Alfred Kroeber, and others. Therefore, in essence this book has been an attempt to address the question of cultural affiliation from an anthropological perspective, not from an archaeological, linguistic, biological, or any other such singular perspective. There are many reasons why this type of analysis and the conclusions presented in the last chapter are so necessary and important, not only for the study of American Indians and issues of cultural affiliation, but for the field of anthropology in general, especially as anthropology attempts to find its direction in the twenty-first century. In this concluding chapter I briefly discuss some of these reasons.

Perhaps the greatest reason for such an approach is that it has become clear over the last hundred years, and especially more recently as a result of postmodernism, relativism, and deconstructionism, is that it is necessary to develop a language and dialogue that is not inherently biased or limiting in its structure, ontology, and epistemology. For example, many prehistorians, by proceeding from a natural science tradition, treat the biological and archaeological record as if it were directly analogous to that of paleontology or geology, with type sites, sequences, and index "tool types" that supposedly embody the full range of variation expected in the material remains of what are often taken to be extinct "cultures" (Sackett, 1982, 1985, 1986). This approach, however, denies types of epistemologies that are often held by the very people under study, and is based on several limiting assumptions. The first limiting assumption is the idea of the existence of toolmaking "traditions," which are thought of as ways of making stone tools transmitted in a social context from one generation to the next. These toolmaking "traditions" are thought to be manifest in the artifact form that are detectable over hundreds of thousands of square miles (i.e., the idea of a Clovis "culture" or peoples). Another limiting assumption is the idea that such "traditions" persisted unchanged and intact over hundreds (or, in the case of the Late Pleistocene and Early Holocene), thousands of years. The third limiting assumption is the conviction that these "traditions" are detectable at points in space (e.g., the Plateau or Great Basin) separated by thousands of miles. Finally, that these "traditions" represent an actual, identifiable people and their culture is the last limiting assumption.

Clark (2002) has made a convincing argument concerning the use of this paradigm and the Lower Paleolithic in Europe, much of which is directly applicable to issues discussed in this book. For example, while internally consistent in respect to its logic of inference, this paradigm cannot be reconciled with the biological or archaeological data. For example, most of the Late Pleistocene "index" tool types such as Clovis, Western Fluted, Desert Side Notch, Folsom, and the like are ubiquitous (or nearly so), and carry little temporal and probably no cultural information whatsoever. Likewise, there is only a minimal and generalized learned behavioral component to the chipped stone artifact form, and not necessarily a largely cultural learned component (Clark, 2002). Similarly, there is an enormous amount of equifinality in the (few) processes by which humans chip stone, such as the formal convergence conditioned by contextual factors such as raw material, size, and distribution in the landscape (Kuhn, 1995). Finally, this formal convergence almost certainly overrides (because of environmental context, rock sources, and mechanics) any hypothetical "cultural" component.

Furthermore, it is important to point out that the time-space distributions of archaeologically defined analytical units, such as Paleoindian or Archaic, exceed by orders of magnitude the time-space distributions of any real or imaginable cultural entity that might have produced and transmitted these units. Unless one resorts to essentialism (e.g., there is an ineffable "Paleoindianness" manifest in the appearance of Clovis lithics), there is simply no behavioral or cultural mechanism whereby a hypothetical toolmaking tradition could have been transmitted over thousands of years and millions of square miles.

Part of the reason for the incongruities in the interpretation of the data has resulted from the massive number of reports, analyses, theories, methods, and articles generated by Plateau and Great Basin archaeologists, and to a larger extent, anthropological specialists:

> Within my lifetime the quantity of original data in archaeology has increased from a relatively small amount, which any competent graduate student could control, to an extraordinary number of site reports, etc., which no student can familiarize himself with in the course of his graduate work. He, therefore, tends to rely on "authorities" or secondary and even tertiary sources as an economical method of acquiring needed information. Unfortunately, well-known "authorities" do not always report the work of others correctly. The graduate student who has relied on his "authority" is misled. (Cressman, 1977, pp. 7-8)

It is understandable that an easy way for anthropologists to grapple with so much data, and the fact that humans who are extremely complex and illogical organisms generated this data, is through numbers and the manageability of statistics. However, this does not give license for anthropologists to dehumanize both the data and the processes that resulted in the data, as well as deny the humanistic link between the people who directly lived, breathed, and created this "data" and their present-day relatives. When this process happens, through the use of circumscribed epistemologies and their inherent language and methods, not only does the integrity of anthropologists and their research lose ground, but the actual, human lives of hundreds, if not thousands or millions, of individuals can become seriously compromised.

Gregory Bateson (1991) identified three types of primary anthropological data: 1) An identified individual in such-and-such a recorded context said such-and-such, and was heard by an individual (usually an anthropologist); 2) An identified individual in such-and-such a recorded context was seen by the anthropologist doing so-and-so; and 3) Artifacts (including tools, works of art, books, clothing, weavings, etc.), made and/or used by such-and-such individuals in such-and-such spatial and geographical contexts (pp. 37-38). Because these are the three basic types of data encountered by anthropologists, Bateson also noted that, "The contexts, the individuals, and the behaviors are too various for their combinations and permutations to be handled in this way [through statistics]. The unit of data which any sample is composed of is too heterogeneous to be legitimately thrown together into a statistical hopper" (p. 39). Furthermore, Bateson (p. 40) stresses that the "normal, non-deviant individual rarely, if ever, becomes a regular informant." A famous example of what happens when anthropologists rely on this circumscribed understanding of people and the "data" they generate is that of the case of the "Windigo Psychosis," which Marano (1982) carefully debunked in his now famous article that demonstrated how this myth had been formulated from a limited understanding of subarctic peoples.

Many great anthropologists have noted the problem of misrepresenting the very people (either their present history through ethnography or their [pre]history through archaeology and biological anthropology) that we are attempting to learn from. A. Irving Hallowell (1960) noted that "a thoroughgoing 'objective' approach to the study of cultures cannot be achieved solely by projecting upon those cultures categorical abstractions derived from Western thought" (p. 21). As discussed in chapters seven through eleven, not only is this precisely what most anthropologists have done in the Plateau and Great Basin, but as was also noted, these Western derived categories ultimately fail in a larger global, cross-cultural framework.

Furthermore, we can see how this circumscribed language has been built into the very legislative process that NAGPRA developed out of for close to a hundred years (and perhaps earlier). As Watkins (2003) points out, "Beginning with the passage of the Antiquities Act in 1906, archaeologists (perhaps unintentionally) began to co-opt the American Indian's unwritten history and material culture" (p. 275). Through this Act the federal government declared that archaeological sites should be protected for the benefit of the "public," and that only through the process of developing a permit system to allow excavation and documentation of these "protected" sites by "qualified" individuals could this protection occur. However, because the federal government deemed only anthropologists as "qualified" to properly excavate, document, and preserve these sites, American Indians were denied both a voice within the process as well as the recognition that these sites were of their cultural manufacture, and thus, ultimately, because they created them, they perhaps knew better than anyone else how to document, interpret, and protect them. Furthermore, it was not until the passage of the Archaeological Resources Protection Act (ARPA) in 1979 that American Indians were even given the explicit right to participate in the process of excavating, documenting, and protecting archaeological sites on their own land (i.e., reservations) for the benefit of the "public."

Finally, with the passage of the Native American Graves Protection and Repatriation Act (NAGPRA) in 1990 and the subsequent Rules in 1995 anthropologists theoretically have begun to arrive full circle back to their foundational roots. NAGPRA mandates that potentially affiliated American Indian tribes must be consulted in the repatriation determination process of cultural patrimony. One of the reasons for this mandate is that, "More archaeologists [and anthropologists in general] are recognizing that professional responsibilities to scholarship and science need to be balanced with ethical responsibilities to indigenous peoples, and that this is not an easy or straightforward task" (Watkins, 2003, p. 278). However, as both the Kennewick Man and the Spirit Cave Mummy cases demonstrate, this collaborative process is only partially working. Furthermore, as this book has attempted to demonstrate, this larger, historically grounded anthropological perspective is absolutely essential if anthropology is to continue working with American Indians and other peoples.

Part of the reason for the continued use of a limited "language" is that because anthropologists are trained in a Western-grounded epistemology, their method and theory of knowing are also grounded in Western ideals. American Indians, however, cannot be assumed to have the same epistemology. A clear example of this is how anthropologists use the idea of cultural evolution (which encompasses technological, social, and other aspects of culture). For example, most anthropologists use the idea of evolution, "the act of unrolling; a series of related changes in a certain direction," only in the limited survival of the fittest sense (e.g., optimal foraging theory, "fitness" of lithic technologies, etc.), and not in the more "humanistic" aspects of evolution (e.g., the complex unrolling of developing a sense of meaning and relationship to place; the series of related changes between people, their culture, and the environment, etc.). Caution must be heeded in this regard, because depending on how one understands evolution (and thus, anthropological theory), it is easy to conclude that evolutionary processes *only* have a beginning, a process influenced by a series of changes in a certain direction, and thus, an end. This would imply that these actions have an ontological, confinable, and measurable status that leads to the erroneous conclusion that these actions can only be studied through a specific ontology and epistemology (i.e., through scientific, empirical analysis of the methods and grounds of knowledge pertaining to being), and not through gnoseology (i.e., through immediate knowledge) or transcendentology (i.e., knowledge that is not directly resolvable by pure logic, mathematics, and sense experience), the latter two of which are valid forms of knowing in many American Indian societies. By denying other forms of knowing, forms that are just as valid for the very people that we are "studying" (and the "data" that they create), we are inherently limiting our understanding while at the same time circumscribing their very being by denying that these other forms of knowing exist and are valid. Examples of other forms of knowing that have recently come to the attention of anthropological investigation include those that can be placed under the categories of Traditional Ecological Knowledge (TEK), ethnoscience, and complementary and alternative medicine (CAM).

As Ridington (1988) has noted for Subarctic hunting peoples, the type of knowledge necessary for successful adaptation to the environment cannot be grasped by merely looking at the artifacts.

> Although they have been capable of producing elaborate hunting implements such as bows and arrows, traps, and deadfalls (Oswalt 1973: 118-119), they also achieve complex interactions with their environment without having recourse to complex material artifacts. Northern hunters have, for instance, traditionally carried out artfully organized communal hunts [This is very similar to both the Plateau tribes methods of communal salmon fishing and the Great Basin tribes methods of communal rabbit and antelope hunting.] with a minimum of material possessions. Using artifacts as simple as snares, they have relied on knowledge held in common to work quietly and autonomously toward a common purpose. In some cases "hunt chiefs" (Ridington 1987a) [again similar to Plateau and Great Basin tribes] visualize and direct the overall hunt plan through dreaming, but success ultimately depends upon the individual's understanding of human and animal behavior in relation to environmental features. Although the physical artifacts required for this form of hunting are minimal, success depends on a complex and sophisticated form of artifice and understanding (Ridington 1983). It is easy for an outside observer to interpret information about dreaming and knowledge differently from infor-

mation about material culture, because of an unexamined assumption that technology *means* material culture. Such an assumption could disguise the full adaptive significance of knowledge for subarctic people and result in what Christian called "a superficial and misleading study" (Christian and Gardner 1977: 100-101). (p. 107)

It is important to stress, however, that as anthropologists we do not want to stray too far to the other extreme (i.e., denying anthropological methods and theories and romanticizing indigenous peoples and their ways of knowing), as many environmentalists, indigenous rights activists, and others have done. Gadamer (1975, 1981, 1994) made this explicit throughout his hermeneutic philosophy. "Understanding" (*Verstehen*) must be historically and linguistically mediated, and there is always some pre-understanding or prejudice (*Vorurteil*) that makes our encounter with tradition possible at all. In other words, both the tradition and those who attempt to interpret it constitute a part of a historical continuum that cannot be artificially separated or segregated. According to Gadamer, the error of the Enlightenment, and to a large extent, Orientalism/Occidentalism and colonial/postcolonial critiques, was and is "prejudice against prejudice," i.e., the refusal to recognize the significance of our own insertion in a tradition that, at some level, we already understand. Thus, Gadamer emphasizes the importance of the "effective history" (*Wirkungsgeschichte*) that underlies any potential "fusion of horizons" (*Horizontsverschmelzung*) that we could hope to achieve. Furthermore, Gadamer also notes the dangerousness of the romantic or psychological approach of classical anthropological theory that sought to collapse historical distance by fostering empathy with the mental attitude, dispositions, and worlds of those who created the traditional texts (or histories, artifacts, oral traditions, and so forth) we interpret. This merely substitutes the Romantic ideal of an ancient, primeval wisdom that could somehow be recuperated for that of the Enlightenment. As Gadamer stresses throughout his work, we are always partners in dialogue, whether it be with texts or histories, and the path to understanding can only be traversed through mutually accepting our different epistemologies with their inherent languages.

Kuper has more recently pointed out this very Romantic fallacy within anthropological interpretations, "there is a strong ecological thread in the indigenous-peoples rhetoric" (Kuper, 2003, p. 390). American Indians naturally subsisted within their environment in the same fashion that other people do (modern Westerners, Asians, Australian aborigines, etc.). By natural, it is meant that because humans are part and parcel of nature, everything we do is in this sense natural. Thus, Kuper notes, "The image of the primitive is often constructed today to suit the Greens and the anti-globalization movement. Authentic natives represent a world to which culture does not challenge nature" (2003, p. 395). This, however, is merely denying one truth and taking the other extreme. It is important to stress that American Indians, prehistorically and historically, manipulated their environment to a large extent, through controlled burning of fires, faunal resource population management/manipulation, construction of various hydrographic features, and many other such actions (see, for example Krech, 1999).

Furthermore, it is important to bring up the question of "Who is Indian?" and

"Whose 'truth' should we listen to?" As Vine Deloria, Jr. (2003) has noted,

> If the decade of Indian activism did anything, it blurred the line between Indians and the rest of society. The popular phrase, "if you say you're an Indian, you are one," made it possible for massive integration of lost young into little networks and communities of Indians where their lack of Indian blood or heritage did not matter as long as they gave support to the goals of that group. Such devotion to the idea of unity was admirable but it also validated people who had little or no commitment to Indians- or even knowledge of Indians. Out of this confusion came the belief that people should not challenge the credentials of anyone who held themselves out to be Indian. (p. 644)

An example of this are the many "indigenous" peoples who now criticize much of anthropological theory by claiming that their epistemology is important (and in many cases, more valid; an ironic colonizing of the colonizers in a sense). These "indigenous" peoples come from a multitude of stances and geographic areas, using much of the same language they lambaste against in their own arguments. A recent example of this rhetoric is that by Smith (1999; see also Carrier 1992, 1995). Smith brings up many good points in her critique against the usual (though not necessarily contemporary), "colonial" anthropological research. For example, Smith states that there are four concepts which underlie *all* Western academic research concerning "indigenous" people: imperialism, history, writing, and theory. Postcolonial discourse, being part of the latter, is not free from the "underlying assumptions, motivations, and values" of these four concepts (Smith, 1999, p. 21). By making these concepts visible, Smith attempts to open them to critical engagement and seeks to "decolonize" (research) methodology.

However, Smith and other critics mistakenly misunderstand the fundamental distinction between imperialism and colonialism in their arguments. For example, many critics of colonialism identify Christopher Columbus as "the one who started it all," who establishes colonialism's (and in some cases, imperialism's) modern time frame, and is representative of its "legacy of suffering and destruction" (Smith, 1999, p. 20). Though Smith is guilty of making this assumption, she does show how colonialism's symbols function differently depending on whether one is the colonizer or the colonized. In her exposition of Columbus, Smith is adopting an indigenous perspective of history, which is how she engages with colonialism and imperialism. Within the discipline of history, however, Columbus did not start the modern time frame of colonialism (nor imperialism for that matter); many factors contributed including the colonization of the Atlantic and the Mediterranean, and the withdrawal of the Chinese from the Indian Ocean and Java (see Fernandez-Armesto, 1987).

Furthermore, imperialism and colonialism are processes that have been a part of human history since the dawn of time. Historians are well aware of the processes of imperialism and colonialism, the continual conquering either physically as is the case of colonialism, or economically as with imperialism of land, resources, and people, as well as the reconquering of these lands, resources, and peoples by other peoples. Two poignant examples that are relevant to the discussion of "colonialism" and to some extent imperialism are that of the Tibetans and American Indians. Many people presently lament the Chinese takeover of Tibet, especially its "colonial" aspects involving destruction and subjugation of the various religious, social, and economic institutions of the Tibetan people. However, what many people fail to realize is that Tibet had previously conquered most of China, as well as much of Kashmir, present-day Nepal, and other areas, often through extremely bloody and brutal battles of "colonial" domination (Snellgrove, 2002). Likewise, we can also look to the Sioux people who had a strong colonial nature in the wars and forced migrations they had with the Blackfeet, Cheyenne, Crow, Pawnee, and other groups of the Plains (see DeMallie, 2001).

Missing, however, in these critiques is an explanation of why the sole focus is on "the form of European imperialism which 'started' in the 15th Century" (Smith, 1999, p. 21), and why there is no clear distinction between imperialism and colonialism within postcolonial discourse. As has been noted above these "processes" of imperialism and colonialism have been part of humankind (and some would argue, human nature) forever. One group of people are always subjugated as an "other" by another dominating group of people, either imperialistically or colonially. This subjugated group usually claims "indigenous" status in order to win sympathy and support, or to claim a more "legitimate" stance in the eyes of potential sympathetic observers. However, these "indigenous" peoples were at one point the dominators of a previous "indigenous" people in most cases, whether culturally, socially, economically, colonially, or imperially. This leads us to the observation that there is a limited amount of awareness and open recognition concerning postcolonial theory, and almost none for "postimperial" theory, for obvious reasons.

Furthermore, "Postcolonial theory has asserted the need to carefully consider how present-day social and cultural practices are marked by histories of colonialism" (Willems-Braun, 1997, p. 3). As noted, colonialism is a process involving a specific type of subjugation that has occurred throughout human history and in different contexts. Modern postcolonial theory recognizes European colonialism, but fails to recognize "indigenous" colonialism, even though it must be understood that the world has never been free of colonization at any point. The primary difference between "modern" colonialism and previous forms is its intimate involvement with specific notions of capitalism (Loomba, 1998). However, it is important to appreciate that colonialism, as a concept, has plural meanings. There is no one colonial experience. Postcolonialism, in truth, is the contestation of colonialism, past and present, rather than the acceptance of a distinct temporal stage of "postcoloniality" (Ashcroft, Griffiths, & Tiffin, 1998; Blunt & Wills, 2000), as many currently use it in the Oriental and Occidental rhetoric. Colonialism only really persists in the discourses and institutions of "postcolonial" states and cultures even though no such postcolonial states or cultures truly exist, for if they did, that would mean that they were no longer colonial in any form, and this is highly unlikely. For if any state or culture is free from colonialism, that would mean that they would need no form of such institutions as government, law, and notions of nations and boundaries. That is, they would be able to let go of their "stateness" or "culturalness." By ignoring the fact that imperialism and colonialism are a part of human history, many critics are

complicit in Western academia's exclusion of voices. Their position as an indigenous or "other" person oppressed under Europe seemingly "privileges" their voice
within the discourse surrounding imperialism and colonialism.

   This is why it is so important to understand both History, and the underlying histories that build History[8]. History and histories are constructed upon and build
ways of knowing. That is, ways of interpreting, constructing, and understanding reality. In this sense, they are also forms of power (see Foucault, 1974, 1980). Many critics and supporters of postcolonial theory pose the question: "Is history important
for indigenous people?" The answer appears simple "yes, history is important"
(Smith, 1999, p. 29). Many claim that history (and one can include anthropological research), as a discipline, however, is not important because it has been and is
being used as a tool of colonialism. These critics claim that history asserts colonial
ideology by negating indigenous ways of knowing and this will do nothing to trans-
form the larger History into justice. This, the critics argue, negates the fact that
"indigenous" histories are important. They are alternative histories that contest
Western ways of knowing. However, by attacking History, and not history, these critics mistakenly confuse the Western history for the larger History that emerges out
of the various histories people hold to be valid. What needs to be recognized is that
histories are part and parcel of History, and though one form of history may have
been used as a "tool" of colonialism in the past, History itself cannot be.

This misunderstanding becomes more apparent when it is realized that the usual
arguments presented are binary and overly simplistic. For example, under
(neo)colonialism "indigenous" people allow their histories to be retold, subsequently becoming outsiders to them, confusing the line between the usual binary of
Western history and "indigenous" history. Furthermore, as relativism has pointed
out, if they are both just ways of knowing, can one be more legitimate than the
other? One problem with Western history was that it considered itself (and to a
large extent, still does) the only legitimate way of knowing. Surely if an alternative
theory of methodology is to be found, it should not make the same mistake?
Furthermore, critics of (post)colonialism and Orientalism use some of the same
problematic notions inherent in the anthropological theory that they critique.
Their own description of the poststructuralist critique of history is an attempted
"totalizing discourse." Likewise, discussions of the "indigenous" experience assume
"universal characteristics" which are of a valid form, and which have been or continue to be of interest and value in a globalized world. As the postmodernists have
pointed out, there is no such thing as a culturally identified group when speaking
in broad terms such as "indigenous." Who is indigenous, and to where, and at what
time, and by whose standards? Furthermore, whose "history" are we supposed to
believe? As Vine Deloria, Jr. (2003) notes,

> A bizarre process of verification developed. When queried about
> their Indian ancestry many people spun delightful tales of how
> their ancestors had refused to go to reservations or take allotments
> and instead melted into white society, preserving always the stories
> and ceremonies that the real tribe, confined on reservations, soon
> forgot. This narrative was a clever ploy and produced a number of

> personalities who were more Indian than reservation people
> because, allegedly, they refused to bow to the government.
> Publishers took the bait and so we have some tribal histories and
> religious books that come from these murky beginnings. (p. 644)

So how does this discussion pertain to this book? First, the conclusions reached in
this book do not rest on any underlying, presumptive *a priori* stances. I am not in
favor of American Indians, nor am I in favor of anthropology. Either one of these
stances fails to provide any meaningful piece of knowledge in a larger context,
instead merely providing assumptive projections that continue the process of imperialism (though not colonialism); the imperialization of knowledge by asserting that
one assumptive projection is better than the other. This process would just add
another binary to the already cluttered arena of binary knowledge, my
opinion/their opinion. As can be noted, such common binaries as we/I,
western/indigenous, inauthentic/authentic, traditional/nontraditional are all overly simplistic and deny any of the complexities involved in each one. Furthermore,
a binary can only be true if one buys into the binary system, thus, one can only be
indigenous if one recognizes that there is an "other," which only further complicates
the problems. Derrida (1976, 1978) pointed this out when he stressed that one can
no longer rely on the essential stability of "signs." For Derrida, a radical "undecid-
ability" surrounds all signification in that there can be no absolute origin or site of
meaning. There can be no I/we, Orient/Occident, traditional/nontraditional, for
these are all signs that are taken out of their particular contextual meaning, in a
sense becoming vacant.

Furthermore, as Walter Benjamin stressed continually through his work (e.g.
Benjamin, 1986), we must also resist the temptation to view history as a neutral and
seamless web, progressing inexorably through "empty" time, yielding a continuous
narrative whole. Through his work, Benjamin has shown how it is essential to
remember the openness of history — open to language, interpretation, and experience — and that embedded within each interpretation of history and it's events are
numerous other levels of interpretation.

Thus, if we are open to the fact that embedded within each interpretation of history and it's events, which make up History, there are numerous further levels of
interpretation, we can begin to understand how important it is to include histories
in History, and as I have argued and attempted to demonstrate in this book, one
must come from an epistemological praxis of epoché. As Geertz (1973) noted,

> The interminable, because unterminable, debate within anthropol-
> ogy as to whether culture is "subjective" or "objective," together
> with the mutual exchange of intellectual insults ('idealist!'- 'mate-
> rialist!'; 'mentalist!' — 'behaviorist!'; 'impressionist!' — 'posi-
> tivist!') which accompanies it, is wholly misconceived. Once
> human behavior is seen as (most of the time; there are true twitch-
> es) symbolic action- action which, like phonation in speech, pig-
> ment in painting, line in writing, or sonance in music, signifies- the
> question as to whether culture is patterned conduct or a frame of

mind, or even the two somehow mixed together, loses sense. The thing to ask about a burlesqued wink or a mock sheep raid is not what their ontological status is. It is the same as that of rocks on the one hand and dreams on the other- they are things of this world. The thing to ask is what their import is: what it is, ridicule or challenge, irony or anger, snobbery or pride, that, in their occurrence and through their agency, is getting said. (p. 10)

Anthropological theory, and the resultant questions that stem from that theory, are vacant of any useful meaning when one divorces the "objects" from the people who made, said, or developed those "objects."

Now, this proposition, that it is not in our interest to bleach human behavior of the very properties that interest us before we begin to examine it, has sometimes been escalated into a larger claim: namely, that as it is only those properties that interest us, we need not attend, save cursorily, to behavior at all.... Though a distinct improvement over 'learned behavior' and 'mental phenomena' notions of what culture is, and the source of some of the most powerful theoretical ideas in contemporary anthropology, this hermetical approach to things seems to me to run the danger (and increasingly to have been overtaken by it) of locking cultural analysis away from its proper object, the informal logic of actual life. There is little profit in extricating a concept from the defects of psychologism only to plunge it immediately into those of schematicism. (Geertz, 1973, p. 17)

Therefore, we come to the current state of the anthropological field concerning American Indians: the collaborative process between American Indians and anthropologists is only partially working despite the fact that this collaborative process is essential to both American Indians and anthropologists. This leads to the question: how is it possible to utilize both anthropological theory and American Indian perspectives and knowledge, while still staying within the various legislative acts set forth by the federal government, in order to ask meaningful, important, and progressive questions for both sides? As Geertz (1973) has again noted,

If anthropological interpretation is constructing a reading of what happens, then to divorce it from what happens- from what, in this time or that place, specific people say, what they do, what is done to them, from the whole vast business of the world- is to divorce it from its applications and render it vacant. (p. 18)

The argument discussed in this book is that first one must begin to recognize the various languages, methods, and theories (and their underlying presumptions and assumptions) employed within the anthropology based epistemology, the American Indian epistemology, and the legislative policies that are a result of these epistemologies. Furthermore, one must correctly observe the phenomena under study in order to understand how these languages, methods, and theories either cloud or illuminate the inquiry. Thus, as I have argued it is essential to begin from an epistemological praxis of epoché. With the observation of phenomena through the suspension of all presumptive and assumptive notions, one can begin to understand not only the phenomena under observation, but also the various languages, methods, and theories that are a result of these observations.

Therefore, by beginning with an epistemological praxis of epoché we begin to understand and incorporate the multitude of histories into History; the multitude of truths into Truth. From this understanding it becomes apparent that the standard binaries of we/I, western/indigenous, inauthentic/authentic, traditional/nontraditional lose much of their ground because they are simplistic conceptualizations based on the assumption that each holds more say towards Truth and History, when in fact they are just one of many truths and histories.

Thus, we arrive at the final point of this book, which is that all histories and truths are valid and important, and that in order to at least begin to possibly strive for History and Truth, we must include the multitude of histories and truths that make up the larger History and Truth. Therefore, anthropology must acknowledge and include American Indians and their histories and truths. Likewise, American Indians must also acknowledge anthropology's histories and truths. Furthermore, we must come to grips with the fact that knowledge is power, and that there are many ways of knowing. We cannot blindly assert one way of knowing over another, for that would lead us back down the dark road of colonialism, romanticism, and the other ugly processes associated with such forms of power. Instead, we must use power as a tool, a tool that can help anthropology, American Indians, and all those in-between. For it is only through the open acknowledgment that the "science of man" (Kroeber, 1923, p. 1) includes all of humankind, and all of humankind's histories and truths, can we, as humans, begin to utilize Truth and History as tools of power for the overall betterment of humankind.

REFERENCES

Adams, R. M. (1997). Things in themselves. *Philosophy and Phenomenological Research, 57*(4), 801-825.

Adams, W. Y., Van Gerven, D. P., & Levy, R. S. (1978). The retreat from migrationism. *Annual Review of Anthropology, 7*, 483-532.

Adelaar, W. F. H. (1989). Review of *language in the Americas* by Joseph H. Greenberg. *Lingua, 78*, 249-255.

Adelung, J. C. (1793). *Grammatisch-kritisches worterbuch der hochdeutschen mundart.* Leipzig.

Adovasio, J. M. (1974). Prehistoric North American basketry. In *Collected papers on aboriginal basketry* (Vol. 16, pp. 98-148). Carson City, NV: Nevada State Museum.

Adovasio, J. M. (1986a). Artifacts and ethnicity: Baskets as an indicator of territoriality and population movement in the prehistoric Great Basin. *University of Utah Anthropological Papers, 110*, 43-88.

Adovasio, J. M. (1986b). Prehistoric basketry. In D'Azevedo, W. (Ed.), *Handbook of North American Indians* (Vol. 11: Great Basin, pp. 194-205). Washington, D.C.: Smithsonian Institution, Government Printing Office.

Adovasio, J. M., & Pedler, D. R. (1994). A tisket, a tasket: Looking at the Numic speakers through the "lens" of a basket. In Madsen, D. B. & Rhode, D. (Eds.), *Across the west: Human population movement and the expansion of the Numa* (pp. 114-123). Salt Lake City: University of Utah Press.

Ager, T. A., & Brubaker, L. B. (1985). Quaternary palynology and vegetational history of Alaska. In Bryant, V. M., Jr. & Holloway, R. G. (Eds.), *Pollen records of late-quaternary North American sediments* (pp. 353-384). Austin, TX: American Association of Stratigraphic Palynologists Foundation.

Aigner, J. S., & Del Bene, T. (1982). Early holocene maritime adaptation in the Aleutian Islands. In Ericson, J. E., Taylor, R. E. & Berger, R. (Eds.), *Peopling of the new world* (pp. 35-68). California: Ballena Press.

Aikens, C. M. (1978). Archaeology of the Great Basin. *Annual Review of Anthropology, 7*, 71-87.

Aikens, C. M. (1982). Archaeology of the northern Great Basin: An overview. In Madsen, D. B. & O'Connell, J. F. (Eds.), *Man and environment in the Great Basin* (pp. 139-155). Washington, D.C.: Society for American Archaeology.

Aikens, C. M. (1998). *Uto-aztecan cultural continuity and adaptive diversity in the desert west of North America: Reaching into deep time from the edge of history.*Unpublished manuscript, Reno, NV.

Akazawa, T. (1999). Pleistocene peoples of Japan and the peopling of the Americas. In Bonnichsen, R. & Turnmire, K. (Eds.), *Ice age people of North America: Environments, origins, adaptations* (pp. 95-103). Corvallis, OR: Oregon State University Press.

Alexseev, V. P., & Gokhman, I. I. (1984). *Antropologia aziatskoi chasti sssr*. Moskwa, Russia: Nauka.

Allen, B. D., & Anderson, R. Y. (1993). Evidence from western North America for rapid shifts in climate during the late glacial maximum. *Science, 260*, 1920-1923.

Allen, B. D., & Anderson, R. Y. (2000). A continuous, high-resolution record of late pleistocene climate variability from the Estancia Basin, New Mexico. *Geological Society of America Bulletin, 112*, 1444-1458.

Alley, J. R., Jr. (1986). *Great Basin Numa: The contact period (Paiutes, Shoshones, Nevada)*. University of California, Santa Barbara, Santa Barbara, CA.

Alroy, J. (2001). A multispecies overkill simulation of the end-pleistocene megafaunal mass extinction. *Science, 292*, 1893-1896.

Alsozatai-Petheo, J. (1986). An alternative paradigm for the study of early man in the new world. In Bryan, A. L. (Ed.), *New evidence for the pleistocene peopling of the Americas* (pp. 15-27). Orono, Maine: Center for the Study of Early Man.

Altheide, T. K., & Hammer, M. F. (1997). Evidence for a possible Asian origin of YAP+ y chromosomes. *American Journal of Human Genetics, 61*, 462-466.

Alves-Silva, J., Santos, M. d. S., Guimaraes, P. E. M., Fereira, A. C. S., Bandelt, H.-J., Pena, S. D. J., et al. (2000). The ancestry of Brazilian mtDNA lineages. *American Journal of Human Genetics, 67*, 444-461.

Ameriks, K. (1985). Hegel's critique of Kant's theoretical philosophy. *Philosophy and Phenomenological Research, 46*(1), 1-35.

Ames, K. (1988). *Instability in prehistoric residential patterns on the intermontane pPateau*. Paper presented at the 41st Northwest Anthropological Conference, Tacoma, WA.

Ames, K. (1991). Sedentism, a temporal shift or a transitional change in hunter-gatherer mobility strategies. In Gregg, S. (Ed.), *Between bands and states* (pp. 103-133). Carbondale, IL: Southern Illinois University Press.

Ames, K. (2000). *Cultural affiliation study of the Kennewick human remains: Review of the archaeological data*. Washington, D.C.: Department of the Interior.

Ames, K., Dummond, D., Galm, J., & Minor, R. (1998). Prehistory of the southern Plateau. In Walker, D. E., Jr. (Ed.), *Plateau* (Vol. 12, pp. 103-119). Washington, D.C.: Smithsonian Institution.

Amoss, P. T. (1993). Hair of the dog: Unraveling pre-contact Coast Salish social stratification. In Mattina, A. & Montler, T. (Eds.), *American indian linguistics and ethnography in honor of Laurence C. Thompson* (pp. 3-35). Missoula, MT: University of Montana.

Anastasio, A. (1972). The southern Plateau: An ecological analysis of intergroup relations. *Northwest Anthropological Research Notes, 6*(2), 109-229.

Anderson, D., & Gillam, J. C. (2000). Paleoindian colonization of the Americas: Implications from an examination of physiography, demography, and artifact distribution. *American Antiquity, 65,* 43-66.

Anderson, D. D. (1984). Prehistory of North Alaska. In Dumas, D. (Ed.), *Handbook of North American Indians* (Vol. 5: Arctic, pp. 80-93). Washington, D.C.: Smithsonian Institution, Government Printing Office.

Anderson, P. M., Bartlein, P. J., & Brubaker, L. B. (1994). Late quaternary history of tundra vegetation in Northwestern Alaska. *Quaternary Research, 41*(3), 306-315.

Anderson, P. M., Lozhkin, A. V., & Brubaker, L. B. (2002). Implications of a 24,000-yr palynological record for a younger dryas cooling and for boreal forest development in Northeastern Siberia. *Quaternary Research, 57,* 325-333.

Anderson, R. Y., Allen, B. D., & Menking, K. M. (2002). Geomorphic expression of abrupt climate change in southwestern North America at the glacial termination. *Quaternary Research, 57,* 371-381.

Anderson, T. W. (1985). Late-quaternary pollen records from Eastern Ontario, Quebec, and Atlantic Canada. In Bryant, V., M., Jr. & Holloway, R. G. (Eds.), *Pollen records of late-quaternary North American sediments* (pp. 281-326). Austin, TX: American Association of Stratigraphic Palynologists Foundation.

Andrews, D. L. (1994). Molecular approaches to the isolation and analysis of ancient nucleic acids. In Bonnichsen, R. & Steele, D. G. (Eds.), *Method and theory for investigating the peopling of the Americas* (pp. 165-176). Corvallis, OR: Center for the Study of the First Americans.

Aoki, H., & Walker, D. E., Jr. (1989). *Nez Perce oral narratives.* Berkeley, CA: University of California Press.

Arkush, B. S. (1999). Numic pronghorn exploitation: A reassessment of Stewardian-derived models of big-game hunting in the Great Basin. In Clemmer, R. O., Myers, L. D. & Rudden, M. E. (Eds.), *Julian Steward and the Great Basin: The making of an anthropologist* (pp. 35-52). Salt Lake City, UT: University of Utah Press.

Asad, T. (Ed.). (1973). *Anthropology and the colonial encounter.* London, UK: Ithaca Press.

Ashcroft, B., Griffiths, G., & Tiffin, H. (1998). *Key concepts in post-colonial studies.* London, UK: Routledge.

Astakhov, V. (1998). The last ice sheet of the Kara Sea: Terrestrial constraints on its age. *Quaternary International, 45/46,* 19-28.

Atwell, R. (1989). *Subsistence variability on the Columbia Plateau.* Unpublished Masters thesis, Portland State University, Portland, OR.

Auffenberg, W., & Milstead, W. W. (1965). Reptiles in the quaternary of North America. In Wright, H. E., Jr. & Frey, D. G. (Eds.), *The quaternary of the United States: A review volume for the VII congress of the international association for quaternary research* (pp. 557-568). Princeton, NJ: Princeton University Press.

Babbitt, B. (2000). *Letter from Secretary of the Interior Bruce Babbitt to Secretary of the Army Louis Caldera regarding disposition of the Kennewick human remains.* Washington, D.C.: Department of the Interior.

Bada, J., Gillespie, R., Gowlett, J. A. J., & Hedges, R. E. M. (1984). Accelerator mass spectrometry radiocarbon ages of amino acid extracts from Californian paleoindian skeletons. *Nature, 312,* 442-444.

Bada, J., & Helfman, P. M. (1975). Amino acid racemization dating of fossil bones. *World Archaeology, 7*(2), 160-173.

Bada, J., & Masters, P. M. (1982). Evidence for a ~50,000-year antiquity of man in the Americas derived from amino-acid racemization of human skeletons. In Ericson, J. E., Taylor, R. E. & Berger, R. (Eds.), *Peopling of the new world* (pp. 171-180). California: Ballena Press.

Bada, J., Schroeder, R. A., & Carter, G. F. (1974). New evidence for the antiquity of man in North America deduced from aspartic acid racemization. *Science, 184,* 791-793.

Baker, R. G., & Waln, K. (1985). Quaternary pollen records from the Great Plains and central United States. In Bryant, V. M., Jr. & Holloway, R. G. (Eds.), *Pollen records of late-quaternary North American sediments* (pp. 191-204). Austin, TX: American Association of Stratigraphic Palynologists Foundation.

Ballinger, S. W., Schurr, T. G., Torroni, A., Gan, Y. Y., Hodge, J. A., Hassan, K., et al. (1992). Southeast Asian mitochondrial DNA analysis reveals genetic continuity of ancient mongoloid migrations. *Genetics, 130,* 139-152.

Bamforth, D. B. (1988). *Ecology and human organization on the Great Plains: Interdisciplinary contributions to archaeology.* New York, NY: Plenum Press.

Bancroft, H. H. (1890). *The history of Nevada, Colorado and Wyoming 1540-1888.* San Francisco: CA: The History Company.

Barbujani, G. (1997). DNA variation and language affinities. *American Journal of Human Genetics, 61,* 1011-1014.

Bard, J. C., Busby, C. L., & Findlay, J. M. (1981). *A cultural resources overview of the Carson and Humboldt sinks, Nevada* (No. Cultural Resource Series No. 2). Carson City, NV: Bureau of Land Management.

Barker, J. P. (1994). *Site damage assessment Elephant Mountain Cave.* Carson City, NV: Bureau of Land Management.

Barker, P., Ellis, C., & Damadio, S. (2000). *Determination of cultural affiliation of ancient human remains from Spirit Cave, Nevada.* Carson City, NV: Bureau of Land Management, Nevada State Office.

Barlow, K. R. (2002). Predicting maize agriculture among the Fremont: An economic comparison of farming and foraging in the American Southwest. *American Antiquity, 67*(1), 65-88.

Barnard, A. (2000). *History and theory in anthropology.* Cambridge, UK: Cambridge University Press.

Barnes, I., Matheus, P., Shapiro, B., Jensen, D., & Cooper, A. (2002). Dynamics of pleistocene population extinctions in beringian brown bears. *Science, 295*, 2267-2270.

Barrett, S. A. (1917). The Washo indians. *Bulletin of the Public Museum of the City of Milwaukee, 2*(1), 1-52.

Barrie, J. V., & Conway, K. W. (1999). Late quaternary glaciation and postglacial stratigraphy of the northern Pacific margin of Canada. *Quaternary Research, 51*, 113-123.

Bascom, W. R. (1965). Four functions of folklore. In Dundes, A. (Ed.), *The study of folklore* (pp. 279-298). Englewood City, NJ: Prentice-Hall, Inc.

Bashkow, I. (2004). A neo-Boasian conception of cultural boundaries. *American Anthropologist, 106*(3), 443-458.

Bateman, R., Goddard, I., O'Grady, R., Funk, W. A., Mooi, R., Kress, W. J., et al. (1990). Speaking of forked tongues: The feasibility of reconciling human phylogeny and the history of language. *Current Anthropology, 31*(1), 1-24.

Bateson, G. (1991). *A sacred unity: Further steps to an ecology of mind.* New York, NY: HarperCollins Publishers.

Bath, J. (1977). *The red-headed giants of Lovelock Cave: Fact or fiction?* Unpublished manuscript, Carson City, NV.

Baugh, T. G., & Nelson, F. W., Jr. (1987). New mexico obsidian sources and exchange on the southern Plains. *Journal of Field Archaeology, 14*(3), 313-329.

Beck, C., & Jones, G. T. (1997). The terminal pleistocene/early holocene archaeology of the Great Basin. *Journal of World Prehistory, 11*(2), 161-236.

Beget, J. E., Keskinen, M. J., & Severin, K. P. (1997). Tephrochronologic constraints on the late pleistocene history of the southern margin of the cordilleran ice sheet, western Washington. *Quaternary Research, 47*, 140-146.

Beltrao, M. C. d. M. C., de Moura, J. R. S., de Vasconcelos, W. S., & Neme, S. M. N. (1986). Sitio arqueologico pleistocenico em ambiente de encosta: Itaborai, RJ, Brasil. In Bryan, A. L. (Ed.), *New evidence for the pleistocene peopling of the americas* (pp. 195-202). Orono, ME: Center for the Study of Early Man.

Benjamin, W. (1986). *Reflections, essays, aphorisms, autobiographical writings.* New York, NY: Schocken Books.

Berger, R., Protsch, R. R., Reynolds, R., Rozaire, C. E., & Sackett, J. R. (1971). New radiocarbon dates based on bone collagen of California paleoindians. *Contributions of the University of California Archaeological Research Facility, 12*, 43-49.

Bettinger, R. L. (1994). How, when, and why Numic spread. In Madsen, D. B. & Rhode, D. (Eds.), *Across the west: Human population movement and the expansion of the Numa* (pp. 44-55). Salt Lake City, UT: University of Utah Press.

Bettinger, R. L., & Baumhoff, M. A. (1982). The Numic spread: Great basin cultures in competition. *American Antiquity, 47*(3), 485-503.

Bettinger, R. L., & Baumhoff, M. A. (1983). Return rates and intensity of resource use in Numic and pre-numic adaptive strategies. *American Antiquity, 48*(4), 830-834.

Bianchi, N., Bailliet, G., Bravi, C., Carnese, R., Rothhammer, F., Martinez-Marignac, V., et al. (1997). Origin of amerindian y-chromosomes as inferred by the analysis of six polymorphic markers. *American Journal of Physical Anthropology, 102*, 79-89.

Bianchi, N. O., Catanesi, C. I., Bailliet, G., Martinez-Marignac, V. L., Bravi, C. M., Vidal-Rioja, L. B., et al. (1998). Characterization of ancestral and derived y-chromosome haplotypes of new world native populations. *American Journal of Human Genetics, 63*, 1862-1871.

Blackman, M. B. (1990). Haida: Traditional culture. In Suttles, W. (Ed.), *Northwest coast* (Vol. 7). Washington, D.C.: Smithsonian Institution.

Blunt, A., & Wills, J. (2000). *Dissident geographies: An introduction to radical ideas and practice.* London, UK: Routledge.

Boas, F. (1896/1948). *Race, language and culture.* New York, NY: Macmillan.

Boas, F. (1911a). *Handbook of American Indian languages* (Vol. Bulletin 40). Washington, DC: Government Printing Office.

Boas, F. (1911b). *The mind of primitive man.* New York, NY: Macmillan.

Boas, F. (1930). Anthropology. In Seligman, E. R. A. & Johnson, A. (Eds.), *Encyclopedia of the social sciences* (Vol. 2, pp. 73-110). New York, NY: Macmillan.

Bonatto, S., & Salzano, F. (1997a). Diversity and age of the four major mtDNA haplogroups, and their implications for the peopling of the new world. *American Journal of Human Genetics, 61*, 1413-1423.

Bonatto, S. L., & Salzano, F. M. (1997b). A single and early migration for the peopling of the americas supported by mitochondrial DNA sequence data. *Proceedings of the National Academy of Sciences of the United States of America, 94*(5), 1866-1871.

Bonnichsen, R., & Bolen, C. W. (1985). A hair, faunal, and flaked stone assemblage: A holocene and late pleistocene record from false Cougar Cave, Montana. In Blackburn, T. C. (Ed.), *Woman, poet, scientist: Essays in new world anthropology honoring dr. Emma Louise Davis* (pp. 4-15). Menlo Park, CA: California.

Bonnichsen, R., & Schneider, A. L. (1999). Breaking the impasse on the peopling of the americas. In Bonnichsen, R. & Turnmire, K. (Eds.), *Ice age people of North America: Environments, origins, adaptations* (pp. 497-519). Corvallis, OR: Oregon State University Press.

Bonnichsen, R., & Steele, D. G. (1994). Introducing first Americans research. In Bonnichsen, R. & Steele, D. G. (Eds.), *Method and theory for investigating the peopling of the Americas* (pp. 1-6). Corvallis, OR: Center for the Study of the First Americans.

Bonnichsen, R., & Turnmire, K. (1999). An introduction to the peopling of the Americas. In Bonnichsen, R. & Turnmire, K. L. (Eds.), *Ice age people in North America: Environments, origins, and adaptations* (pp. 1-26). Corvallis, OR: Oregon State University Press.

Borrero, L. A. (1986). Cazadores de *mylodon* en la patagonia austral. In Bryan, A. L. (Ed.), *New evidence for the pleistocene peopling of the Americas* (pp. 281-294). Orono, ME: Center for the Study of Early Man.

Boxberger, D. (2000). *Cultural affiliation study of the Kennewick human remains: Review of traditional historical and ethnographic information.* Washington, D.C.: Department of the Interior.

Boyd, R. (1990). Demographic history, 1774-1874. In Suttles, W. (Ed.), *Northwest coast* (Vol. 7). Washington, D.C.: Smithsonian Institution.

Boyd, R. (1999). *The coming of the spirit of pestilence: Introduced infectious diseases and population decline among northwest coast Indians, 1774-1874.* Vancouver, BC: UBC Press.

Brace, C. L., Nelson, A. R., Seguchi, N., Oe, H., Sering, L., Qifeng, P., et al. (2001). Old world sources of the first new world human inhabitants: A comparative craniofacial view. *Proceedings of the National Academy of Sciences of the United States, 98*(17), 10017-10022.

Bradman, N., & Thomas, M. (1998). Why y? The y chromosome in the story of human evolution, migration, and prehistory. *Science Spectra, 14*, 1-8.

Brantingham, P. J., Krivoshapkin, A. I., Jinzeng, L., & Tserendagva, Y. (2001). The initial upper paleolithic in Northeast Asia. *Current Anthropology, 42*(5), 735-746.

Bratlinger, P. (1990). *Crusoe's footprints: Cultural studies in Britain and America.* New York, NY: Routledge.

Breschini, G. (1979). The Marmes burial casts. *Northwest Anthropological Research Notes, 13*(2), 111-158.

Brewer, D. J. (1985). Herpetofaunas in the late pleistocene: Extinctions and extralimital forms. In Mead, J. I. & Meltzer, D. J. (Eds.), *Environments and extinctions: Man in late glacial North America* (pp. 31-52). Orono, ME: Center for the Study of Early Man.

Bright, W. (1970). On linguistic unrelatedness. *International Journal of American Linguistics, 36*, 288-290.

Briner, J. P., & Kaufman, D. S. (2000). Late pleistocene glaciation of the southwestern Ahklun mountains, Alaska. *Quaternary Research, 53*, 13-22.

Brooks, S. T., & Brooks, R. H. (1977). A proposed model for palaeodemography and archaeology in the Great Basin. In Fowler, D. (Ed.), *Models and Great Basin prehistory: A symposium* (Vol. 12, pp. 169-194). Reno, NV: Desert Research Institute Publications in the Social Sciences.

Brooks, S. T., & Brooks, R. H. (1990). Who were the Stillwater Marsh people? *Halcyon, 12*, 63-74.

Brooks, S. T., Haldeman, M. B., & Brooks, R. H. (1988). *Osteological analyses of the Stillwater skeletal series: Stillwater marsh, Churchill county, Nevada.* Carson City, NV: U.S. Department of the Interior.

Broughton, J. M., Madsen, D. B., & Quade, J. (2000). Fish remains from Homestead Cave and lake levels of the past 13,000 years in the Bonneville Basin. *Quaternary Research, 53*, 392-401.

Brown, M. D., Hosseini, S. H., Torroni, A., Bandelt, H.-J., Allen, J. C., Schurr, T. G., et al. (1998). MtDNA haplogroup x: An ancient link between Europe/Western Asia and North America. *American Journal of Human Genetics, 63*, 1852-1861.

Bryan, A. L. (1969). Early man in America and the late pleistocene chronology of western Canada and Alaska. *Current Anthropology, 10*(4), 339-365.

Bryan, A. L. (1986). Paleoamerican prehistory as seen from South America. In Bryan, A. L. (Ed.), *New evidence for the pleistocene peopling of the Americas* (pp. 1-14). Orono, MI: Center for the Study of Earl May.

Bryan, A. L. (1991). The fluted-point tradition in the Americas- one of several adaptations to late pleistocene American environments. In Bonnichsen, R. & Turnmire, K. (Eds.), *Clovis origins and adaptations.* Corvallis, OR: Center for the Study of the First Americans, Oregon State University.

Bryan, A. L., & Tuohy, D. R. (1999). Prehistory of the Great Basin/Snake River plain to about 8,500 years ago. In Bonnichsen, R. & Turnmire, K. (Eds.), *Ice age people of North America: Environments, origins, adaptations* (pp. 249-263). Corvallis, OR: Oregon State University Press.

Bryant, V. M., Jr., & Holloway, R. G. (1985a). A late-quaternary paleoenvironmental record of Texas: An overview of the pollen evidence. In Bryant, V. M., Jr. & Holloway, R. G. (Eds.), *Pollen records of late-quaternary North American sediments* (pp. 39-70). Austin, TX: American Association of Stratigraphic Palynologists Foundation.

Bryant, V. M., Jr., & Holloway, R. G. (Eds.). (1985b). *Pollen records of late-quaternary North American sediments.* Dallas, TX: American Association of Stratigraphic Palynologists Foundation.

Bunzl, M. (2004). Boas, Foucault, and the "native anthropologist": Notes toward a neo-Boasian anthropology. *American Anthropologist, 106*(3), 435-442.

Butler, B. R. (1981). Late period cultural sequences in the northeastern Great Basin subarea and their implications for the Upper Snake and Salmon River country. *Journal of California and Great Basin Anthropology, 3*(2), 245-256.

Butler, V. L. (1996). Tui chub taphonomy and the importance of marsh resources in the western Great Basin of North America. *American Antiquity, 61*(4), 699-717.

Campbell, L. (1997). *American Indian languages: The historical linguistics of Native America.* New York, NY: Oxford University Press.

Campbell, S. (1985a). *Summary of results, Chief Joseph dam cultural resources project, Washington.* Seattle, WA: Office of Public Archaeology, Institute of Environmental Studies, University of Washington.

Campbell, S. (1985b). Synthesis. In Campbell, S. (Ed.), *Summary of Results, Chief Joseph Dam Cultural Resources Project, Washington.* (Vol. 481-514): University of Washington, Office of Public Archaeology: Seattle.

Cann, R. L., Stoneking, M., & Wilson, A. C. (1987). Mitochondrial DNA and human evolution. *Nature, 325*, 31-36.

Carlson, R. L. (1994). Trade and exchange in prehistoric British Columbia. In Ericson, T. G. B. a. J. E. (Ed.), *Prehistoric Exchange Systems in North America* (Vol. 307-362): Plenum Press: New York.

Carrier, J. G. (1992). Occidentalism: The world turned upside-down. *American Ethnologist, 19*(2), 195-212.

Carrier, J. G. (Ed.). (1995). *Occidentalism: Images of the west.* Oxford, UK: Oxford University Press.

Cavalli-Sforza, L. L., & Bodmer, W. F. (1971). *The genetics of human populations.* San Francisco, CA: W.H. Freeman and Company.

Cavalli-Sforza, L. L., Menozzi, P., & Piazza, A. (1994). *The history and geography of human genes.* New Jersey, NJ: Princeton University Press.

Cavalli-Sforza, L. L., Piazza, A., Menozzi, P., & Mountain, J. L. (1988). Reconstruction of human evolution; bringing together genetic, archaeological, and linguistic data. *Proceedings of the National Academy of Sciences, 85,* 6002-6006.

Caviglia, S. E., Yacobaccio, H. D., & Borrero, L. A. (1986). Las buitreras: Convivencia del hombre con fauna extinta en patagonia meridional. In Bryan, A. L. (Ed.), *New evidence for the pleistocene peopling of the Americas* (pp. 295-318). Orono, ME: Center for the Study of Early Man.

Chafe, W. L. (1987). Review of *language in the Americas* by Joseph H. Greenberg. *Current Anthropology, 28,* 652-653.

Chalfant, S. A. (1974). Aboriginal territories of the Flathead, Pend d'Oreille and Kutenai indians of western Montana. In *American Indian ethnohistory: Indians of the Northwest* (pp. 25-116). New York, NY: Garland.

Chartkoff, J. L. (1985). Shores: Perspectives on paleoamerican habitat, subsistence, and society in the far west. In Blackburn, T. C. (Ed.), *Woman, poet, scientist: Essays in new world anthropology honoring Dr. Emma Louis Davis* (pp. 37-55). Menlo Park, CA: Ballena Press.

Chatters, J. (1989). Resource intensification and sedentism on the southern Plateau. *Archaeology in Washington, 1,* 1-20.

Chatters, J. (1995). Population growth, climatic cooling, and the development of collector strategies on the southern Plateau, western North America. *Journal of World Prehistory, 9,* 341-400.

Chatters, J. (1998). Environment. In Walker, D. E., Jr. (Ed.), *Handbook of north American Indians* (Vol. 12: Plateau, pp. 29-48). Washington, D.C.: Smithsonian Institution.

Chatters, J. (2000). The recovery and first analysis of an early holocene human skeleton from Kennewick, Washington. *American Antiquity, 65,* 291-316.

Chatters, J., & Pokotylo, D. (1998). Prehistory: Introduction. In Deward E. Walker, J. (Ed.), *Plateau* (Vol. 12, pp. 73-80). Washington, D.C.: Smithsonian Institution.

Chen, Y.-S., Olckers, A., Schurr, T. G., Kogelnik, A. M., Huoponen, K., & Wallace, D. C. (2000). MtDNA variation in the south African Kung and Khwe- and their genetic relationship to other African populations. *American Journal of Human Genetics, 66,* 1362-1383.

Claims Commission, I. (1974). *Paiute Indians v: Commission findings on the Paiute Indians.* New York, NY: Garland.

Clark, E. E. (1953). *Indian legends of the Pacific Northwest.* Berkeley, CA: University of California Press.

Clark, G. A. (2002). Neandertal archaeology- implications for our origins. *American Anthropologist, 104*(1), 50-67.

Clemmer, R. O., Myers, D., & Rudden, M. E. (Eds.). (1999). *Julian Steward and the Great Basin: The making of an anthropologist.* Salt Lake City: University of Utah Press.

Cohodas, M. (1999). Elizabeth Hickox and Karuk basketry: A case study in debates on innovation and paradigms of authenticity. In Steiner, R. B. P. a. C. B. (Ed.), *Unpacking Culture: Art and Commodity in Colonial and Postcolonial Worlds* (Vol. 143-161): University of California Press: Berkeley.

Collier, D., Hudson, A. E., & Ford, A. (1942). *Archaeology of the upper Columbia region* (Vol. 9). Seattle, WA: University of Washington Press.

Collins, M. B., & Dillehay, T. D. (1986). The implications of the lithic assemblage from Monte Verde for early man studies. In Bryan, A. L. (Ed.), *New evidence for the peopling of the Americas* (pp. 339-356). Orono, ME: Center for the Study of Early Man.

Coltrain, J. B., and Steven W. Leavitt. (2002). Climate and diet in Fremont prehistory: Economic variability and abandonment of maize agriculture in the Great Salt Lake Basin. *American Antiquity, 67*(3), 453-485.

Colville, C. T. o. (2000). *Native American graves protection and repatriation act claim to the ancient one (aka Kennewick man)*. Nespelem, WA: Confederated Tribes of the Colville Reservation.

Commission, U. S. I. C. (1973-1975). *Nez Perce tribe claims: D175-a, d175-b, d180-a*. Washington, DC: Government Printing Office.

Connolly, T. J. (1999). *Newberry Crater: A ten-thousand-year record of human occupation and environmental change in the Basin-Plateau borderlands* (Vol. 121). Salt Lake City: University of Utah Press.

Cook, S. (1978). Historical demography. In Heizer, R. F. (Ed.), *California* (Vol. 8). Washington, D.C.: Smithsonian Institution.

Coues, E. (Ed.). (1965). *History of the expedition under the command of Lewis and Clark*. New York, NY: Dover Publications.

Court, N. C. (2003). *Appeal from the United States district court for the district of Oregon, 1579 Bonnichsen v. United States: Opinion by Judge Gould*. Portland, OR.

Crandell, D. R. (1965). The glacial history of western Washington and Oregon. In Wright, H. E., Jr. & Frey, D. G. (Eds.), *The quaternary of the United States: A review volume for the VII congress of the international association for quaternary research*. Princeton, NJ: Princeton University Press.

Crapanzano, V. (1992). The postmodern crisis: Discourse, parody, memory. In Marcus, G. E. (Ed.), *Rereading cultural anthropology* (pp. 87-102). Durham, NC: Duke University Press.

Cressman, L. S. (1977). *Prehistory of the far west: Home of vanished peoples*. Salt Lake City, UT: University of Utah Press.

Crone, G. (1969). *The discovery of America*. New York, NY: Weybright and Talley.

Dangberg, G. (1968). *Washo tales: Translated with an introduction*. Minden, NV.

Darnell, R. (1969). *The development of American anthropology, 1879-1920: From the Bureau of American Ethnology to Franz Boas*. Unpublished Dissertation, University of Pennsylvania, Philadelphia, PA.

Davidson, I. (1999). The game of the name: Continuity and discontinuity in language origins. In King, B. J. (Ed.), *The origin of language: What nonhuman primates can tell us* (pp. 229-268). Santa Fe, NM: School of American Research Press.

Davis, E. L. (1982). The geoarchaeology and history of China Lake, California. In Ericson, J. E., Taylor, R. E. & Berger, R. (Eds.), *Peopling of the new world* (pp. 203-228). Menlo Park, CA: Ballena Press.

Davis, L. G., & Muehlenbachs, K. (2001). A late pleistocene to holocene record of precipitation reflected in Margaritifera falcata shell (delta)18° from three archaeological sites in the lower Salmon River canyon, Idaho. *Journal of Archaeological Science, 28*, 291-303.

Dawson, G. M. (1892). Notes on the Shuswap people of British Columbia. *Proceedings and Transactions of the Royal Society of Canada for the Year 1891, 9*(1), 3-44.

D'Azevedo, W. (Ed.). (1986). *Great Basin* (Vol. 11). Washington, D.C.: Smithsonian Institution.

De Laguna, F. (1975). *Matrilineal kin groups in northwestern North America.* Paper presented at the Northern Athapaskan Conference, Ottawa.

de Smet, P.-J. (1843). *Letters & sketches: With a narrative of a year's residence among the Indian tribes of the Rocky Mountains, 1841-1842.* Philadelphia: M. Fithian.

de Smet, P.-J. (1847). *Oregon missions and travels over the Rocky Mountains in 1845-46.* New York, NY: E. Dunigan.

de Smet, P.-J. (1859). *Western missions and missionaries: A series of letters.* New York, NY: P.J. Kenedy.

de Smet, P.-J. (1863). *New Indian sketches.* New York, NY: D. and J. Sadler.

deFrance, S. D., Keefer, D. K., Richardson, J. B., & Alvarez, A. A. (2001). Late paleo-indian coastal foragers: Specialized extractive behavior at Quebrada Tacahuay, Peru. *Latin American Antiquity, 12*(4), 413-426.

Delacorte, M. G. (1994). *Late prehistoric resource intensification in the Numic heartland.* Paper presented at the 20th Annual Great Basin Anthropological Conference.

Deloria, V., Jr. (2003). Anti-indianism in modern America: A voice from Tatekeya's earth. *American Anthropologist, 105*(3), 643-644.

DeMallie, R. J. (Ed.). (2001). *The Plains* (Vol. 13). Washington, D.C.: Smithsonian Institution.

Demarchi, D. A., Panzetta-Dutari, G. M., Motran, C. C., Lopez de Basualdo, M. d. l. A., & Marcellino, A. J. (2001). Absence of the 9-bp deletion of mitochondrial DNA in pre-hispanic inhabitants of Argentina. *Human Biology, 73*(4), 575-582.

Derrida, J. (1976). *Of grammatology* (Spivak, G. C., Trans.). Baltimore, MD: Johns Hopkins University Press.

Derrida, J. (1978). *Writing and difference* (Bass, A., Trans.). Chicago, IL: University of Chicago Press.

Dillehay, T. D. (1986). The cultural relationships of Monte Verde: A late pleistocene settlement site in the subantarctic. In Bryan, A. L. (Ed.), *New evidence for the pleistocene peopling of the Americas* (pp. 319-338). Orono, ME: Center for the Study of Early Man.

Dillehay, T. D. (2000). *The settlement of the Americas: A new prehistory.* New York, NY: Basic Books.

Dixon, J. (1999). *Bones, boats, and bison: Archeology and the first colonization of North America.* Albuquerque, NM: University of New Mexico Press.

Dobyns, H. F. (1983). *Their number become thinned: Native American population dynamics in eastern North America.* Knoxville, TN: University of Tennesse Press.

Dobyns, H. F. (1992). Native American trade centers as contagious disease foci. In Verano, J. W. & Ubelaker, D. H. (Eds.), *Disease and demography in the Americas* (pp. 215-222). Washington, D.C.: Smithsonian Institution Press.

Donnelly, P., & Tavare, S. (1995). Coalescents and genealogical structure under neutrality. *Annual Review of Genetics, 29,* 401-421.

Douglas, D. (1914). *Journal kept by David Douglas during his travels in North America, 1823-1827. Together with a particular description of thirty-three species of American oak and eighteen species of pinus, with appendices containing a list of the plants introduced by douglas and an account of his death in 1834.* London: W. Wesley and Son.

Douglas, D. (1959). *Journal kept by David Douglas during his travels in North America, 1823-1827.* New York, NY: Antiquarian Press.

Drews, R. (1988). *The coming of the Greeks: Indo-european conquests in the Aegean and the Near East.* Princeton, Conn.: Princeton University Press: Princeton.

Driver, H. W., & Massey, W. C. (1957). *Comparative studies of North American Indians* (Vol. 47). Philadelphia.

Dugas, D. P. (1998). Late quaternary variations in the level of paleo-lake Malheur, eastern Oregon. *Quaternary Research, 50,* 276-282.

Dumond, D. D. (1984). Prehistory: Summary. In Dumas, D. (Ed.), *Handbook of North American Indians* (Vol. 5: Arctic). Washington, D.C.: Smithsonian Institution Press.

Dumond, D. D. (1987). *The Eskimos and Aleuts* (Revised ed.). London, UK: Thames and Hudson.

Dundes, A. (1965a). Structural typology in North American Indian folktales. In Dundes, A. (Ed.), *The study of folklore* (pp. 206-215). Englewood City, NJ: Prentice-Hall, Inc.

Dundes, A. (1965b). *The study of folklore.* Englewood Cliffs, NJ: Prentice-Hall Inc.

Dundes, A. (1980). *Interpreting folklore.* Bloomington, IN: Indiana University Press.

Duranti, A. (2003). Language as culture in U.S. anthropology: Three paradigms. *Current Anthropology, 44*(3), 323-347.

Easterbrook, D. J. (1963). Late pleistocene glacial events and relative sea level changes in the northern Puget lowland, Washington. *Geological Society of America Bulletin, 74*(12), 1465-1484.

Easterbrook, D. J. (1992). Advance and retreat of cordilleran ice sheets in Washington, U.S.A. *Geographie Physique et Quaternaire, 46,* 51-68.

Easton, R. D., Merriwether, A., Crews, D. E., & Ferrell, R. E. (1996). MtDNA variation in the Yanomami: Evidence for additional new world founding lineages. *American Journal of Human Genetics, 59,* 213-225.

Edwards, M. E., Anderson, P. M., Brubaker, L. B., Ager, T. A., Andreev, A. A., Bigelow, N. H., et al. (2000). Pollen-based biomes for Beringia 18,000, 6000 and 0 [14]c yr bp. *Journal of Biogeography, 27*(3), 521-554.

Eerkens, J. W. (2003). Residential mobility and pottery use in the western Great Basin. *Current Anthropology, 44*(5), 728-738.

Ehle, J. (1988). *Trail of tears: The rise and fall of the Cherokee nation.* New York, NY: Anchor Books.

Ellis, D. C. (1995). *Cree legends and narratives.* Winnipeg, Canada: University of Manitoba Press.

Elston, R. G. (1982). Good times, hard times: Prehistoric culture change in the western Great Basin. *Society for American Archaeology Papers, 2,* 186-206.

Elston, R. G. (1986). Prehistory of the western area. In D'Azevedo, W. (Ed.), *Handbook of North American Indians* (Vol. 11: Great Basin, pp. 135-148). Washington, D.C.: Smithsonian Institution.

Elston, R. G., & Zeanah, D. W. (2002). Thinking outside the box: A new perspective on diet breadth and sexual division of labor in the prearchaic Great Basin. *World Archaeology, 34*(1), 103-130.

Emerson, E. R. (1965). *Indian myths.* New York, NY: Ross and Haines, Inc.

Erickson, K. (1990). Marine shell in the Plateau culture area. *Northwest Anthropological Research Notes, 24*(1), 91-144.

Erlandson, J. (1994). *Early hunter-gatherers of the California coast.* New York, NY: Plenum Press.

Erlandson, J. M., & Moss, M. L. (2001). Shellfish feeders, carrion eaters, and the archaeology of aquatic adaptations. *American Antiquity, 66*(3), 413-432.

Ferguson, T. J. (1996). *Human remains and associated grave goods from Lovelock Cave, Neavada: Final research report.* Washington, D.C.: National Museum of the American Indian, Smithsonian Institution, Department of Repatriation.

Fernandez-Armesto, F. (1987). *Before Columbus: Exploration and colonisation from the Mediterranean to the Atlantic, 1229-1492.* London, UK: Macmillian Education.

Fidalgo, F., Guzman, L. M. M., Politis, G. G., Salemme, M. C., & Tonni, E. P. (1986). Investigaciones arqueologicas en el sitio 2 de arroyo seco (pdo. De tres arroyos- pcia. De Buenos Aires- repulica Argentina). In Bryan, A. L. (Ed.), *New evidence for the pleistocene peopling of the Americas* (pp. 221-270). Orono, ME: Center for the Study of Early Man.

Fine-Dare, K. S. (2002). *Grave injustice: The American Indian repatriation movement and NAGPRA.* Lincoln, NE: University of Nebraska Press.

Fix, A. G. (2002). Colonization models and initial genetic diversity in the Americas. *Human Biology, 74*(1), 1-10.

Fladmark, K. R. (1985). *Glass and ice: The archaeology of Mt. Edziza* (Vol. 14). Burnaby, B.C.: Department of Archaeology, Simon Fraser University.

Flannery, K. V., & Marcus, J. (1994). *Early formative pottery of the valley of Oaxaca, Mexico* (Vol. 27). Ann Arbor, MI: Department of Anthropology.

Flores, D. (1991). Bison ecology and bison diplomacy: The southern Plains from 1800 to 1850. *Journal of American History, 78*(2), 465-485.

Follett, W. I. (1977). Fish remains from thea Heye Cave, nv-wa-385 Washoe county, Nevada, *Great Basin Anthropological Papers* (Vol. 35: 59-80): Berkeley, CA: University of California, Department of Anthropology.

Forman, S. L., Ingolfsson, O., Gataullin, V., Manley, W., & Lokrantz, H. (2002). Late quaternary stratigraphy, glacial limits, and paleoenvironments of the marresale area, western Yamal peninsula, Russia. *Quaternary Research, 57,* 355-370.

Forster, P., Harding, R., Torroni, A., & Bandelt, H.-J. (1996). Origin and evolution of Native American mtDNA variation: A reappraisal. *American Journal of Human Genetics, 59,* 935-945.

Forster, P., & Toth, A. (2003). Toward a phylogenetic chronology of ancient Gaulish, Celtic, and Indo-european. *Proceedings of the National Academy of Sciences, 100*(15), 9079-9084.

Foster, M. K. (1996). Language and the culture history of North America. In Goddard, I. (Ed.), *Language* (Vol. 17, pp. 64-110). Washington, D.C.: Smithsonian Institution.

Foucault, M. (1974). *The archaeology of knowledge and the discourse on language* (Sheridan-Smith, A. M., Trans.). London, UK: Tavistock Publications.

Foucault, M. (1977). *Discipline and punish: The birth of the prison* (Sheridan, A., Trans.). London, UK: Allen Lane.

Foucault, M. (Ed.). (1980). *Power/knowledge: Selected interviews and other writings.* New York, NY: Pantheon Books.

Fowler, C. S., and Sven Liljeblad. (1986a). Northern paiute. In D'Azevedo, W. (Ed.), *Handbook of North American Indians, Vol. 11: Great Basin* (Vol. 435-465): Smithsonian Institution: Government Printing Office, Washington, D.C.

Fowler, D., & Fowler, C. S. (1970). Stephen Powers' "the life and culture of the Washoe and Paiutes". *Ethnohistory, 17*(3-4), 117-149.

Fowler, D., & Fowler, C. S. (1971). *Anthropology of the Numa: John Wesley Powell's manuscripts on the Numic peoples of western North America, 1868-1880* (Vol. 14). Washington, DC: Smithsonian Institution.

Fowler, N. (1986b). The role of competition in plant communities in arid and semi-arid regions. *Annual Reviews of Ecology and Systematics, 17,* 89-110.

Fraser, S. (1889). *Journal of a voyage from the Rocky Mountains to the Pacific Coast, 1808.* Quebec, Canada: A. Cote.

Fraser, S. (1960). *The letters and journals of Simon Fraser 1806-1808.* New York, NY: Macmillan.

Fremont, J. C. (1845). *Report on the exploring expedition to the Rocky Mountains in the year 1842 and to Oregon and northern California in the years 1843-1844.* Washington, DC: Gales and Seaton.

Frison, G. C. (1974). *The Casper site: A Hell Gap bison kill on the high Plains.* New York, NY: Academic Press.

Frison, G. C. (1976). The chronology of paleo-indian and altithermal period groups in the Bighorn Basin, Wyoming. In Cleland, C. E. (Ed.), *Cultural change and continuity: Essays in honor of James Bennett Griffin* (pp. 147-173). New York, NY: Academic Press.

Frison, G. C. (1984). The Carter/Kerr-McGee paleoindian site: Cultural resource management and archaeological research. *American Antiquity, 49*(2), 288-314.

Frison, G. C. (1999). The late pleistocene prehistory of the northwestern Plains, the adjacent mountains, and intermontane basins. In Bonnichsen, R. & Turnmire, K. (Eds.), *Ice age peoples of North America: Environments, origins, adaptations* (pp. 264-280). Corvallis, OR: Oregon State University Press.

Frison, G. C., & Todd, L. C. (Eds.). (1987). *The Horner site: The type site of the Cody cultural complex.* New York, NY: Academic Press.

Frye, J. C., & Leonard, A. B. (1965). Quaternary of the southern Great Plains. In Wright, H. E., Jr. & Frey, D. G. (Eds.), *The quaternary of the United States: A review volume for the VII congress of the international association for quaternary research* (pp. 203-216). Princeton, NJ: Princeton University Press: New Jersey.

Fuller, G. W. (1931). *A history of the Pacific Northwest.* New York, NY: A. Knopf.

Gadamer, H.-G. (1975). *Truth and method.* New York, NY: Seabury Press.

Gadamer, H.-G. (1981). *Reason and the age of science.* Cambridge, MA: MIT Press.

Gadamer, H.-G. (1994). *Literature and philosophy in dialogue.* Albany, NY: State University of New York Press.

Gairdner, M. (1841). Notes on the geography of the Columbia River. *Journal of the Royal Geographical Society of London, 11*(2), 250-257.

Galm, J. (1994). Prehistoric trade and exchange in the interior Plateau of northwestern North America. In Baugh, T. & Ericson, J. (Eds.), *Prehistoric exchange systems in North America* (pp. 275-305). New York, NY: Plenum Press.

Geertz, C. (1973). *The interpretation of cultures.* New York, NY: Basic Books.

Gehr, K. D. (1980). *Late pleistocene and recent archaeology and geomorphology of the south shore of Harney Lake, Oregon.* Unpublished Masters Thesis, Portland State University, Portland.

Geist, V. (1999). Periglacial ecology, large mammals, and their significance to human biology. In Bonnichsen, R. & Turnmire, K. (Eds.), *Ice age people of North America: Environments, origins, adaptations* (pp. 78-94). Corvallis, OR: Oregon State University Press.

Gellner, E. (1985). *Relativism and the social sciences.* London, UK: Cambridge University Press.

Gellner, E. (1992). *Postmodernism, reason and religion.* London, UK: Routledge.

Gibbons, A. (1996). The peopling of the Americas. *Science, 274*(5284), 31-3.

Gigli, J. G. (1974). Dat so la lee, queen of the Washo basketmakers. In Tuohy, D. & Rendall, D. L. (Eds.), *Collected papers on aboriginal basketry* (Vol. 16, pp. 1-27). Carson City, NV: Nevada State Museum.

Glassow, M. A., Wilcoxon, L. R., & Erlandson, J. (1988). Cultural and environmental change during the early period of Santa Barbara channel prehistory. In Bailey, G. & Parkington, J. (Eds.), *The archaeology of prehistoric coastlines* (pp. 64-77). Cambridge, MA: Cambridge University Press.

Goddard, I. (1978). A further note on pidgin English. *International Journal of American Linguistics, 44*(1), 73.

Goddard, I. (1996a). Introduction. In Goddard, I. (Ed.), *Languages* (Vol. 17). Washington, D.C.: Smithsonian Institution.

Goddard, I. (Ed.). (1996b). *Languages* (Vol. 17). Washington, D.C.: Smithsonian Institution.

Goddard, I., & Campbell, L. (1994). The history and classification of American Indian languages: What are the implications for the peopling of the Americas? In Bonnichsen, R. & Steele, D. G. (Eds.), *Method and theory for investigating the peopling of the Americas* (pp. 189-207). Corvallis, OR: Center for the Study of the First Americans.

Goebel, T., & Slobodin, S. B. (1999). The colonization of western Beringia: Technology, ecology, and adaptations. In Bonnichsen, R. & Turnmire, K. (Eds.), *Ice age people of North America: Environments, origins, adaptations* (pp. 104-155). Corvallis, OR: Oregon State University Press.

Goebel, T., Waters, M. R., & Dikova, M. (2003). The archaeology of Ushki Lake, Kamchatka, and the pleistocene peopling of the Americas. *Science, 301*, 501-505.

Golla, V. K. (1988). Review of *language in the Americas* by Joseph H. Greenberg. *American Anthropologist, 90*, 434-435.

Gonzalez-Jose, R., Dahinten, S. L., Luis, M. A., Hernandez, M., & Pucciarelli, H. M. (2001). Craniometric variation and the settlement of the americas: Testing hypotheses by means of r-matrix and matrix correlation analyses. *American Journal of Physical Anthropology, 116*, 154-165.

Gonzalez-Jose, R., Gonzalez-Martin, A., Hernandez, M., Pucciarelli, H. M., Sardi, M., Rosales, A., et al. (2003). Craniometric evidence for palaeoamerican survival in Baja California. *Nature, 425*, 62-65.

Goodman, A. H., & Martin, D. L. (1999). *Biological analysis of the Spirit Cave human remains (ahur 2064): Implications for cultural affiliation.* Reno, NV: Report on file at the BLM Nevada State Office.

Goody, J. (1996). *The east in the west.* Cambridge: Cambridge University Press.

Goss, J. A. (1977). Linguistic tools for the Great Basin prehistorian. In Fowler, D. D. (Ed.), *Models and Great Basin prehistory* (Vol. 12, pp. 49-70). Reno, NV: Desert Research Institute Publications in the Social Sciences.

Goss, J. A. (1999). *Fallon Paiute-Shoshone tribe repatriation of the Spirit Cave Mummy and associated artifacts.* Reno, NV: Ms on file at BLM Nevada office.

Gould, S. J. (1981). *The mismeasure of man.* New York, NY: W.W. Norton & Company.

Gould, S. J., & Lewontin, R. C. (1979). The spandrels of San Marco and the panglossian paradigm: A critique of the adaptationist programme. *Proceedings of the Royal Society of London, 205*, 581-598.

Gravlee, C. C., Bernard, H. R., & Leonard, W. R. (2003). Boas's changes in bodily form: The immigrant study, cranial plasticity, and boas's physical anthropology. *American Anthropologist, 105*(2), 326-332.

Grayson, D. (1993). *The desert's past: A natural history of the Great Basin.* Washington, D.C.: Smithsonian Institution Press.

Grayson, D. (2000a). *An archaeological perspective on the Spirit Cave human remains.* Reno, NV: Ms on file in BLM Nevada office.

Grayson, D. (2000b). Mammalian responses to middle holocene climatic change in the great basin of the western United States. *Journal of Biogeography, 27*(1), 181-192.

Green, T., Pavesic, M., Woods, J., & Titmus, G. (1986). The Demoss burial locality: Preliminary observations. *Idaho Archaeologist, 9*(2), 31-40.

Green, T. B. C., Fenton, T., Woods, J., Titmus, G., Tiezen, L., & Miller, S. (1998). The Buhl burial: A paleoindian woman from southern Idaho. *American Antiquity, 63*, 437-456.

Greenberg, J. (1987). *Language in the Americas.* San Jose, CA: Stanford University Press.

Greenberg, J., Turner, C. G. I., & Zegura, S. (1986). The settlement of the Americas: A comparison of the linguistic, dental, and genetic evidence. *Current Anthropology, 27*, 477-497.

Greenspan, R. L. (1998). Gear selectivity models, mortality profiles and the interpretation of archaeological fish remains: A case study from the Harney basin, Oregon. *Journal of Archaeological Science, 25*, 973-984.

Greiser, S. T. (1985). Predictive models of hunter-gatherer subsistence and settlement strategies on the central High Plains. *Plains Anthropologist Memoir, 20*(110).

Grigg, L. D., & Whitlock, C. (1998). Late-glacial vegetation and climate change in western Oregon. *Quaternary Research, 49*, 287-298.

Grosscup, G. L. (1974). Northern paiute archaeology. In Horr, D. A. (Ed.), *Paiute Indians VI* (pp. 9-51). New York, NY: Garland Publishing Inc.

Grosswald, M. G. (1999). Ice age environments of northern Eurasia with specific reference to the beringian margin of Siberia. In Bonnichsen, R. & Turnmire, K. L. (Eds.), *Ice age people of North America: Environments, origins, and adaptations* (pp. 27-41). Corvallis, OR: Oregon State University Press.

Grosswald, M. G., & Hughes, T. J. (1999). The case for an ice shelf in the pleisocene Arctic ocean. *Polar Geography, 23*(1), 23-54.

Gruhn, R. (1994). The pacific coast route of initial entry: An overview. In Steele, R. B. a. D. G. (Ed.), *Method and Theory for the Investigation of the Peopling of the Americas* (Vol. 249-256): Center for the Study of the First Americans: Corvallis, Oregon.

Gustafson, C. (1972). *Faunal remains from the marmes rockshelter and related archaeological sites in the Columbia River.* Unpublished Dissertation, Washington State University, Pullman, WA.

Guthrie, R. D. (1980). Bison and man in North America. *Canadian Journal of Anthropology, 1*, 55-73.

Haas, M. R. (1965). Is Kutenai related to Algonkian? *Canadian Journal of Linguistics, 10*(2-3), 77-92.

Hackenberger, S. (2000). *Cultural affiliation study of the Kennewick human remains: Review of bio-archaeological information.* Washington, D.C.: Department of the Interior.

Haines, F. (1938a). The northward spread of horses among the Plains Indians. *American Anthropologist, 40*(3), 429-437.

Haines, F. (1938b). Where did the Plains Indians get their horses? *American Anthropologist, 40*(1), 112-117.

Hale, H. (1846). *Ethnography and philology* (Vol. 6). Philadelphia: PA: Lea and Blanchard.

Hall, S. A. (1985a). Bibliography of quaternary palynology in Arizona, Colorado, New Mexico, and Utah. In Bryant, V. M., Jr. & Holloway, R. G. (Eds.), *Pollen records of late-quaternary North American sediments* (pp. 407-426). Austin, TX: American Association of Stratigraphic Palynologists Foundation.

Hall, S. A. (1985b). Quaternary pollen analysis and vegetational history of the Southwest. In Bryant, V. M., Jr. & Holloway, R. G. (Eds.), *Pollen records of late-quaternary North American sediments* (pp. 95-124). Austin, TX: American Association of Stratigraphic Palynologists Foundation.

Hallowell, A. I. (1960). Ojibwa ontology, behavior, and world view. In Diamond, S. (Ed.), *Culture and history* (pp. 19-52). New York, NY: Columbia University Press.

Hamilton, T. D., & Goebel, T. (1999). Late pleistocene peopling of Alaska. In Bonnichsen, R. & Turnmire, K. (Eds.), *Ice age people of North America: Environments, origins, adaptations* (pp. 156-199). Corvallis, OR: Oregon State University Press.

Handler, R. (2004). Afterword: Mysteries of culture. *American Anthropologist, 106*(3), 488-494.

Harper, J. R. (Ed.). (1971). *Paul Kane's frontier.* Austin, TX: The University of Texas Press.

Harris, M. (1968). *The rise of anthropological theory.* New York, NY: Thomas Y. Crowell.

Hayden, B. (Ed.). (1992). *A complex culture of the British Columbia plateau: Traditional Stl'atl'imx resource use.* Vancouver, B.C.: UBC Press.

Hayden, B., & Schulting, R. (1997). The Plateau interaction sphere and late prehistoric cultural complexity. *American Antiquity, 62,* 51-85.

Helm, J. (Ed.). (1981). *Subarctic* (Vol. 6). Washington, D.C.: Smithsonian Institution.

Helm, J., Rogers, E. S., & Smith, J. G. E. (1981). Intercultural relations and cultural change in the Shield and Mackenzie borderlands. In Helm, J. (Ed.), *Subarctic* (Vol. 6, pp. 146-157). Washington, D.C.: Smithsonian Institution Press.

Hess, S. (1997). *Rocks, range, and Renfrew: Using distance-decay effects to study late pre-Mazama period obsidian acquisition and mobility in Oregon and Washington.* Unpublished Dissertation, Washington State University, Pullman, WA.

Hester, J. J., & Nelson, S. M. (Eds.). (1978). *Studies in Bella Bella prehistory.* Burnaby, B.C.: Department of Archaeology, Simon Fraser University.

Heusser, C. J. (1965). A pleistocene phytogeographical sketch of the Pacific Northwest and Alaska. In Wright, H. E., Jr. & Frey, D. G. (Eds.), *The quaternary of the United States: A review volume for the VII congress of the international association for quaternary research* (pp. 469-484). Princeton, NJ: Princeton University Press.

Heusser, C. J. (1985). Quaternary pollen records from California. In Bryant, V. M., Jr. & Holloway, R. G. (Eds.), *Pollen records of late-quaternary North American sediments* (pp. 125-140). Austin, TX: American Association of Stratigraphic Palynologists Foundation.

Hibbard, C. W. (1960). An interpretation of pliocene and pleistocene climates in North America. *Michigan Academy of Science, Arts and Letters Presidential Address Annual Report, 62,* 5-30.

Hicks, B. (2000a). *Summary of the southern Plateau/lower Snake River archaeological record: Statement in support of affiliation with the ancient one.* Nespelem, WA: Confederated Tribes of the Colville Reservation, History/Archaeology Department.

Hicks, B. (2000b). *Supplemental archaeological information relative to the Colville tribes' affiliation with Kennewick man submitted in response to Dr. F. Mcmanamon's letter of July 24, 2000.* Nespelem, WA: Confederated Tribes of the Colville Reservation, History/Archaeology Department.

Hicks, J. W. (1977). *Microscopy of hairs: A practical guide and manual.* Washington, D.C.: Federal Bureau of Investigation.

Hildebrandt, W. R., & McGuire, K. R. (2002). The ascendance of hunting during the California middle archaic: An evolutionary perspective. *American Antiquity, 67*(2), 231-256.

Hill, J. H. (2000). *Why is Uto-Aztecan so big?* Reno, NV: Ms on file at BLM Nevada State Office.

Hobler, P. M. (Ed.). (1982). *Papers on central coast archaeology.* Burnaby, B.C.: Department of Archaeology, Simon Fraser University.

Hockett, B. S. (2000). Paleobiogeographic changes at the pleistocene-holocene boundary near Pintwater Cave, southern Nevada. *Quaternary Research, 53,* 263-269.

Hoelzer, G. A., Wallman, J., & Melnick, D. J. (1998). The effects of social structure, geographical structure, and population size on the evolution of mitochondrial DNA: Ii. Molecular clocks and the lineage sorting period. *Journal of Molecular Evolution, 47,* 21-31.

Hoffecker, J. F., Powers, W. R., & Goebel, T. (1993). The colonization of Beringia and the peopling of the new world. *Science, 259,* 46-53.

Hofle, C., Mary E. Edwards, David M. Hopkins, and Daniel H. Mann. (2000). The full-glacial environment of the northern Seward peninsula, Alaska, reconstructed from the 21,500-year-old Kitluk paleosol, *Quaternary Research* (Vol. 53:143-153).

Hofmann, R. R. (1983). Evolutionaere und saisonbedingte anpassung des verdauungsapparates des gamswildes (rupicapra rupicapra). *Wildbiologische Informationen fuer den Jaeger, VI,* 85-93.

Holliday, V. T. (2000). Folsom drought and episodic drying on the southern High Plains from 10,900-10,200 14c yr bp. *Quaternary Research, 53,* 1-12.

Holloway, R. G., & Bryant, V. M., Jr. (1985). Late-quaternary pollen records and vegetational history of the Great Lakes region: United states and Canada. In Bryant, V. M., Jr. & Holloway, R. G. (Eds.), *Pollen records of late-quaternary North American sediments* (pp. 205-244). Austin, TX: American Association of Stratigraphic Palynologists Foundation.

Holman, J. A. (1976). Paleoclimatic implications of "ecologically incompatible" herpetological species (late pleistocene: Southeastern United States). *Herpetologica, 32,* 290-295.

Holmes, W. H. (1914). Areas of American culture characterization tentatively outlined as an aid in the study of the antiquities. *American Anthropologist, 16*(3), 413-446.

Horai, S., & Matsunaga, E. (1986). Mitochondrial DNA polymorphism in Japanese: Ii. Analysis with restriction enzymes of four or five base pair recognition. *Human Genetics, 72,* 105-117.

Horting, C. (2000). A case of mistaken identity: The misuse of artifactual basketry in the prehistoric Great Basin. *Idaho Archaeologist, 23*(2), 15-22.

Huckleberry, G., Beck, C., Jones, G. T., Holmes, A., Cannon, M., Livingston, S., et al. (2001). Terminal pleistocene/early holocene environmental change at the Sunshine locality, north-central Nevada, USA. *Quaternary Research, 55,* 303-312.

Huddletson, L. E. (1967). *Origins of the American Indians: European concepts, 1492-1729.* Austin, TX: University of Texas Press.

Hudson, R. R. (1990). Gene genealogies and the coalescent process. In Futuyma, D. & Antonovics, J. (Eds.), *Oxford surveys in evolutionary biology* (Vol. 7, pp. 1-44). Oxford, UK: University of Oxford Press.

Hughes, R. (1994). Methodological observations on Great Basin prehistory. In Madsen, D. & Rhode, D. (Eds.), *Across the west: Human population movement and the expansion of the Numa* (pp. 67-70). Salt Lake City: University of Utah Press.

Hultkrantz, A. (1986). Mythology and religious concepts. In D'Azevedo, W. (Ed.), *Great Basin* (Vol. 11, pp. 630-640). Washington D.C.: Smithsonian Institution.

Hunn, E. S. (1999). Mobility as a factor limiting resource use on the Columbia plateau. In Goble, D. D. & Hirt, P. W. (Eds.), *Northwest lands, northwest people: Readings in environmental history* (pp. 156-172). Seattle, WA: University of Washington Press.

Hunn, E. S. (2000). *Cultural affiliation study of the Kennewick human remains: Review of linguistic information.* Washington, D.C.: Department of the Interior.

Ignace, M. B. (1992). *Aboriginal territories of the Shuswap nation.* Kamloops, BC: Shuswap Nation Tribal Council.

Ikawa-Smith, F. (1982). The early prehistory of the Americas as seen from northeast Asia. In Ericson, J. E., Taylor, R. E. & Berger, R. (Eds.), *Peopling of the new world* (pp. 13-34). Menlo Park, CA: Ballena Press.

Interior, D. o. (2000). *Human culture in the southeastern Columbia Plateau, 9500-9000bp and cultural affiliation with present-day tribes.* Washington, D.C.: Department of the Interior.

Irving, W. (1836). *The adventures of Captain Bonneville, U.S.A., in the Rocky Mountains and the far west.* New York, NY: G.P. Putnam.

Isaacs, J. (1980). *Australian dreaming: 40,000 years of aboriginal history.* Sydney: Lansdowne Press.

Isayeva, L. L. (1984). Late pleistocene glaciation of north-central Siberia. In Velichko, A. A. (Ed.), *Late quaternary environments of the Soviet Union* (pp. 21-30). Minneapolis, MN: University of Minnesota Press.

Jackson, D. D. (1978). *Letters of the Lewis and Clark expedition with related documents, 1783-1854* (Vol. 2). Urbana, IL: University of Illinois Press.

Jacobs, M. (1959). *The content and style of oral literature* (Vol. 26). New York, NY: Wenner-Gren Foundation for Anthropological Research.

Jacobs, P. M., Knox, J. C., & Mason, J. A. (1997). Preservation and recognition of middle and early pleistocene loess in the driftless area, Wisconsin. *Quaternary Research, 47,* 147-154.

Jacobsen, W. H., Jr. (1986). Washoe language. In D'Azevedo, W. (Ed.), *Great Basin* (Vol. 11, pp. 107-112). Washington, D.C.: Smithsonian Institution.

Jaehnig, M. (1984). *Archaeological investigations at site 45-ok-18, Chief Joseph dam project, Washington.* Seattle, WA: Office of Public Archaeology, Institute for Environmental Studies, University of Washington.

Jaehnig, M. (2000). *Establishing cultural continuity between Kennewick man and modern Columbia Plateau tribes.* Pendleton, OR: Confederated Tribes of the Umatilla Indian Reservation, Cultural Resources Protection Program.

James, L. A., Harbor, J., Fabel, D., Dahms, D., & Elmore, D. (2002). Late pleistocene glaciations in the northwestern Sierra Nevada, California. *Quaternary Research, 55*, 1-11.

Janetski, J. C., and David B. Madsen. (1990). Wetland adaptations in the Great Basin, *Museum of Peoples and Cultures, Occasional Papers No. 1*: Brigham Young University.

Jantz, R., & Owsley, D. (1997). Pathology, taphonomy, and cranial morphometrics of the Spirit Cave mummy. *Nevada Historical Society Quarterly, 40*, 62-84.

Jantz, R., & Owsley, D. (1998). How many populations of early North American were there? *American Journal of Physical Anthropology, Supplement 26*, 128.

Jantz, R., & Owsley, D. (2001). Variation among early North American crania. *American Journal of Physical Anthropology, 114*, 146-155.

Jennings, J. D. (1978). *Prehistory of utah and the eastern Great Basin* (Vol. 98). Salt Lake City, UT: University of Utah.

Johansen, D. O., & Gates, C. M. (1957). *Empire of the Columbia: A history of the Pacific Northwest.* New York, NY: Harper and Row.

Johnson, E. C. (1975). *Walker River Paiutes: A tribal history.* Schurz, NV: Walker River Paiute Tribe.

Jones, G. T., Beck, C., Jones, E. E., & Hughes, R. E. (2003). Lithic source use and paleoarchaic foraging territories in the Great Basin. *American Antiquity, 68*(1), 5-38.

Jones, K. T., & Madsen, D. B. (1989). Calculating the cost of resource transportation: A Great Basin example. *Current Anthropology, 30*(4), 529-534.

Jones, P. N. (2002). American Indian demographic history and cultural affiliation: A discussion of certain limitations on the use of mtDNA and y chromosome testing. *AnthroGlobe Journal, Winter*, 1-32.

Jones, P. N. (2003). Old world infectious diseases in the Plateau area of North America during the protohistoric: Rethinking our understanding of "contact" in the Plateau. *Journal of Northwest Anthropology, 37*(1), 1-26.

Jones, P. N. (2004a). *American Indian cultural affiliation and cultural continuity in the Plateau and Great Basin culture regions of the American west.* Saybrook Graduate School, San Francisco.

Jones, P. N. (2004b). *American Indian mtDNA, y chromosome genetic data, and the peopling of North America.* Boulder, Co.: Bauu Institute Press.

Jones, P. N., & Stapp, D. (2003). An anthropological perspective on Magistrate Jelderks' Kennewick man decision. *High Plains Applied Anthropologist, 23*(1), 1-16.

Jones, T. L., Fitzgerald, R. T., Kennett, D. J., Miksicek, C. H., Fagan, J. L., Sharp, J., et al. (2002). The Cross Creek site (ca-slo-1797) and its implications for new world colonization. *American Antiquity*, 213-230.

Jorgensen, J. (1994). Synchronic relations among environment, language, and culture as clues to the Numic expansion. In Madsen, D. B. & Rhode, D. (Eds.), *Across the west: Human population movement and the expansion of the Numa* (pp. 84-102): Salt Lake City: University of Utah Press.

Kaestle, F. (1995). Mitochondrial DNA evidence for the identity of the descendants of the prehistoric Stillwater Marsh populations. In Larsen, C. S. & Kelly, R. L. (Eds.), *Bioarchaeology of the Stillwater Marsh: Prehistoric human adaptation in the western Great Basin* (Vol. 77, pp. 73-80). Washington, D.C.: American Museum of Natural Hisotry.

Kaestle, F. (1997). Molecular analysis of ancient Native American DNA from western Nevada. *Nevada Historical Society Quarterly, 40*(1), 85-96.

Kaestle, F. (1998). *Molecular evidence for prehistoric Native American population movement: The Numic expansion.* Unpublished Dissertation, University of California, Davis, Davis, CA.

Kaestle, F. (2000). *Comment on the repatriation of the "Spirit Cave Man" remains.* Reno, NV: Ms on file in BLM Nevada office.

Kaestle, F. A., & Smith, D. G. (2001). Ancient mitochonrial DNA evidence for prehistoric population movement: The Numic expansion. *American Journal of Physical Anthropology, 115*, 1-12.

Kane, P. (1856). Notes on travels among the Walla Walla Indians. *Canadian Journals, 1*(5), 417-424.

Kane, P. (1859). *Wanderings of an artist among the Indians of North America, from Canada to Vancouver's Island and Oregon through the Hudson's Bay territory and back again.* London: Longmans Brown.

Karafet, T., Xu, L., Du, R., Wang, W., Feng, S., Wells, R. S., et al. (2001). Paternal population history of east Asia: Sources, patterns, and microevolutionary processes. *American Journal of Human Genetics, 69*, 615-628.

Karafet, T., Zegura, S. L., Vuturo-Brady, J., Posukh, O., Osipova, L., Wiebe, V., et al. (1997). Y chromosome markers and trans-bering strait dispersals. *American Journal of Physical Anthropology, 102*, 301-314.

Karafet, T. M., Zegura, S. L., Posukh, O., Osipova, L., Bergen, A., Long, J., et al. (1999). Ancestral Asian source(s) of new world y-chromosome founder haplotypes. *American Journal of Human Genetics, 64*, 817-831.

Kaufman, D. S., William F. Manley, Alexander P. Wolfe, Feng Sheng Hu, Shari J. Preece, John A. Westgate, and Steve L. Forman. (2001). The last interglacial to glacial transition, Togiak Bay, southwestern Alaska, *Quaternary Research* (Vol. 55:190-202).

Kelley, M. A., and Clark Spencer Larsen. (1991). Advances in dental anthropology: Wiley-Liss: New York.

Kelly, I. T. (1932). Ethnography of the Surprise Valley Paiute. *University of California Publications in American Archaeology and Ethnology, 31*(3), 67-210.

Kelly, I. T., & Van Valkenburgh, R. F. (1976). *Paiute Indians II.* New York, NY: Garland Publishing.

Kelly, R. L. (1995). Hunter gatherer lifeways in the Carson desert: A context for bioarchaeology. In Kelly, C. S. L. a. R. L. (Ed.), *Bioarchaeology of the Stillwater Marsh: Prehistoric Human Adaptation in the Western Great Basin* (Vol. 77:12-32): American Museum of Natural History, Anthropological Papers.

Kennedy, D. I. D., & Bouchard, R. T. (1998). Northern Okanagan, Lakes, and Colville. In Walker, D. E., Jr. (Ed.), *Plateau* (Vol. 12, pp. 238-252). Washington, DC: Smithsonian Institution.

Kinkade, M. D., Elmendorf, W. W., Rigsby, B., & Aoki, H. (1998). Languages. In Walker, D. E., Jr. (Ed.), *Plateau* (Vol. 12, pp. 49-72). Washington, D.C.: Smithsonian Institution.

Knight, A., Batzer, M. A., Stoneking, M., Tiwari, H. K., Scheer, W. D., Herrera, R. J., et al. (1996). DNA sequences of alu elements indicate a recent replacement of the human autosomal genetic complement. *Proceedings of the National Academy of Sciences, 93*, 4360-4364.

Kovanen, D. J., & Easterbrook, D. J. (2002). Timing and extent of allerod and younger dryas age (ca. 12,500-10,000 14c yr bp) oscillations of the cordilleran ice sheet in the Fraser lowland, western North America. *Quaternary Research, 57*, 208-224.

Krantz, G. S. (1979). Oldest human remains from the Marmes site. *Northwest Anthropological Research Notes, 13*(2), 159-174.

Krauss, M. E., & Golla, V. K. (1981). Northern Athapaskan languages. In Helm, J. (Ed.), *Subarctic* (Vol. 6, pp. 67-85). Washington, D.C.: Smithsonian Institution Press.

Krech, S., III. (1999). *The ecological Indian: Myth and history*. New York, NY: W.W. Northon & Company.

Krider, P. R. (1998). Paleoclimatic significance of late quaternary lacustrine and alluvial stratigraphy, Animas Valley, New Mexico. *Quaternary Research, 50*, 283-289.

Kroeber, A. L. (1920). California culture provinces. *University of California Publications in American Archaeology and Ethnology, 17*(2), 151-169.

Kroeber, A. L. (1923). *Anthropology*. New York, NY: Harcourt, Brace and Company.

Kroeber, A. L. (1925a). Paiute. In Kroeber, A. L. (Ed.), *Handbook of the Indians of California* (Vol. 78, pp. 593-600). Washington, DC: Smithsonian Institution.

Kroeber, A. L. (1925b). Paviotso. In Kroeber, A. L. (Ed.), *Handbook of Indians of California* (Vol. 78, pp. 581-584). Washington, DC: Smithsonian Institution.

Kroeber, A. L. (1939). Cultural and natural areas of native North America. *University of California Publications in American Archaeology and Ethnology, 31*(4), 211-256.

Kroeber, A. L., & Gifford, E. W. (1980). *Karok myths*. Berkeley, CA: University of California Press.

Kuhn, S. L. (1995). *Mousterian lithic technology*. Princeton, NJ: Princeton University Press.

Kuhn, T. S. (1970). *The structure of scientific revolutions* (2 ed.). Chicago, IL: University of Chicago Press.

Kuper, A. (2003). The return of the native. *Current Anthropology, 44*(3), 389-402.

Kurten, B., & Anderson, E. (1980). *Pleistocene mammals of North America*. New York, NY: Columbia University Press.

Kuzmin, Y. V., & Tankersley, K. B. (1996). The colonization of eastern Siberia: An evaluation of the paleolithic age radiocarbon dates. *Journal of Archaeological Science, 23*(4), 577-585.

Lahren, C. H. (1997). *Report letter on hair sample 2064 to Dr. Doug Owsley, January 23, 1997*. Reno, NV: Ms. on File at Bureau of Land Management.

Lamb, S. M. (1958). Linguistic prehistory in the Great Basin. *International Journal of American Linguistics, 24*(2), 95-100.

Lamb, S. M. (1964a). The classification of the Uto-Aztecan languages: A historical survey. In Bright, W. (Ed.), *Studies in Californian linguistics* (pp. 106-125). Berkeley, CA: University of California Press.

Lamb, S. M. (1964b). Linguistic diversification and extinction in North America. *International Congress of Americanists, 34*(2), 457-464.

Lamberg-Karlovsky, C. C. (2002). Archaeology and language: The Indo-Iranians. *Current Anthropology, 43*(1), 63-88.

Larsen, C. S. (1997). *Bioarchaeology: Interpreting behavior from the human skeleton*. Cambridge, MA: Cambridge University Press.

Larson, M. L. (1997). Housepits and mobile hunter-gatherers: A consideration of the Wyoming evidence. *Plains Anthropologist, 42*(161), 353-369.

Leahey, T. H. (1987). *A history of psychology: Main currents in psychological thought* (Second ed.). Englewood Cliffs, NJ: Prentice-Hall.

Lee, D., & Frost, J. H. (1844). *Ten years in Oregon*. New York, NY: J. Collord.

Lekson, S. (2000). *The Chaco meridian: Centers of political power in the ancient Southwest*. Walnut Creek, CA: Altamira Press.

Lemke, R. W., Laird, W. M., Tipton, M. J., & Lindvall, R. M. (1965). Quaternary geology of northern Great Plains. In Wright, H. E., Jr. & Frey, D. C. (Eds.), *The quaternary of the United States: A review volume for the VII congress of the international association for quaternary research* (pp. 15-28). Princeton, NJ: Princeton University Press.

Leonhardy, F., & Rice, D. (1970). A proposed culture typology for the Lower Snake River region, southeastern Washington. *Northwest Anthropological Research Notes, 4*(1), 1-29.

Lightner, T. M. (1971). On Swadesh and Voegelin's 'a problem in phonological alternation'. *International Journal of American Linguistics, 37*, 227-237.

Liljeblad, S. (1957). *Indian peoples in Idaho*. Pocatello, ID: Idaho State College.

Liljeblad, S. (1986). Oral tradition: Content and style of verbal arts. In D'Azevedo, W. (Ed.), *Great Basin* (Vol. 11, pp. 641-659). Washington, D.C.: Smithsonian Institution.

Lohse, E., & Sammons-Lohse, D. (1986). Sedentism on the southern Plateau: A matter of degree related to the easy and efficient exploitation of resources. *Northwest Anthropological Research Notes, 20*(2), 115-136.

Loomba, A. (1998). *Colonialism/postcolonialism*. London, UK: Routledge.

Lorenz, J., & Smith, D. G. (1996). Distribution of four founding mtDNA haplogroups among native North Americans. *American Journal of Physical Anthropology, 101*, 307-323.

Lowe, D. J., Green, J. D., Northcote, T. G., & Hall, K. J. (1997). Holocene fluctuations of a Meromictic Lake in southern British Columbia. *Quaternary Research, 48*, 100-113.

Lowie, R. (1924). Notes on Shoshonean ethnography. *American Museum of Natural History Anthropological Papers, 20*(3), 187-312.

Lowie, R. (1993). *Myths and traditions of the Crow Indians*. Lincoln, NE: University of Nebraska Press.

Lyman, R. L. (1985). Cultural resource management and archaeological research in the interior Pacific Northwest: A note to NARN readers and the translucency of Northwest archaeology. *Northwest Anthropological Research Notes, 19*(2), 161-168.

Lyman, R. L. (1997). Impediments to archaeology: Publishing and the (growing) translucency of archaeological research. *Northwest Anthropological Research Notes, 31*(1-2), 5-22.

Lyneis, M. M. (1982). Prehistory in the southern Great Basin. In Madsen, D. B. & O'Connell, J. F. (Eds.), *Man and environment in the Great Basin* (pp. 172-185). Washington, D.C.: Society of American Archaeology.

MacDonald, D. H. (1998). Subsistence, sex, and cultural transmission in Folsom culture. *Journal of Anthropological Archaeology, 17*, 217-239.

MacEachern, S. (2000). Genes, tribes, and African history. *Current Anthropology, 41*(3), 357-384.

Madsen, D. B. (1982). Get it where the getting's good: A variable model of Great Basin subsistence and settlement based on data from the eastern Great Basin. In Madsen, D. B. & O'Connell, J. F. (Eds.), *Man and environment in the Great Basin* (pp. 207-226). Washington, D.C.: Society for American Archaeology.

Madsen, D. B., & Schmitt, D. N. (1998). Mass collecting and the diet breadth model: A Great Basin example. *Journal of Archaeological Science, 25*, 445-455.

Madsen, D. B., & Simms, S. R. (1998). The Fremont complex: A behavioral perspective. *Journal of World Prehistory, 12*(3), 255-336.

Mann, D. H., & Peteet, D. M. (1994). Extent and timing of the last glacial maximum in southwestern Alaska. *Quaternary Research, 42*(2), 136-148.

Marano, L. (1982). Windigo psychosis: The anatomy of an emic-etic confusion. *Current Anthropology, 23*(4), 385-412.

Markgraf, V., & Scott, L. (1981). Lower timberline in central Colorado during the past 15,000 yr. *Geology, 9*, 231-234.

Martin, L. D., Rogers, R. A., & Neuner, A. M. (1985). The effect of the end of the pleistocene on man in North America. In Mead, J. I. & Meltzer, D. J. (Eds.), *Environments and extinctions: Man in late glacial North America* (pp. 15-30). Orono, ME: Center for the Study of Early Man.

Martin, P. S. (1982). The pattern and meaning of holarctic mammoth extinction. In Hopkins, D. M., Matthews, J. V., Schweger, C. E. & Young, S. (Eds.), *Paleocology of Beringia* (pp. 399-408). New York, NY: Academic Press.

Martin, P. S., & Mehringer, P. J., Jr. (1965). Pleistocene pollen analysis and biogeography of the Southwest. In Wright, H. E., Jr. & Frey, D. G. (Eds.), *The quaternary of the United States: A review volume for the VII congress of the international association for quaternary research* (pp. 433-452). Princeton, NJ: Princeton University Press.

Martin, P. S., & Szuter, C. R. (1999). Megafauna of the Columbia Basin, 1800-1840: Lewis and clark in a game sink. In Goble, D. D. & Hirt, P. W. (Eds.), *Northwest lands, northwest peoples: Readings in environmental history* (pp. 229-263). Seattle, WA: University of Washington Press.

Martin, P. S., Thompson, R. S., & Long, A. (1985). Shasta ground sloth extinction: A test of the blitzkrieg model. In Mead, J. I. & Meltzer, D. J. (Eds.), *Environments and extinctions: Man in late glacial North America* (pp. 5-14). Orono, ME: Center for the Study of Early Man.

Martynov, A. I. (1981). Siberia before the mongols: New findings and problems. *Journal of the Stewart Anthropological Society, 12*(2), 441-506.

Mason, O. T. (1896). Influence of the environment upon human industries or arts. In *Annual report of the board of regents of the Smithsonian Institution, showing the operations, expenditures, and conditions of the institution to July, 1895* (pp. 639-665). Washington, D.C.: Smithsonain Institution.

Matisoff, J. A. (1990). On megalo-comparison: A discussion note. *Language, 66,* 106-120.

McCartney, A. P. (1984). Prehistory of the Aleutian region. In Dumas, D. (Ed.), *Arctic* (Vol. 5, pp. 119-135). Washington, D.C.: Smithsonian Institution.

McDonald, R. W., Carmack, E. C., McLaughlin, F. A., Falkner, K. K., & Swift, J. H. (1999). Connections among ice, runoff and atmospheric forcing in the beaufort gyre. *Geophysical Research Letters, 26*(15), 2223-2226.

McGimsey, C. R., III. (2003). The four fields of archaeology. *American Antiquity, 68*(4), 611-618.

Mehringer, J., Peter J. (1985a). Late-quaternary pollen records from the interior Pacific Northwest and northern Great Basin of the United States. In Bryant, V. M., Jr. & Holloway, R. G. (Eds.), *Pollen records of late-quaternary North American sediments* (pp. 167-190). Austin, TX: American Association of Stratigraphic Palynologists Foundation: Texas.

Mehringer, J., Peter J. (1985b). Quaternary pollen records from the interior Pacific Northwest coast: Aleutians to the Oregon-California boundary. In Bryant, V. M., Jr. & Holloway, R. G. (Eds.), *Pollen records of late-quaternary North American sediments* (pp. 167-190). Austin, TX: American Association of Stratigraphic Palynologists Foundation.

Meltzer, D. J., & Mead, J. I. (1985). Dating late pleistocene extinctions: Theoretical issues, analytical bias, and substantive results. In Mead, J. I. & Meltzer, D. J. (Eds.), *Environments and extinctions: Man in late glacial North America* (pp. 145-174). Orono, ME: Center for the Study of Early Man.

Menking, K. M., James L. Bischoff, John A. Fitzpatrick, James W. Burdette, and Robert O. Rye. (1997). Climatic/hydrologic oscillations since 155,000 yr bp at Owens Lake, California, reflected in abundance and stable isotope composition of sediment carbonate, *Quaternary Research* (Vol. 48:58-68).

Mensing, S. A. (2001). Late-glacial and early holocene vegetation and climate change near Owens Lake, eastern California. *Quaternary Research, 55,* 57-65.

Merculieff, I. (1994). Western society's linear systems and aboriginal cultures: The need for two-way exchanges for the sake of survival. In Burch, E. S., Jr. & Ellanna, L. (Eds.), *Key issues in hunter-gatherer research* (pp. 405-415). Oxford, UK: Berg Publishers Ltd.

Merriwether, A., Hell, W. W., Vahlne, A., & Ferrell, R. E. (1996). MtDNA variation indicates Mongolia may have been the source for the founding population for the new world. *American Journal of Human Genetics, 59*, 204-212.

Merriwether, A., Rothhammer, F., & Ferrell, R. E. (1995). Distribution of the four founding lineage haplotypes in Native Americans suggests a single wave of migration for the new world. *American Journal of Physical Anthropology, 98*, 411-430.

Merriwether, D. A., Huston, S., Iyengar, S., Hamman, R., Norris, J. M., Shetterly, S. M., et al. (1997). Mitochondrial versus nuclear admixture estimates demonstrate a past history of directional mating. *American Journal of Physical Anthropology, 102*, 153-159.

Miller, S. J. (1982). The archaeology and geology of an extinct megafauna/fluted-point association at Owl Cave, the wadsen site, Idaho: A preliminary report. In Jonathon E. Ericson, R. E. T., and Rainer Berger (Ed.), *Peopling of the New World* (Vol. 81-96): Ballena Press: California.

Miller, W. R. (1986). Numic languages. In D'Azevedo, W. (Ed.), *Great Basin* (Vol. 11, pp. 98-106). Washington, D.C.: Smithsonian Institution.

Milner, G., and C. Larsen. (1991). Teeth as artifacts of human behavior: Intentional mutilation and accidental modification. In Larsen, M. K. a. C. (Ed.), *Advances in Dental Anthropology* (Vol. 357-378): Wiley-Liss: New York.

Mithun, M. (1990). Studies of North American Indian languages. *Annual Review of Anthropology, 19*, 309-330.

Moss, M., & Erlandson, J. (1995). *A comparative chronology of Northwest Coast fishing features.* Paper presented at the Hidden Dimensions: The Cultural Significance of, University of British Columbia, Canada.

Moulton, G. E. (Ed.). (1991). *The journals of the Lewis and Clark expedition.* Lincoln, NE: University of Nebraska Press.

Mountain, J. L., & Cavalli-Sforza, L. L. (1997). Multilocus genotypes, a tree of individuals, and human evolutionary history. *American Journal of Human Genetics, 61*, 705-718.

Murdock, G. P. (1941). *Ethnographic bibliography of North America* (Vol. 1). New Haven, CT: Yale University, Department of Anthropology.

Nelson, M. C., & Hegmon, M. (2001). Abandonment is not as it seems: An approach to the relationship between site and regional abandonment. *American Antiquity, 66*(2), 213-235.

Nelson, M. C., & Schachner, G. (2002). Understanding abandonments in the North American Southwest. *Journal of Archaeological Research, 10*, 167-206.

Newman, M. T. (1962). Evolutionary changes in body size and head form in American Indians. *American Anthropologist, 64*(2), 237-257.

Nials, F. L. (1999). *Geomorphic systems and stratigraphy in internally-drained watersheds of the northern Great Basin: Implications for archaeological studies* (No. Technical Paper No. 5). Reno, NV: University of Nevada, Department of Anthropology, Sundance Archaeological Research Fund.

Nicholas, G. P. (1998). Wetlands and hunter-gatherers: A global perspective. *Current Anthropology, 39*(5), 720-731.

O'Connell, J. F., Jones, K. T., & Simms, S. R. (1982). Some thoughs on prehistoric archaeology in the Great Basin. In Madsen, D. B. & O'Connell, J. F. (Eds.), *Man and environment in the Great Basin* (pp. 227-240). Washington, D.C.: Society for American Archaeology.

Ogden, P. S. (1909). Journals of the Snake expedition, 1825-1827. *Oregon Historical Quarterly, 10*(4), 331-365.

Ogden, P. S. (1910). Journals of the Snake expedition, 1825-1827. *Oregon Historical Quarterly, 11*(2), 201-222.

Ogden, P. S. (1950). *Ogden's Snake country journals.* London, UK: Hudson's Bay Record Society.

O'Grady, R., Goddard, I., Bateman, R., Di Michele, W. A., Funk, V. A., Kress, W. J., et al. (1989). Genes and tongues. *Science, 243*, 1651.

Olrik, A. (1965). Epic laws of folk narrative. In Dundes, A. (Ed.), *The study of folklore* (pp. 129-141). Englewood City, NJ: Prentice-Hall, Inc.

Opler, M. E. (1983). The Apachean culture pattern and its origins. In Ortiz, A. (Ed.), *The Southwest* (Vol. 10). Washington, D.C.: Smithsonian Institution.

O'Rourke, D. H., Hayes, M. G., & Carlyle, S. W. (2000). Spatial and temporal stability of mtDNA haplogroup frequencies in native North America. *Human Biology, 72*(1), 15-34.

Orta, A. (2004). The promise of particularism and the theology of culture: Limits and lessons of "neo-Boasianism". *American Anthropologist, 106*(3), 473-487.

Ortiz, A. (Ed.). (1983). *The Southwest* (Vol. 10). Washington, D.C.: Smithsonian Institution.

Ossenberg, N. S. (1976). Within and between race distances in population studies based on discrete traits of the human skull. *American Journal of Physical Anthropology, 45*, 701-716.

Ossenberg, N. S. (1977). Congruence of distance matrices based on cranial discrete traits, cranial measurements, and linquistic-geographic criteria in five Alaskan populations. *American Journal of Physical Anthropology, 47*, 93-98.

Ossenberg, N. S. (1986). Isolate conservatism and hybridization in the population history of Japan: The evidence of nonmetric cranial traits. *University Museum Bulletin, 27*, 199-215.

Ossenberg, N. S. (1994). Origins and affinities of the native peoples of Northwestern North America: The evidence of cranial nonmetric traits. In Bonnichsen, R. & Steele, D. G. (Eds.), *Method and theory for investigating the peopling of the Americas* (pp. 79-115). Corvallis, OR: Center for the Study of the First Americans.

Oviatt, C. G., Thompson, R. S., Kaufman, D. S., Bright, J., & Forester, R. M. (1999). Reinterpretation of the burmester core, Bonneville Basin, Utah. *Quaternary Research, 52*, 180-184.

Owsley, D. (1992). Demography of prehistoric and early historic northern Plains populations. In Ubelaker, J. W. V. a. D. H. (Ed.), *Disease and Demography in the Americas* (Vol. 75-86): Smithsonian Institution: Washington D.C.

Owsley, D. (1996). Lab notes: 9f-nsm-2064 Spirit Cave Mummy: Ms on file at Nevada State Museum.

Owsley, D., & Jantz, R. (1999). Databases for paleo-american skeletal biology research. In Bonnichsen, R. (Ed.), *Who were the first Americans? Proceedings of the 58th annual biology colloquium, Oregon State University* (pp. 76-96). Corvallis, OR: Center for the Study of the First Americans.

Owsley, D., & Jantz, R. (2001). Archaeological politics and public interest in paleoamerican studies: Lessons from Gordon Creek Woman and Kennewick man. *American Antiquity, 66*(4), 565-575.

Page, R. D. M., & Charleston, M. A. (1990). Reconciled trees and incongruent gene and species trees. *DIMACS Series in Discrete Mathematics and Theoretical Computer Science, 00,* 1-14.

Palmer, G. B. (1975). Cultural ecology in the Canadian plateau: Pre-contact to the early contact period in the territory of the southern Shuswap Indians of British Columbia. *Northwest Anthropological Research Notes, 9*(2), 199-245.

Palmer, J. (1847). *Journal of travels over the Rocky Mountains to the mouth of the Columbia River: Made during the years of 1845 and 1846.* Cincinnati: OH: J.A. and V.P. Janes.

Pamilo, P., & Nei, M. (1998). Relationships between gene trees and species trees. *Molecular Biological Evolution, 5*(5), 568-583.

Parker, S. A. M. (1846). *Journal of an exploring tour beyond the Rocky Mountains, under the direction of the A.B.C.F.M. Containing a description of the geography, geology, climate, productions of the country, and the numbers, manners, and customs of the natives: With a map of oregon territory.* Auburn, NY: J.C. Derby & Co.

Pellatt, M. G., & Mathewes, R. W. (1997). Holocene tree line and climate change on the Queen Charlotte Islands, Canada. *Quaternary Research, 48,* 88-99.

Pendleton, L. S. A., McLane, A. R., & Thomas, D. H. (1982). *Cultural resource overview, Carson City district, west central Nevada* (Vol. 5). New York, NY: American Museum of Natural History.

Pielou, E. C. (1991). *After the ice age: The return of life to glaciated North America.* Chicago, IL: University of Chicago Press.

Pitulko, V. V., Nikolsky, P. A., Girya, E. Y., Basilyan, A. E., Tumskoy, V. E., Koulakov, S. A., et al. (2004). The Yana RHS site: Humans in the arctic before the last glacial maximum. *Science, 303,* 52-56.

Pluciennik, M. (1995). A perilous but necessary search: Archaeology and European identities. In Atkinson, J. & O'Sullivan, J. (Eds.), *Nationalism and archaeology: Scottish archaeological forum* (pp. 35-58). Glasgow: Cruithne Press.

Point, N. (1967). *Wilderness kingdom: Indian life in the Rocky Mountains: 1840-1847: The journal and paintings of Nicolas Point.* New York, NY: Holt, Rinehart and Winston.

Poloni, E. S., Semino, O., Passarino, G., Santachiara-Benerecetti, A. S., Dupanloup, I., Langaney, A., et al. (1997). Human genetic affinities for y-chromosome p49a,f/taq1 haplotypes show strong correspondence with linguistics. *American Journal of Human Genetics, 61,* 1015-1035.

Porcasi, J. F., Jones, T. L., & Raab, L. M. (2000). Trans-holocene marine mammal exploitation on San Clemente Island, California: A tragedy of the commons revisited. *Journal of Anthropological Archaeology, 19,* 200-220.

Porinchu, D. F., & Cwynar, L. C. (2002). Late-quaternary history of midge communities and climate from a tundra site near the lower Lena River, northeast Siberia. *Journal of Paleolimnology, 27*(1), 59-69.

Porter, S. C., Pierce, K. L., & Hamilton, T. D. (1983). Late wisconsin mountain glaciation in the western United States. In Porter, S. C. (Ed.), *Late-quaternary environments of the United States: Volume 1, the late pleistocene* (pp. 71-111). Minneapolis, MN: University of Minnesota Press.

Powell, J., & Rose, J. (1999). *Report on the osteological assessment of the "Kennewick man" skeleton (cenwww.97.Kennewick)*. Washington, D.C.: Department of the Interior.

Powell, J. F., & Neves, W. A. (1999). Craniofacial morphology of the first Americans: Pattern and process in the peopling of the new world. *Yearbook of Physical Anthropology, 42*, 153-188.

Powell, J. W. (1891a). Indian linguistic families of America north of Mexico. In *Seventh annual report, Bureau of American Ethnology* (pp. 1-142). Washington, D.C.: Government Printing Office.

Powell, J. W. (1891b). The study of Indian languages. *Science, 17*(418), 71-74.

Quade, J., Forester, R. M., Pratt, W. L., & Carter, C. (1998). Black mats, spring-fed streams, and late-glacial-age recharge in the southern Great Basin. *Quaternary Research, 49*, 129-148.

Quimby, G. I. (1985). Japanese wrecks, iron tools, and prehistoric Indians of the Northwest Coast. *Arctic Anthropology, 22*(2), 7-15.

Radin, P. (1919). *The genetic relationship of the North American Indian languages* (Vol. 14). Berkeley, CA: University of California Press.

Ramsey, J. (1977). *Coyote was going there: Indian literature of the Oregon country.* Seattle, WA: University of Washington Press.

Rankin, R. L. (1992). Review of *language in the Americas* by Joseph H. Greenberg. *International Journal of American Linguistics, 58*, 324-351.

Raven, C., & Elston, R. G. (Eds.). (1988). *Preliminary investigations in Stillwater Marsh: Human prehistory and geoarchaeology* (Vol. 1). Reno, NV: Department of the Interior.

Raven, C., & Elston, R. G. (Eds.). (1991). *Looking for the marsh: Past, present, and future archaeological research in the Carson Desert.* Portland, OR: U.S. Fish and Wildlife Service.

Ray, V. F. (1936). Native villages and groupings of the Columbia Basin. *Pacific Northwest Quarterly, 27*(2), 99-152.

Ray, V. F. (1939). *Cultural relations in the plateau of Northwestern America* (Vol. 3). Los Angeles, CA: Southwestern Museum.

Ray, V. F., Murdock, G. P., Blyth, B., Stewart, O. C., Harris, J., Hoebel, E. A., et al. (1938). Tribal distribution in eastern Oregon and adjacent regions. *American Anthropologist, 40*(3), 384-415.

Raymond, A. W., & Parks, V. M. (1990). Archaeological sites exposed by recent flooding of Stillwater Marsh, Carson Desert, Churchill county, Nevada. In Janetski, J. C. & Madsen, D. (Eds.), *Wetland adaptations in the Great Basin* (Vol. 1). Provo, UT: Museum of Peoples and Cultures, Brigham Young University.

Reheis, M. (1999). Highest pluvial-lake shorelines and pleistocene climate of the western Great Basin. *Quaternary Research, 52*, 196-205.

Relethford, J. H. (2001). Global analysis of regional differences in craniometric diversity and population substructure. *Human Biology, 73*(5), 629-636.

Rhode, D., & Madsen, D. B. (1998). Pine nut use in the early holocene and beyond: The Danger Cave archaeobotanical record. *Journal of Archaeological Science, 25*, 1199-1210.

Richman, J. R., & Forsyth, M. P. (Eds.). (2004). *Legal perspectives on cultural resources.* Walnut Creek, CA: Altamira Press.

Richmond, G. M. (1965). Glaciation of the Rocky Mountains. In Wright, H. E., Jr. & Frey, D. G. (Eds.), *The quaternary of the United States: A review volume for the VII congress of the international association for quaternary research* (pp. 217-230). Princeton, NJ: Princeton University Press.

Richmond, G. M., Fryxell, R., Neff, G. E., & Weis, P. (1965). The cordilleran ice sheet of the northern Rocky Mountains and related quaternary history of the Columbia Plateau. In Wright, H. E., Jr. & Frey, D. G. (Eds.), *The quaternary of the United States: A review volume for the VII congress of the international association for quaternary research* (pp. 231-242). Princeton, NJ: Princeton University Press.

Rick, T. C., & Erlandson, J. M. (2000). Early holocene fishing strategies on the California coast: Evidence from ca-sba-2057. *Journal of Archaeological Science, 27*, 621-633.

Rick, T. C., Erlandson, J. M., & Vellanoweth, R. L. (2001). Paleocoastal marine fishing on the Pacific coast of the Americas: Perspectives from Daisy Cave, California. *American Antiquity, 66*(4), 595-614.

Ridington, R. (1988). Knowledge, power, and the individual in subarctic hunting societies. *American Anthropologist, 90*(1), 98-110.

Rigsby, B. (1969). The Waiilatpuan problem: More on Cayuse-Molala relatability. *Northwest Anthropological Research Notes, 3*(1), 68-146.

Ritchie, J. C. (1985). Quaternary pollen records from the western interior and the arctic of Canada. In Bryant, V. M., Jr. & Holloway, R. G. (Eds.), *Pollen records of late-quaternary North American sediments* (pp. 327-352). Austin, TX: American Association of Stratigraphic Palynologists Foundation.

Robson bonnichsen et al. Vs. United states of america et al. 2002.

Rogers, A., & Jorde, L. B. (1995). Genetic evidence on modern human origins. *Human Biology, 67*, 1-36.

Rogers, L. A., Rogers, R. A., & Martin, L. D. (1992). How the door opened: The peopling of the new world. *Human Biology, 64*(3), 281-302.

Roll, T., & Hackenberger, S. (1998). Prehistory of the eastern Plateau. In Walker, D. E., Jr. (Ed.), *Plateau* (Vol. 12, pp. 120-137). Washington, D.C.: Smithsonian Institution.

Rosenblatt, D. (2004). An anthropology made safe for culture: Patterns of practice and the politics of difference in Ruth Benedict. *American Anthropologist, 106*(3), 459-472.

Ross, A. (1904). *Adventures of the first settlers on the Oregon or Columbia River: Being a narrative of the expedition fitted out by John Jacob Astor, to establish the "Pacific Fur Company"; with an account of some Indian tribes on the coast of the Pacific. By Alexander Ross, one of the adventurers* (Vol. 7). Cleveland, OH: Arthur H. Clark.

Ross, A. (1913). Journal of Alexander Ross. *Oregon Historical Quarterly, 14*(3), 366-385.

Ross, A. (1956). *The fur hunters of the far west.* Norman, OK: University of Oklahoma Press.

Roy-Engel, A. M., Carroll, M. L., Vogel, E., Garber, R. K., Nguyen, S. V., Salem, A.-H., et al. (2001). Alu insertion polymorphisms for the study of human genomic diversity. *Genetics, 159*, 279-290.

Ruby, R. H., & Brown, J. A. (1972). *The Cayuse Indians: Imperial tribesman of old Oregon.* Norman, OK: University of Oklahoma Press.

Rudolph, T. (1995). *The Hetrick site: 11,000 years of prehistory in the Weiser river valley.* Boise, ID: Science Applications International Corporation.

Ruhlen, M. (1986). *A guide to the world's languages* (Vol. 1). Stanford, CA: Stanford University Press.

Ruhlen, M. (1987). Voices from the past. *Natural History, 96*(3), 6-10.

Ruhlen, M. (1994). Linguistic evidence for the peopling of the Americas. In Bonnichsen, R. & Steele, D. G. (Eds.), *Method and theory for investigating the peopling of the Americas* (pp. 177-188). Corvallis, OR: Center for the Study of the First Americans.

Sabin, A. L., & Pisias, N. G. (1996). Sea surface temperature changes in the northeastern Pacific ocean during the past 20,000 years and their relationship to climate change in northwestern North America. *Quaternary Research, 46*, 48-61.

Sack, D. (1999). The composite nature of the Provo level of Lake Bonneville, Great Basin, western North America. *Quaternary Research, 52*, 316-327.

Sackett, J. R. (1982). Approaches to style in lithic archaeology. *Journal of Anthropological Archaeology, 1*, 59-112.

Sackett, J. R. (1985). Style, ethnicity, and stone tools. In Thompson, M., Garcia, M. T. & Kense, F. J. (Eds.), *Status, structure and stratification: Current archaeological reconstructions* (pp. 277-282). Calgary, Canada: University of Calgary.

Sackett, J. R. (1986). Isochrestism and style: A clarification. *Journal of Anthropological Archaeology, 5*, 266-277.

Said, E. W. (1978). *Orientalism.* New York, NY: Pantheon.

Said, E. W. (2000). *Reflections on exile and other essays.* Cambridge, MA: Harvard University Press.

Sandweiss, D. H., McInnis, H., Burger, R. L., Cano, A., Ojeda, B., Paredes, R., et al. (1998). Quebrada Jaguay: Early South American maritime adaptations. *Science, 281*, 1830-1832.

Sandweiss, D. H., Rothhammer, F., Reitz, J. H., & Feldman, R. (1989). Early maritime adaptations at the Ring Site, Peru. In Rice, D. & Stanish, C. (Eds.), *Ecology, settlement, and history in the Osmore Basin.* London, UK: British Archaeological Reports, International Series.

Santos, F. R., Pandya, A., Tyler-Smith, C., Pena, S. D. J., Schanfield, M., Leonard, W. R., et al. (1999). The central Siberian origin for Native American y chromosomes. *American Journal of Human Genetics, 64*, 619-628.

Sapir, E. (1917). Linguistic publications of the Bureau of American Ethnology, a general view. *International Journal of American Linguistics, 1*, 280-290.

Sappington, R. L. (1989). The Lewis and Clark expedition among the Nez Perce Indians: The first ethnographic study in the Columbia Plateau. *Northwest Anthropological Research Notes, 23*(1), 1-33.

Saussure, F. d. (1916/1974). *Course in general linguistics* (Baskin, W., Trans.). Glasgow: Fontana/Collins.

Schalk, R., & Cleveland, G. (1983). A sequence of adaptations in the Columbia-Fraser plateau. In Schalk, R. (Ed.), *Cultural resource investigations for the Lyons fish hatchery, Lyons Ferry, Washington* (pp. 11-56). Pullman, WA: Washington State University, Laboratory of Archaeology and History.

Schalk, R., Dillian, C., Hamilon, S., Hodges, C., Olsen, D., & Stratford, M. (1998). *Archaeological investigations at 45ok2a, 45ok5, and 45ok20 in the Chief Joseph reservoir.* Honolulu, HI: International Archaeological Research Institute, Inc.

Schneider, A. L. (2004). Kennewick man: The three-million-dollar skeleton. In Richman, J. R. & Forsyth, M. P. (Eds.), *Legal perspectives on cultural resources* (pp. 202-215). Walnut Creek, CA: AltaMira Press.

Schurr, T., Ballinger, S., Gan, Y.-Y., Hodge, J. A., Weiss, K. M., & Wallace, D. (1990). Amerindian mitochondrial DNAs have rare Asian mutations at high frequencies, suggesting they derived from four primary maternal lineages. *American Journal of Human Genetics, 46*, 613-623.

Schurr, T., & Wallace, D. (1999). MtDNA variation in Native Americans and Siberians and its implications for the peopling of the new world. In Bonnichsen, R. (Ed.), *Who were the first Americans? Proceedings of the 58th annual biology colloquium, Oregon State University* (pp. 41-77). Covallis, OR: Center for the Study of the First Americans.

Schurr, T. G., Sukernik, R. I., Starikovskaya, Y. B., & Wallace, D. C. (1999). Mitochondrial DNA variation in Koryaks and Itel'men: Population replacement in the Okhotsk sea-bering sea region during the neolithic. *American Journal of Physical Anthropology, 108*, 1-39.

Schuster, H. (1998). Yakima and neighboring groups. In Walker, D. E., Jr. (Ed.), *Plateau* (Vol. 12, pp. 327-351). Washington, D.C.: Smithsonian Institution.

Scott, G. R. (1965). Nonglacial quaternary geology of the southern and middle Rocky Mountains. In Wright, H. E., Jr. & Frey, D. G. (Eds.), *The quaternary of the United States: A review volume for the VII congress of the international association for quaternary research* (pp. 243-254). Princeton, NJ: Princeton University Press.

Scoulcr, J. (1848). On the Indian tribes inhabiting the north-west coast of America. *Journal of the Ethnological Society of London, 1*, 228-252.

Scozzari, R., Cruciani, F., Santolamazza, P., Malaspina, P., Torroni, A., Sellitto, D., et al. (1999). Combined use of biallelic and microsatellite y-chromosome polymorphisms to infer affinities among African populations. *American Journal of Human Genetics, 65*, 829-846.

Seeman, M. F. (1994). Inter-cluster patterning at nobles pond: A case for "disembedded" procurement among early paleoindian societies. *American Antiquity, 59*, 273-287.

Service, N. P. (2003). *Kennewick man.* Retrieved February 19, 2003, from http://www.cr.nps.gov/aad/kennewick

Sherzer, J. (1973). Areal linguistics in North America. In Sebeok, T. A. (Ed.), *Linguistics in North America* (pp. 749-795). The Hague: Mouton.

Sherzer, J. (1976). *An areal-typological study of American Indian languages north of Mexico.* Amsterdam: North-Holland.

Shields, E. D. (1996). Quantitative complete tooth variation among East Asians and Native Americans: Developmental biology as a tool for the assessment of human divergence. *Journal of Craniofacial Genetics and Developmental Biology, 16*(4), 193-207.

Shields, E. D., & Jones, G. (1996). Heterochronic quantitative microevolution: Dental divergence in aboriginal Americans. *American Journal Of Physical Anthropology, 100*(3), 355-365.

Shields, E. D., & Jones, G. (1998). Dorset and Thule divergence from east central Asian roots. *American Journal of Physical Anthropology, 106*(2), 207-18.

Shimkin, D. B. (1980). Comanche-Shoshone words of acculturation, 1786-1848. *Journal of the Steward Anthropological Society, 11*(2), 195-248.

Shipley, W. (1980). Penutian among the ruins: A personal assessment. *Proceedings of the Annual Meeting of the Berkeley Linguistics Society, 6*, 437-441.

Simms, S. (1990). Fremont transitions. *Utah Archaeology, 3*, 1-18.

Simms, S. (1994). Unpacking the Numic spread. In Madsen, D. & Rhode, D. (Eds.), *Across the west: Human population movement and the expansion of the Numa* (pp. 76-83). Salt Lake City, UT: University of Utah Press.

Simpson, G. (1931). *Fur trade and empire. George Simpson's journal; remarks connected with the fur trade in the course of a voyage from York factory to Fort George and back to York factory, 1824-1825; together with accompanying documents.* Cambridge, MA: Harvard University Press.

Slaughter, B. H. (1975). Ecological interpretation of the brown sand wedge local fauna. In Wendorf, F. & Hester, J. J. (Eds.), *Late pleistocene environments of the southern High Plains* (Vol. 9, pp. 179-192). Fort Burgwin, NM: Fort Burgwin Research Center.

Smith, D. G., Lorenz, J., Rolfs, B. K., Bettinger, R. L., Green, B., Eshleman, J., et al. (2000). Implications of the distribution of albumin naskapi and albumin mexico for new wold prehistory. *American Journal of Physical Anthropology, 111*, 557-572.

Smith, D. G., Malhi, R., Eshleman, J., Lorenz, J. G., & Kaestle, F. A. (1999). Distribution of mtDNA haplogroup x among native North Americans. *American Journal of Physical Anthropology, 110*, 271-284.

Smith, G. I. (1979). *Subsurface stratigraphy and geochemistry of late quaternary evaporites, Searles Lake, California* (No. Professional Paper 1043). Washington, D.C.: U.S. Geological Survey.

Smith, G. I. (1985). Possible impacts on early man of late quaternary lake fluctuations in the great basin. In Blackburn, T. C. (Ed.), *Woman, poet, scientist: Essays in new world anthropology honoring Dr. Emma Louis Davis* (pp. 118-125). Menlo Park, CA: Ballena Press.

Smith, J. W., & Smith, R. A. (1982). New light on early sociocultural evolution in the Americas. In Ericson, J. E., Taylor, R. E. & Berger, R. (Eds.), *Peopling of the new world* (pp. 229-262). Menlo Park, CA: Ballena Press.

Snellgrove, D. (2002). *Indo-tibetan buddhism: Indian buddhists and their Tibetan successors.* Boston, MA: Shambhala.

Sparks, C. S., & Jantz, R. L. (2002). A reassessment of human cranial plasticity: Boas revisited. *Proceedings of the National Academy of Sciences, 99*(23), 14636-14639.

Speth, J. D. (1983). *Bison kills and bone counts: Decision making by ancient hunters.* Chicago, IL: University of Chicago Press.

Sprague, R. (2000a). *Great Basin burial pattern change.* Reno, NV: Ms on file at BLM Nevada office.

Sprague, R. (2000b). *A review of southern plateau burial practices. Attachment 1.* Pendleton, OR: Confederated Tribes of the Umatilla Indian Reservation, Cultural Resources Protection Program.

Stafford, T., Hull, A. J. T., Zabel, T. H., Donahue, D. J., Duhamel, R. C., Brendel, K., et al. (1984). Holocene ages of Yuha burial: Direct radiocarbon determination by accelerator mass spectronomy. *Nature, 308*, 446-447.

Stanford, D. (1991). Clovis origins and adaptations: An introductory perspective. In Bonnichsen, R. & Turnmire, K. (Eds.), *Clovis origins and adaptations.* Corvallis, OR: Center for the Study of First Americans, Oregon State University.

Stanford, D. (1999). Paleoindian archaeology and late pleistocene environments in the Plains and Southwestern United States. In Bonnichsen, R. & Turnmire, K. (Eds.), *Ice age people of North America: Environments, origins, adaptations* (pp. 281-339). Corvallis, OR: Oregon State University Press.

Steele, D. G., & Powell, J. (1992). Peopling of the Americas: Paleobiological evidence. *Human Biology, 64*(3), 303-336.

Steele, D. G., & Powell, J. (1994). Paleobiological evidence for the peopling of the Americas: A morphometric view. In Bonnichsen, R. & Steele, D. G. (Eds.), *Method and theory for investigating the peopling of the Americas* (pp. 141-163). Corvallis, OR: Center for the Study of the First Americans.

Steele, D. G., & Powell, J. (1999). Peopling of the Americas: A historical and comparative perspective. In Bonnichsen, R. (Ed.), *Who were the first Americans? Proceedings of the 58th annual biology colloquium, Oregon State University* (pp. 97-126). Covallis, OR: Center for the Study of the First Americans.

Stern, T. (1963). Klamath myth abstracts. *Journal of American Folklore, 76*(299), 31-41.

Stern, T. (1998). Columbia River trade network. In Walker, D. E., Jr. (Ed.), *Plateau* (Vol. 12, pp. 641-652). Washington, D.C.: Smithsonian Institution.

Steward, J. (1955). *Theory of culture change.* Urbana, IL: University of Illinois Press.

Steward, J. (1970). *Aboriginal sociopolitical groups.* Salt Lake City, UT: University of Utah Press.

Steward, J. H. (1937). Linguistic distributions and political groups of the Great Basin Shoshoneans. *American Anthropologist, 39*(4), 625-634.

Steward, J. H. (1938). *Basin-Plateau aboriginal sociopolitical groups* (Vol. 120). Washington, DC: Government Printing Office.

Steward, J. H. (1940). Native cultures of the intermontane (great basin) area. In Institution, S. (Ed.), *Essays in historical anthropology of North America: Published in honor of John R. Swanton* (Vol. Miscellaneous Collections 100, pp. 445-502). Washington, DC: Smithsonian Institution.

Stewart, O. C. (1939). The Northern Paiute bands. *University of California Anthropological Records, 2*(3), 127-149.

Stewart, O. C. (1941). Culture element distributions, XIV: Northern Paiute. *University of California Anthropological Records, 4*(3), 361-446.

Stewart, O. C. (1966). Tribal distributions and boundaries in the Great Basin. In D'Azevedo, W. (Ed.), *The current status of anthropological research in the Great Basin* (Vol. Social Sciences and Humanities Publications 1, pp. 167-238). Reno, NV: University of Nevada, Desert Research Institute.

Stewart, O. C. (1982). *Indians of the Great Basin: A critical bibliography.* Bloomington, IN: Indiana University Press.

Surovell, T. A. (2003). Simulating coastal migration in new world colonization. *Current Anthropology, 44*(4), 580-591.

Suttles, W. (Ed.). (1990). *Northwest Coast* (Vol. 7). Washington, D.C.: Smithsonian Institution.

Sutton, M. Q. (1993). The Numic expansion in great basin oral tradition. *Journal of California and Great Basin Anthropology, 15*(1), 111-128.

Swadesh, M. (1954). On the penutiam vocabulary survey. *International Journal of American Linguistics, 20*(2), 123-133.

Swanson, E. H., Jr. (1972). *Birch creek: Human ecology in the cool desert of the northern Rocky Mountains 9,000 b.C. - a.D. 1850.* Pocatello, ID: Idaho State University Press.

Swedlund, A., & Anderson, D. (2003). Gordon Creek Woman meets Spirit Cave Man: A response to comment by Owsley and Jantz. *American Antiquity, 68*(1), 161-168.

Szathmary, E. J. E. (1979). Blood groups of Siberian, Eskimos, Subarctic and Northwest Coast Indians: The problem of origins and genetic relationships. In Laughlin, W. S. & Harper, A. B. (Eds.), *The first Americans: Origings, affinities, and adaptations* (pp. 185-209). New York, NY: Gustav Fisher.

Szathmary, E. J. E. (1984). Human biology of the Arctic. In Dumas, D. (Ed.), *Arctic* (Vol. 5, pp. 64-71). Washington, D.C.: Smithsonian Institution.

Szathmary, E. J. E. (1985). Search for genetic factors controlling plasma glucose levels in Dogrib Indians. In Chakraborty, R. & Szathmary, E. J. E. (Eds.), *Diseases of complex etiology in small populations* (pp. 199-225). New York, NY: Alan R. Liss.

Szathmary, E. J. E. (1994). Modelling ancient population relationships from modern population genetics. In Bonnichsen, R. & Steele, D. G. (Eds.), *Method and theory for the investigation of the peopling of the Americas* (pp. 117-130). Corvallis, OR: Center for the Study of the First Americans.

Szathmary, E. J. E., & Ossenberg, N. S. (1978). Are the biological differences between North American Indians and Eskimos truly profound? *Current Anthropology, 19*, 673-701.

Taylor, R. E., Payen, L. A., Gerow, B., Donahue, D. J., Zabel, T. H., Jull, A. J. T., et al. (1983). Middle holocene age of the Sunnyvale human skeleton. *Science, 220*, 1271-1273.

Teit, J. (1909/1975). *The Shuswap.* New York, NY: AMS Press.

Teit, J. (1912). Traditions of the Lillooet Indians of British Columbia. *Journal of American Folk-Lore, 25*(98), 287-371.

Teit, J. (1914). Indian tribes of the interior. In Shortt, A. & Dought, A. G. (Eds.), *Canada and its provinces* (Vol. XXI, pp. 283-314). Toronto: Canada: Edinburgh University Press.

Templeton, A. R. (1993). The "eve" hypotheses: A genetic critique and reanalysis. *American Anthropologist, 95*(1), 51-72.

Templeton, A. R. (2002). Out of Africa again and again, *Nature* (Vol. 416:45-51).

Thackray, G. D. (2001). Extensive early and middle Wisconsin glaciation on the western Olympic peninsula, Washington, and the variability of Pacific moisture delivery to the northwestern United States. *Quaternary Research, 55*, 257-270.

Thomas, D. H. (1981). An overview of central Great Basin prehistory. In Madsen, D. B. & O'Connell, J. F. (Eds.), *Man and environment in the Great Basin* (pp. 156-171). Washington, D.C.: Society for American Archaeology.

Thomas, D. H. (1994). Chronology and the Numic expansion. In Madsen, D. B. & Rhode, D. (Eds.), *Across the west: Human population movement and the expansion of the Numa* (pp. 56-62). Salt Lake City, UT: University of Utah Press.

Thomas, D. H. (1999). *Archaeology of Hidden Cave, Nevada*. Washington, D.C.: American Museum of Natural History.

Thompson, D. (1914). Journal of David Thompson. *Oregon Historical Quarterly, 15*(2), 104-125.

Thompson, D. (1916). *David Thompson's narrative of his explorations in western America, 1784-1812*. Toronto, Canada: The Champlain Society.

Thompson, D. (1917). David Thompson's journey's in Spokane country. *Washington Historical Quarterly, 8*(4), 261-264.

Thompson, D. (1920). David Thompson's journeys in Spokane country. *Washington Historical Quarterly, 8*(4), 261-264.

Thompson, R. H. (Ed.). (1958). *Migrations in new world culture history*. Tucson, AZ: University of Arizona Press.

Thompson, R. S. (1984). *Late pleistocene and holocene environments in the Great Basin*. Unpublished Ph.D. Dissertation, University of Arizona, Tucson, AZ.

Thompson, R. S. (1985). The age and environment of the Mount Moriah (Lake Mohave) occupation at Smith Creek Cave, Nevada. In Mead, J. I. & Meltzer, D. J. (Eds.), *Environments and extinctions: Man in late glacial North America* (pp. 111-120). Orono, ME: Center for the Study of Early Man.

Thompson, R. S., & Hattori, E. M. (1983). Paleobotany of Gatecliff Shelter: Packrat (neotoma) middens from Gatecliff Shelter and holocene migrations of woodland plants. In Thomas, D. H. (Ed.), *The archaeology of Monitor Valley. 2. Gatecliff Shelter* (Vol. 59(1), pp. 157-167). Washington, D.C.: American Museum of Natural History.

Thompson, S. (1977). *The folktale*. Berkeley, CA: University of California Press.

Thoms, W. (1965). Folklore. In Dundes, A. (Ed.), *The study of folklore* (pp. 4-6). Englewood Cliffs, NJ: Prentice-Hall, Inc.

Torroni, A., Schurr, T., Cabell, M. D., Brown, M. D., Neel, J. V., Larson, M., et al. (1993). Asian affinities and continental radiation of the four founding Native American mtDNAs. *American Journal of Human Genetics, 53*, 563-590.

Torroni, A., Theodore G. Schurr, T. G., Yang, C.-C., Szathmary, E. J. E., Williams, R. C., Schanfield, M. S., et al. (1992). Native American mitochondrial DNA analysis indicates that the Amerind and the Nadene populations were founded by two independent migrations. *Genetics, 130*, 153-162.

Townsend, J. K. (1970). *Across the rockies to the Columbia*. Lincoln, NE: University of Nebraska Press.

Tuohy, D., & Dansie, A. (1997). New information regarding early holocene manifestations in the western Great Basin. *Nevada Historical Society Quarterly, 40*(1), 24-40.

Tuohy, D. R. (1988a). Artifacts from the northwestern Pyramid Lake shoreline. In Willig, J. A., Aikens, C. M. & Fagan, J. L. (Eds.), *Early human occupation in far western North America: The clovis-archaic interface* (Vol. 21, pp. 201-217). Carson City, NV: Nevada State Museum.

Tuohy, D. R. (1988b). Paleoindian and early archaic cultural complexes from three central Nevada locations. In Willig, J. A., Aikens, C. M. & Fagan, J. L. (Eds.), *Early human occupation in far western North America: The clovis-archaic interface* (Vol. 21, pp. 217-230). Carson City, NV: Nevada State Museum.

Tuohy, D. R. (1990). Pyramid Lake fishing: The archaeological record. In Janetski, J. C. & Madsen, D. B. (Eds.), *Wetland adaptations in the Great Basin* (pp. 121-158). Provo, UT: Brighman Yound University.

Tuohy, D. R., & Clark, D. T. (1979). *Excavations at Marble Bluff dam and Pyramid Lake fishway, Nevada*. Reno, NV: US Bureau of Reclamation Contract Report, Contract #C2520.

Tuohy, D. R., Dansie, A. J., & Haldeman, M. B. (1987). *Final report on the excavations in the Stillwater Marsh archaeological district, Nevada*. Carson City, NV: Nevada State Museum Archaeological Services Reports.

Turner, C., Nichol, C., & Scott, G. (1991). Scoring procedures for key morphological traits of the permanent dentition: The Arizona State University dental anthropology system. In Kelley, M. & Larsen, C. (Eds.), *Advances in dental anthropology* (pp. 13-31). New York, NY: Wiley-Liss.

Turner, C. G., II. (1974). *Three-rooted mandibular first permanent molars and the question of American Indian origins*. New York, NY: MSS Information Corporation.

Turner II, C. G. (1967). *The dentition of Arctic peoples*. Unpublished Dissertation, University of Wisconsin, Madison.

Turner II, C. G. (1985). The dental search for Native American origins. *The Journal of Pacific History, 4*, 31-78.

Turner II, C. G. (1989). *Out of southeast Asia: Dentition and the peopling of the Pacific Basin and adjoining areas*. Paper presented at the Circum-Pacific Prehistory Conference, Seattle, WA.

Turner II, C. G. (1994). Relating Eurasian and Native American populations through dental morphology. In Bonnichsen, R. & Steele, D. G. (Eds.), *Method and theory for investigating the peopling of the Americas* (pp. 131-140). Corvallis, OR: Center for the Study of the First Americans.

Tylor, E. B. (1871/1924). *Primitive culture*. New York, NY: Brentano's.

Tylor, E. B. (1881/1924). *Anthropology: An introduction to the study of man and civilization*. New York, NY: D. Appleton.

Uebelacker, M. L. (2000). *Cultural affiliation determination for the Kennewick remains: A critical review of the evidence.* Toppenish, WA: Confederated Tribes and Bands of the Yakama Nation.

United States Indian Claims, C. (1974). *Paiute Indians v. Commission findings.* New York, NY: Garland Publishing.

Unruh, J. D., Jr. (1979). *The plains across: The overland emigrants and the trans-Mississippi west, 1840-60.* Urbana: IL: University of Illinois Press.

Valero-Garces, B. L., Laird, K. R., Fritz, S. C., Kelts, K., Ito, E., & Grimm, E. C. (1997). Holocene climate in the northern Great Plains inferred from sediment stratigraphy, stable isotopes, carbonate geochemistry, diatoms, and pllen at Moon Lake, North Dakota. *Quaternary Research, 48,* 359-369.

Van Stone, J. W. (1984). Exploration and contact history of western Alaska. In Dumas, D. (Ed.), *Arctic* (Vol. 5, pp. 149-160). Washington, D.C.: Smithsonian Institution.

Vansina, J. (1985). *Oral tradition as history.* Madison, WI: University of Washington Press.

Vehik, S. C., and Timothy G. Baugh. (1994). Prehistoric Plains trade. In Ericson, T. G. B. a. J. E. (Ed.), *Prehistoric Exchange Systems in North America* (Vol. 249-274): Plenum Press: New York.

Vierling, L. A. (1998). Palynological evidence for late- and postglacial environmental change in central Colorado. *Quaternary Research, 49,* 222-232.

Voegelin, C. F., & Voegelin, F. M. (1966). *Map of north American Indian languages.* New York, NY: Rand McNally.

Wahrhaftig, C., & Birman, J. H. (1965). The quaternary of the pacific mountain system in California. In Wright, H. E., Jr. & Frey, D. G. (Eds.), *The quaternary of the United States: A review volume for the VII congress of the international association for quaternary research* (pp. 299-340). Princeton, NJ: Princeton University Press.

Waitt, R. B., Jr. (1980). About forty last-glacial Missoula jokulhlaups through southern Washington. *Journal of Geology, 88,* 653-679.

Waitt, R. B., Jr. (1983). *Tens of successive, colossal Missoula floods at north and east margins of channeled scabland.* Washington, D.C.: U.S. Geological Survey, Department of the Interior.

Waitt, R. B., Jr. (1984). Periodic jokulhlaups from pleistocene glacial lake Missoula - new evidence from varved sediment in northern Idaho and Washington. *Quaternary Research, 22,* 46-58.

Waitt, R. B., Jr., & Thornson, R. M. (1983). The cordilleran ice sheet in Washington, Idaho, and Montana. In Porter, S. C. (Ed.), *Late-quaternary environments of the United States, volume 1: The late pleistocene* (pp. 53-70). Minneapolis, MN: University of Minnesota Press.

Walker, D. E., Jr. (Ed.). (1998). *Plateau* (Vol. 12). Washington, D.C.: Smithsonian Institution.

Walker, D. E., Jr., & Matthews, D. N. (1994). *Blood of the monster: The Nez Perce coyote cycle.* Worland, WY: High Plains Publishing.

Wallace, D., & Torroni, A. (1992). American Indian prehistory as written in the mitochondrial DNA: A review. *Human Biology, 64*(3), 403-416.

Walpoff, M. (1999). *Paleoanthropology* (2 ed.). New York, NY: McGraw-Hill.

Ward, R. H., Alan Redd, A., Valencia, D., Frazier, B., & Paabo, S. (1993). Genetic and linguistic differentiation in the Americas. *Proceedings of the National Academy of Sciences, USA, 90,* 10663-10667.

Warre, S. H. J. (1848). *Sketches in North America and the Oregon territory.* London: Dickinson.

Waters, M. R., & Ravesloot, J. C. (2001). Landscape change and the culture evolution of the Hohokam along the middle Gila River and other river valleys in south-central Arizona. *American Antiquity, 66*(2), 285-299.

Watkins, C. (1990). Etymologies, equations, and comparanda: Types and values, and criteria for judgement. In Baldi, P. (Ed.), *Linguistic change and reconstruction methodology.* Berlin: Mouton de Gruyter.

Watkins, J. E. (2003). Beyond the margin: American Indians, First Nations, and archaeology in North America. *American Antiquity, 68*(2), 273-285.

Watkins, W. S., Bamshad, M., Dixon, M. E., Rao, B. B., Naidu, J. M., Reddy, P. G., et al. (1999). Multiple origins of the mtDNA 9-bp deletion in populations of south India. *American Journal of Physical Anthropology, 109,* 147-158.

Watson, E., Forster, P., Richards, M., & Bandelt, H.-J. (1997). Mitochondrial footprints of human expansions in Africa. *American Journal of Human Genetics, 61,* 691-704.

Wauchope, R. (1962). *Lost tribes and sunken continents.* Chicago, IL: University of Chicago Press.

Weidenreich, F. (1945). The brachycephalization of recent mankind. *Southwest Journal of Anthropology, 1,* 1-54.

Weiss, K. M. (1994). American origins. *Proceedings of the Academy of Sciences, USA, 91,* 833-835.

Wells, P. V. (1983). Paleobiogeography of montane grasslands in the Great Basin since the last glaciopluvial. *Ecological Monographs, 53,* 341-382.

West, F. H. (Ed.). (1996). *American beginnings: The prehistory and palaeoecology of Beringia.* Chicago, IL: University of Chicago Press.

Wheeler, M. (1954). *Archaeology from the earth.* Oxford, UK: Oxford University Press.

Wheeler, S. M., & Wheeler, G. N. (1940). *Field notes: 1940.* Reno, NV: Ms. On file at the BLM Nevada State Office.

Wheeler, S. M., & Wheeler, G. N. (1969). Cave burials near Fallon, Churchhill county, Nevada. In Rendall, D. L. & Tuohy, D. R. (Eds.), *Miscellaneous papers* (pp. 71-78). Carson City, NV: Nevada State Museum.

Whistler, K. W. (1977). Wintun prehistory: An interpretation based on linguistic reconstruction of plant and animal nomenclature. *Proceedings of the Annual Meeting of the Berkeley Linguistics Society, 3,* 157-174.

Whitney-Smith, E. (2001). *Second-order predation and pleistocene extinctions: A system dynamics model.* Unpublished Dissertation, Columbian School of Arts and Sciences, George Washington University, St. Louis, MO.

Wilcox, R. E. (1965). Volcanic-ash chronology. In Wright, H. E., Jr. & Frey, D. G. (Eds.), *The quaternary of the United States: A review volume for the VII congress of the international association for quaternary research* (pp. 807-816). Princeton, NJ: Princeton University Press.

Wiles, G. C., Post, A., Muller, E. H., & Molina, B. F. (1999). Dendrochronology and late holocene history of bering piedmont glacier, Alaska. *Quaternary Research, 52*, 185-195.

Wilkinson, C. F., Buffalohead, W. R., Hart, E. R., & Johnson, E. C. (1986). The Indian claims commission. Salt Lake City, UT: Howe Brothers.

Willems-Braun, B. (1997). Buried epistemologies: The politics of nature in (post)colonial British Columbia. *Annals of the Association of American Geographers, 87*(1), 3-31.

Williams, J. W., Webb, T., Richard, P. H., & Newby, P. (2000). Late quaternary biomes of Canada and the eastern United States. *Journal of Biogeography, 27*(3), 585-607.

Williams, M. L. (1991). *Schoolcraft's Indian legends.* East Lansing, MI: Michigan State University Press.

Willig, J. A. (1988). Paleo-archaic adaptations and lakeside settlement patterns in the northern Alkali Basin, Oregon. In Willig, J. A., Aikens, C. M. & Fagan, J. (Eds.), *Early human occupation in far western North America: The clovis-archaic interface* (Vol. 21, pp. 417-482). Carson City, NV: Nevada State Museum.

Willig, J. A. (1991). Clovis technology and adaptation in far western North America: Regional pattern and environmental context. In Bonnichsen, R. & Turnmire, K. (Eds.), *Clovis origins and adaptations.* Corvallis, OR: Center for the Study of First Americans, Oregon State University.

Willig, J. A., & Aikens, C. M. (1988). The clovis-archaic interface in far western North America. In Willig, J. A., Aikens, C. M. & Fagan, J. (Eds.), *Early human occupation in far western North America: The clovis-archaic interface* (Vol. 21, pp. 1-40). Carson City, NV: Nevada State Museum.

Wissler, C. (1914). Material cultures of the north American Indians. *American Anthropologist, 16*(3), 447-505.

Wissler, C. (1917). *The American Indian: An introduction to the anthropology of the new world.* New York, NY: Douglas C. McMurtrie.

Wolpoff, M. H. (1999). *Paleoanthropology* (2 ed.). New York, NY: McGraw-Hill.

Work, J. (1909). Journal of John Work, April 30th to May 31st, 1830. *Oregon Historical Quarterly, 10*(3), 296-313.

Work, J. (1912a). Journal of John Work, November and December, 1824. *Washington Historical Quarterly, 3*(3), 198-228.

Work, J. (1912b). Journal of John Work's Snake country expedition of 1830-31. *Oregon Historical Quarterly, 13*(4), 363-371.

Work, J. (1914a). Journal of John Work, December 15, 1825 to June 12, 1826. *Washington Historical Quarterly, 5*(4), 258-287.

Work, J. (1914b). Journal of John Work, June-October, 1825. *Washington Historical Quarterly, 5*(2), 85-115.

Work, J. (1914c). Journal of John Work, September 7th - Dec. 14th, 1825. *Washington Historical Quarterly, 5*(3), 163-191.

Work, J. (1915). The journal of John Work, July 5, - September 15, 1826. *Washington Historical Quarterly, 6*(1), 26-49.

Work, J. (1920). John Work's journal of a trip from Fort Colville to Fort Vancouver and return in 1828. *Washington Historical Quarterly, 11*(2), 104-114.

Wright, H. E., Jr., & Frey, D. C. (Eds.). (1965). *The quaternary of the United States: A review volume for the VII congress of the international association for quaternary research.* Princeton, NJ: Princeton University Press.

Wright, H. E., Jr., & Ruhe, R. V. (1965). Glaciation of Minnesota and Iowa. In Wright, H. E., Jr. & Frey, D. G. (Eds.), *The quaternary of the United States: A review volume for the VII congress of the international association for quaternary research* (pp. 29-42). Princeton, NJ: Princeton University Press.

Wright, K. (1999). First Americans. *Discover, Febuary,* 52-63.

Wrischnik, L. A., Higuchi, R. H., Stoneking, M., Erlich, H. A., Anheim, N., & Wilson, A. C. (1987). Length mutations in human mitochondrial DNA: Direct sequencing of enzymatically amplified DNA. *Nucleic Acid Research, 15,* 529-542.

Yao, Y.-G., Watkins, W. S., & Zhang, Y.-P. (2000). Evolutionary history of the mtDNA 9-bp deletion in Chinese populations and its relevance to the peopling of east and southeast Asia. *Human Genetics, 107*(5), 504-512.

Young, D. A., & Bettinger, R. L. (1992). The Numic spread: A computer simulation. *American Antiquity, 57*(1), 85-99.

Zazula, G. D., Froese, D. G., Schweger, C. E., Mathewes, R. W., Beaudoin, A. B., Telka, A. M., et al. (2003). Ice-age steppe vegetation in east Beringia. *Nature, 423,* 603.

Zhu, R. X., Hoffman, K. A., Potts, R., Deng, C. L., Pan, Y. X., Guo, B., et al. (2001). Earliest presence of humans in northeast Asia. *Nature, 413,* 413-417.

Zier, C. J., & Kalasz, S. M. (1999). *Colorado prehistory: A context for the Arkansas River Basin.* Denver, CO: Colorado Council of Professional Archaeologists.

NOTES

1 For the purposes of this book, the author uses the definition of American Indian tribes set forth in NAGPRA (Section 2, part 7) as:

"Indian tribe" means any tribe, band, nation, or other organized group or community of Indians, including any Alaska Native village (as defined in, or established pursuant to, the Alaska Native Claims Settlement Act), which is recognized as eligible for the special programs and services provided by the United States to Indians because of their status as Indians.

It is important to note that this definition does not include the numerous American Indian groups not formally recognized by the federal government, as well as not formally recognizing First Nations and other indigenous peoples of Central and South America for whom this book may be relevant or for whom at one point or another inhabited or utilized parts of the present-day United States.

2 Throughout this book, the author uses both "Truth" and truth, as well as "History" and histories. truth and history refer to the relative level of these words, in the sense that for all individuals, their epistemology and ontology form their notion of truth and history, and this fact cannot be denied. "Truth" and "History," in the more ultimate sense, however, does not deny truths and histories, but instead subsumes them into a larger understanding of all truths and histories, arriving at a more peliomorphoic understanding of "what is." This understanding will be discussed in more depth in the conclusion.

3 By Truth, it is understood that there is some larger noumena that encompasses all of the individually understood and perceived truths (i.e., phenomena). A similar stance is taken with History. This implies that though all truths, and all histories, are valid, there is still a larger pleiomorphic Truth and History that encompasses all

of the truths and histories.

4 It is recognized that NAGPRA and its guidelines of inquiry are ethnocentric to a Western epistemology, and thus do not necessarily allow for various forms of American Indian knowledge to be considered on equal ground. That is why I have also approached the question of cultural affiliation from an epistemological praxis of epoché.

5 As noted in chapter one, I do not attempt to give a full account of the legal and sociological history of the Kennewick Man skeleton. Instead, this chapter is meant to give a brief history of the case to help contextualize the question of cultural affiliation and its theoretical reach into ancient history.

6 The Spirit Cave Mummy case has not been covered within the anthropological or media literature like the Kennewick Man case has been. The best summary of the case is found in Barker, Ellis, & Damadio (2000).

7 Although Clovis and Folsom were originally used to designate a specific lithic point style, over time archaeologists have used these terms to denote an entire "culture" that utilized these lithic point styles during a specific time. This understanding is very circumscribed and erroneous, but because of its pervasiouvness in the literature, I use these words throughout this book with the following understandings: Clovis and Folsom only designate a specific lithic point style that occurred over a long period of time and a large geographic area, and in no way designates a particular, identifiable group of people. Likewise, this same understanding is also valid for other such lithic point styles as Plano, Dalton, Western Fluted, Agate, etc.

8 As was discussed in chapter two, History is understood to mean the larger, unified understanding of the individual histories that every individual and society constructs. Thus, no history is privledged over another, but is encompassed into a larger understanding of History in an attempt to come as close as possible to Truth. Truth, as with History, encompasses all of the individually held and known truths of individuals and societies.

INDEX

Aleut 91, 154, 157, 158
Alfred Kroeber 9, 11, 157, 197
Algonquian 77, 106, 152, 162
Amerind 106, 152, 154, 157, 248
Ancient DNA 109
      aDNA 109, 110
Anthropological Theory 21, 23, 25, 136, 201, 202, 203, 205, 207, 228
Apache 92, 107, 108, 109
Army Corps of Engineers 28
Athapaskan 33, 77, 91, 92, 152, 221, 233
Bannock 35, 83, 108, 161
Basketry 140, 145, 146, 147, 182, 183, 184, 185, 187, 188, 211, 219, 225, 229
Bering land bridge 40, 43, 99, 112, 120
      Beringian 41, 42, 43, 46, 215, 227
      Beringia 41, 42, 46, 119, 120, 192, 222, 226, 229, 235, 250, 252
      Bering Sea 41, 46, 243
Biological Continuity 89, 98, 192
Bison 121, 125, 131, 132, 133, 221, 223, 224, 227, 245
Bottleneck 103
British Columbia 33, 47, 48, 49, 50, 51, 53, 54, 56, 77, 78, 138, 218, 221, 228, 234, 237, 239, 246, 251
Buhl skeleton 95, 136
Bureau of Ethnology 10
Bureau of Land Management 30, 139, 214, 234
Burial Complex 133

Camas 76, 78, 117, 132, 133, 135, 137

Carrier 18, 34, 203, 218

Carson Sink 117

Cascade Point 133

Cayuse 33, 76, 79, 108, 109, 159, 183, 241, 242

Cephalic Index 89

Chatters, J. 28, 53, 55, 96, 134, 136, 137, 219

Chemehuevi 82, 161

Chinook 10, 79, 159, 176

Chuska Mountains 66

Clark Fork River 53, 78

Clearwater River 76

Clovis 9, 121, 122, 131, 133, 139, 198, 218, 245, 248, 251, 254

Clyde Kluckhohn 9

Coalescent Times 98, 100, 101

Coastal Refugias 43, 46, 47, 51

Coeur d'Alene 33, 76, 78, 108

Colby Mammoth 131

Colonialism 18, 203, 204, 205, 206, 208, 234
        See also, Postcolonialism

Columbia Basin 135, 160, 161, 167, 236, 240

Columbia River 28, 30, 33, 53, 56, 76, 78, 79, 116, 117, 160, 166, 167, 169, 225,
        227, 239, 241, 245

Colville Reservation 23, 220, 228, 229

Cordilleran Ice Sheet 49, 50, 51, 52, 53, 54, 58, 215, 233, 241, 249

Cranial Morphology 88, 89

Cross Creek Site 127, 231

Cultural Affiliation 1, 5, 6, 7, 8, 9, 11, 12, 13, 14, 15, 16, 17, 21, 22, 25, 28, 30, 32,
        37, 38, 71, 75, 82, 84, 85, 89, 94, 113, 115, 117, 121, 127, 145, 146, 151,
        152, 156, 168, 179, 188, 190, 191, 192, 193, 194, 195, 197, 212, 214, 217,
        226, 227, 230, 231, 249, 254

Cultural Particularists 9

Cultural Resource Management 116, 224, 235
        CRM 116, 117, 136, 141

Danger Cave 145, 241

Deconstructionist 16

DeMoss Site 138

Department of Interior 93, 95

Derrida, J. 17, 206, 221

Desert Culture 139, 144

Desert Side Notch 198

Diego Duran 7

Diffusion 9, 11, 13, 14, 157, 159, 182, 183, 185, 187
        see also, Migrations

Displacement 110, 115, 134, 135, 136, 139, 140, 148, 167, 171, 177, 179, 185, 186,
        188, 190, 192, 193, 194

Dogrib 107, 246

E.B. Tylor 10

Early Holocene 37, 41, 45, 47, 49, 52, 55, 56, 58, 59, 61, 63, 64, 66, 67, 68, 70, 71, 75, 84, 87, 88, 91, 93, 94, 95, 96, 97, 110, 111, 112, 113, 115, 116, 117, 118, 119, 120, 121, 122, 123, 124, 125, 126, 127, 128, 129, 130, 131, 132, 133, 135, 137, 138, 139, 140, 141, 142, 143, 146, 148, 160, 161, 163, 166, 167, 177, 179, 190, 191, 192, 193, 194, 198, 212, 215, 219, 230, 236, 241, 248

Eastern Mono 81

Edward Sapir 9, 157

Eel Point Site 128

Elephant Mountain Cave 142, 214

Emireh Points 118

Epistemology 7, 8, 11, 12, 15, 16, 23, 25, 127, 198, 200, 201, 203, 207, 253, 254

Eskimos 91, 107, 222, 246

Flathead 33, 34, 76, 78, 108, 219

Fluted Point 139

Folsom 70, 131, 198, 229, 235, 254

Foucault, M. 17, 18, 205, 218, 224

Francis Bacon 8, 16

Franz Boas 9, 10, 89, 157, 197, 220

Fraser River 53, 77

Fraser River Valley 53

Fremont 73, 80, 146, 147, 185, 189, 214, 220, 224, 235, 244

Gila River 64, 65, 250

Glacial Lake Missoula 53, 56, 166, 176, 249

Gordon Creek woman 93, 95, 239, 246

Grand Coulee 53, 166

Great Salt Lake 59, 80, 220

Green River 77

Haida 92, 107, 216

Haplogroups 98, 101, 102, 103, 216, 234

Haplotype 98, 100, 101, 102, 107, 109

Harney Basin 59, 227

Hetrick Site 137, 242

High Plains 68, 224, 227, 229, 231, 244, 249

Historical Linguistics 151, 153, 154, 163, 218

Hogup Cave 145

Hokan 35, 81

Imperialism 18, 203, 204, 205, 206

Indigirka Basins 42

Intergroup Marriage 99, 102

Interior Salish 77, 78, 162

Interpretivism 17, 18

Kalispel 33, 78

Kamchatka 41, 106, 119, 226

Kara Glaciation 41

Kawaiisu 35, 82, 161

258

Kennewick Man 3, 5, 6, 8, 12, 13, 25, 27, 28, 29, 30, 32, 34, 37, 53, 55, 75, 85, 87, 89, 92, 93, 94, 95, 96, 110, 111, 112, 113, 120, 133, 172, 176, 191, 192, 193, 194, 200, 220, 229, 231, 239, 240, 243, 254
Ancient One 6, 8, 27, 220, 228
Klamath 34, 36, 79, 108, 159, 160, 173, 183, 245
Kolyma Basin 41, 42, 119
Kootenai 33, 34, 77, 108, 159, 183
Lake Bonneville 59, 62, 242
Lake Estancia 65, 66
Lake Lahotan 59
Lake Malheur 59, 222
Lake Pend Oreille 53, 78
Lakeside Cave 130
Late Holocene 55, 64, 66, 70, 128, 130, 132, 140, 142, 143, 251
Late Pleistocene 13, 37, 41, 42, 45, 49, 52, 53, 54, 55, 56, 58, 60, 61, 63, 64, 65, 66, 67, 68, 70, 71, 75, 84, 86, 87, 88, 91, 96, 112, 115, 116, 117, 118, 119, 121, 122, 123, 124, 125, 126, 127, 128, 129, 132, 133, 136, 137, 140, 143, 148, 160, 166, 167, 177, 179, 187, 190, 191, 192, 193, 194, 198, 212, 215, 216, 217, 218, 221, 222, 224, 225, 228, 229, 230, 231, 236, 240, 244, 245, 247, 249
Late Pliocene 45, 46
Laurentide 40, 52, 56, 67, 71
Lena Basin 41
Lillooet 33, 34, 77, 99, 246
Lovelock Cave 141, 185, 189, 215, 223
Lovelock Wickerware 182, 183, 188
Lower Salmon River 55, 221
Magistrate Jelderks 23, 28, 30, 172, 176, 231
Mahoney Lake 55
Mammoths 121
Marmes burials 95, 138
Mastodon 121, 122
Megafauna 3, 118, 120, 121, 122, 123, 124, 125, 126, 236, 237
Middle Columbia River Salishans 33, 78
Middle Holocene 45, 60, 63, 64, 67, 95, 116, 125, 126, 128, 129, 131, 132, 142, 143, 160, 192, 226, 246
Migrations 4, 50, 85, 97, 98, 103, 104, 112, 136, 165, 166, 179, 181, 182, 183, 190, 194, 204, 214, 247, 248
Milankovitch Cycles 38
Milling Stone Horizon 128
Mimbres 189
Modoc 34, 36, 79, 108
Mojave Desert 60, 130, 144
Molala 33, 34, 79, 159, 160, 183, 241
mtDNA 97, 98, 100, 101, 102, 103, 104, 105, 110, 111, 212, 216, 217, 219, 222, 224, 231, 234, 237, 238, 243, 244, 250, 252
Multilateral Word Comparison 153, 154, 155, 162, 163, 193
Na-Dene 106, 154, 157, 158, 159

NAGPRA 3, 6, 7, 12, 13, 14, 15, 16, 21, 22, 25, 28, 30, 37, 75, 84, 85, 117, 151, 179, 191, 194, 197, 200, 223, 253, 254

Native Hawaiian 12, 21, 22

Navajo 82, 92, 103, 108

Newberry Volcano 137

Nez Perce 23, 33, 34, 76, 79, 107, 108, 109, 159, 160, 194, 213, 220, 243, 249

Nicola 33, 77, 159, 183

Non-random Mating 102

Northern Okanagan 33, 78, 233

Northwest Coast 3, 4, 34, 38, 46, 47, 48, 49, 51, 53, 56, 71, 76, 92, 99, 100, 107, 112, 138, 157, 158, 159, 160, 216, 217, 236, 237, 240, 246

Numic 14, 35, 81, 82, 83, 95, 98, 140, 142, 144, 145, 146, 147, 148, 152, 161, 162, 163, 168, 170, 179, 180, 182, 183, 184, 185, 186, 187, 189, 190, 193, 211, 213, 215, 221, 224, 232, 237, 244, 246, 247, 252

Occidental 16, 18, 204

Occidentalism 17, 18, 202, 218

Okanagan Valley 53, 55, 56

Olivella Shell Beads 138

Olympic Peninsula 50, 247

Ontology 7, 23, 25, 127, 198, 201, 228, 253

Pptimal Foraging Theory 130, 185, 186, 187, 188, 190, 201

Oral Traditions 4, 6, 27, 165, 166, 167, 168, 169, 170, 171, 172, 175, 176, 177, 179, 183, 194, 202

Oregon Trail 76, 80

Orientalism 17, 18, 202, 205, 242

Orientalists 17

Overkill 121, 123, 124, 126, 212

Overland Trail 80

Owens Lake 56, 58, 236

Owens Valley 35, 56, 81, 82, 168, 169

Paiute 23, 30, 32, 35, 36, 76, 81, 82, 83, 94, 109, 141, 146, 161, 162, 168, 169, 189, 194, 219, 224, 226, 227, 231, 232, 233, 246, 249

Palouse 33, 79, 160, 166, 167

Panglossism 188

Paviotso 161, 233

Pend d'Oreille 33, 34, 78, 219

Penutian 153, 159, 160, 161, 162, 163, 193, 244

Pint Nut 117

Pinto Series Points 142

Pithouse 116, 117, 134, 136

Positivism 19

Postcolonial theory 204, 205

Postcolonialism 17, 204, 234

Postmodern 16, 220

Postmodernism 18, 19, 197, 225

Postmodernists 18, 19, 205

Poststructuralism 17

Praxis of Epoché 3, 5, 12, 14, 15, 16, 17, 19, 21, 32, 37, 75, 85, 165, 179, 191, 194, 197, 206, 208, 254

Purcell Trench Lobe 49, 53, 54

Pyramid Lake 59, 95, 248

Quebrada Tacahuay 127, 221

Queen Charlotte Islands 47, 49, 50, 239

Relativism 10, 17, 18, 19, 197, 205, 225

Renaissance 7, 8

RFLP 101

Robert Lowie 9, 11

Rocky Mountains 33, 35, 52, 53, 54, 55, 56, 70, 71, 78, 80, 82, 83, 159, 185, 221, 224, 230, 239, 241, 243, 246

Roman Empire 8

Sahaptian 33, 76, 78, 79, 159, 160, 161, 166, 183, 193

Saidukah 168

Salmon 55, 76, 77, 78, 79, 80, 83, 117, 132, 133, 134, 136, 166, 167, 172, 201, 218, 221

San Juan Basin 64, 66

Searles Lake 63, 244

Sekani 34

Shoshone 23, 30, 32, 34, 35, 36, 76, 82, 83, 109, 162, 169, 170, 226, 244

Shouldered Lanceolate Points 133

Shuswap 33, 34, 77, 162, 221, 230, 239, 246

Sinodont 86, 87

Snake River 33, 55, 56, 60, 76, 79, 83, 134, 162, 218, 228, 234

Spirit Cave Mummy 3, 5, 6, 12, 13, 25, 27, 30, 32, 35, 37, 58, 75, 85, 87, 89, 92, 93, 94, 95, 110, 111, 112, 113, 120, 139, 140, 143, 172, 176, 191, 192, 193, 194, 200, 226, 231, 238, 254

Spokane 33, 78, 109, 247

Stemmed Point 139

Stillwater Marsh 94, 98, 131, 149, 186, 217, 232, 233, 240, 248

Strait of Juan de Fuca 50

Sundadont 86, 87

Surprise Valley 36, 168, 232

The Dalles 79, 99, 138

Thomas Jefferson 8

Thompson 33, 34, 59, 63, 76, 77, 121, 122, 123, 166, 168, 170, 171, 172, 180, 182, 213, 236, 238, 242, 247

Tlingit 92, 100

Traditional Ecological Knowledge 201

Tucannon phase 134

Umatilla 23, 33, 79, 109, 160, 194, 231, 245

CTUIR 4, 23, 109

Upper Cowlitz 160

Ushki-I 119

Ute 35, 82, 161, 169, 183, 184

Uto-Aztecan 35, 82, 152, 159, 161, 162, 163, 193, 212, 229, 234

Vantage 134

Walker River 23, 231
Walla Walla 33, 79, 109, 232
Warm Springs Indians 79
Wasco 33, 34, 79, 109, 183
Washoe 35, 73, 81, 83, 146, 152, 161, 162, 169, 223, 224, 230
Weaving 145, 146
Western Columbia River Sahaptins 33, 79
Western Fluted 133, 198, 254
Western Pluvial Lake 142
Windust 133, 134, 138
Wisconsin Glaciation 38, 40, 47, 52, 67, 247
Wishram 33, 34, 79, 109, 183
Yakama 23, 54, 78, 107, 108, 109, 160, 194, 249
Yamal peninsula 41, 42, 223
Y-chromosome 98, 100, 102, 103, 107, 110, 111, 216, 232, 239, 243
Yerington 23
Younger Dryas 42, 51, 54, 61, 66, 213, 233